CW00969531

Capital
In Manga!

By: Karl Marx

Narrated and Illustrated by:
VARIETY ART WORKS

Translated by:
GUY YASKO

Cover by:
VICTOR SERRA

Ottawa

www.redquillbooks.com

ISBN 978-1-926958-19-4

Printed on acid-free paper. The paper used in this book incorporates post-consumer waste and has not been sourced from endangered old growth forests, forests of exceptional conservation value or the Amazon Basin. Red Quill Books subscribes to a one-book-at-a-time manufacturing process that substantially lessens supply chain waste, reduces greenhouse emissions, and conserves valuable natural resources.

This title previously published in Japanese as:
Manga De Dokuha: Das Kapital

Karl Marx, 1818-1883: German economist, philosopher and revolutionary. He is considered the most influential thinker of the 20th century. Marx analyzed the capitalist economy, and with Engels, built communist thought. The ideas of revolutionary class struggle and the abolition of class systems are still alive today. Marx devoted his later years to writing Capital and died in his chair at home. He also wrote the *Communist Manifesto, The German Ideology, The Eighteenth Brumaire* and other influential works.

RED QUILL BOOKS

RQB is a radical publishing house.

Part of the proceeds from the sale of this book will support student scholarships.

Preface

The methods developed in the Industrial Revolution of the early 19th century made possible the mass production of goods, but the gap between rich and poor became wider and wider. People became either prosperous or poor. It became clear that new value was created in the production process through the exploitation of workers. Marx stood against the capitalist system his entire life. This is the manga version of his representative work.

This manga is a narrative version of the contents of Volume I of Capital. The original work is a masterpiece. It illuminates the structures of capitalism while incorporating revolutionary thought and philosophy. Our hope is that this manga may act as a faithful bridge to the original work.

TABLE OF CONTENTS

Main Characters

ROBIN: JOINS WITH DANIEL TO REALIZE HIS DREAMS BY OPENING A FACTORY, BUT STRUGGLES WITH FEELINGS OF GUILT ABOUT SQUEEZING "SURPLUS-VALUE" FROM EXPLOITED WORKERS.

HEINRICH: ROBIN'S FATHER. VALUES A LIFE OF MODERATION AND UNDERSTANDS THAT THE BASIS OF ALL WEALTH IS LABOUR.

CARL: A FACTORY WORKER. HE HAS AS DOUBTS ABOUT CAPITALISTS, WHO FORCE HARSH LABOUR ON WORKERS.

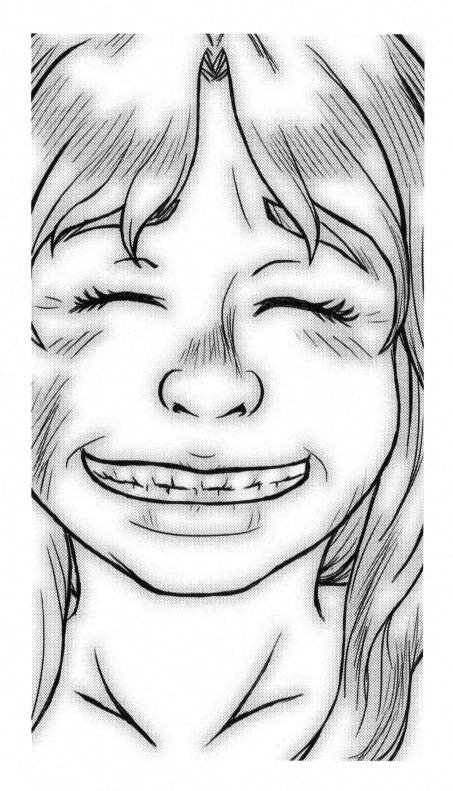

HELENA: ROBIN'S CHILDHOOD FRIEND. WORKS HARD FOR HER
FAMILY.

DANIEL: A CAPITALIST AND INVESTOR. A COOL STRATEGIST WHO PLAYS PEOPLE LIKE HE PLAYS CHESS.

THE FOREMAN: WATCHES OVER THE WORKERS CLOSELY.

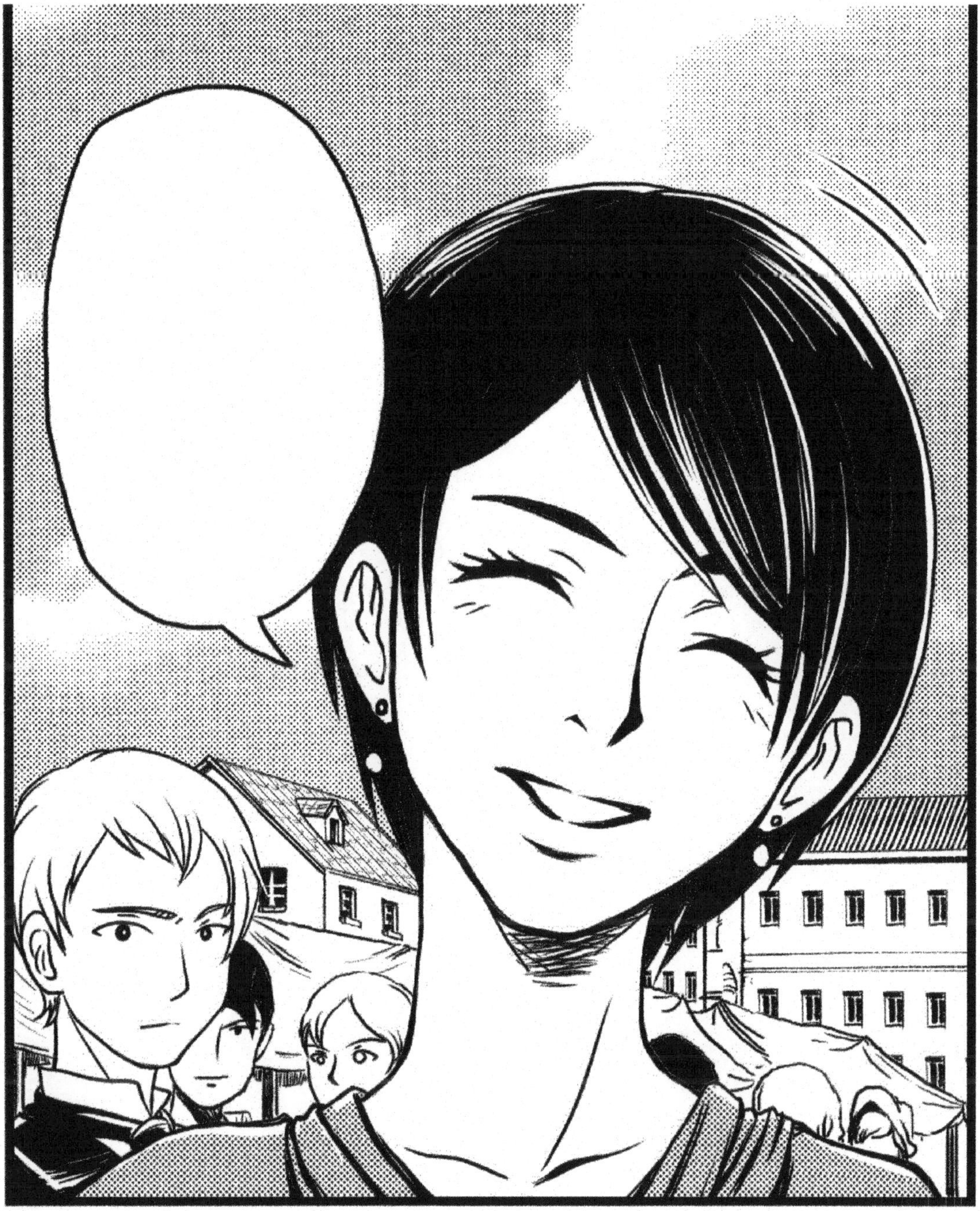

ENNY: THE DAUGHTER OF A MAJOR BANKER. THE WOMAN OF ROBIN'S FANCY.

THE PROCESS OF CAPITALIST PRODUCTION

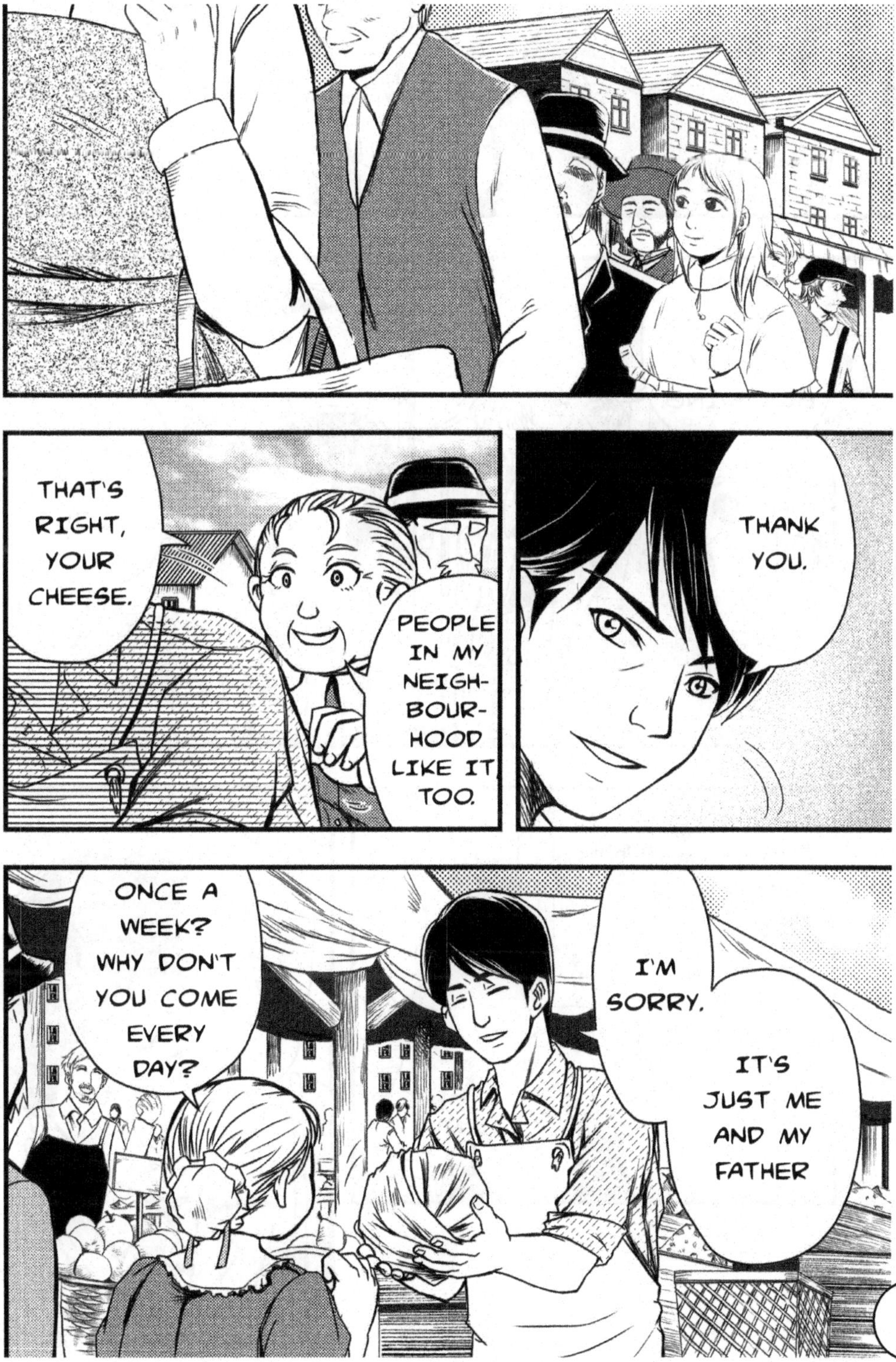
THAT'S RIGHT, YOUR CHEESE.
PEOPLE IN MY NEIGHBOURHOOD LIKE IT TOO.
THANK YOU.
ONCE A WEEK? WHY DON'T YOU COME EVERY DAY?
I'M SORRY.
IT'S JUST ME AND MY FATHER

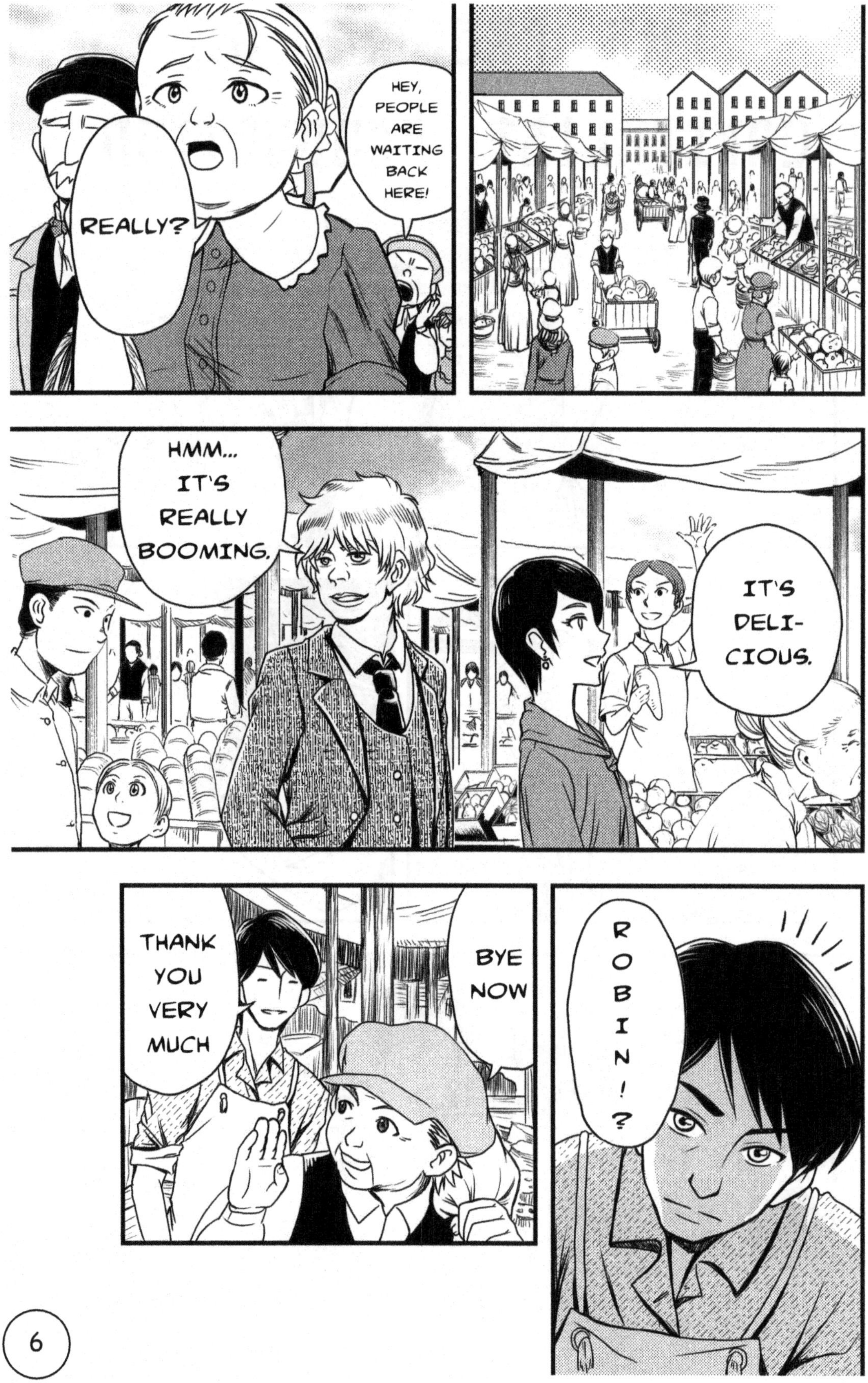
REALLY?
HEY, PEOPLE ARE WAITING BACK HERE!
HMM... IT'S REALLY BOOMING.
IT'S DELICIOUS.
THANK YOU VERY MUCH
BYE NOW
ROBIN!?

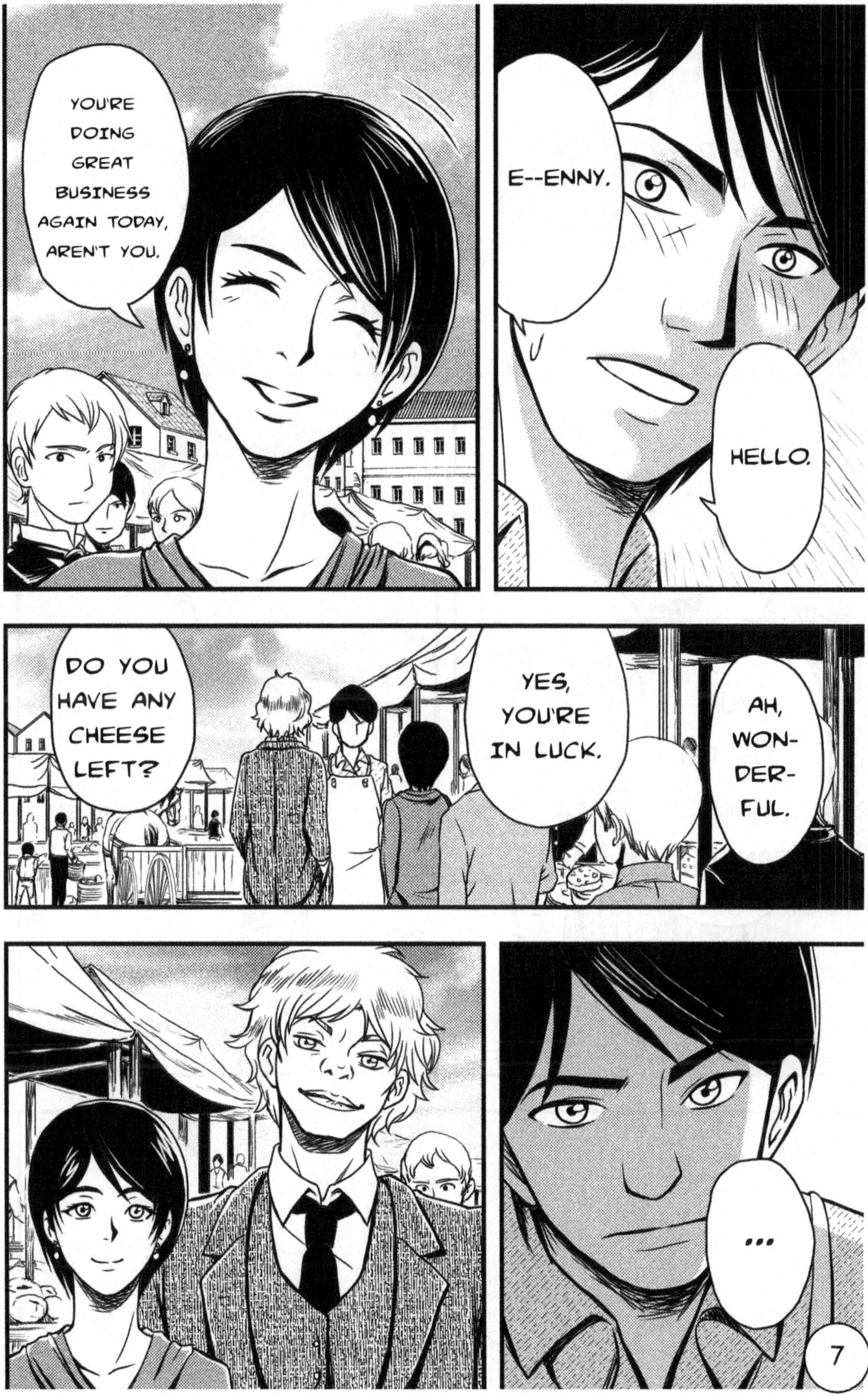
YOU'RE DOING GREAT BUSINESS AGAIN TODAY, AREN'T YOU.
E--ENNY.
HELLO.
DO YOU HAVE ANY CHEESE LEFT?
YES, YOU'RE IN LUCK.
AH, WON-DER-FUL.
...

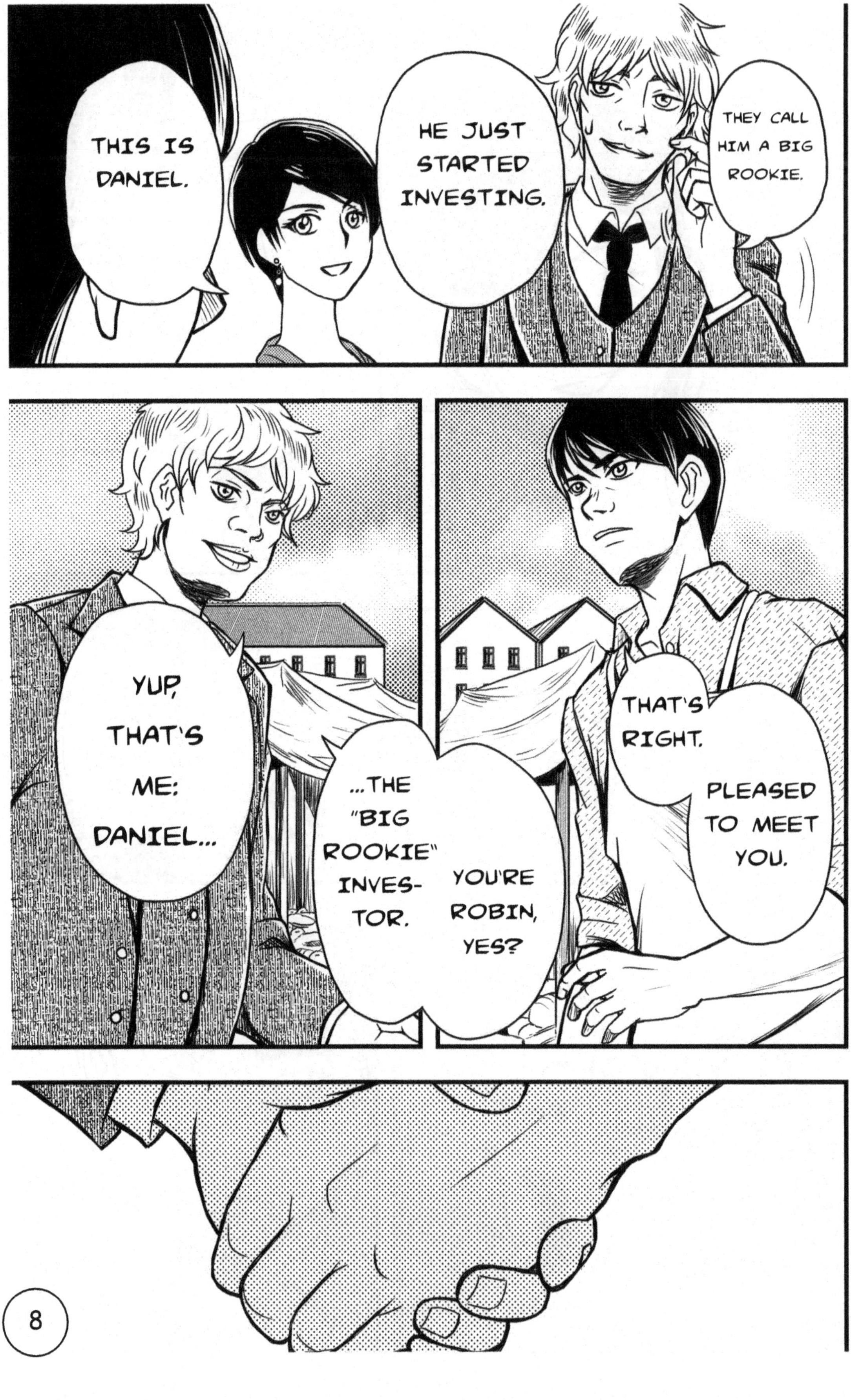
THIS IS DANIEL.
HE JUST STARTED INVESTING.
THEY CALL HIM A BIG ROOKIE.
YUP, THAT'S ME: DANIEL...
...THE "BIG ROOKIE" INVES-TOR.
YOU'RE ROBIN, YES?
THAT'S RIGHT.
PLEASED TO MEET YOU.

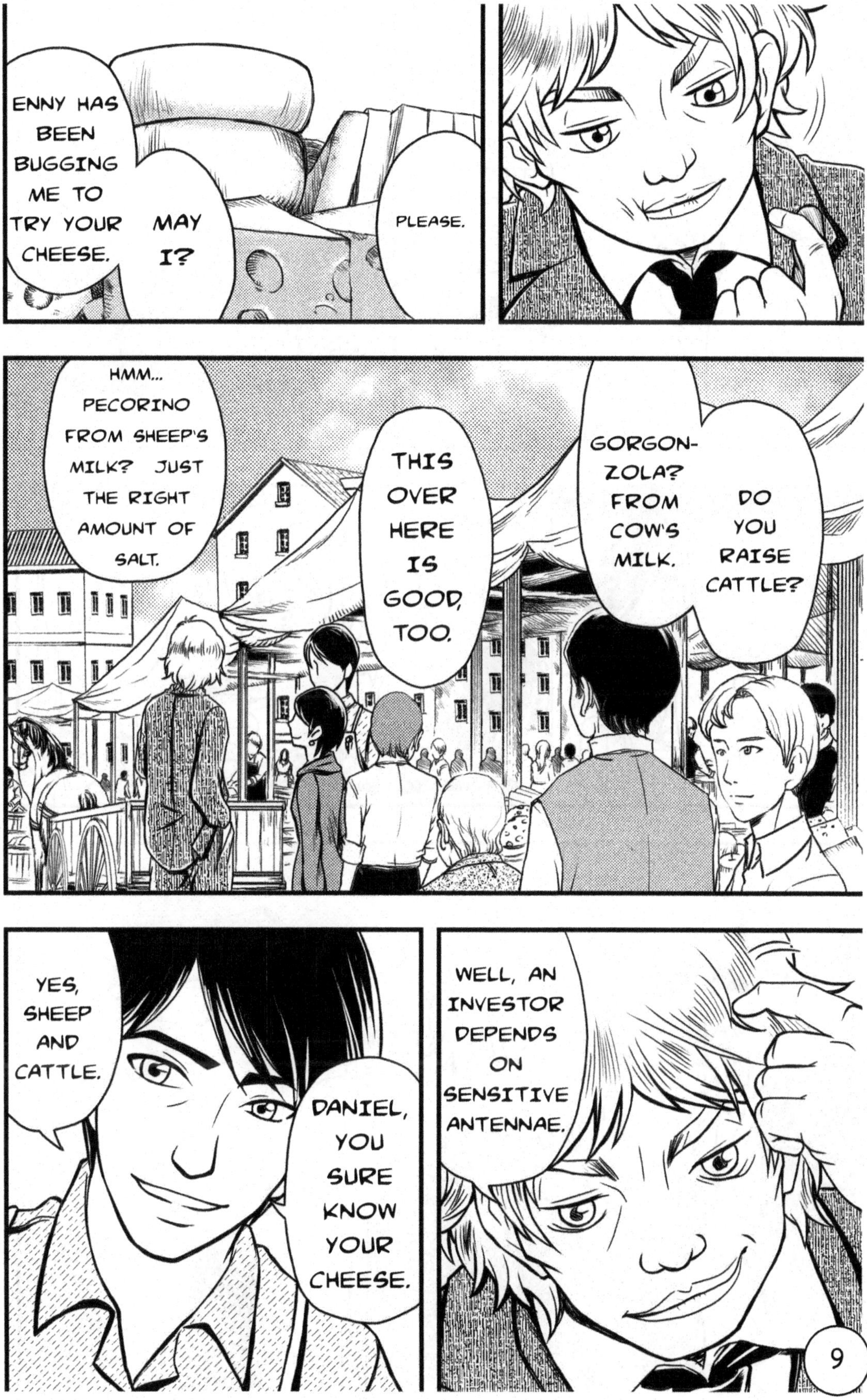
ENNY HAS BEEN BUGGING ME TO TRY YOUR CHEESE.
MAY I?
PLEASE.
HMM... PECORINO FROM SHEEP'S MILK? JUST THE RIGHT AMOUNT OF SALT.
THIS OVER HERE IS GOOD, TOO.
GORGON-ZOLA? FROM COW'S MILK.
DO YOU RAISE CATTLE?
YES, SHEEP AND CATTLE.
DANIEL, YOU SURE KNOW YOUR CHEESE.
WELL, AN INVESTOR DEPENDS ON SENSITIVE ANTENNAE.

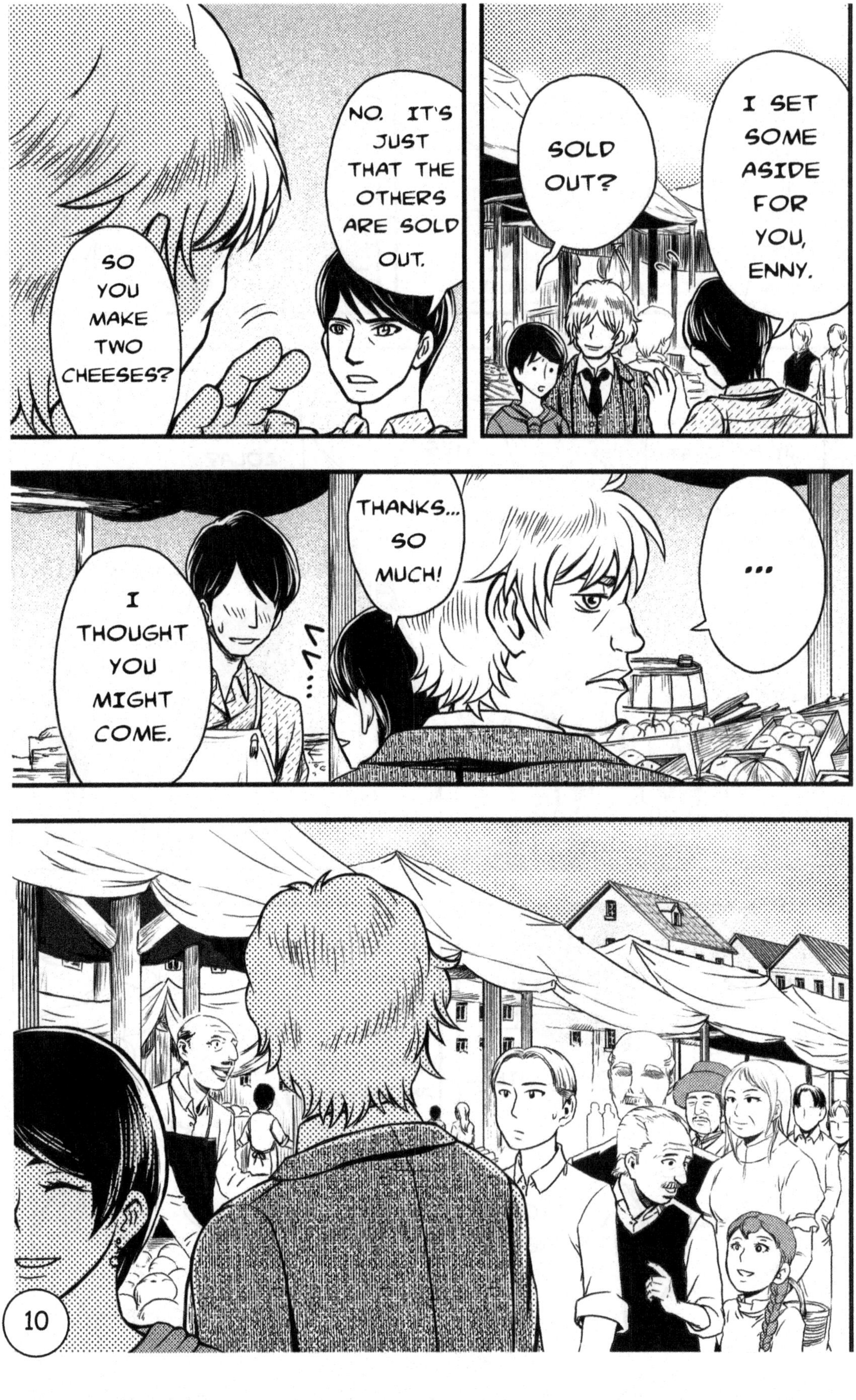
SO YOU MAKE TWO CHEESES?
NO. IT'S JUST THAT THE OTHERS ARE SOLD OUT.
SOLD OUT?
I SET SOME ASIDE FOR YOU, ENNY.
I THOUGHT YOU MIGHT COME.
THANKS... SO MUCH!
...

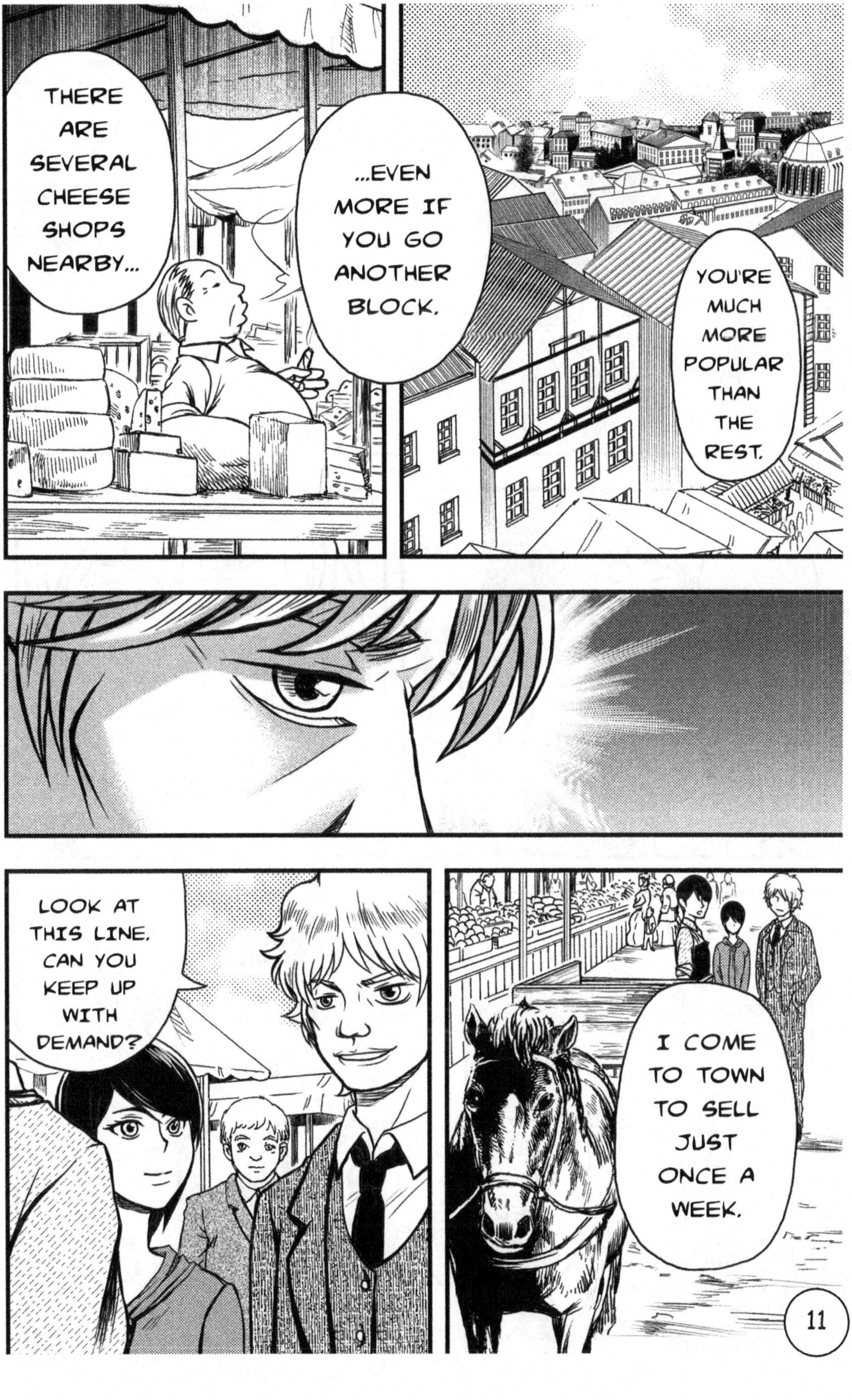
THERE ARE SEVERAL CHEESE SHOPS NEARBY...
...EVEN MORE IF YOU GO ANOTHER BLOCK.
YOU'RE MUCH MORE POPULAR THAN THE REST.
LOOK AT THIS LINE. CAN YOU KEEP UP WITH DEMAND?
I COME TO TOWN TO SELL JUST ONCE A WEEK.

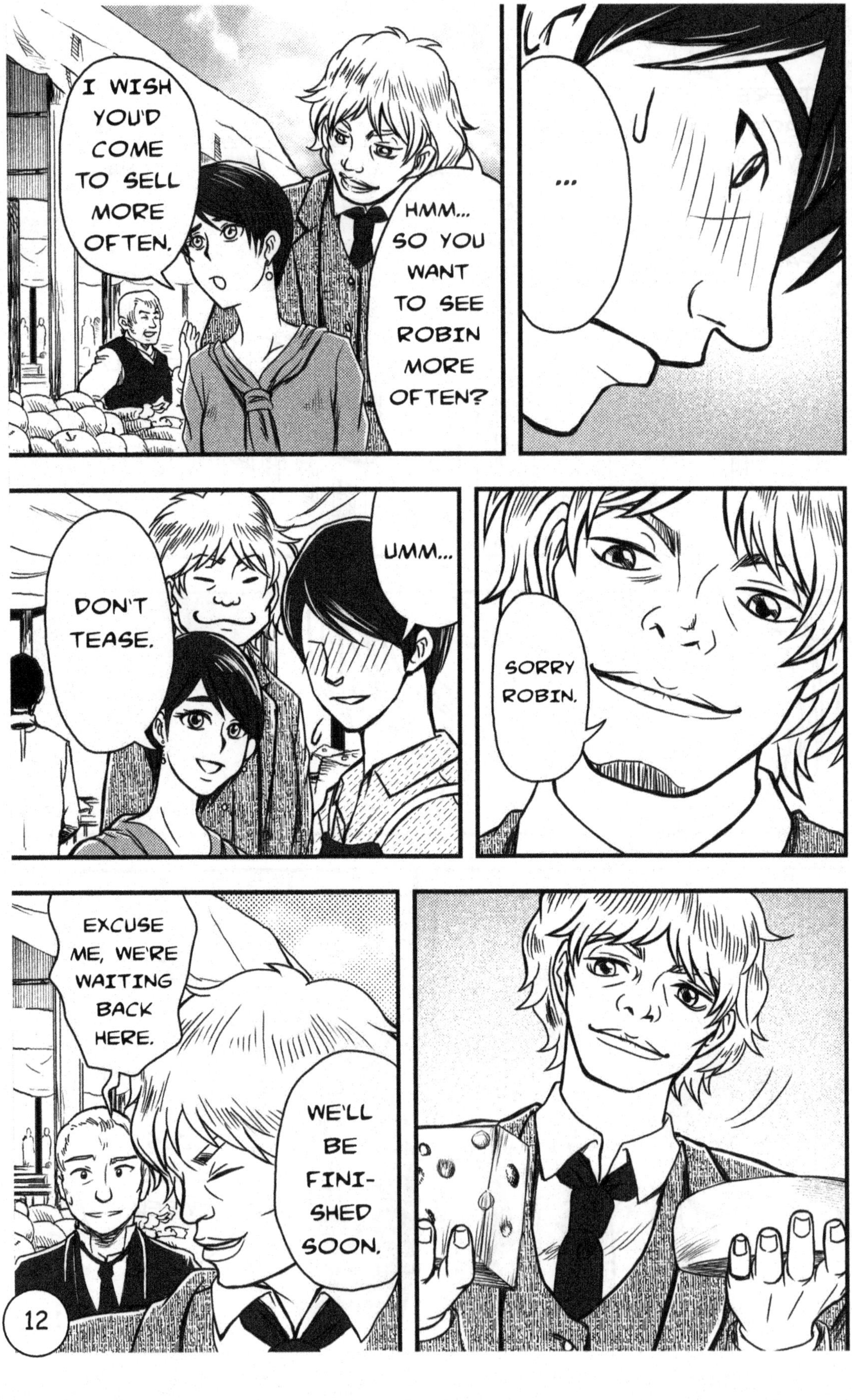
I WISH YOU'D COME TO SELL MORE OFTEN.
HMM... SO YOU WANT TO SEE ROBIN MORE OFTEN?
...
DON'T TEASE.
UMM...
SORRY ROBIN.
EXCUSE ME, WE'RE WAITING BACK HERE.
WE'LL BE FINI-SHED SOON.

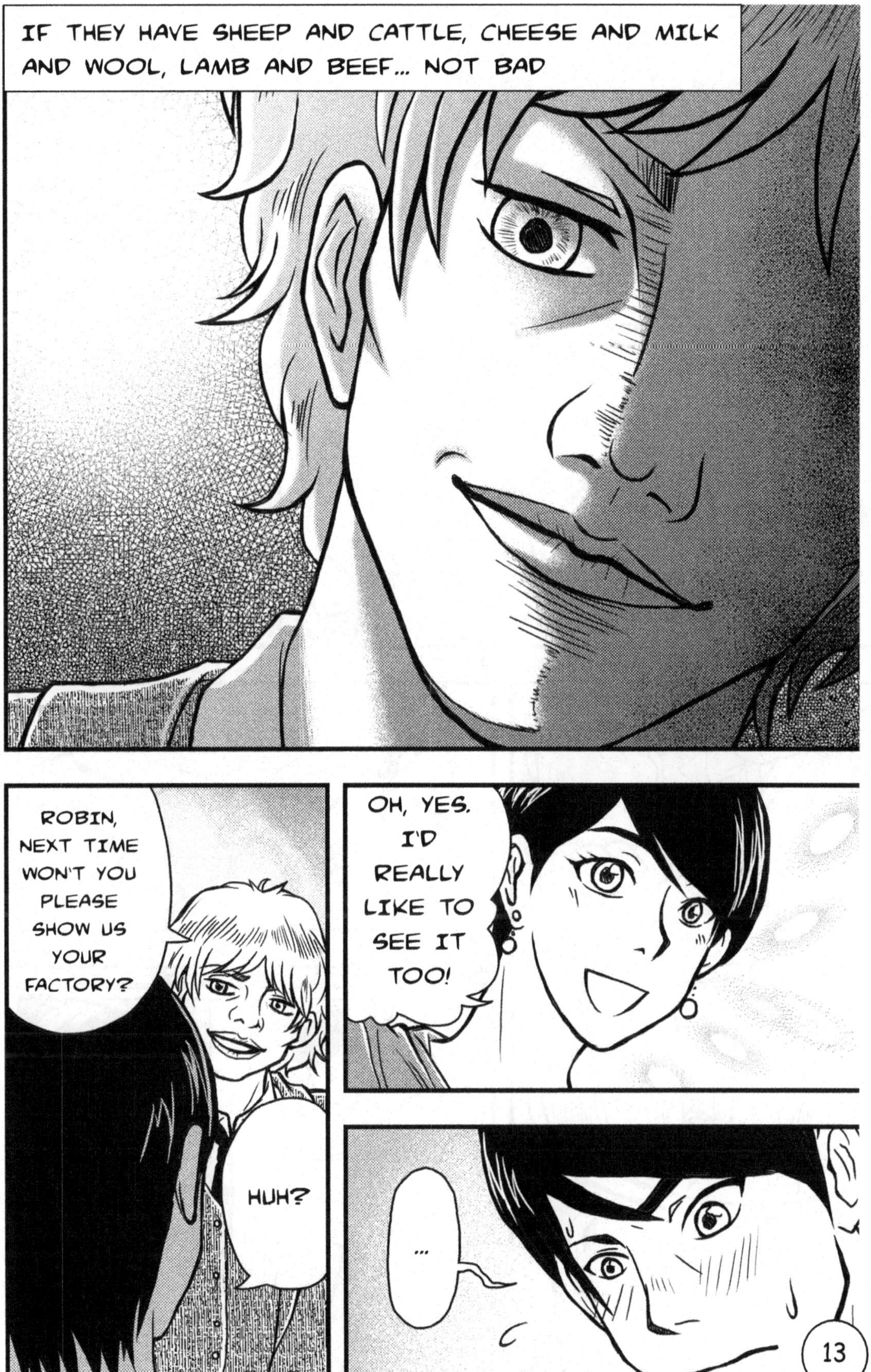
IF THEY HAVE SHEEP AND CATTLE, CHEESE AND MILK AND WOOL, LAMB AND BEEF... NOT BAD
ROBIN, NEXT TIME WON'T YOU PLEASE SHOW US YOUR FACTORY?
HUH?
OH, YES. I'D REALLY LIKE TO SEE IT TOO!
...

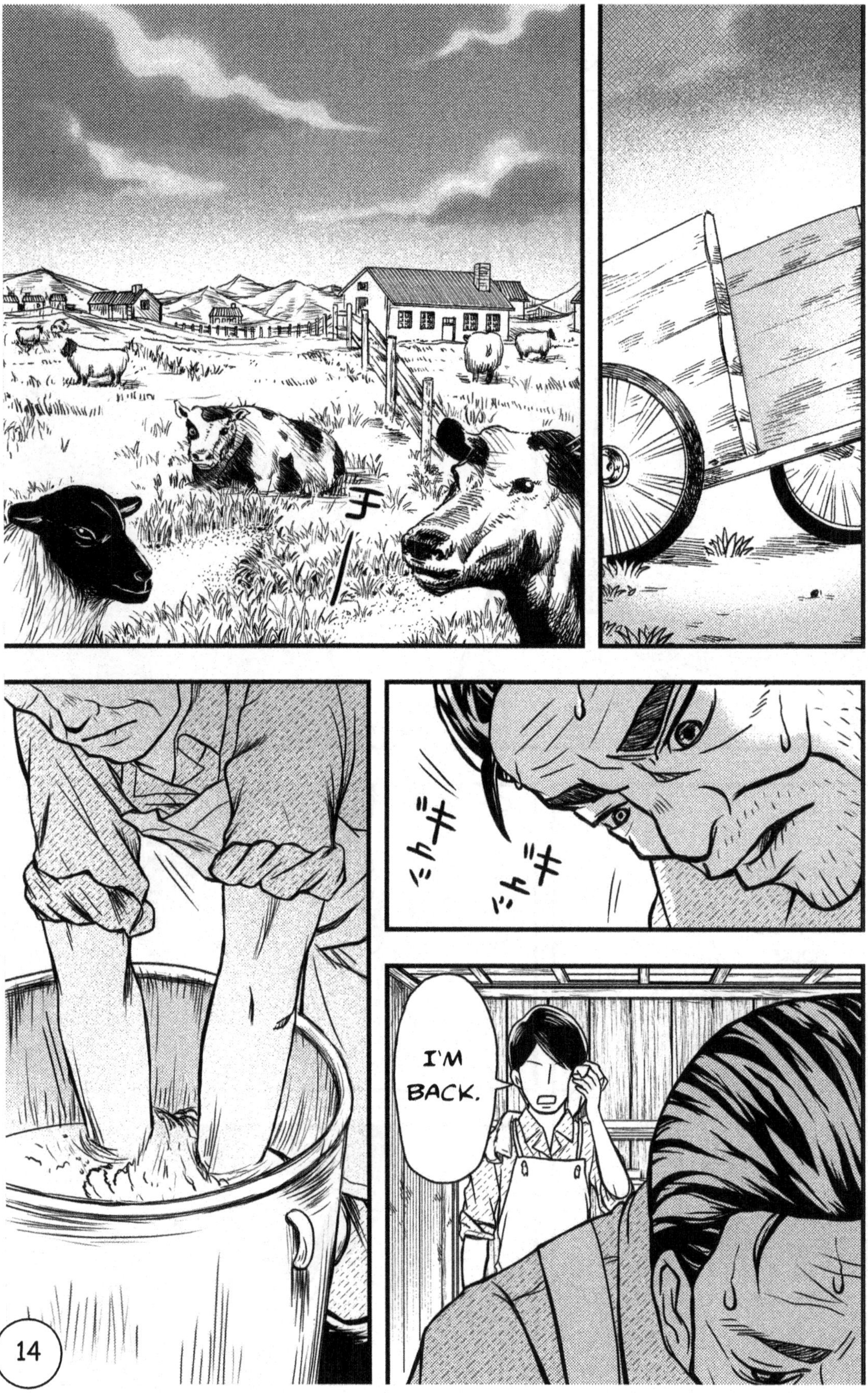
チー
ドキッ
ドキッ
I'M BACK.

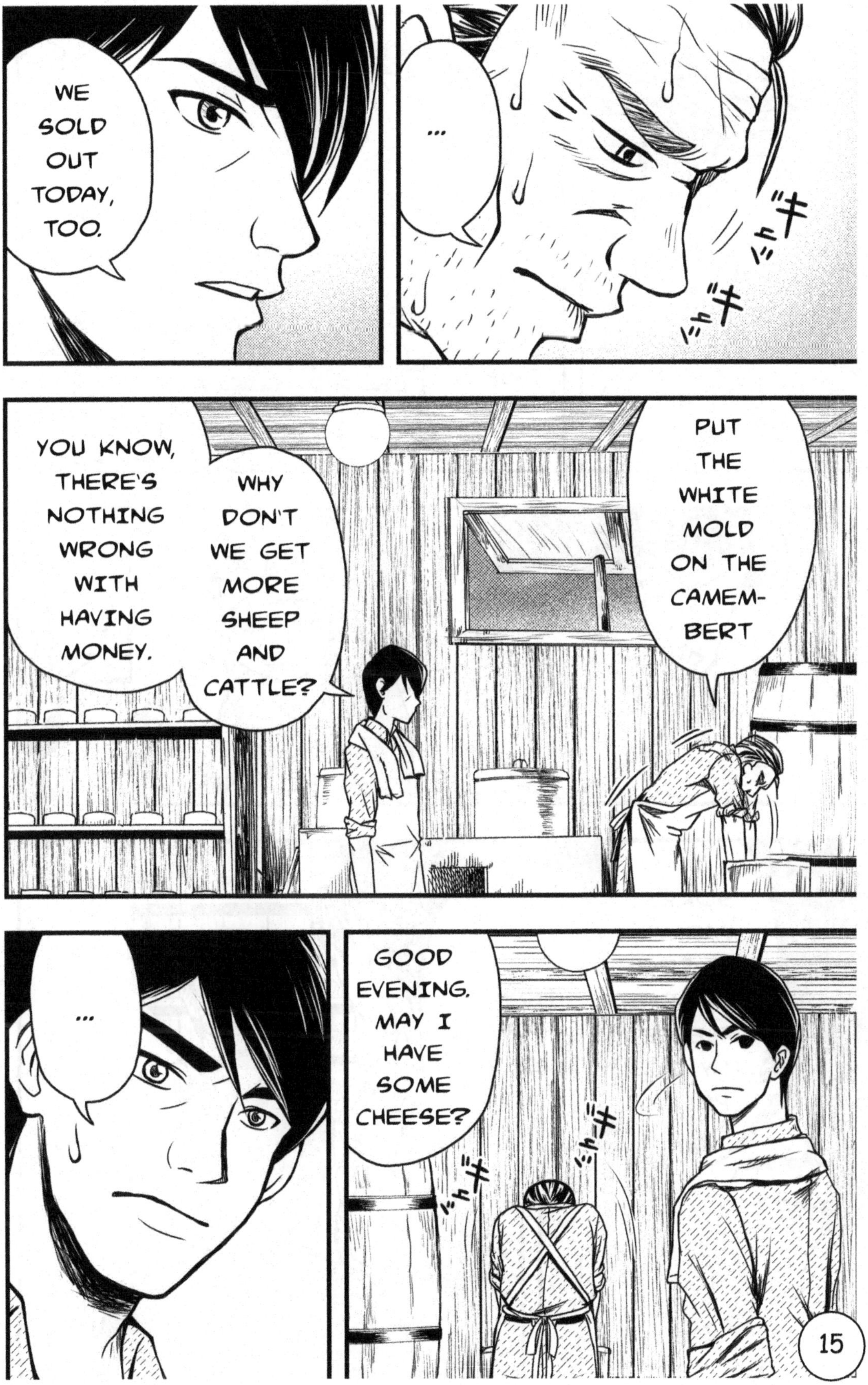
WE SOLD OUT TODAY, TOO.
...
YOU KNOW, THERE'S NOTHING WRONG WITH HAVING MONEY.
WHY DON'T WE GET MORE SHEEP AND CATTLE?
PUT THE WHITE MOLD ON THE CAMEMBERT
...
GOOD EVENING. MAY I HAVE SOME CHEESE?

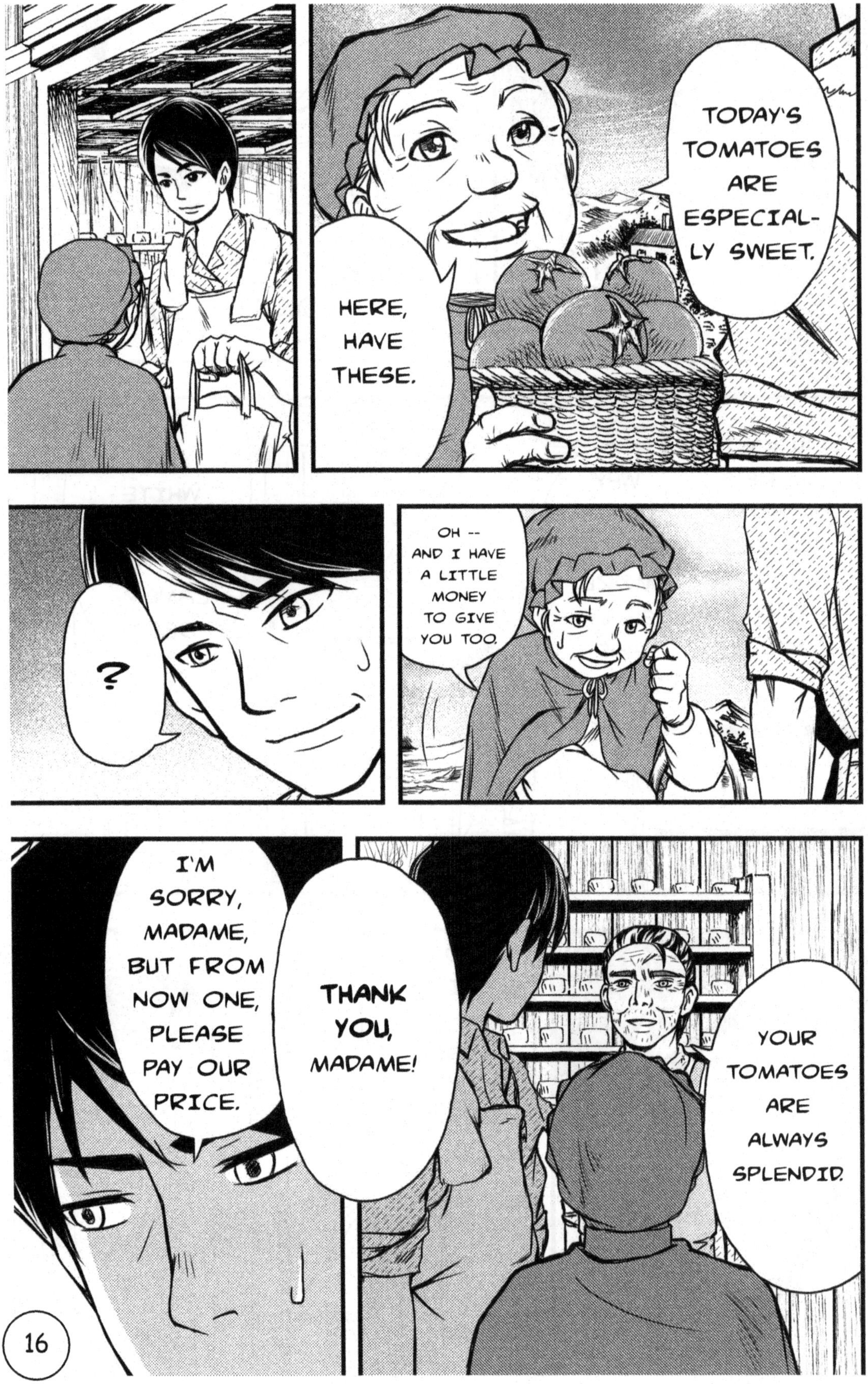
TODAY'S TOMATOES ARE ESPECIAL-LY SWEET.
HERE, HAVE THESE.
?
OH -- AND I HAVE A LITTLE MONEY TO GIVE YOU TOO.
I'M SORRY, MADAME, BUT FROM NOW ONE, PLEASE PAY OUR PRICE.
THANK YOU, MADAME!
YOUR TOMATOES ARE ALWAYS SPLENDID.

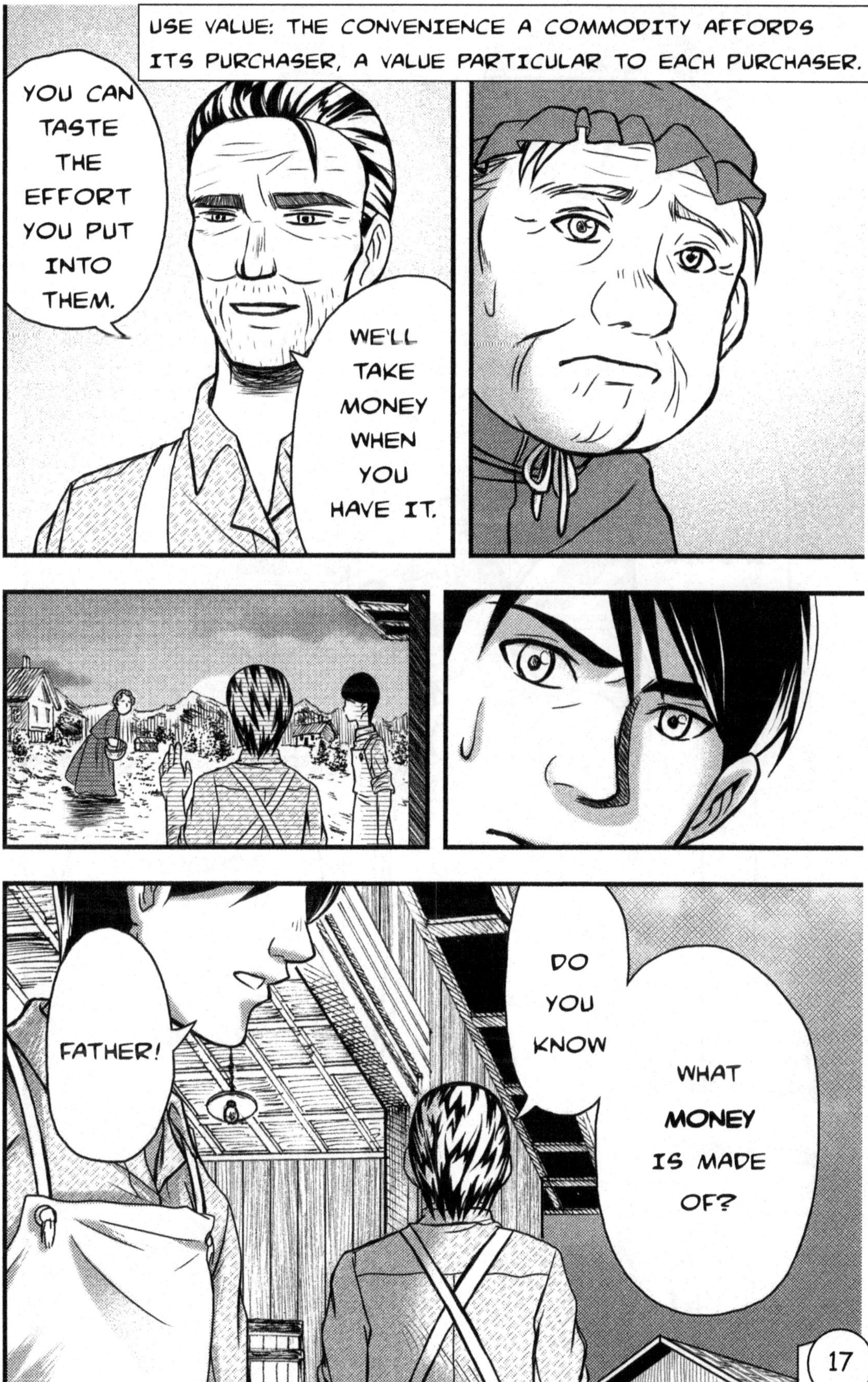
USE VALUE: THE CONVENIENCE A COMMODITY AFFORDS ITS PURCHASER, A VALUE PARTICULAR TO EACH PURCHASER.
YOU CAN TASTE THE EFFORT YOU PUT INTO THEM.
WE'LL TAKE MONEY WHEN YOU HAVE IT.
FATHER!
DO YOU KNOW
WHAT **MONEY** IS MADE OF?

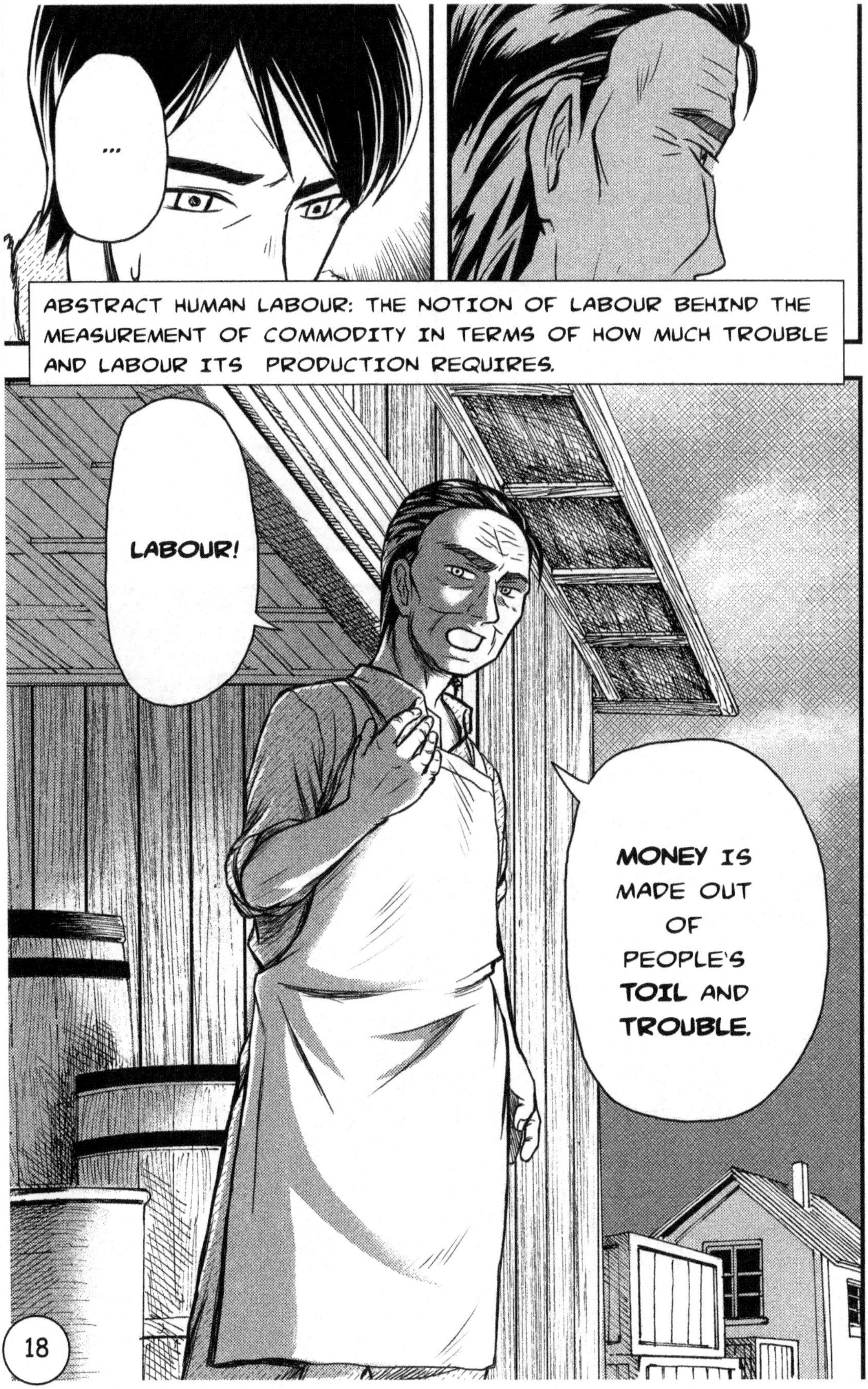
...
ABSTRACT HUMAN LABOUR: THE NOTION OF LABOUR BEHIND THE MEASUREMENT OF COMMODITY IN TERMS OF HOW MUCH TROUBLE AND LABOUR ITS PRODUCTION REQUIRES.
LABOUR!
MONEY IS MADE OUT OF PEOPLE'S TOIL AND TROUBLE.

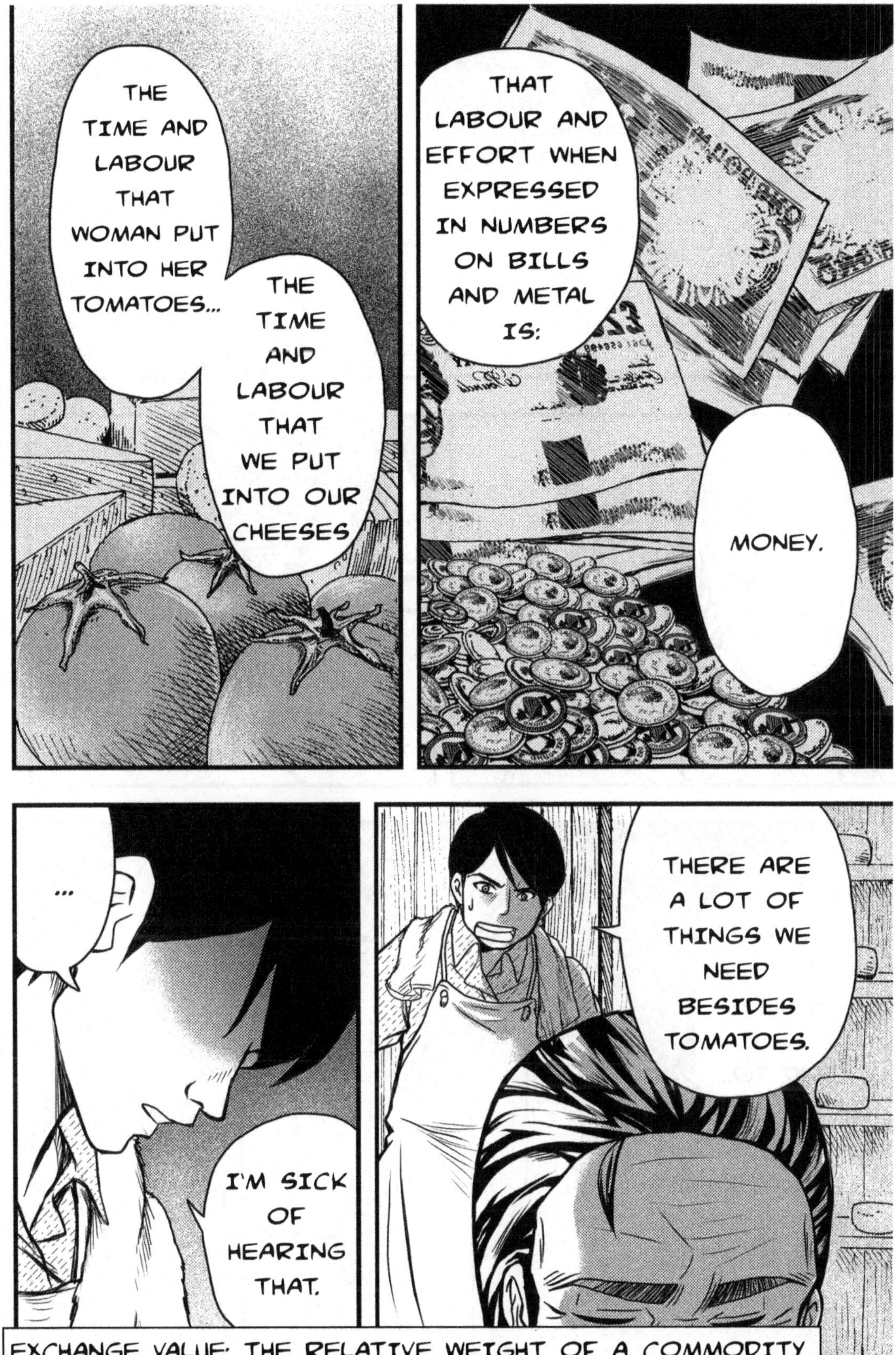
THE TIME AND LABOUR THAT WOMAN PUT INTO HER TOMATOES...
THE TIME AND LABOUR THAT WE PUT INTO OUR CHEESES
THAT LABOUR AND EFFORT WHEN EXPRESSED IN NUMBERS ON BILLS AND METAL IS:
MONEY.
...
I'M SICK OF HEARING THAT.
THERE ARE A LOT OF THINGS WE NEED BESIDES TOMATOES.
EXCHANGE VALUE: THE RELATIVE WEIGHT OF A COMMODITY WHEN MEASURED AGAINST OTHER COMMODITIES. A COMPARATIVE MEASURE.

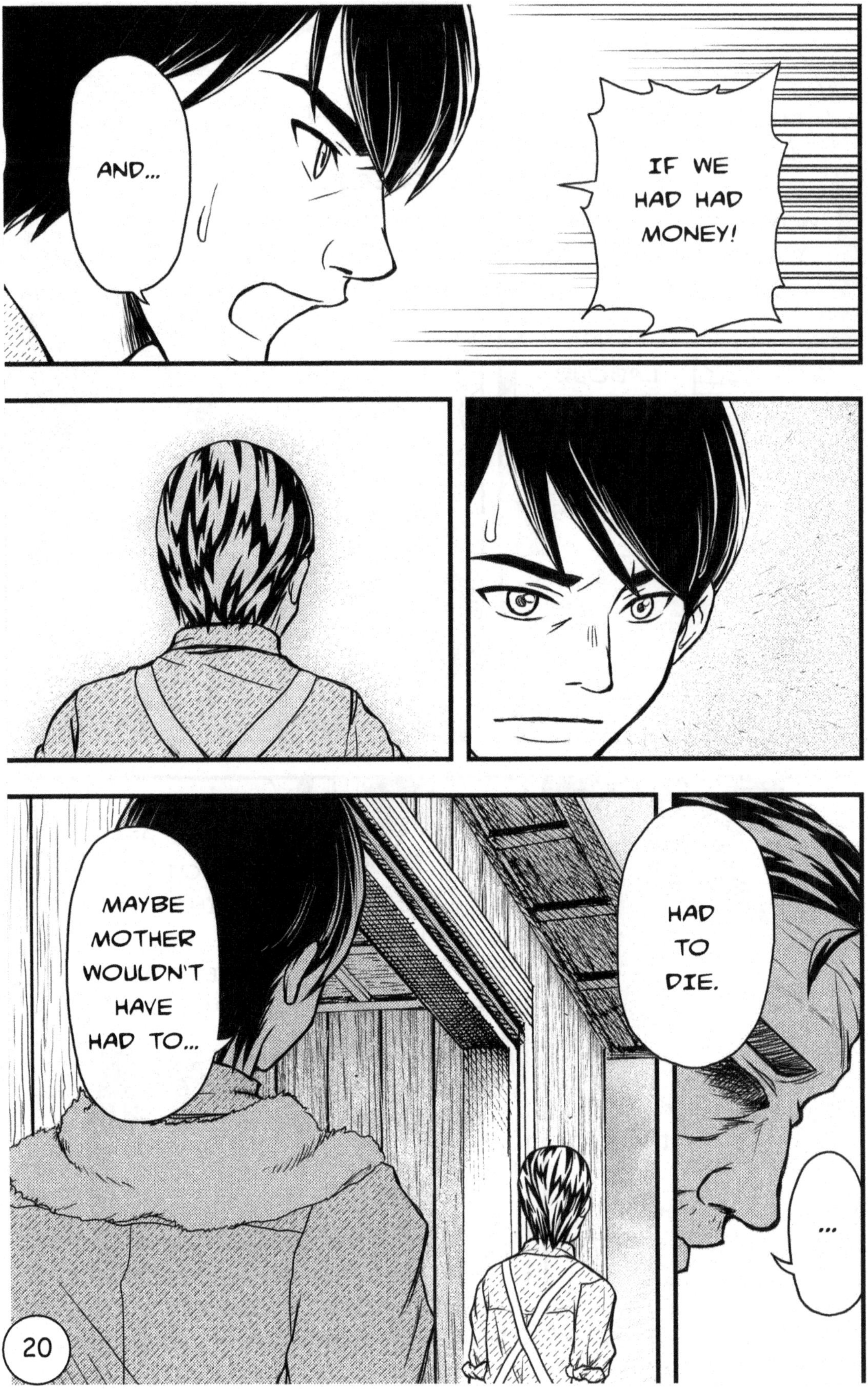
AND...
IF WE HAD HAD MONEY!
MAYBE MOTHER WOULDN'T HAVE HAD TO...
HAD TO DIE.
...

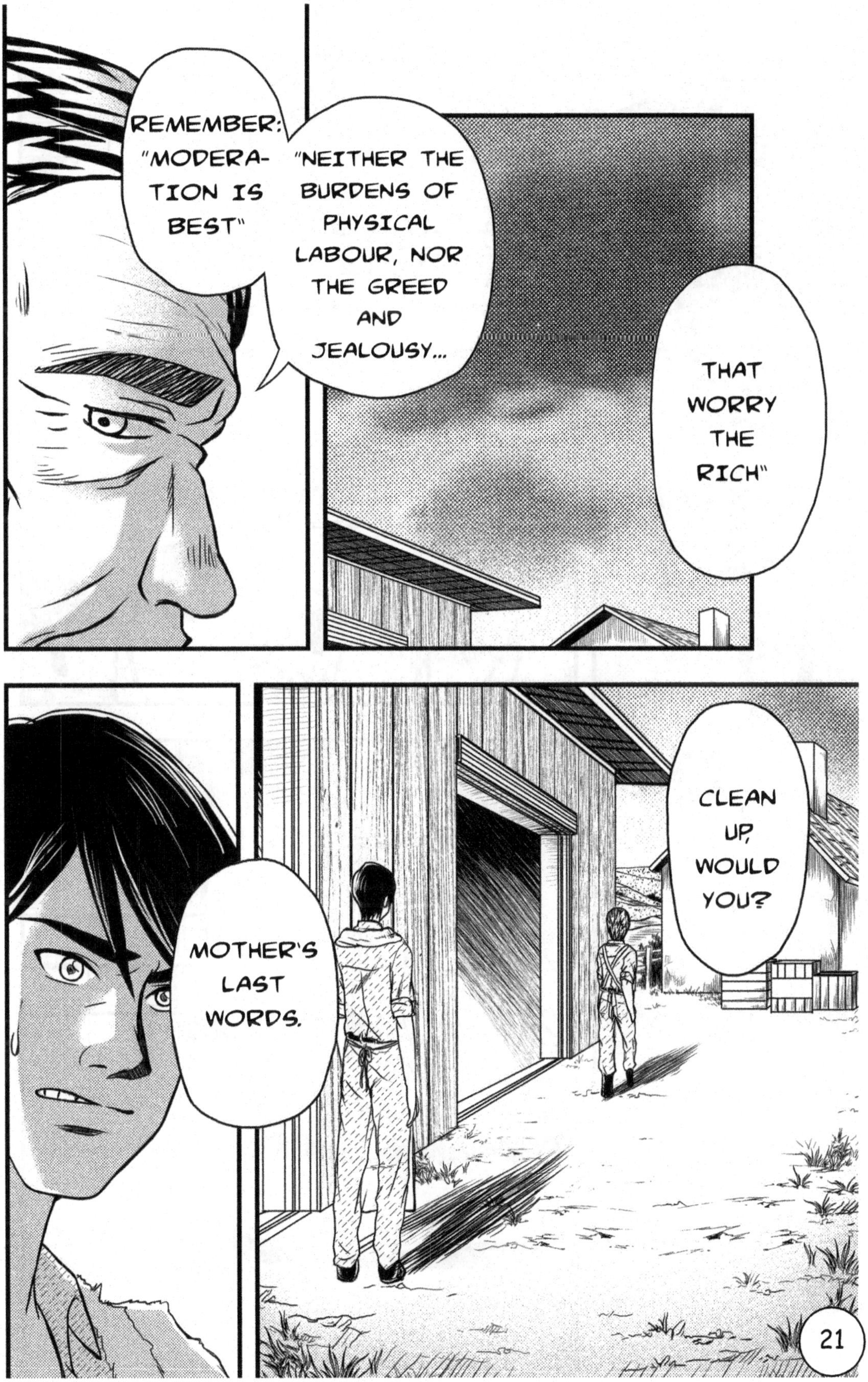
REMEMBER: "MODERATION IS BEST"
"NEITHER THE BURDENS OF PHYSICAL LABOUR, NOR THE GREED AND JEALOUSY...
THAT WORRY THE RICH"
MOTHER'S LAST WORDS.
CLEAN UP, WOULD YOU?

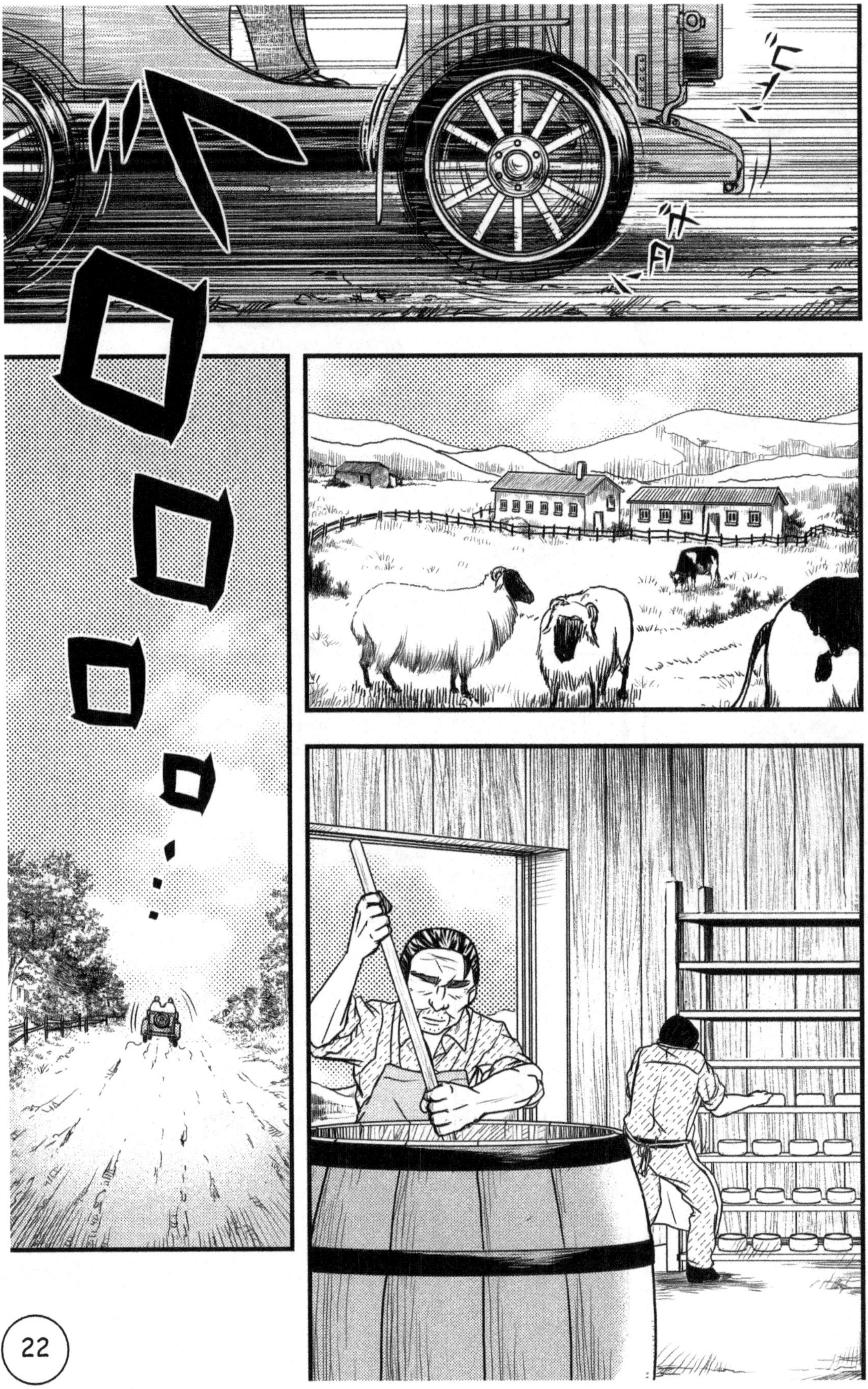
ブロロロロ…
ゴトン
ガタン

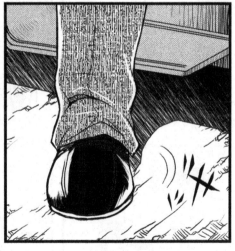

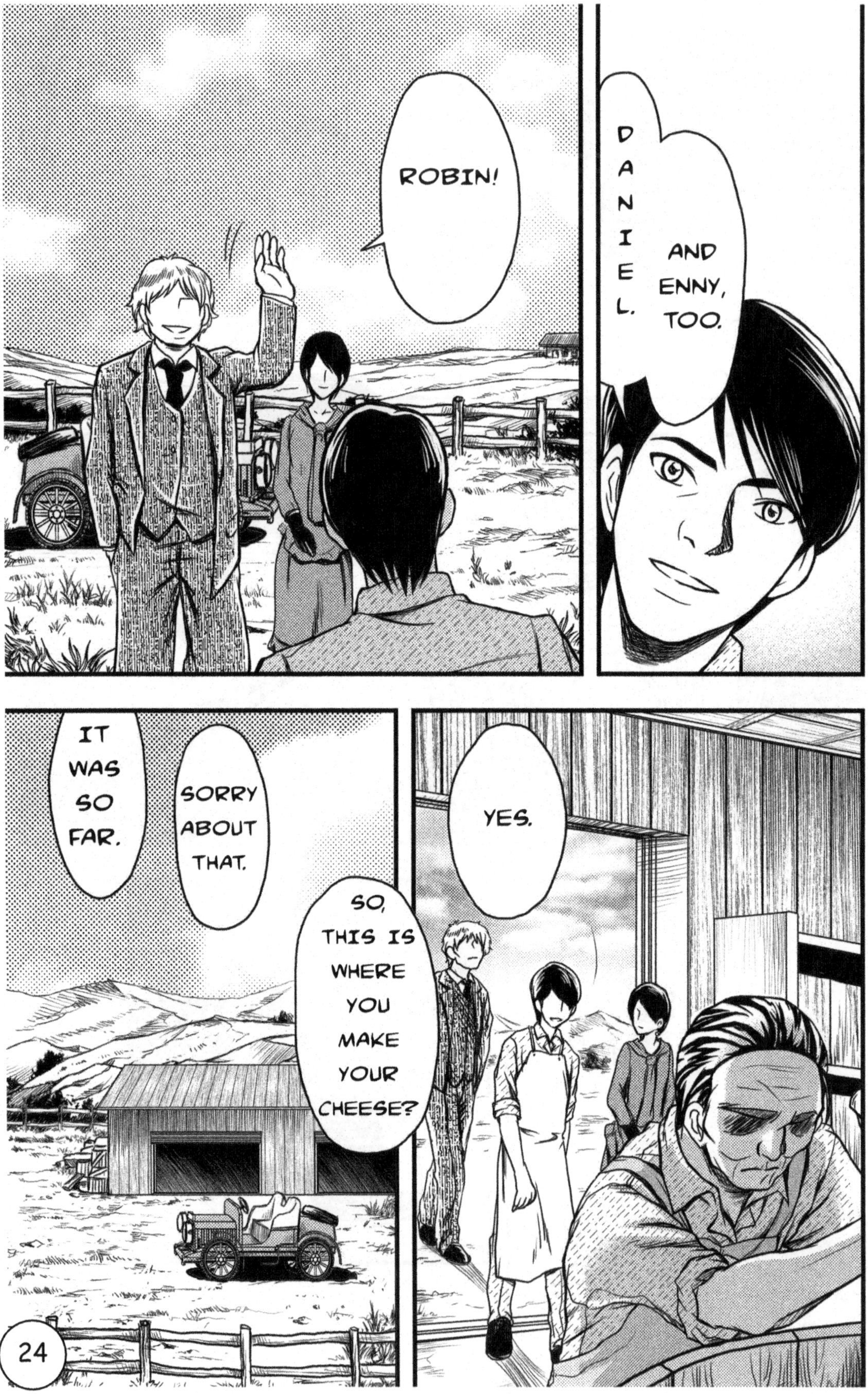
ROBIN!
DANIEL.
AND ENNY, TOO.
IT WAS SO FAR.
SORRY ABOUT THAT.
SO, THIS IS WHERE YOU MAKE YOUR CHEESE?
YES.

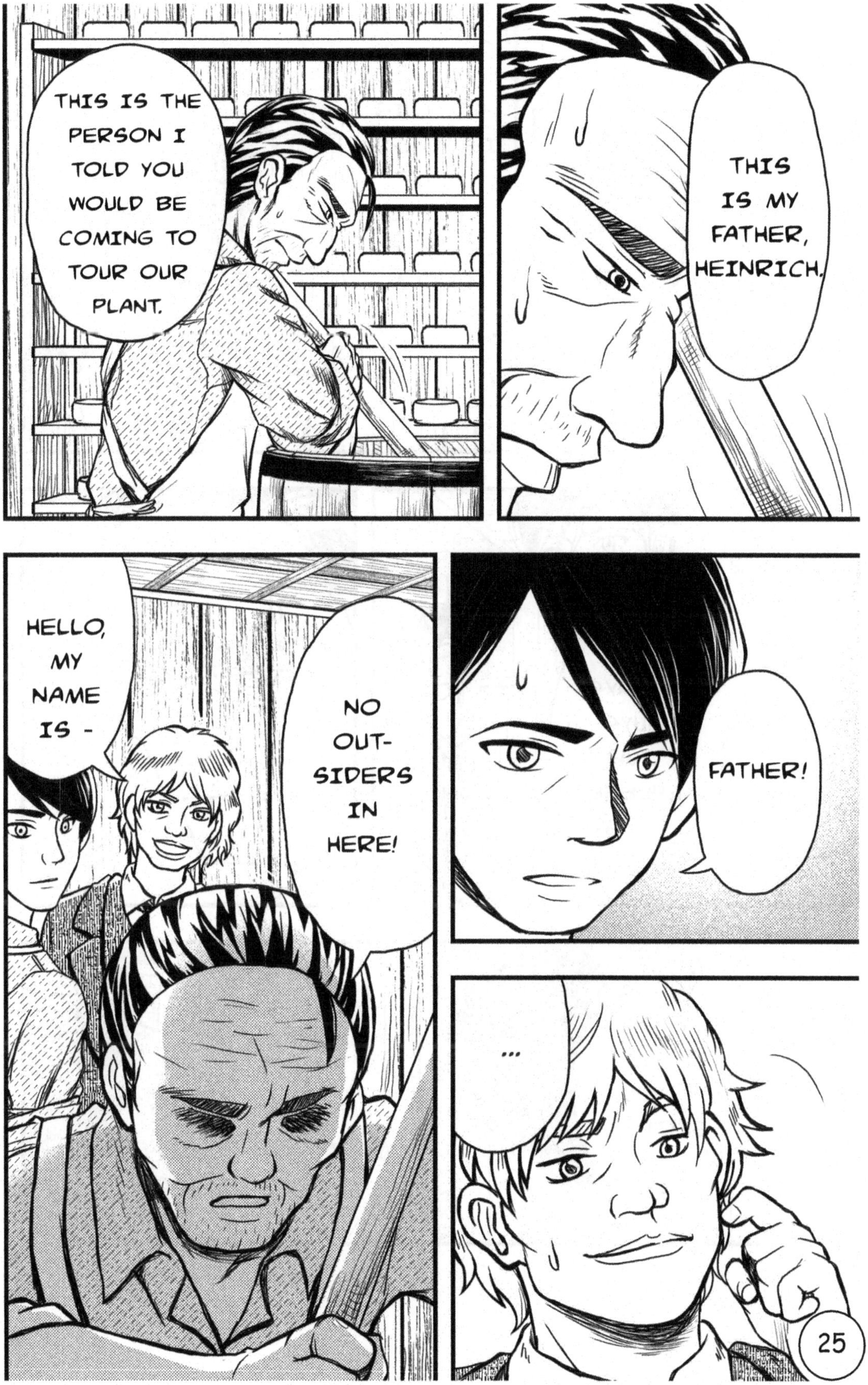
THIS IS THE PERSON I TOLD YOU WOULD BE COMING TO TOUR OUR PLANT.
THIS IS MY FATHER, HEINRICH.
HELLO, MY NAME IS -
NO OUT-SIDERS IN HERE!
FATHER!
...

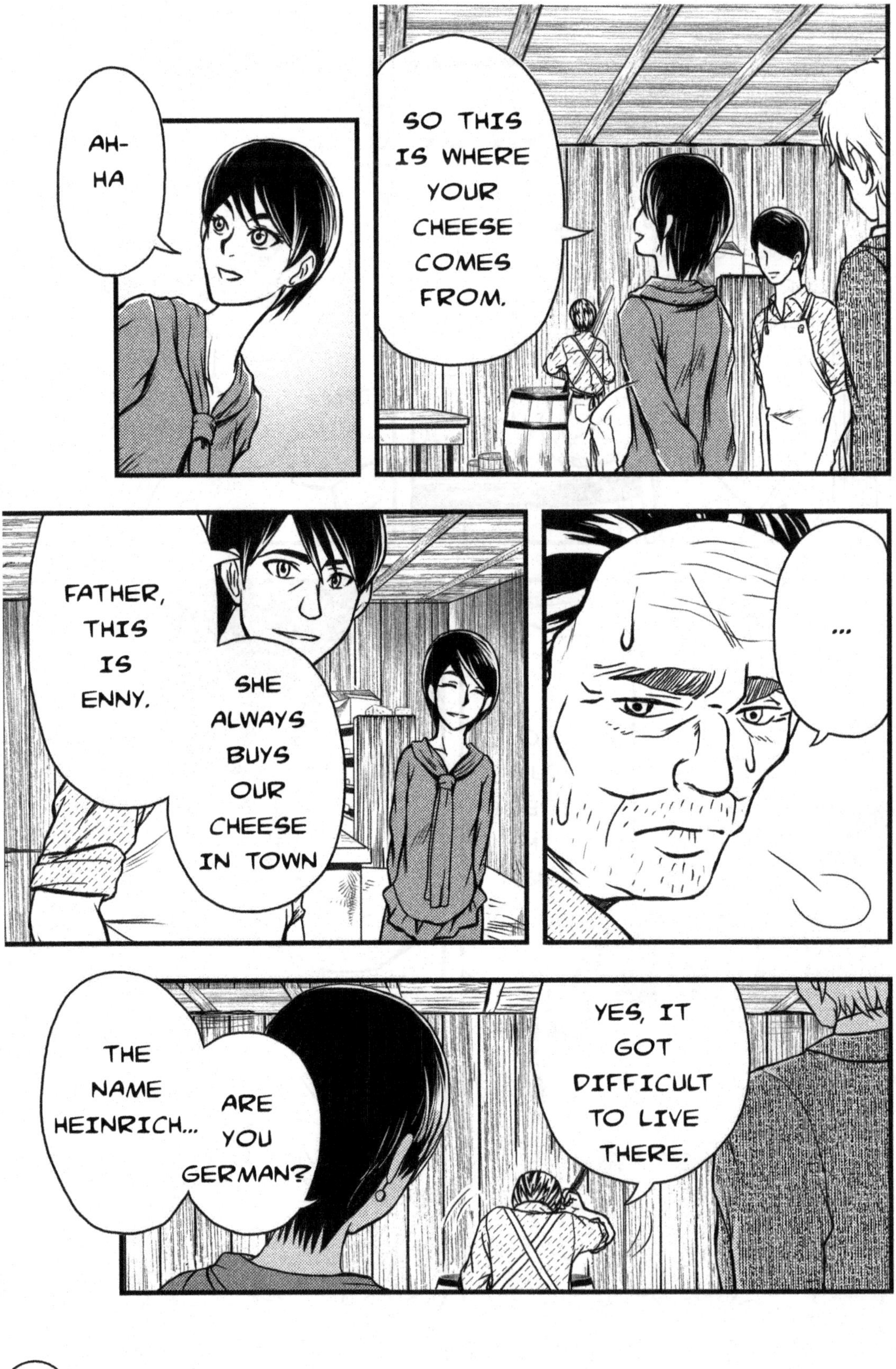
AH-
HA
SO THIS IS WHERE YOUR CHEESE COMES FROM.
FATHER, THIS IS ENNY.
SHE ALWAYS BUYS OUR CHEESE IN TOWN
...
THE NAME HEINRICH...
ARE YOU GERMAN?
YES, IT GOT DIFFICULT TO LIVE THERE.

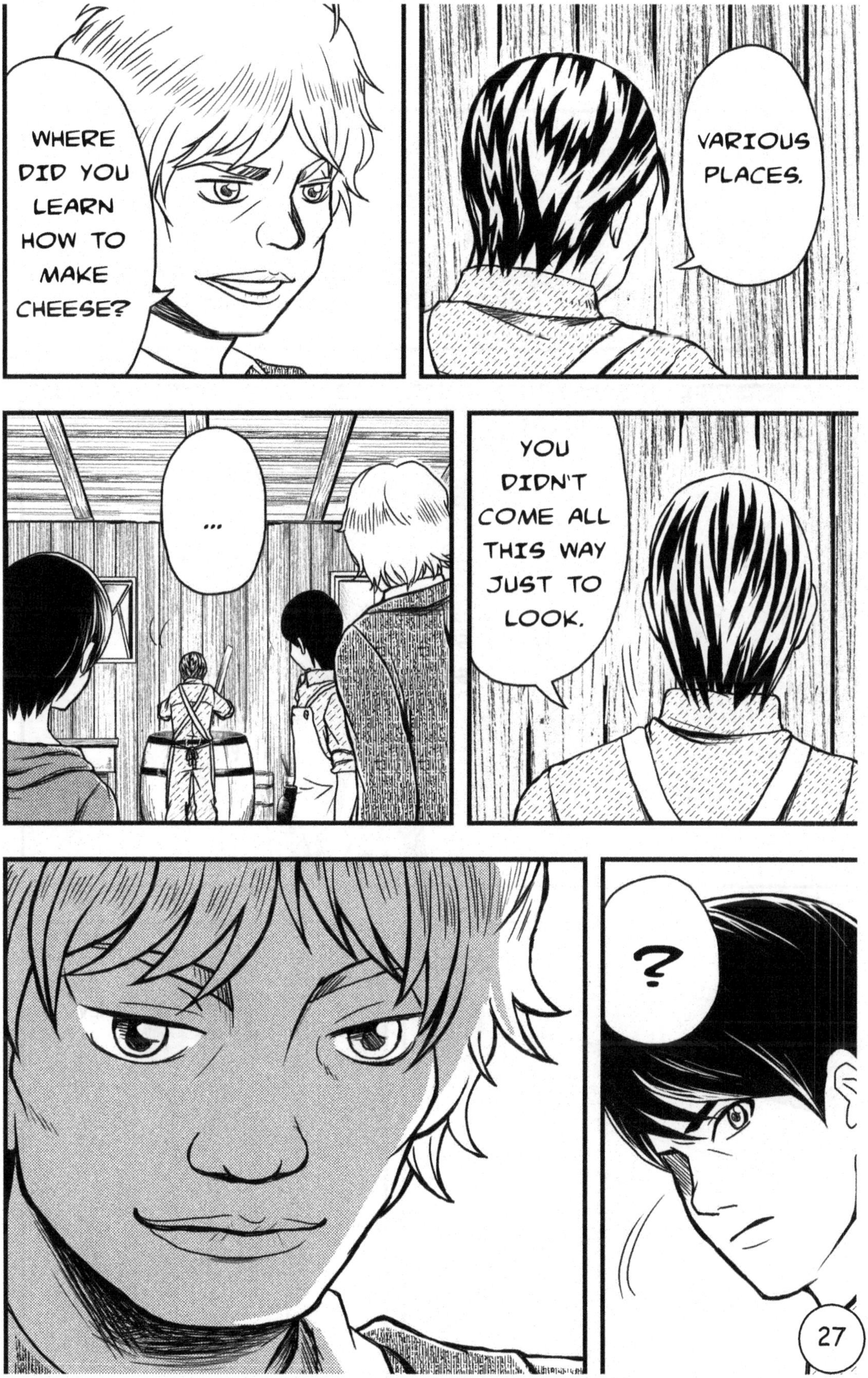
WHERE DID YOU LEARN HOW TO MAKE CHEESE?
VARIOUS PLACES.
...
YOU DIDN'T COME ALL THIS WAY JUST TO LOOK.
?

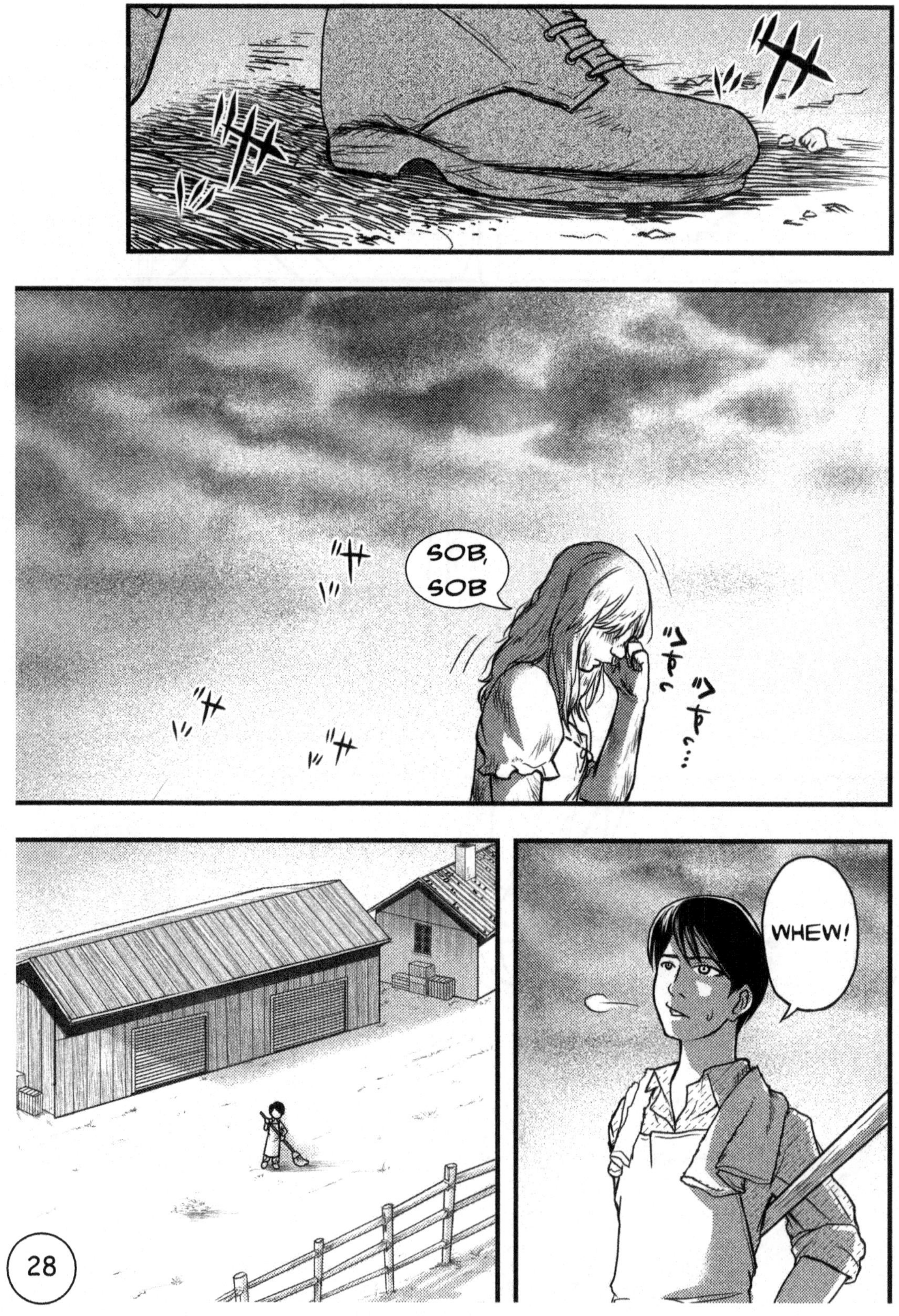
SOB, SOB
WHEW!

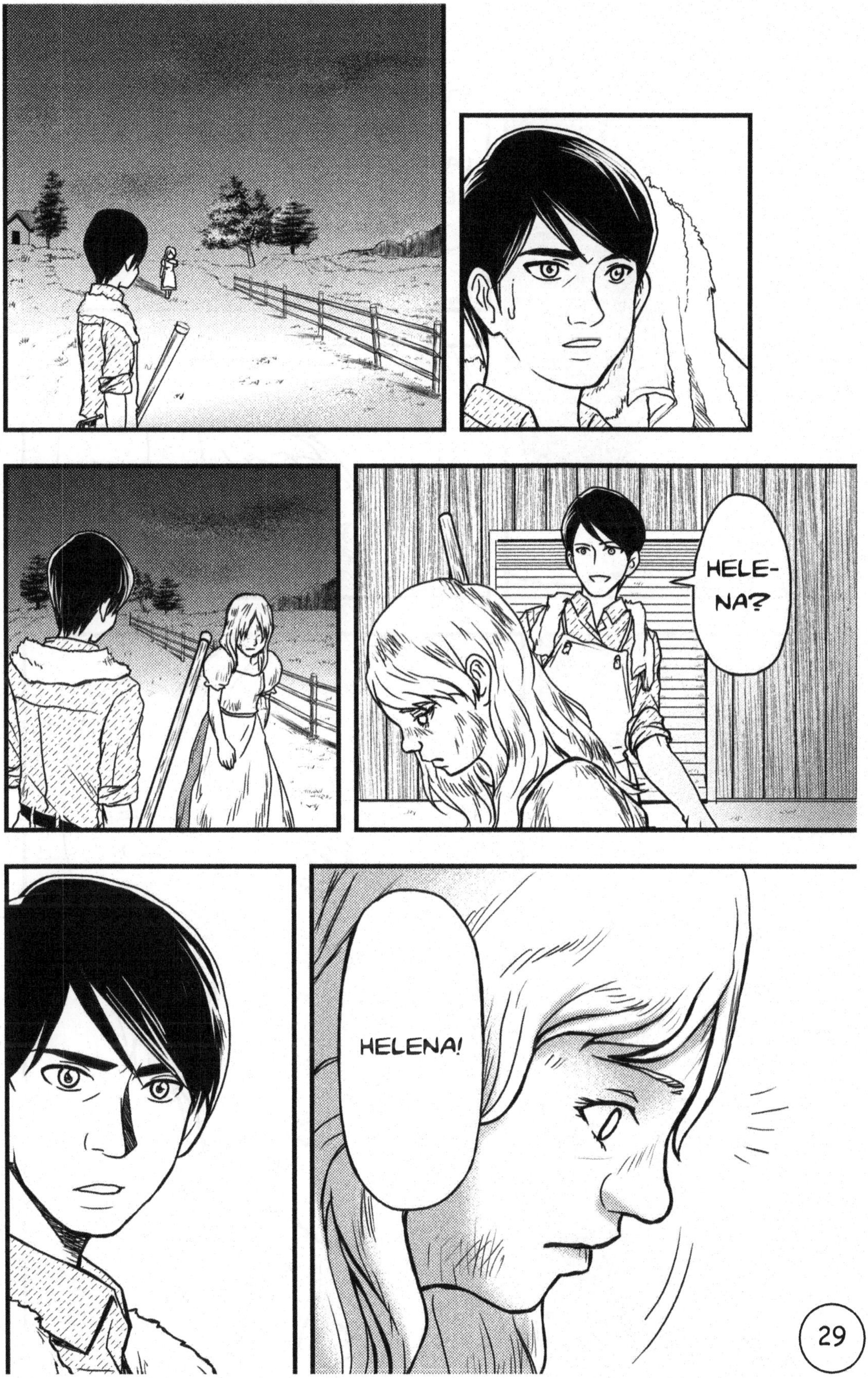
HELE-
NA?
HELENA!

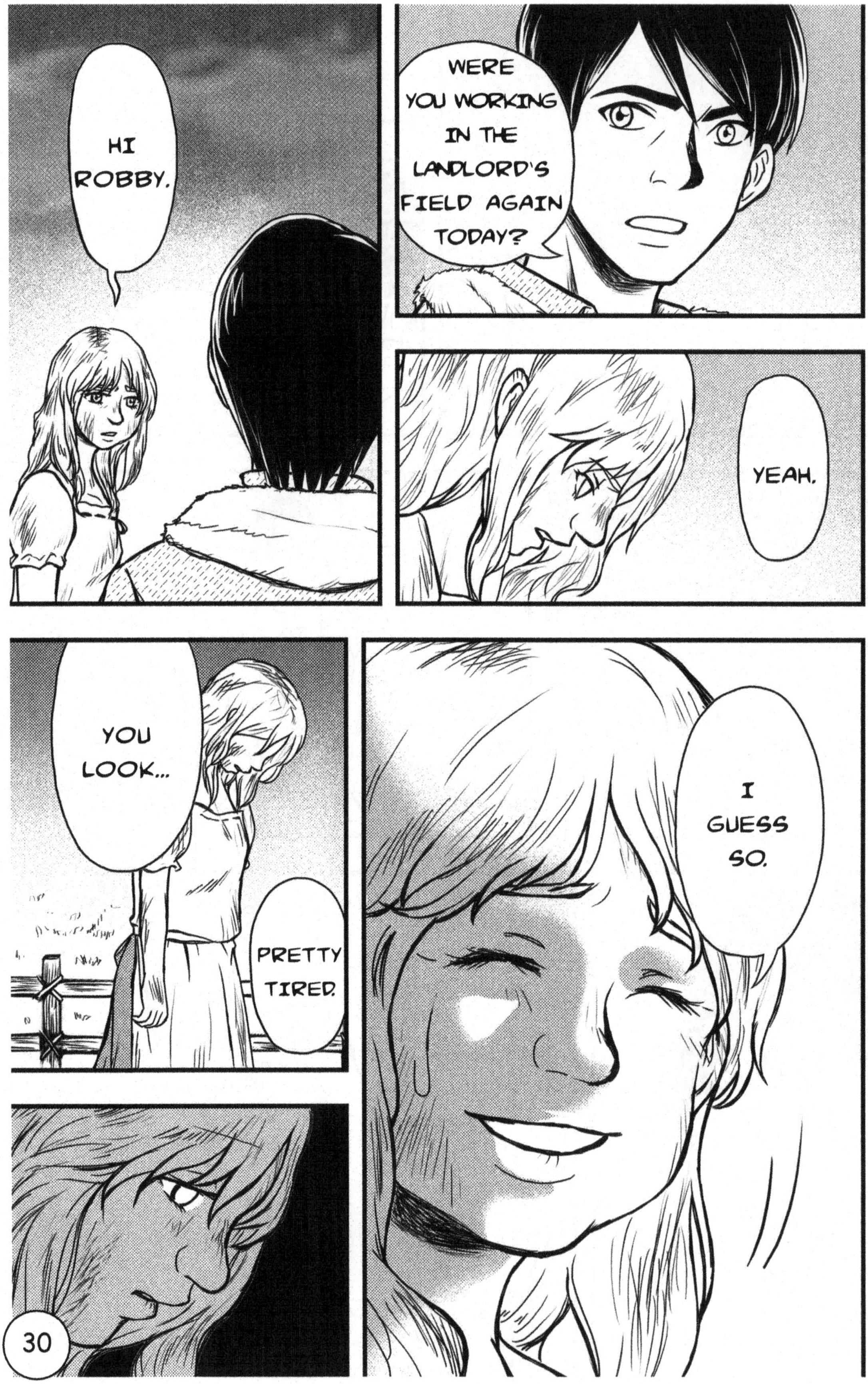
HI ROBBY.
WERE YOU WORKING IN THE LANDLORD'S FIELD AGAIN TODAY?
YEAH.
YOU LOOK...
PRETTY TIRED.
I GUESS SO.

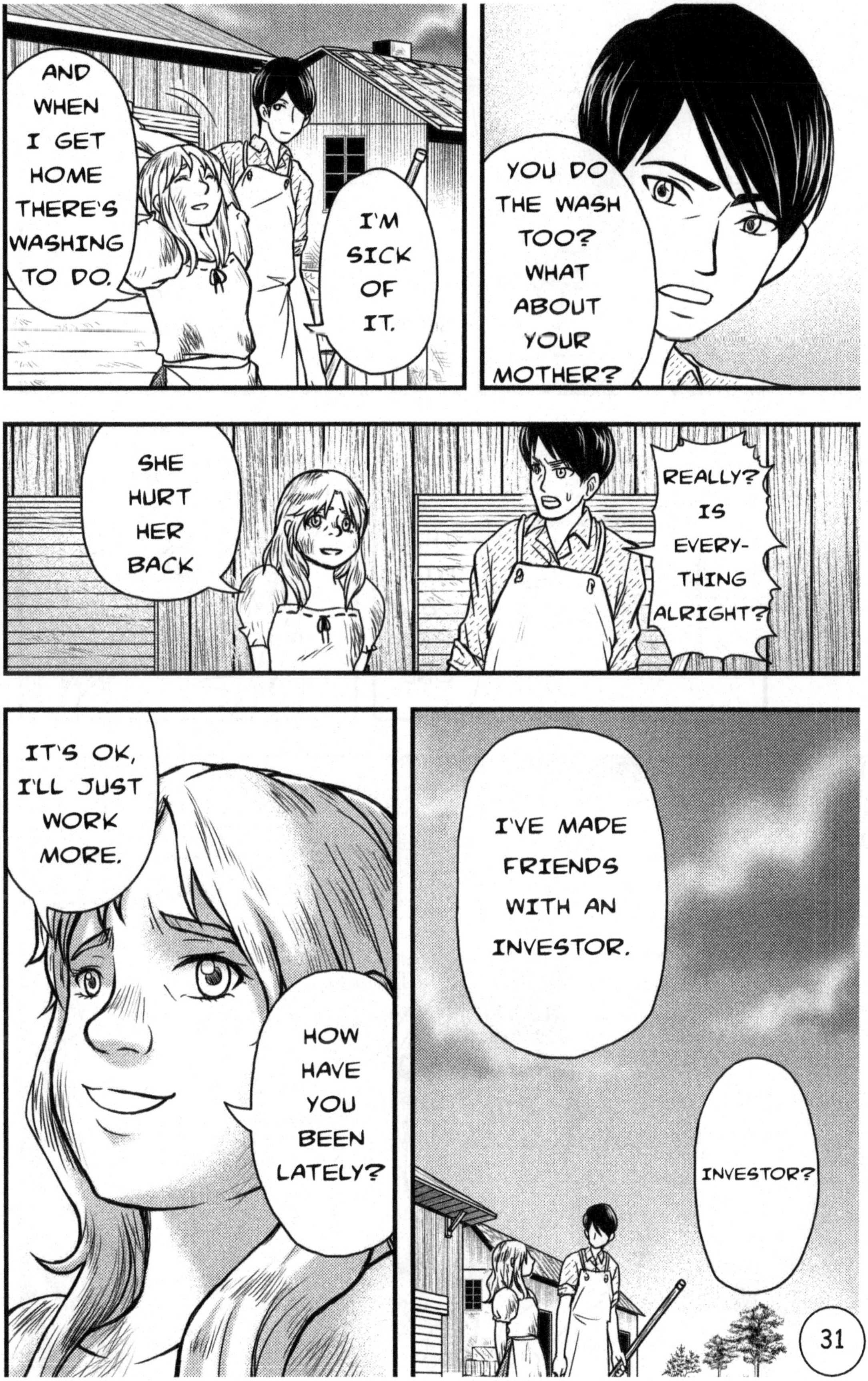
AND WHEN I GET HOME THERE'S WASHING TO DO.
I'M SICK OF IT.
YOU DO THE WASH TOO? WHAT ABOUT YOUR MOTHER?
SHE HURT HER BACK
REALLY? IS EVERY-THING ALRIGHT?
IT'S OK, I'LL JUST WORK MORE.
HOW HAVE YOU BEEN LATELY?
I'VE MADE FRIENDS WITH AN INVESTOR.
INVESTOR?

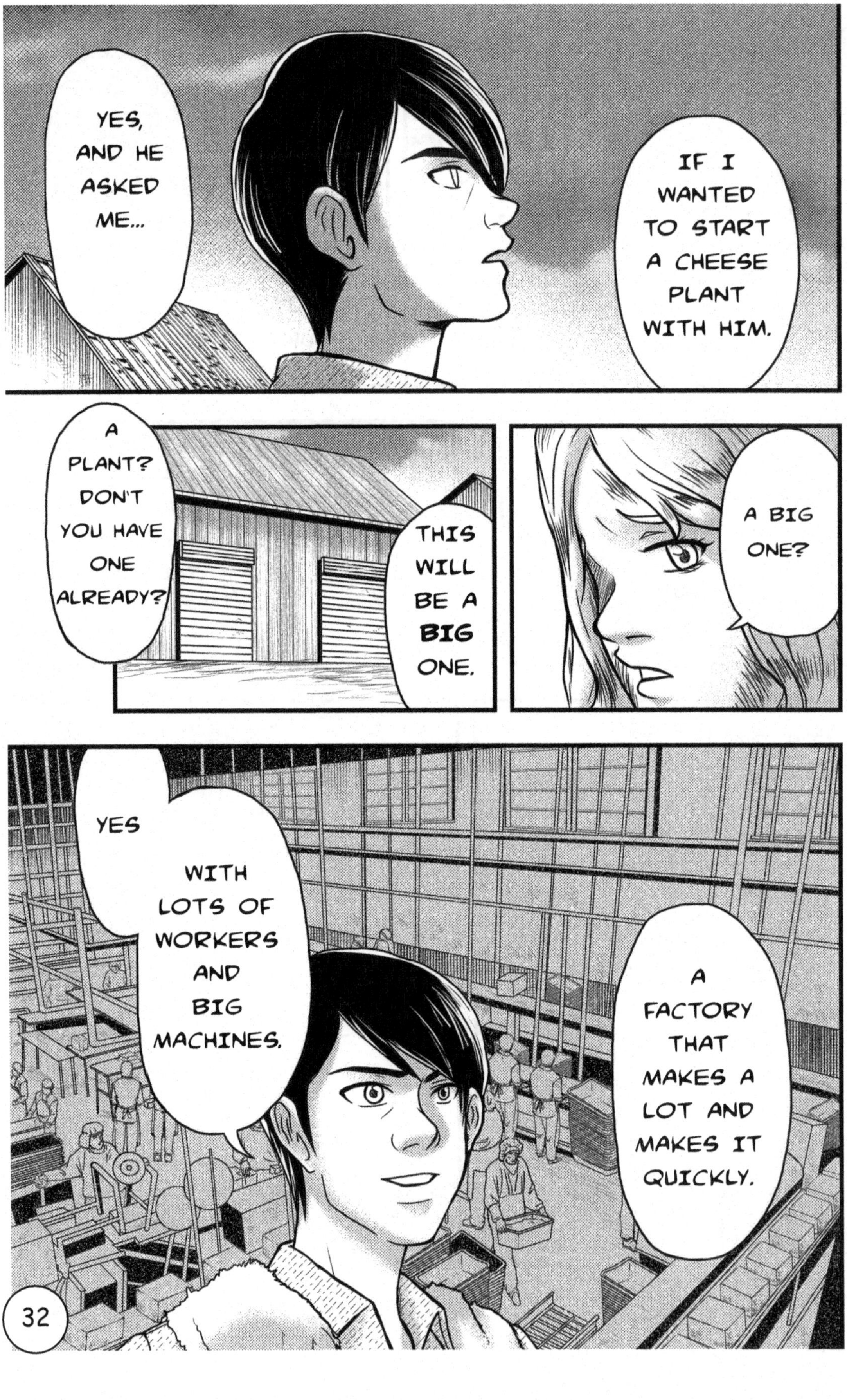
YES, AND HE ASKED ME...
IF I WANTED TO START A CHEESE PLANT WITH HIM.
A PLANT? DON'T YOU HAVE ONE ALREADY?
THIS WILL BE A **BIG** ONE.
A BIG ONE?
YES
WITH LOTS OF WORKERS AND BIG MACHINES.
A FACTORY THAT MAKES A LOT AND MAKES IT QUICKLY.

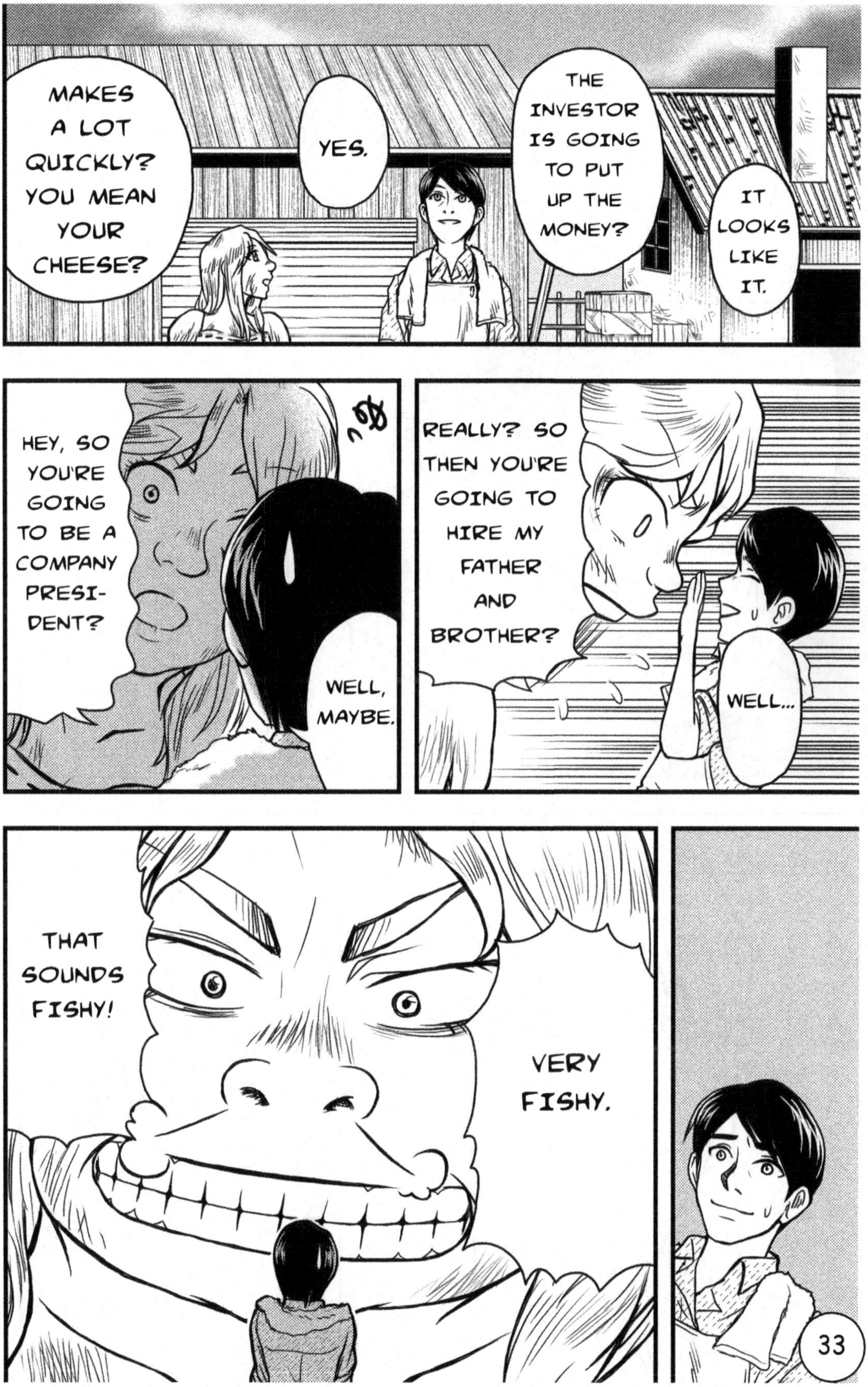

MAKES A LOT QUICKLY? YOU MEAN YOUR CHEESE?
YES.
THE INVESTOR IS GOING TO PUT UP THE MONEY?
IT LOOKS LIKE IT.
HEY, SO YOU'RE GOING TO BE A COMPANY PRESI-DENT?
WELL, MAYBE.
REALLY? SO THEN YOU'RE GOING TO HIRE MY FATHER AND BROTHER?
WELL...
THAT SOUNDS FISHY!
VERY FISHY.

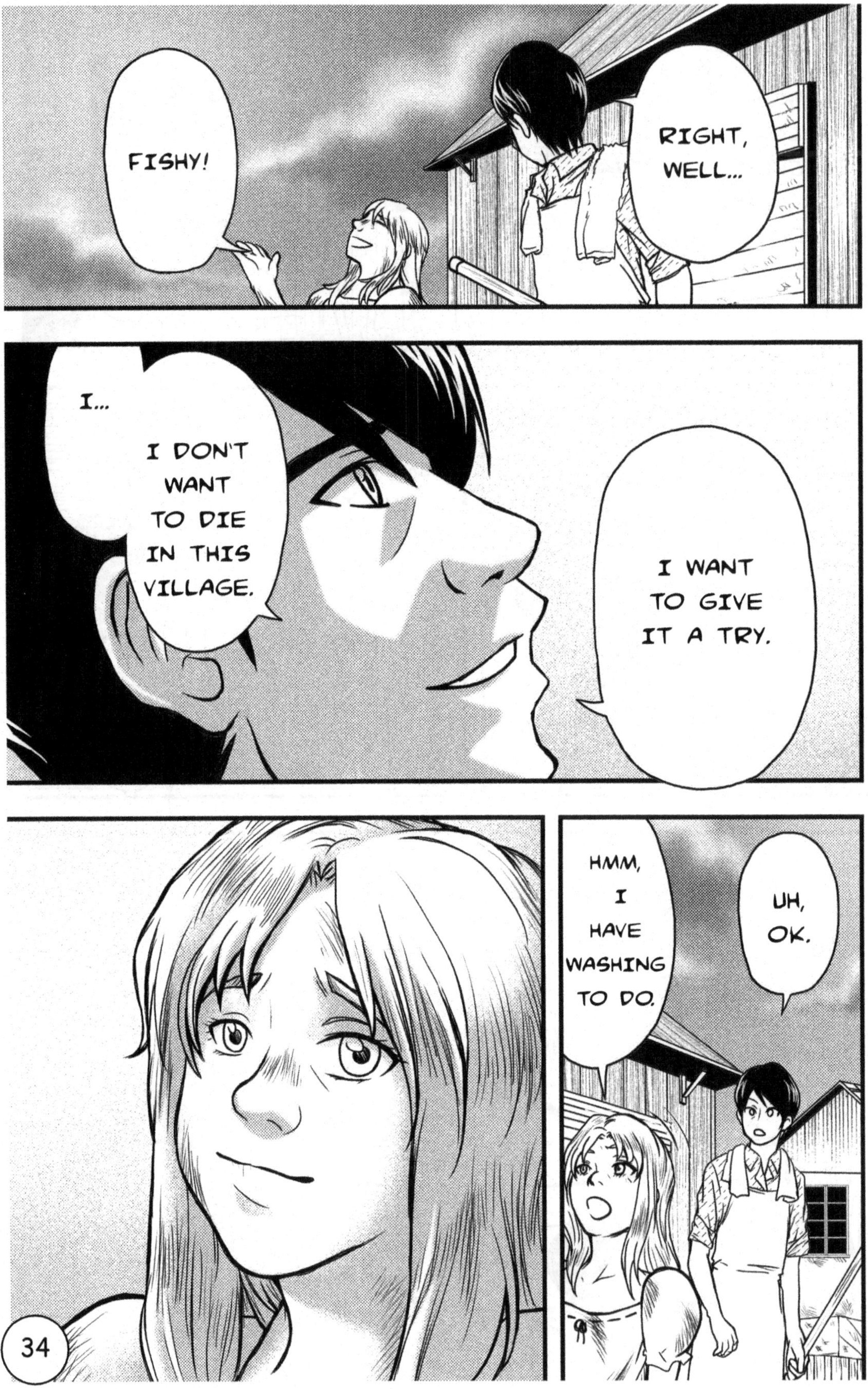
FISHY!
RIGHT, WELL...
I...
I DON'T WANT TO DIE IN THIS VILLAGE.
I WANT TO GIVE IT A TRY.
HMM, I HAVE WASHING TO DO.
UH, OK.

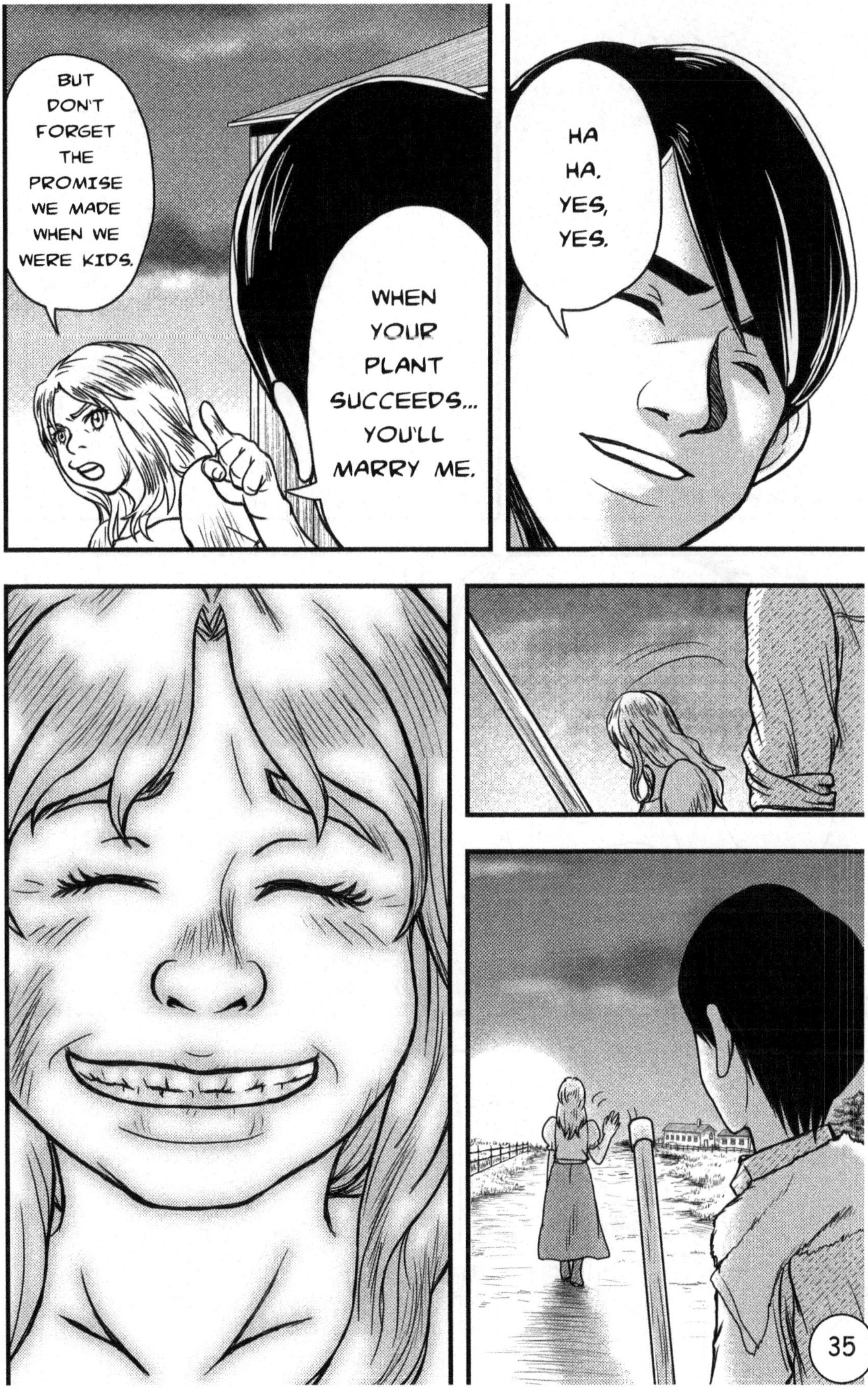
BUT DON'T FORGET THE PROMISE WE MADE WHEN WE WERE KIDS.
WHEN YOUR PLANT SUCCEEDS... YOU'LL MARRY ME.
HA HA. YES, YES.

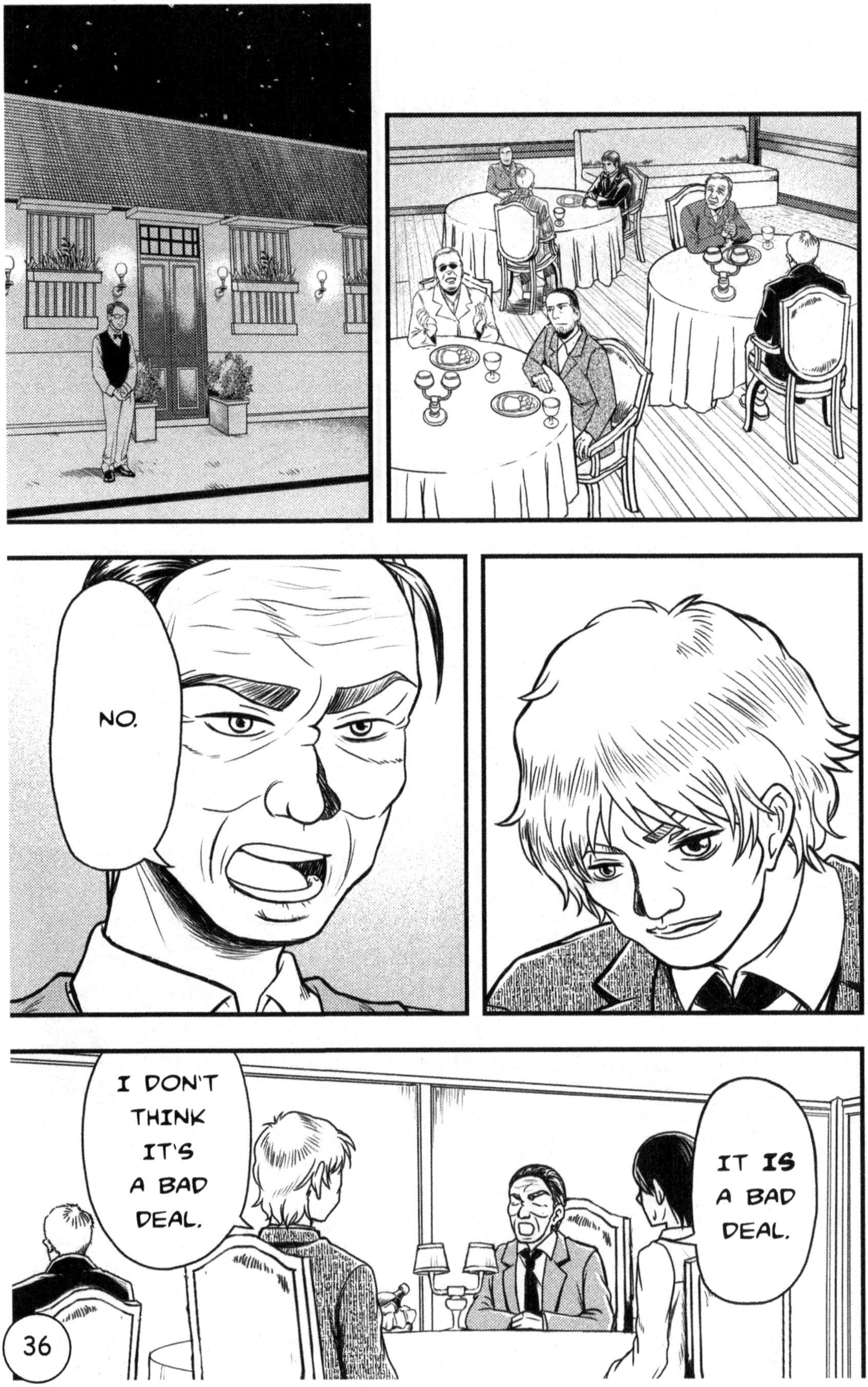
NO.
I DON'T THINK IT'S A BAD DEAL.
IT IS A BAD DEAL.

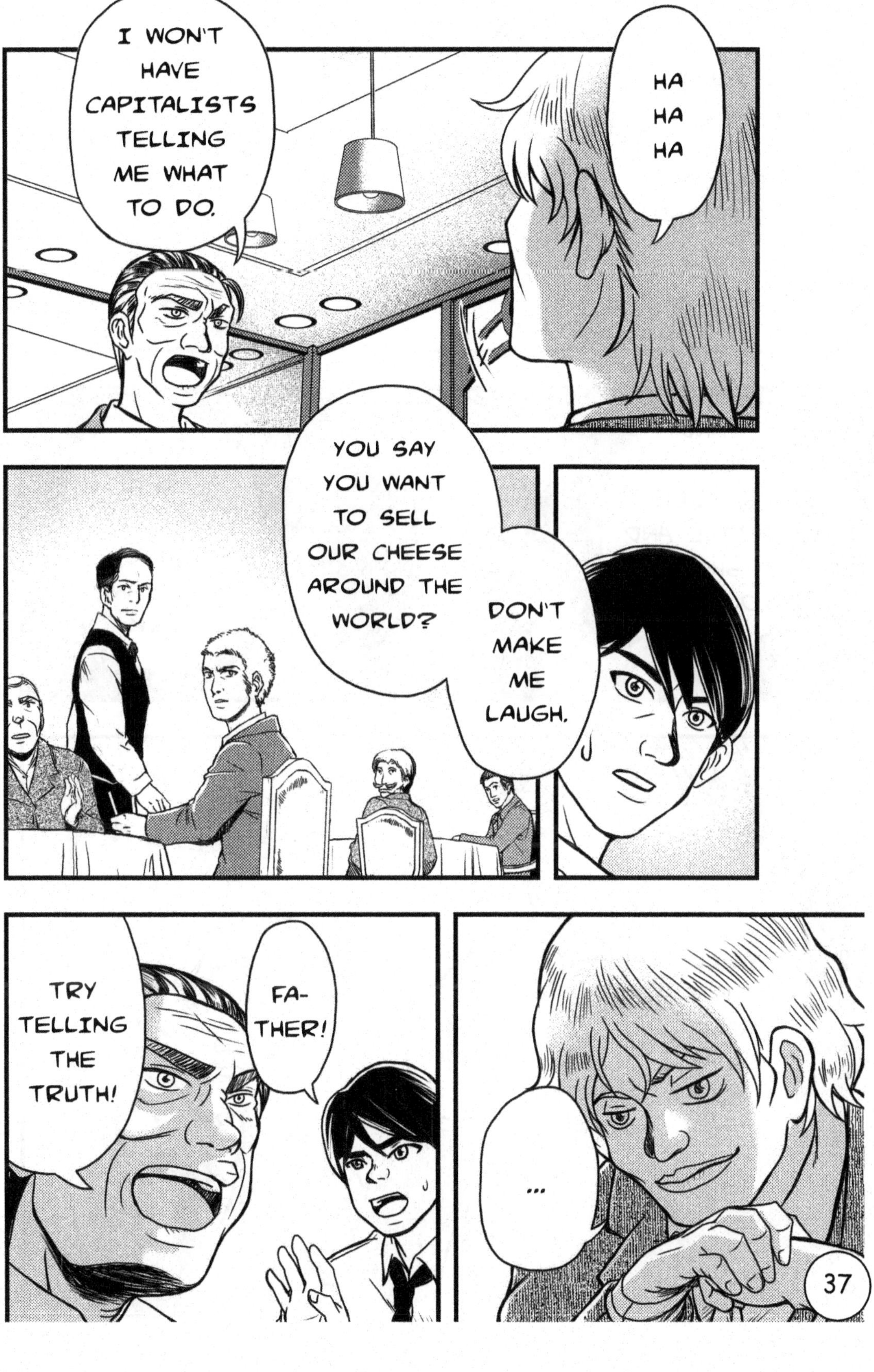
I WON'T HAVE CAPITALISTS TELLING ME WHAT TO DO.
HA HA HA
YOU SAY YOU WANT TO SELL OUR CHEESE AROUND THE WORLD?
DON'T MAKE ME LAUGH.
TRY TELLING THE TRUTH!
FA-THER!
...

CIRCUIT OF THE COMMODITY: A CYCLICAL MECHANISM OF CAPITALISM IN WHICH THE COMMODITY (C) IS EXCHANGED FOR MONEY (M), WHICH IN TURN BECOMES ANOTHER COMMODITY (C).

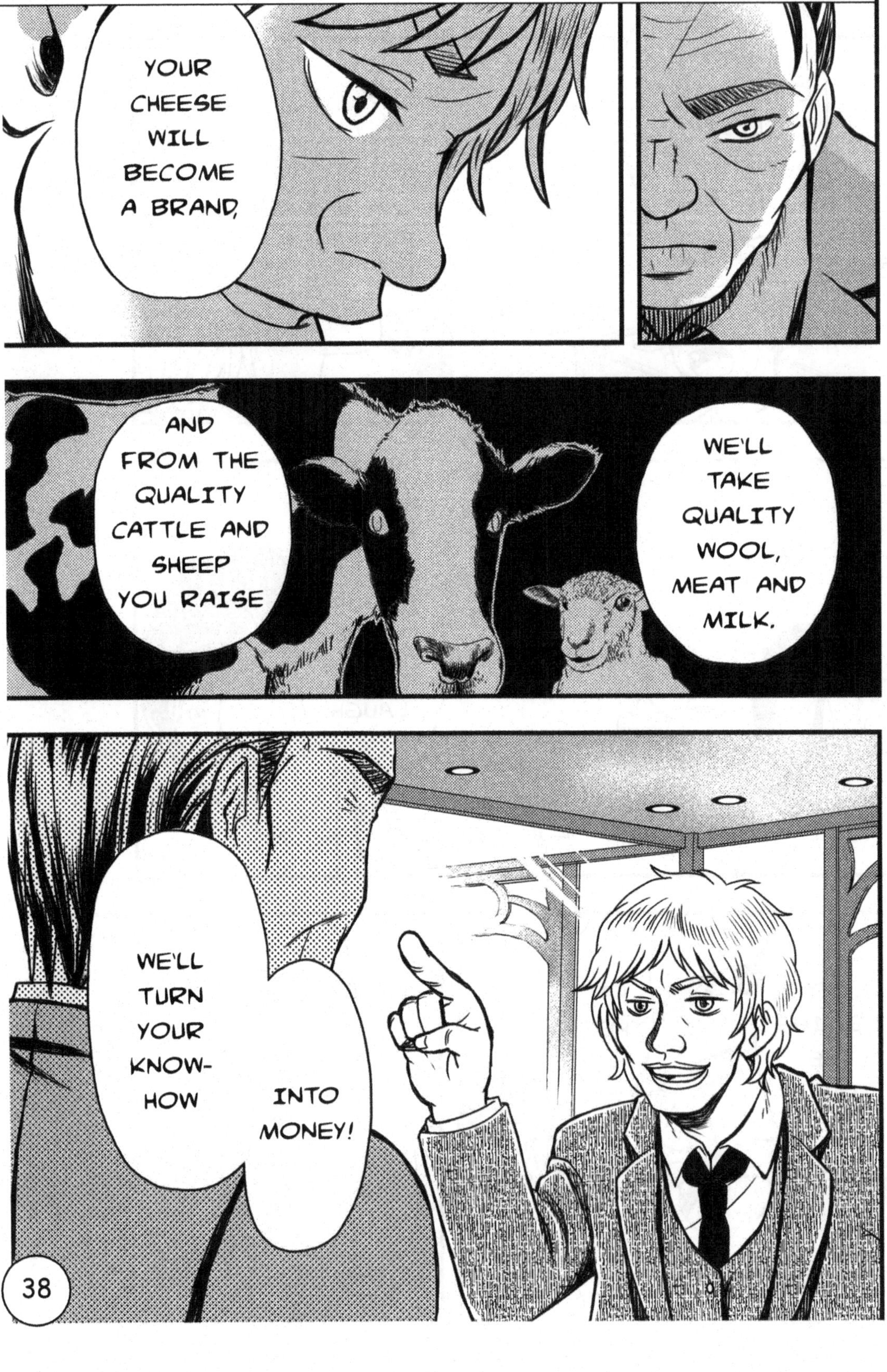
YOUR CHEESE WILL BECOME A BRAND,
AND FROM THE QUALITY CATTLE AND SHEEP YOU RAISE
WE'LL TAKE QUALITY WOOL, MEAT AND MILK.
WE'LL TURN YOUR KNOW-HOW
INTO MONEY!

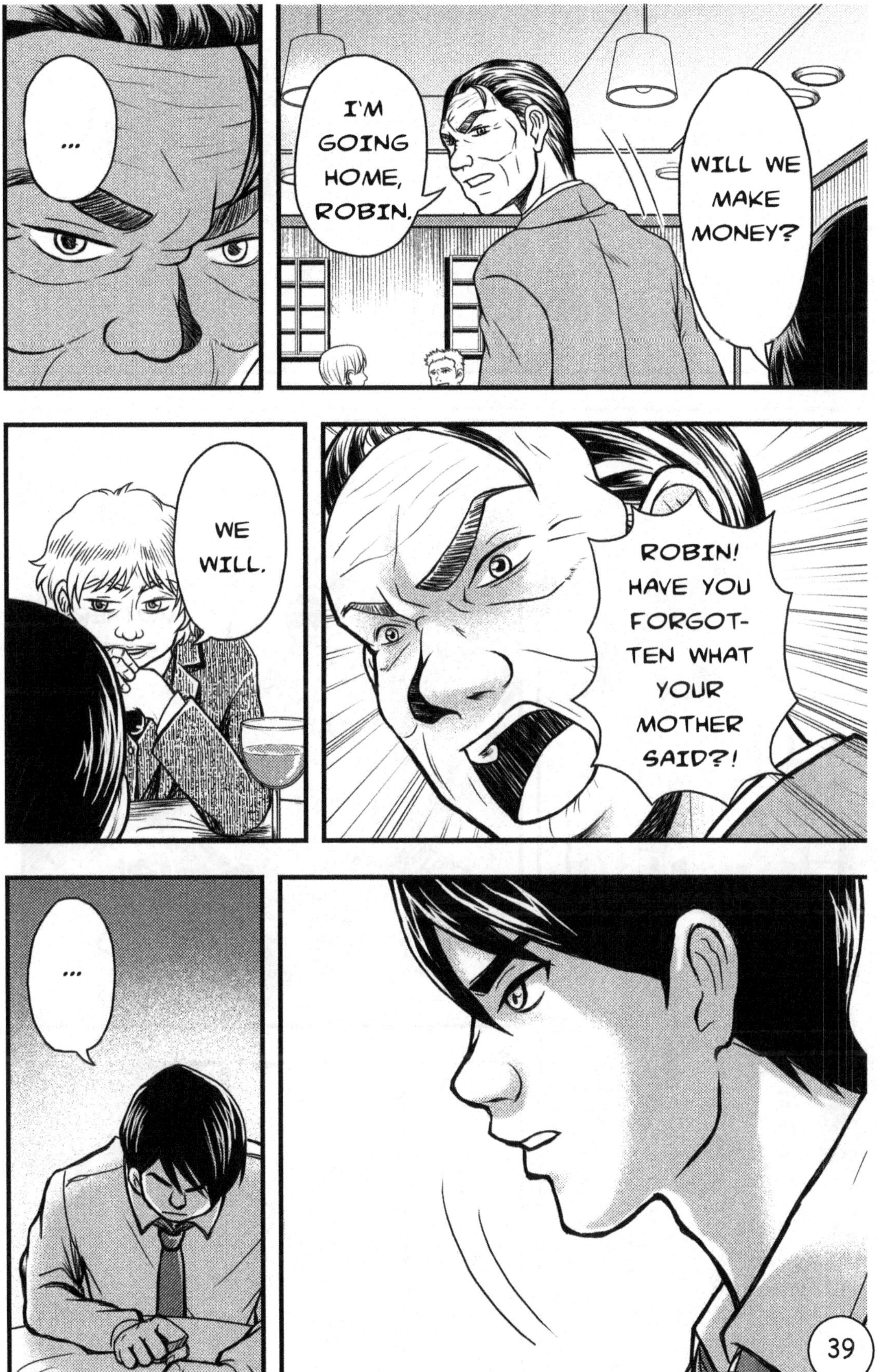
...
I'M GOING HOME, ROBIN.
WILL WE MAKE MONEY?
WE WILL.
ROBIN! HAVE YOU FORGOTTEN WHAT YOUR MOTHER SAID?!
...

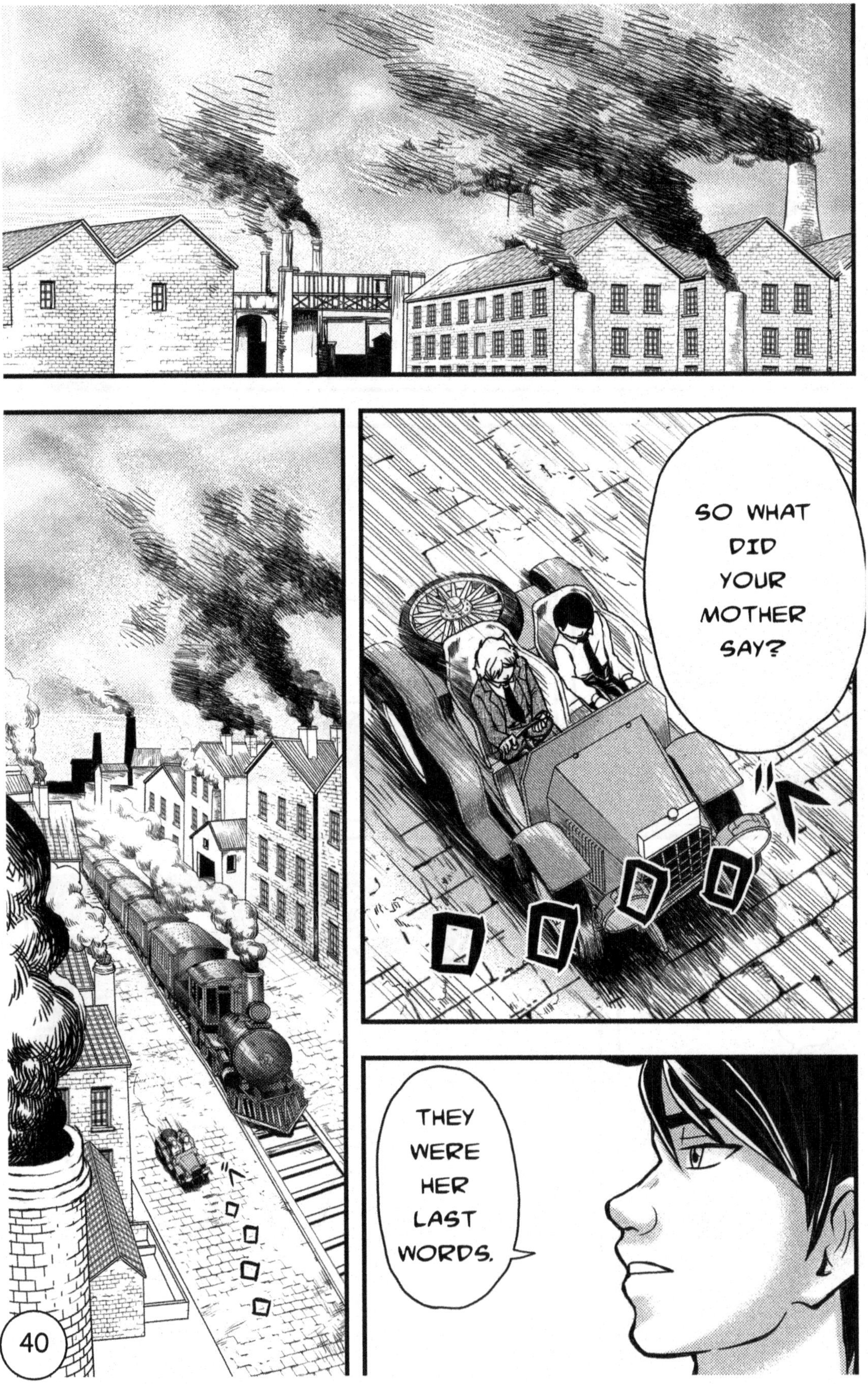
SO WHAT DID YOUR MOTHER SAY?
THEY WERE HER LAST WORDS.

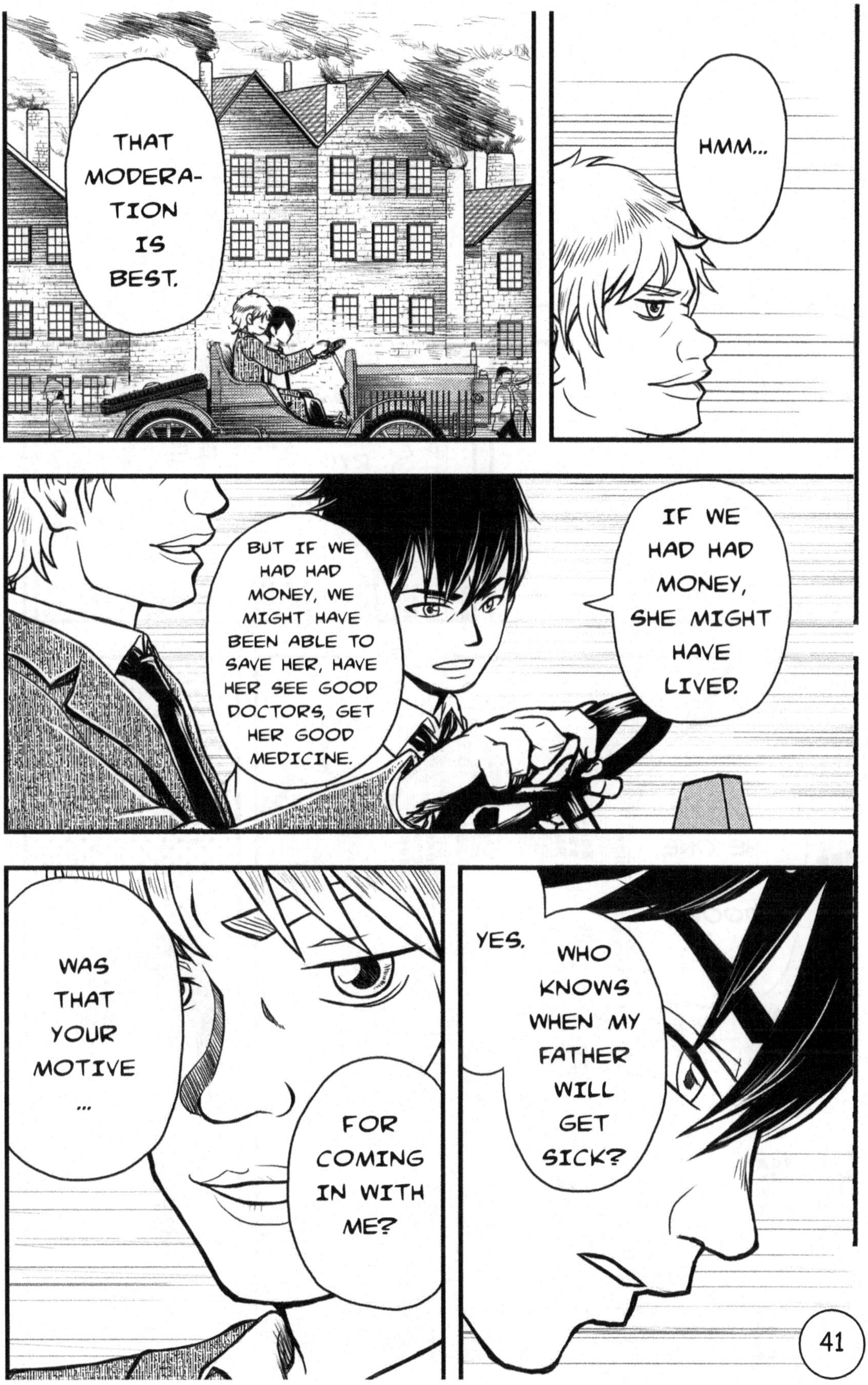
THAT MODERATION IS BEST.
HMM...
BUT IF WE HAD HAD MONEY, WE MIGHT HAVE BEEN ABLE TO SAVE HER, HAVE HER SEE GOOD DOCTORS, GET HER GOOD MEDICINE.
IF WE HAD HAD MONEY, SHE MIGHT HAVE LIVED.
WAS THAT YOUR MOTIVE ...
FOR COMING IN WITH ME?
YES.
WHO KNOWS WHEN MY FATHER WILL GET SICK?

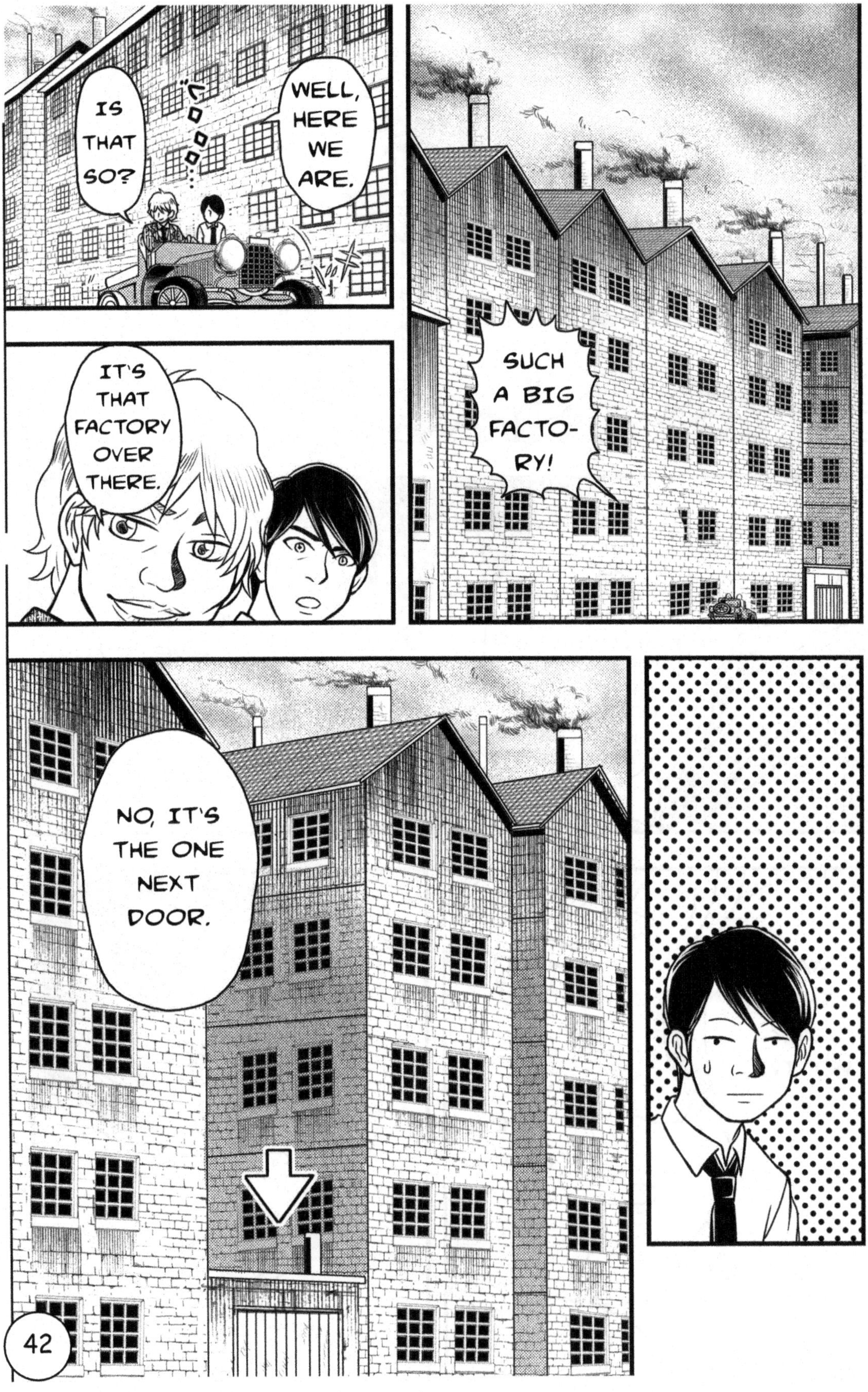
WELL, HERE WE ARE.
IS THAT SO?
IT'S THAT FACTORY OVER THERE.
SUCH A BIG FACTO-RY!
NO, IT'S THE ONE NEXT DOOR.

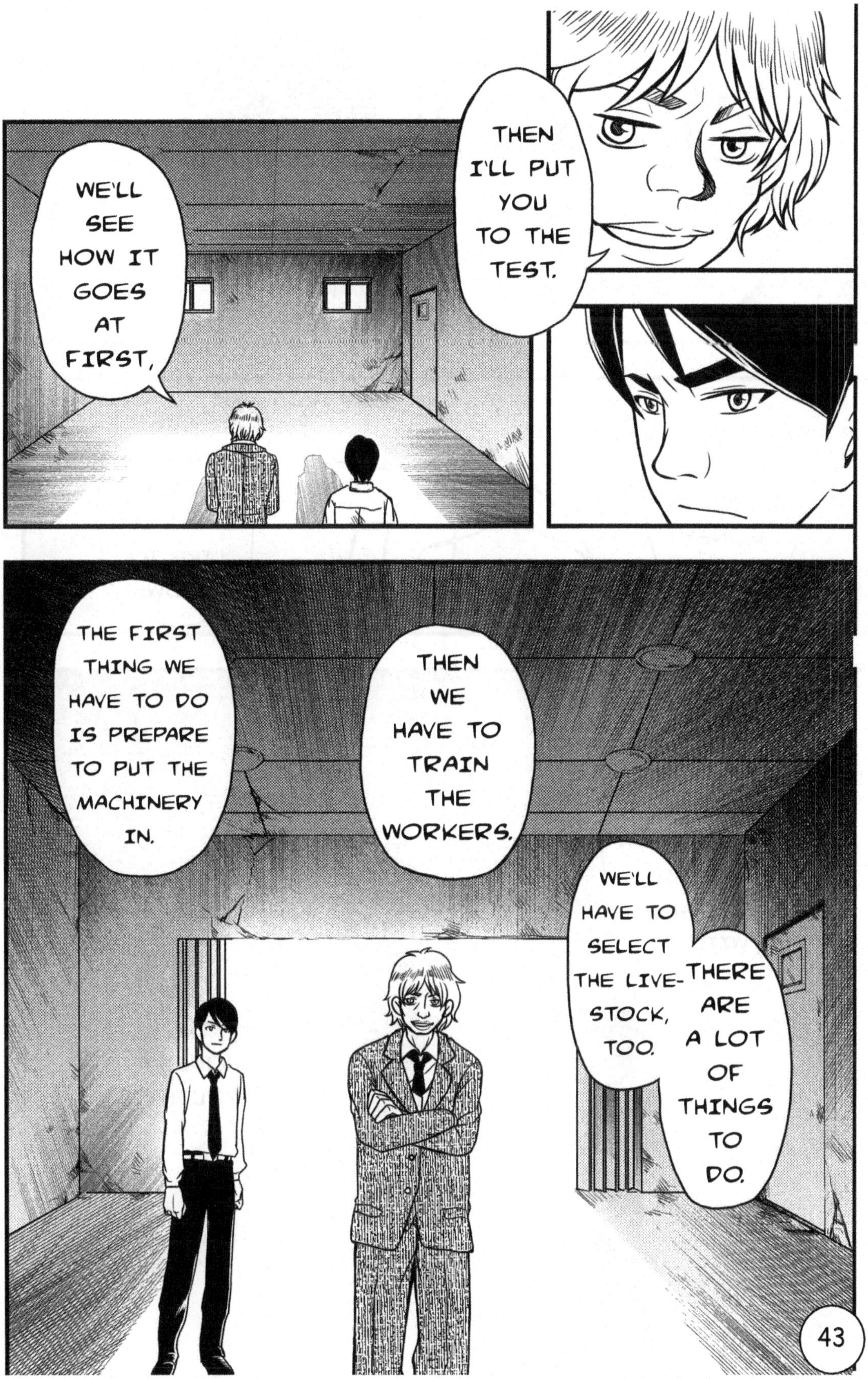
WE'LL SEE HOW IT GOES AT FIRST,
THEN I'LL PUT YOU TO THE TEST.
THE FIRST THING WE HAVE TO DO IS PREPARE TO PUT THE MACHINERY IN.
THEN WE HAVE TO TRAIN THE WORKERS.
WE'LL HAVE TO SELECT THE LIVE-STOCK, TOO.
THERE ARE A LOT OF THINGS TO DO.

YOU'LL BE REALLY BUSY.

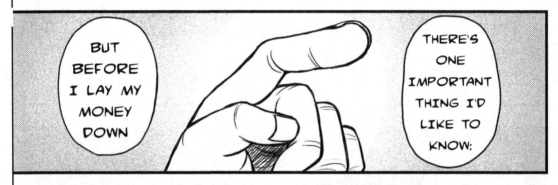

BUT BEFORE I LAY MY MONEY DOWN

THERE'S ONE IMPORTANT THING I'D LIKE TO KNOW:

WHAT YOU SAID ABOUT YOUR MOTIVATION FOR COMING IN WITH ME...

WAS THAT THE HONEST TRUTH?

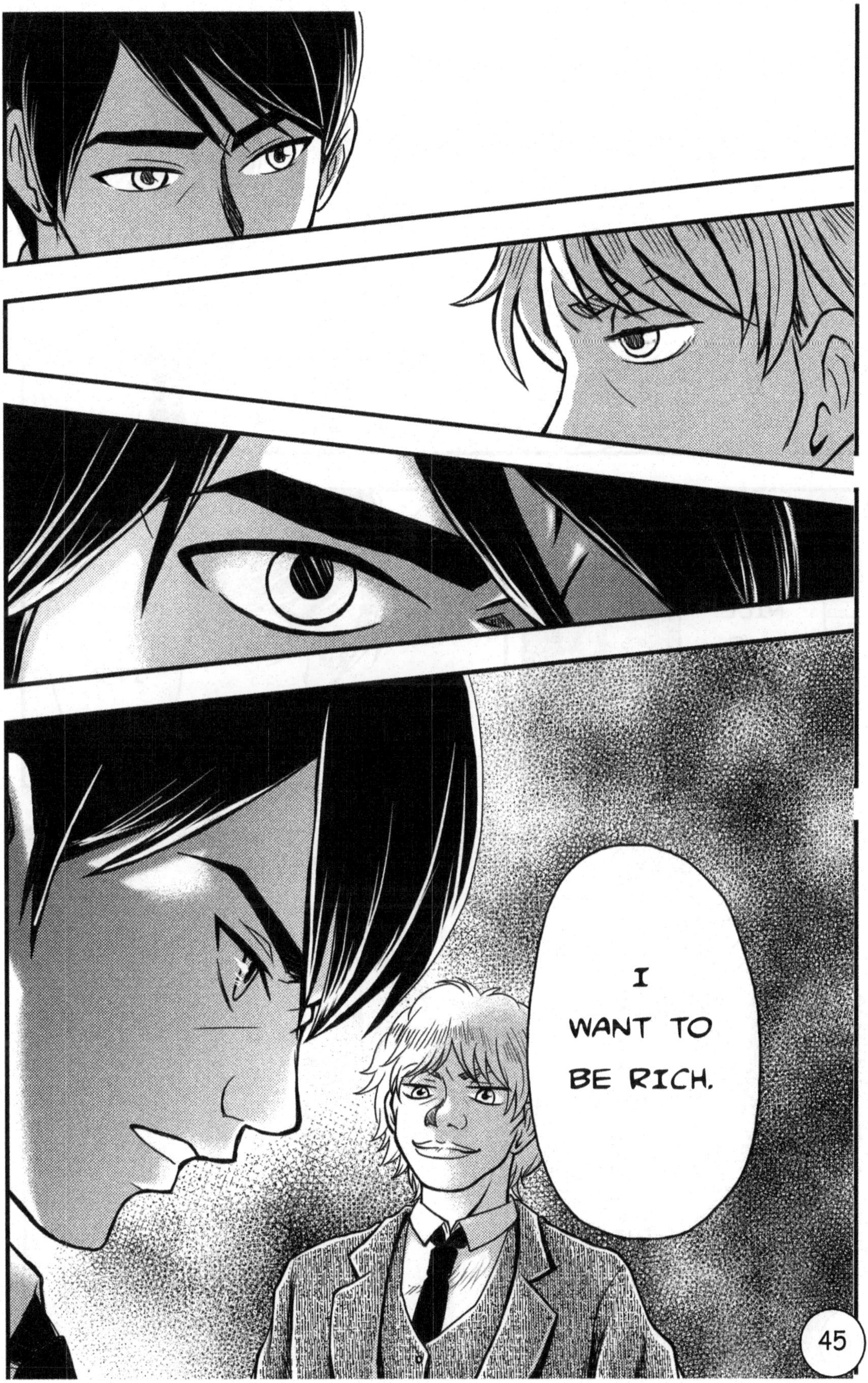
I WANT TO BE RICH.

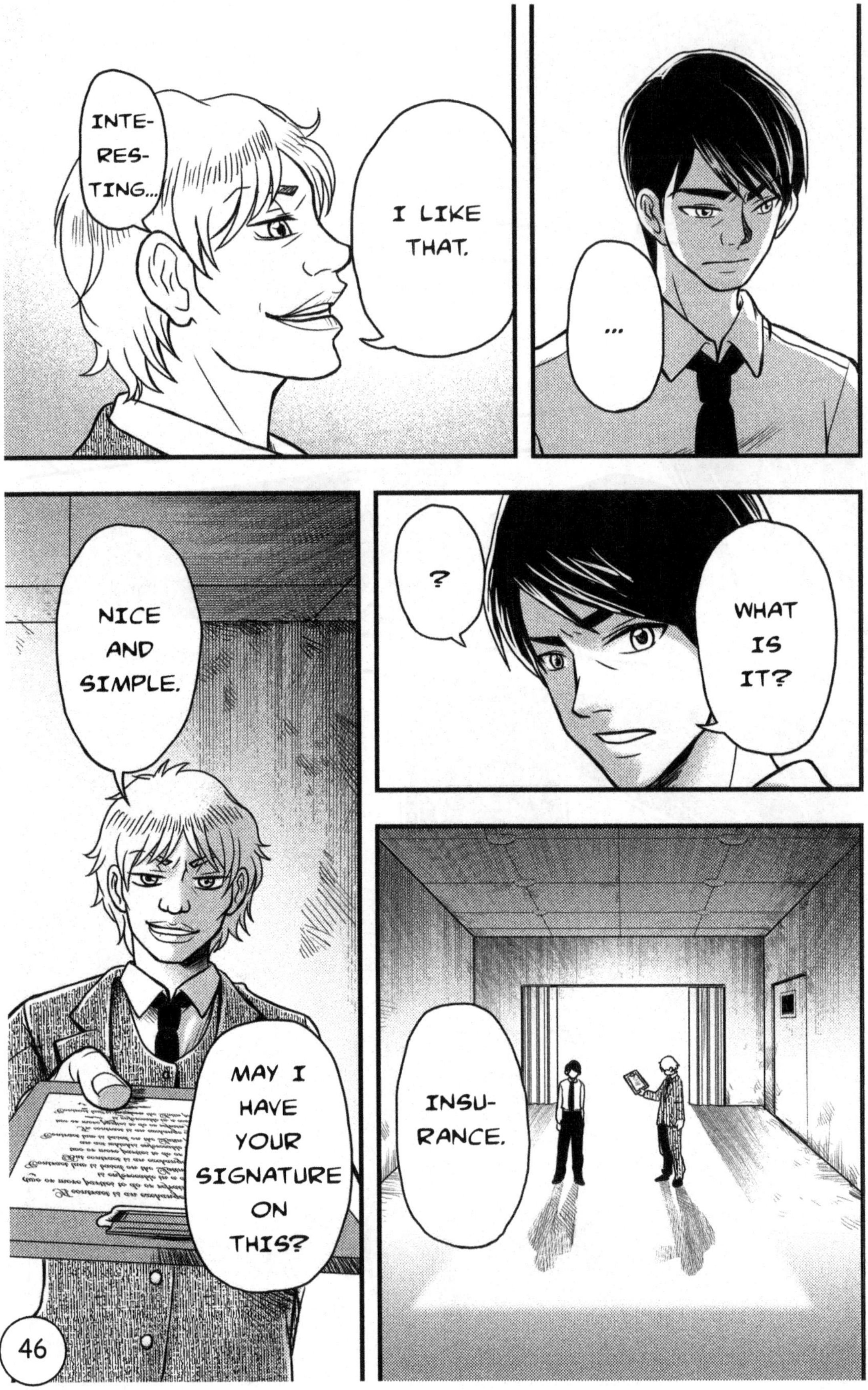
INTE-RES-TING...
I LIKE THAT.
...
NICE AND SIMPLE.
MAY I HAVE YOUR SIGNATURE ON THIS?
?
WHAT IS IT?
INSU-RANCE.

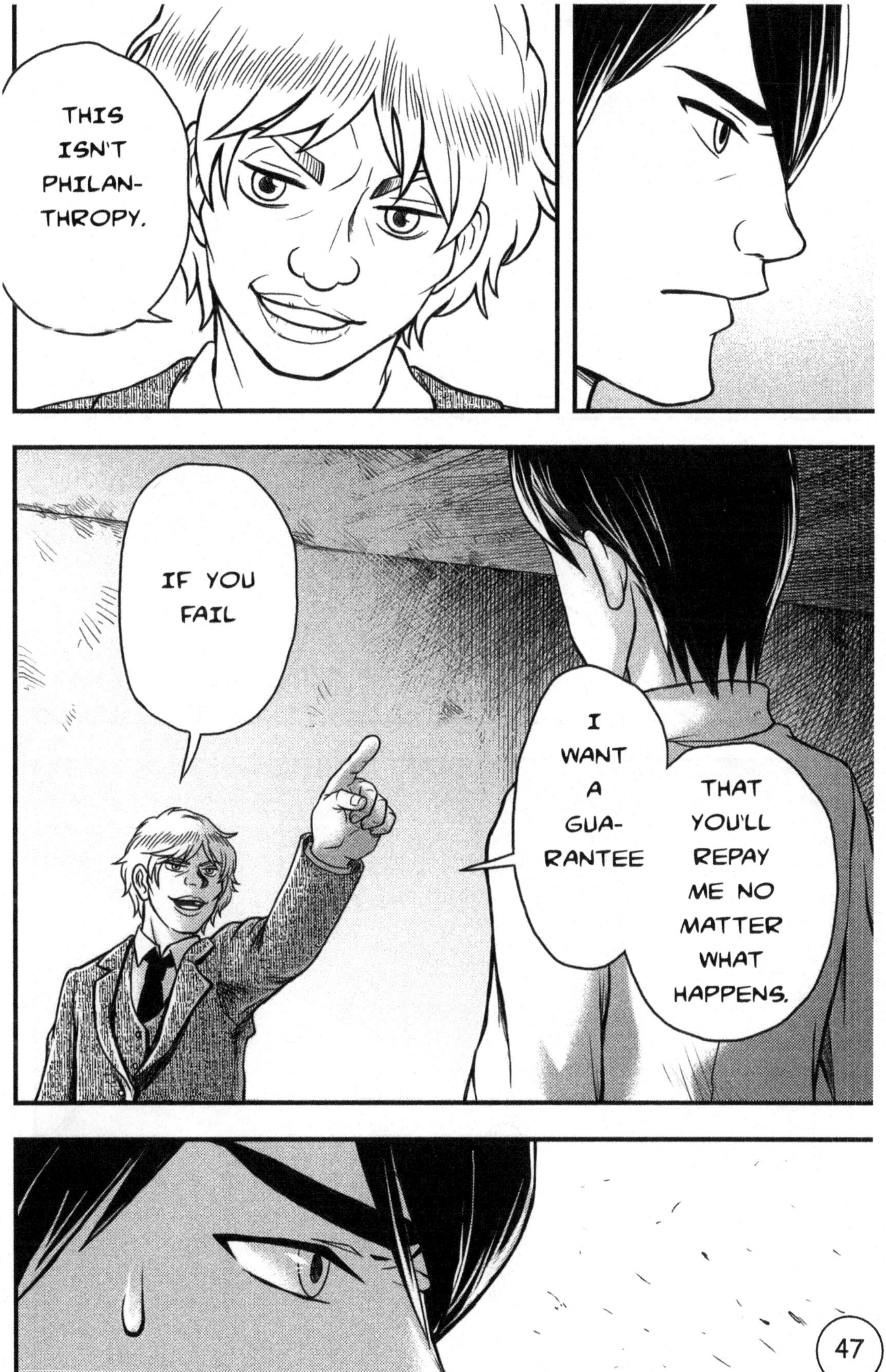
THIS ISN'T PHILAN-THROPY.
IF YOU FAIL
I WANT A GUA-RANTEE
THAT YOU'LL REPAY ME NO MATTER WHAT HAPPENS.

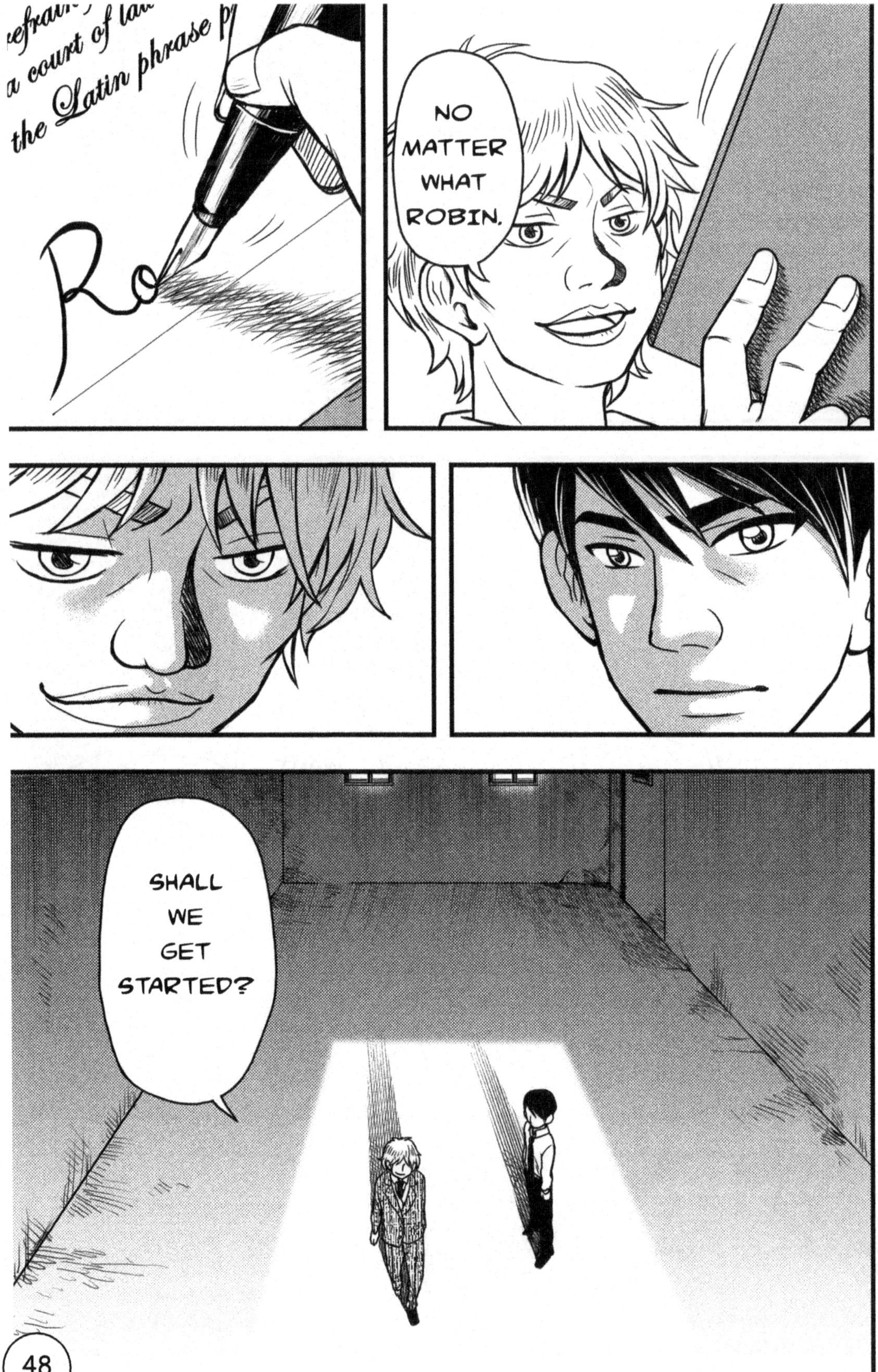
a court of
the Latin phrase
Ro
NO MATTER WHAT ROBIN.
SHALL WE GET STARTED?

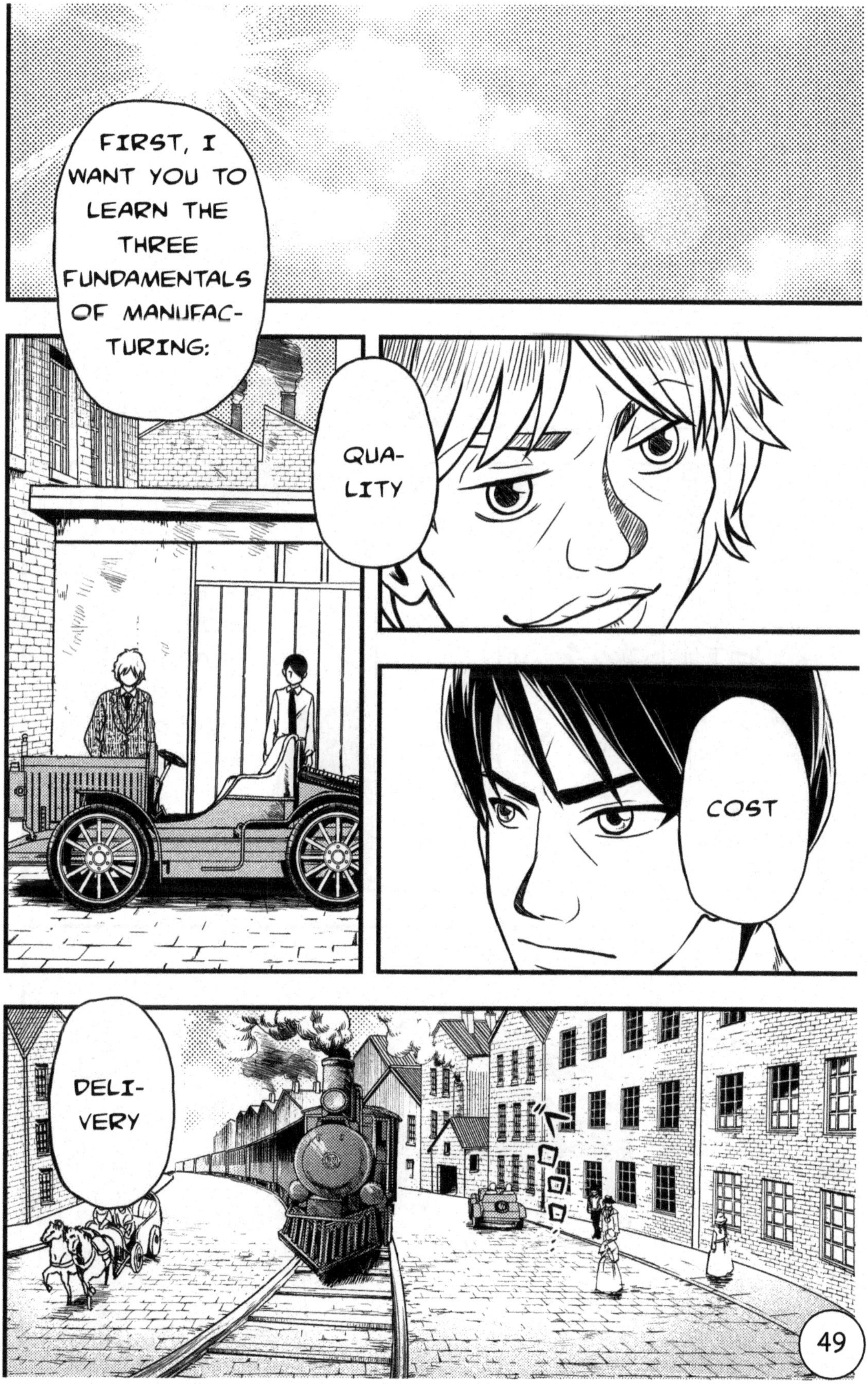

FIRST, I WANT YOU TO LEARN THE THREE FUNDAMENTALS OF MANUFAC-TURING:
QUA-LITY
COST
DELI-VERY

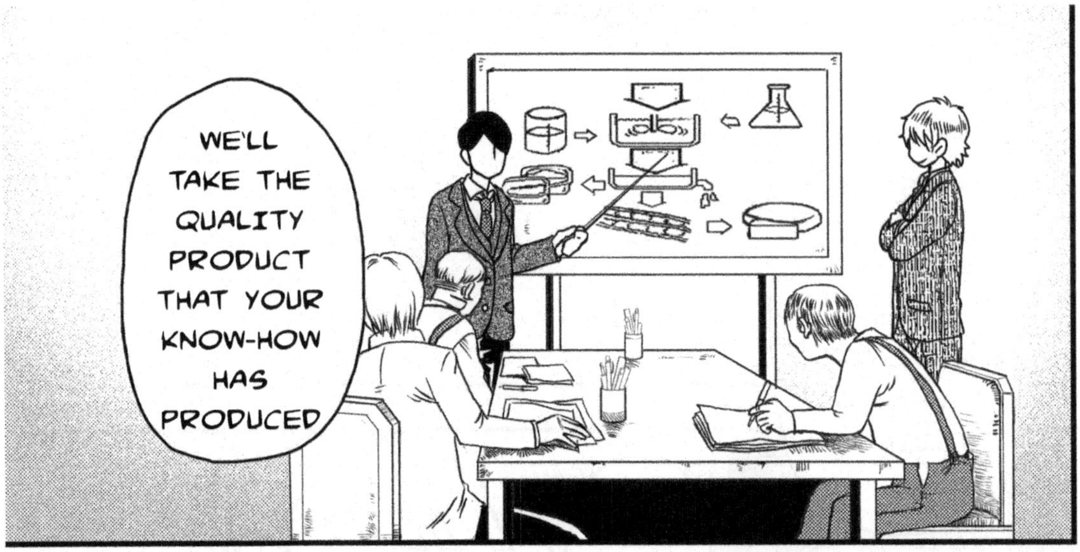
WE'LL TAKE THE QUALITY PRODUCT THAT YOUR KNOW-HOW HAS PRODUCED

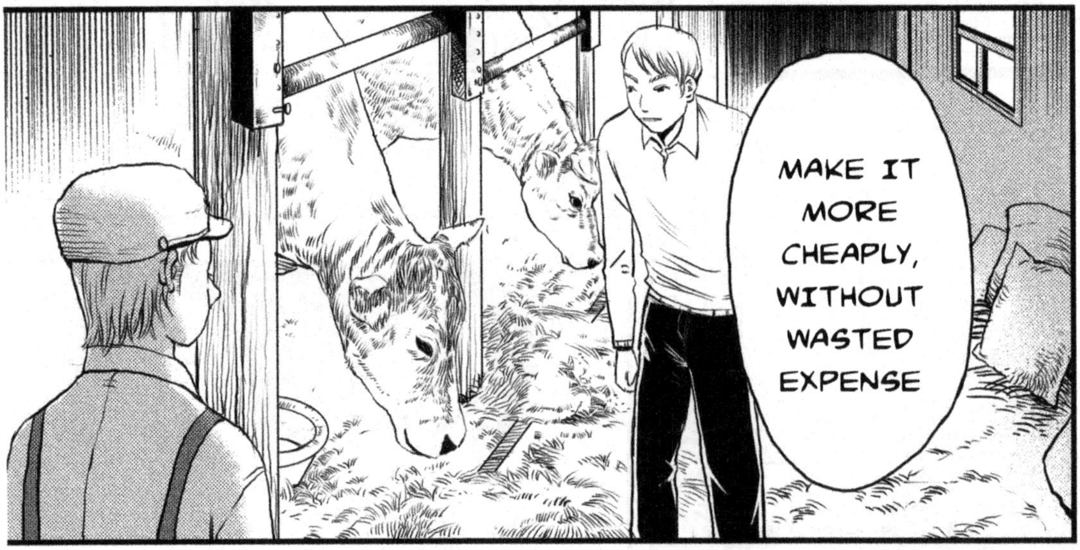
MAKE IT MORE CHEAPLY, WITHOUT WASTED EXPENSE

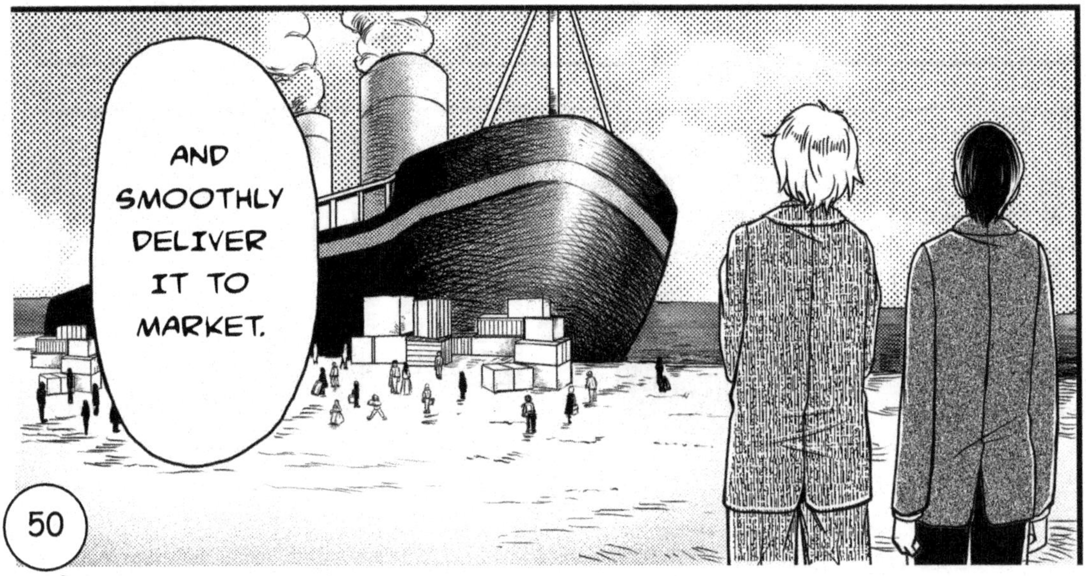
AND SMOOTHLY DELIVER IT TO MARKET.

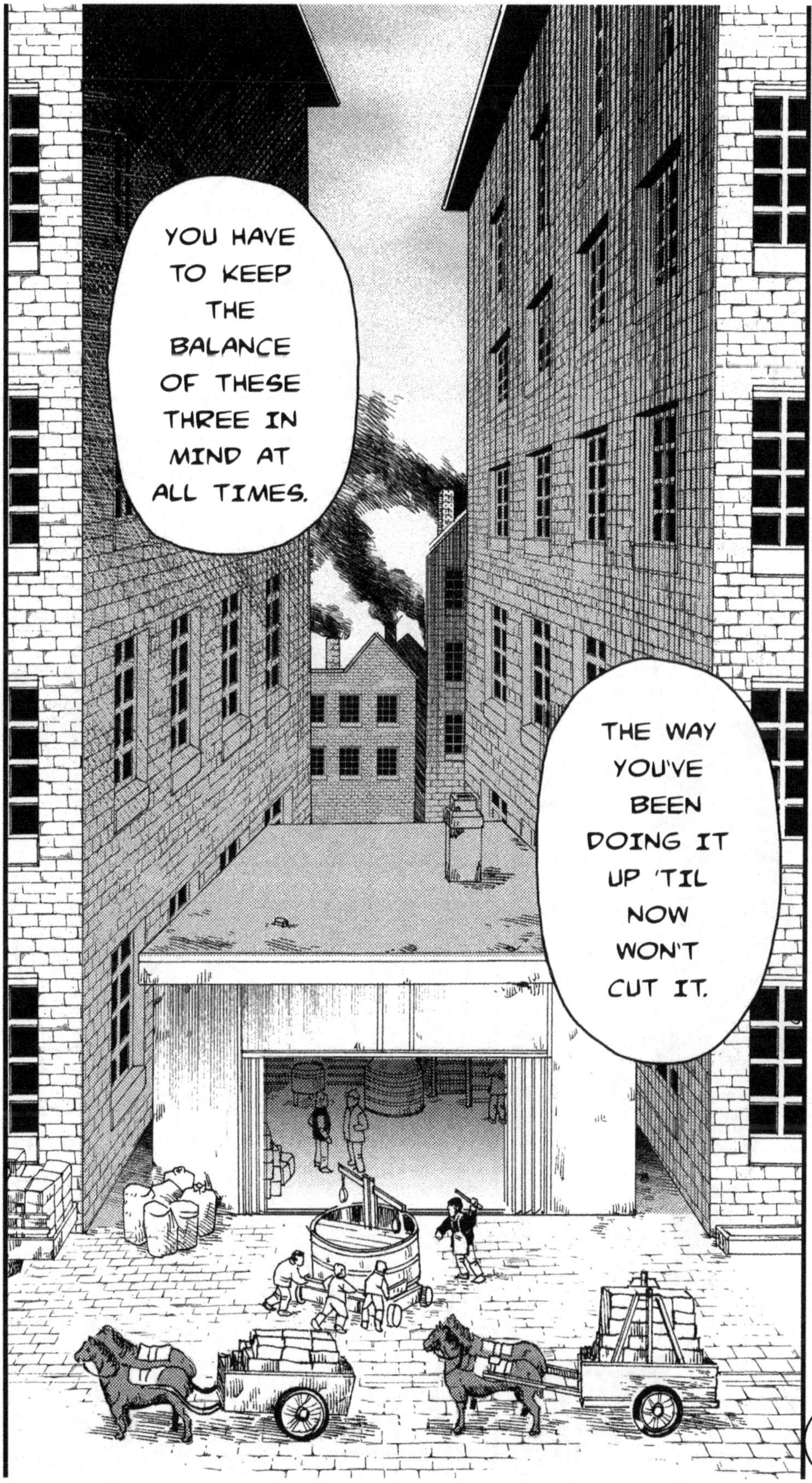
YOU HAVE TO KEEP THE BALANCE OF THESE THREE IN MIND AT ALL TIMES.
THE WAY YOU'VE BEEN DOING IT UP 'TIL NOW WON'T CUT IT.

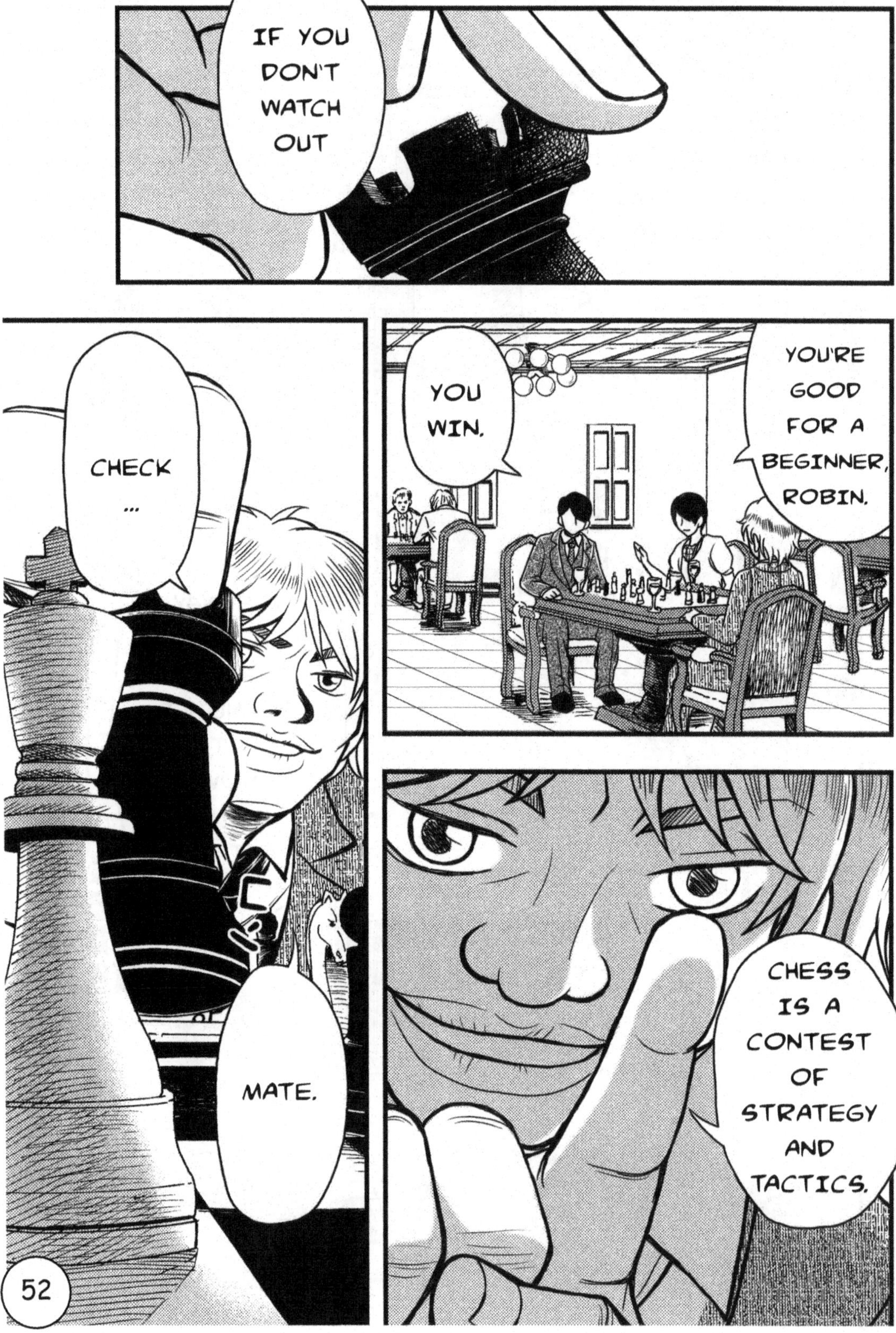
IF YOU DON'T WATCH OUT
CHECK ...
MATE.
YOU WIN.
YOU'RE GOOD FOR A BEGINNER, ROBIN.
CHESS IS A CONTEST OF STRATEGY AND TACTICS.

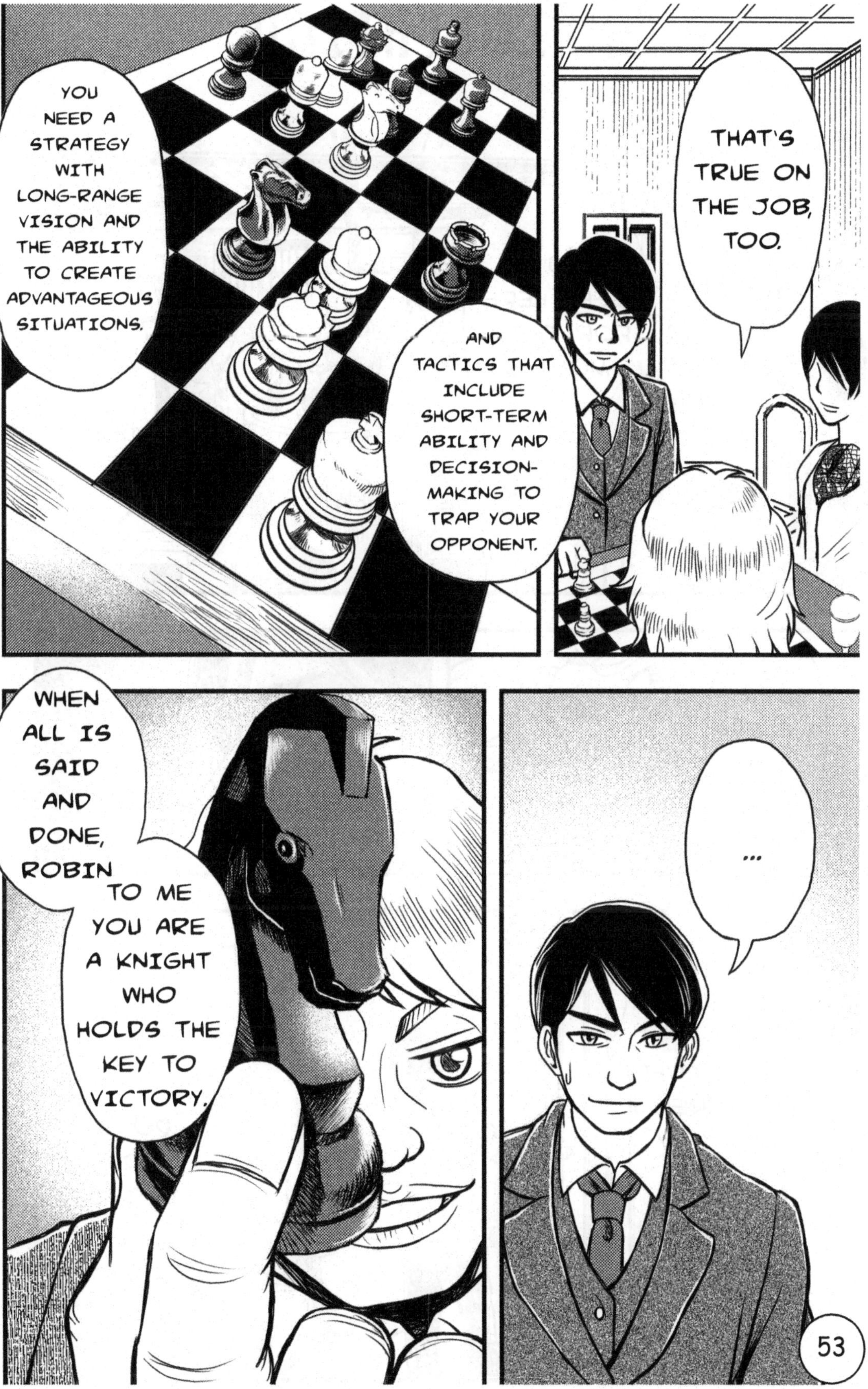
YOU NEED A STRATEGY WITH LONG-RANGE VISION AND THE ABILITY TO CREATE ADVANTAGEOUS SITUATIONS.
AND TACTICS THAT INCLUDE SHORT-TERM ABILITY AND DECISION-MAKING TO TRAP YOUR OPPONENT.
THAT'S TRUE ON THE JOB, TOO.
WHEN ALL IS SAID AND DONE, ROBIN
TO ME YOU ARE A KNIGHT WHO HOLDS THE KEY TO VICTORY.
...

EXPLOITATION

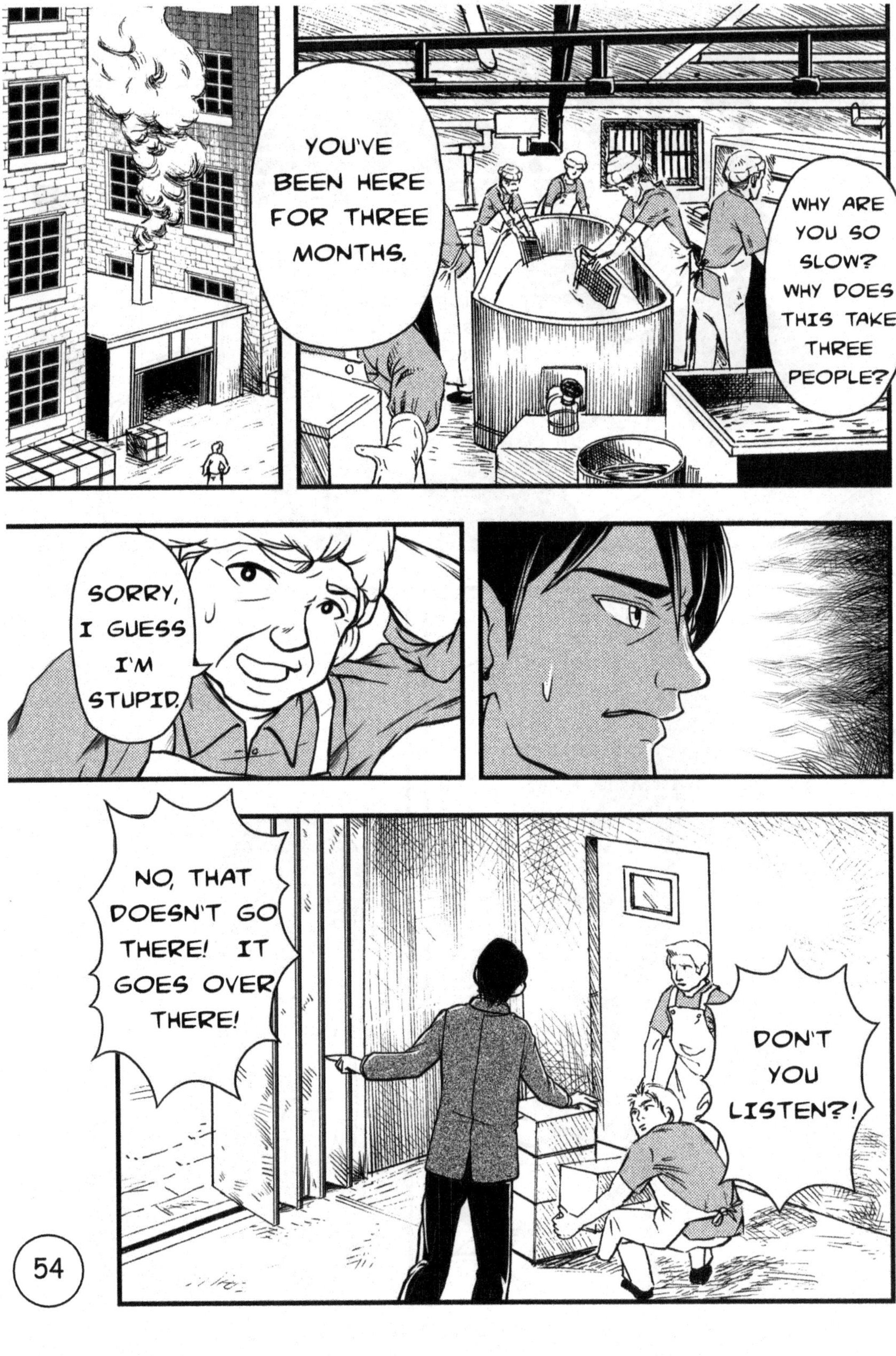
YOU'VE BEEN HERE FOR THREE MONTHS.
WHY ARE YOU SO SLOW? WHY DOES THIS TAKE THREE PEOPLE?
SORRY, I GUESS I'M STUPID.
NO, THAT DOESN'T GO THERE! IT GOES OVER THERE!
DON'T YOU LISTEN?!

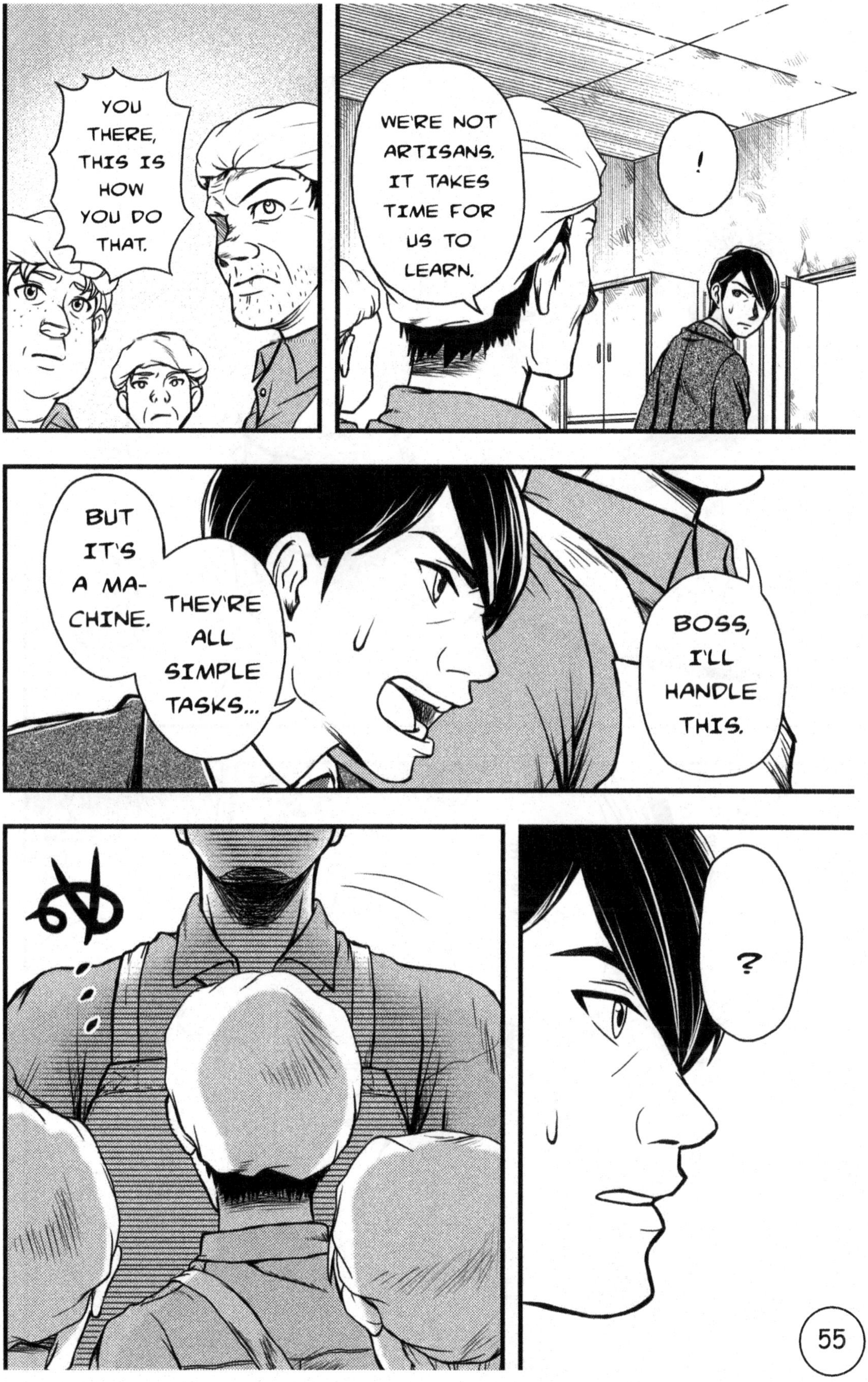
YOU THERE, THIS IS HOW YOU DO THAT.
WE'RE NOT ARTISANS. IT TAKES TIME FOR US TO LEARN.
!
BUT IT'S A MA- CHINE.
THEY'RE ALL SIMPLE TASKS...
BOSS, I'LL HANDLE THIS.
...
?

WHAT ARE YOU...?

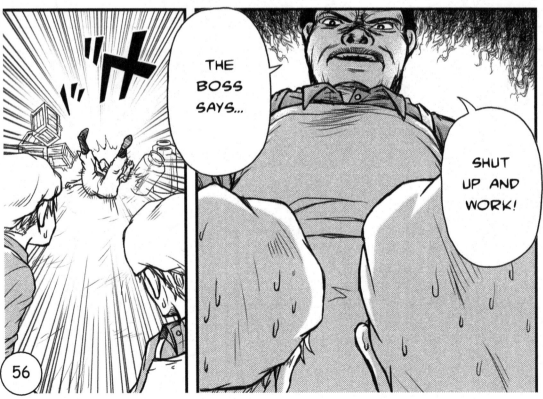

THE BOSS SAYS...

SHUT UP AND WORK!

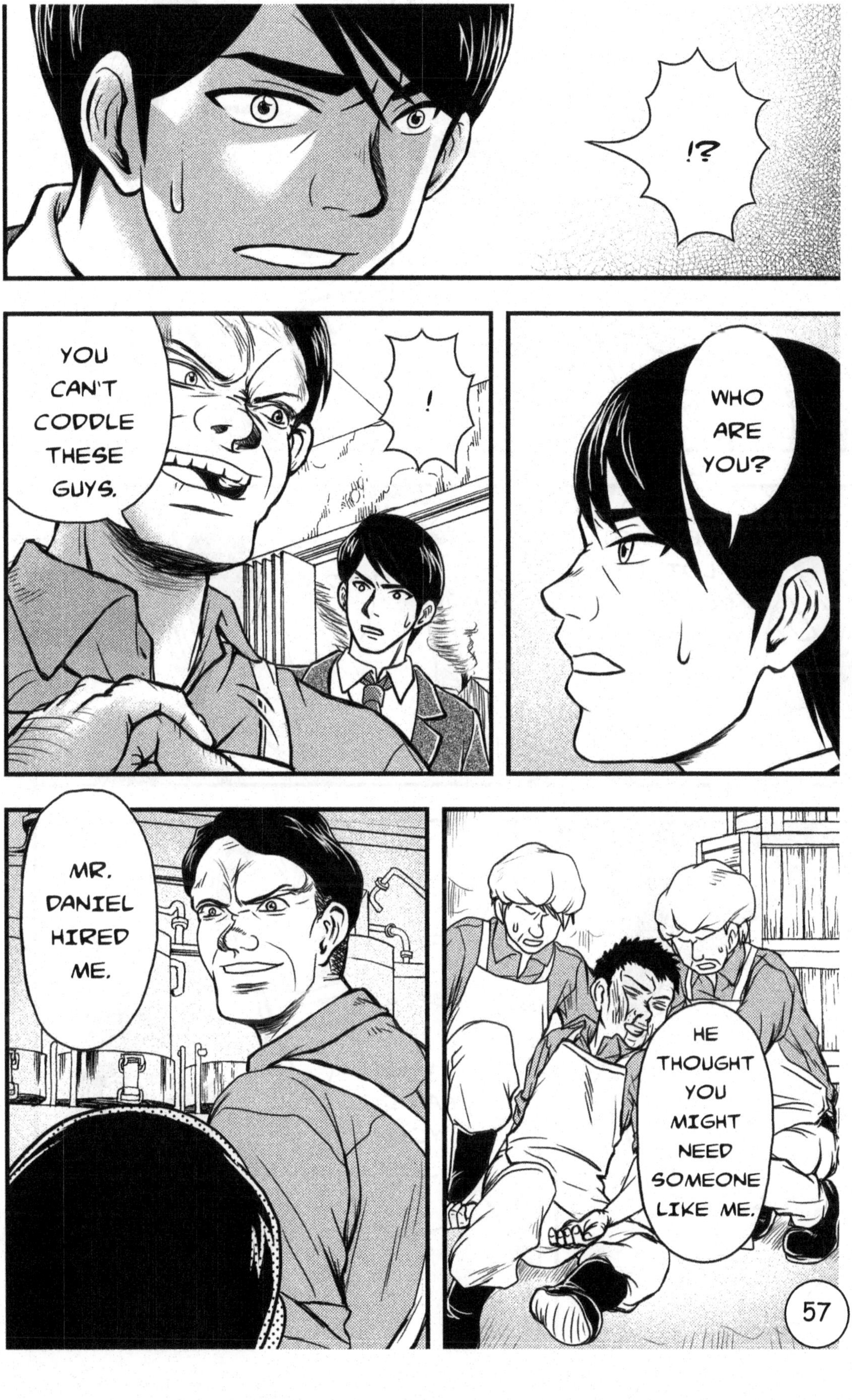
!?
YOU CAN'T CODDLE THESE GUYS.
!
WHO ARE YOU?
MR. DANIEL HIRED ME.
HE THOUGHT YOU MIGHT NEED SOMEONE LIKE ME.

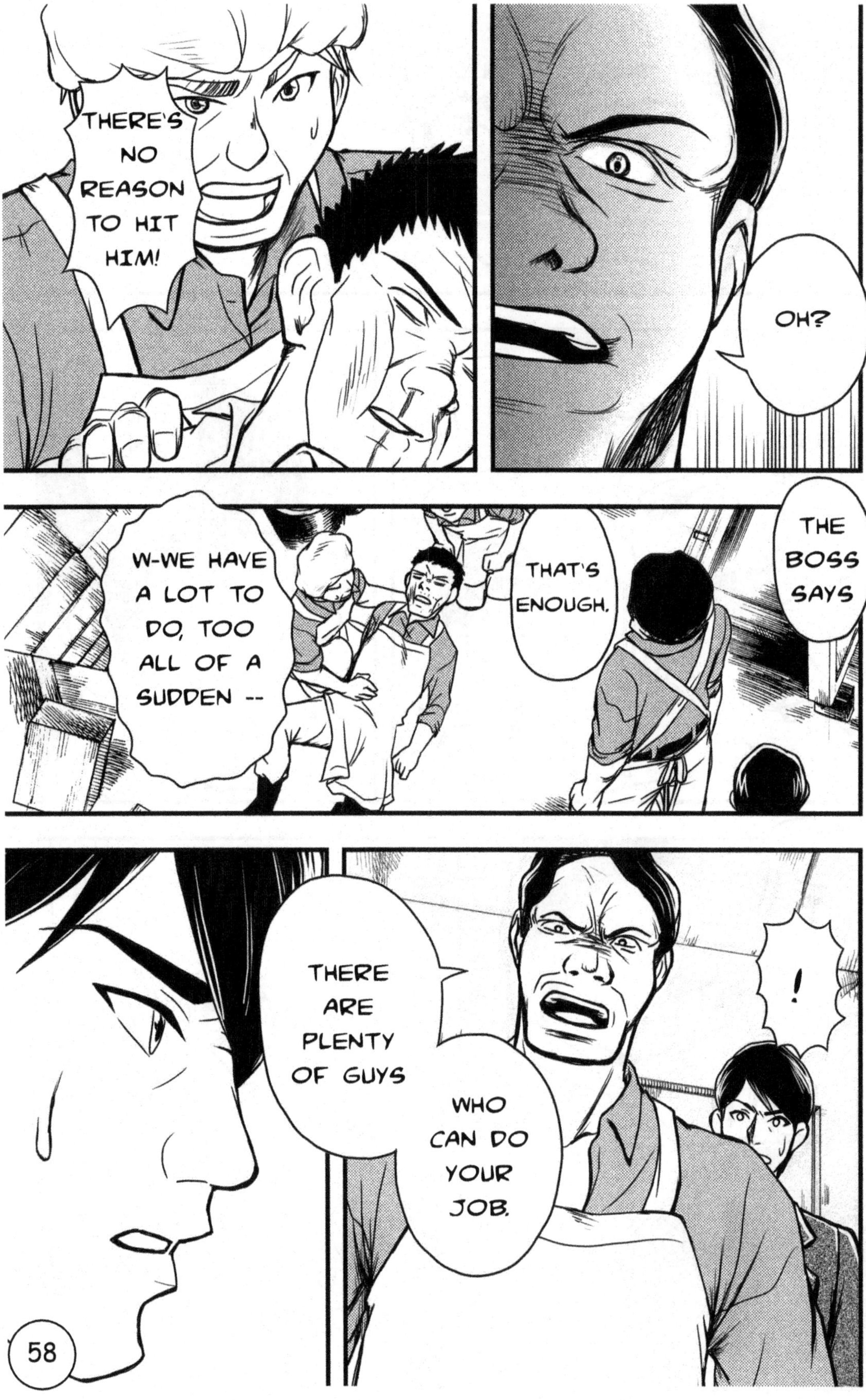
THERE'S NO REASON TO HIT HIM!
OH?
W-WE HAVE A LOT TO DO, TOO ALL OF A SUDDEN --
THAT'S ENOUGH.
THE BOSS SAYS
THERE ARE PLENTY OF GUYS
WHO CAN DO YOUR JOB.
!

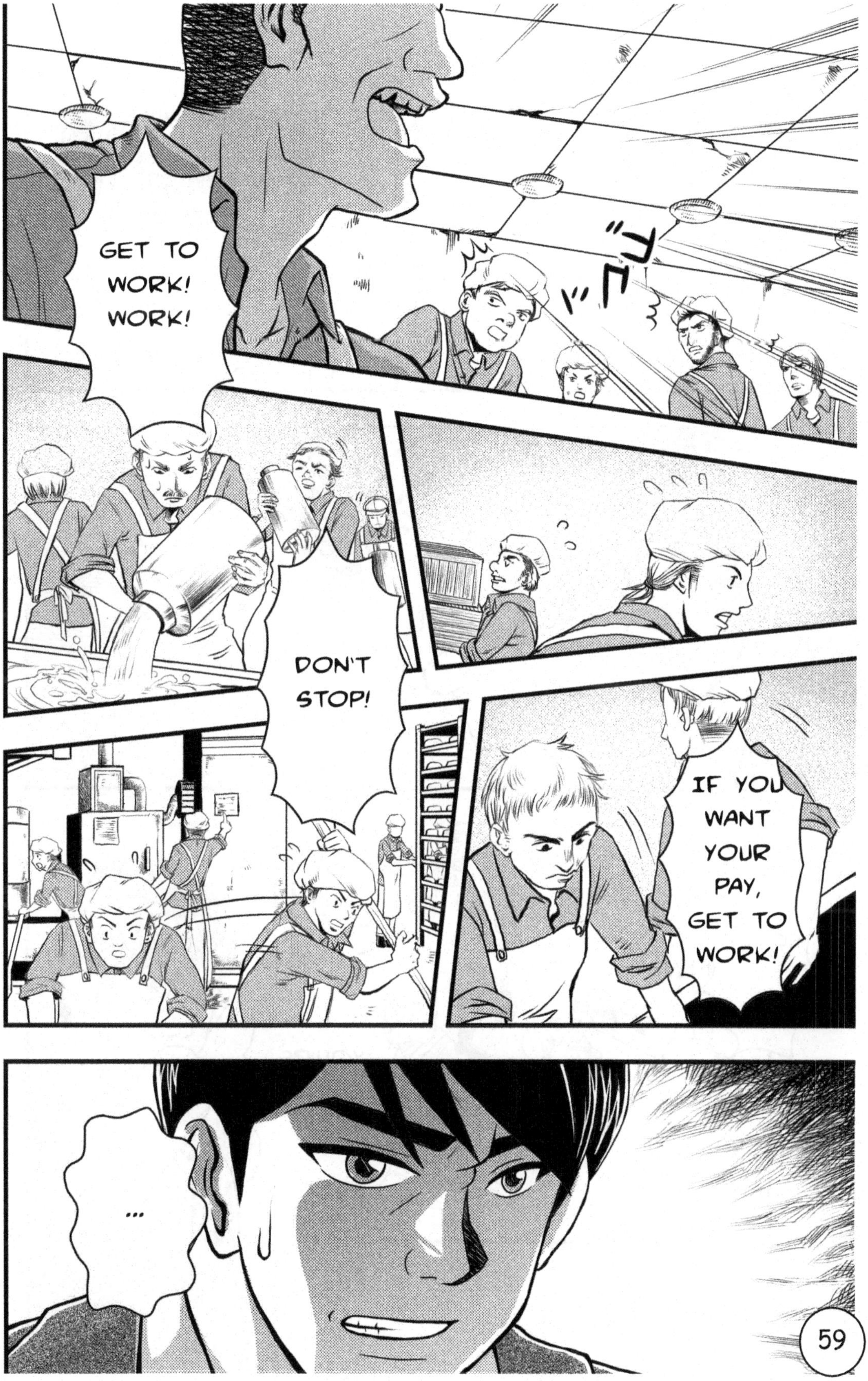
GET TO WORK! WORK!
DON'T STOP!
IF YOU WANT YOUR PAY, GET TO WORK!
...

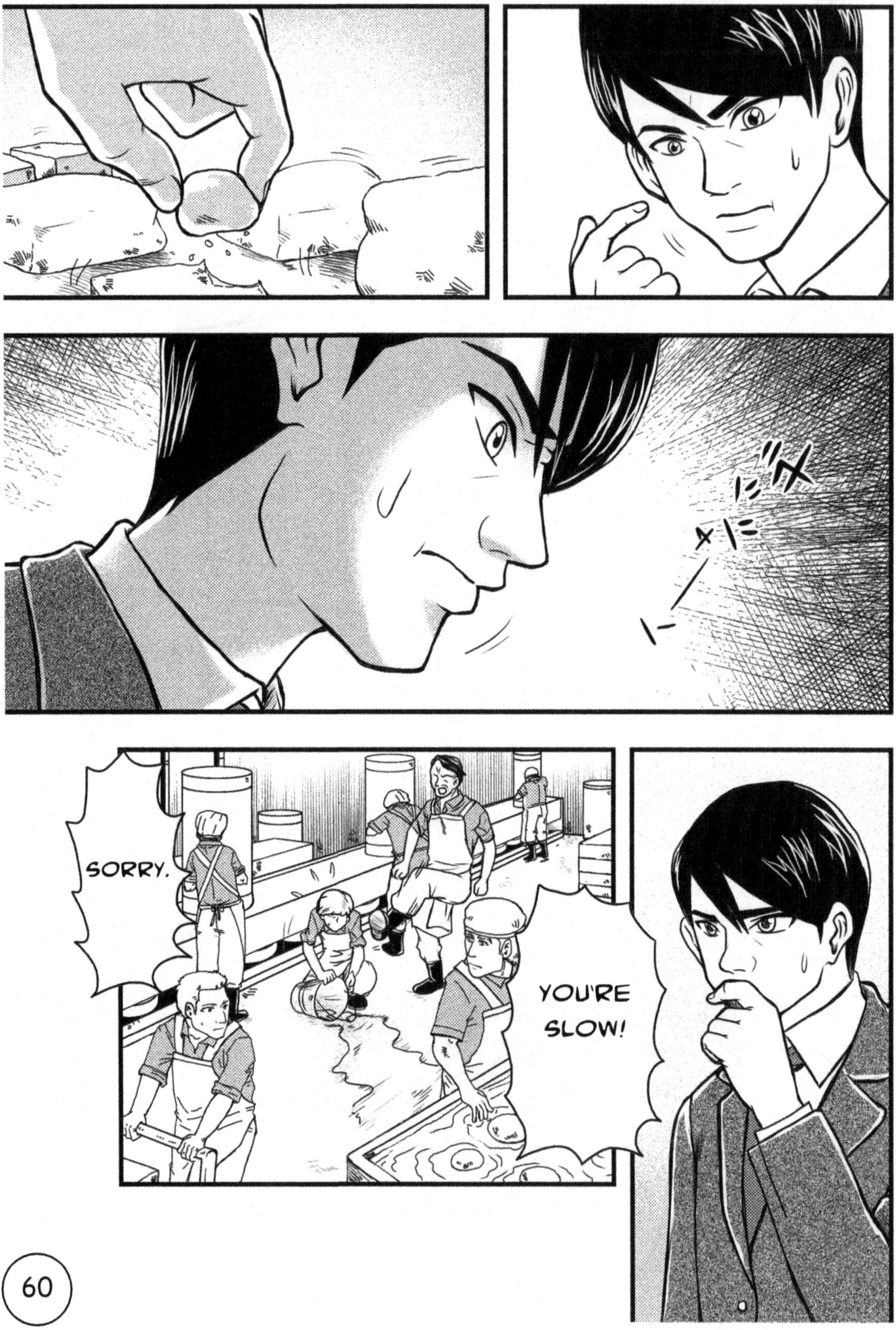
SORRY.
YOU'RE SLOW!

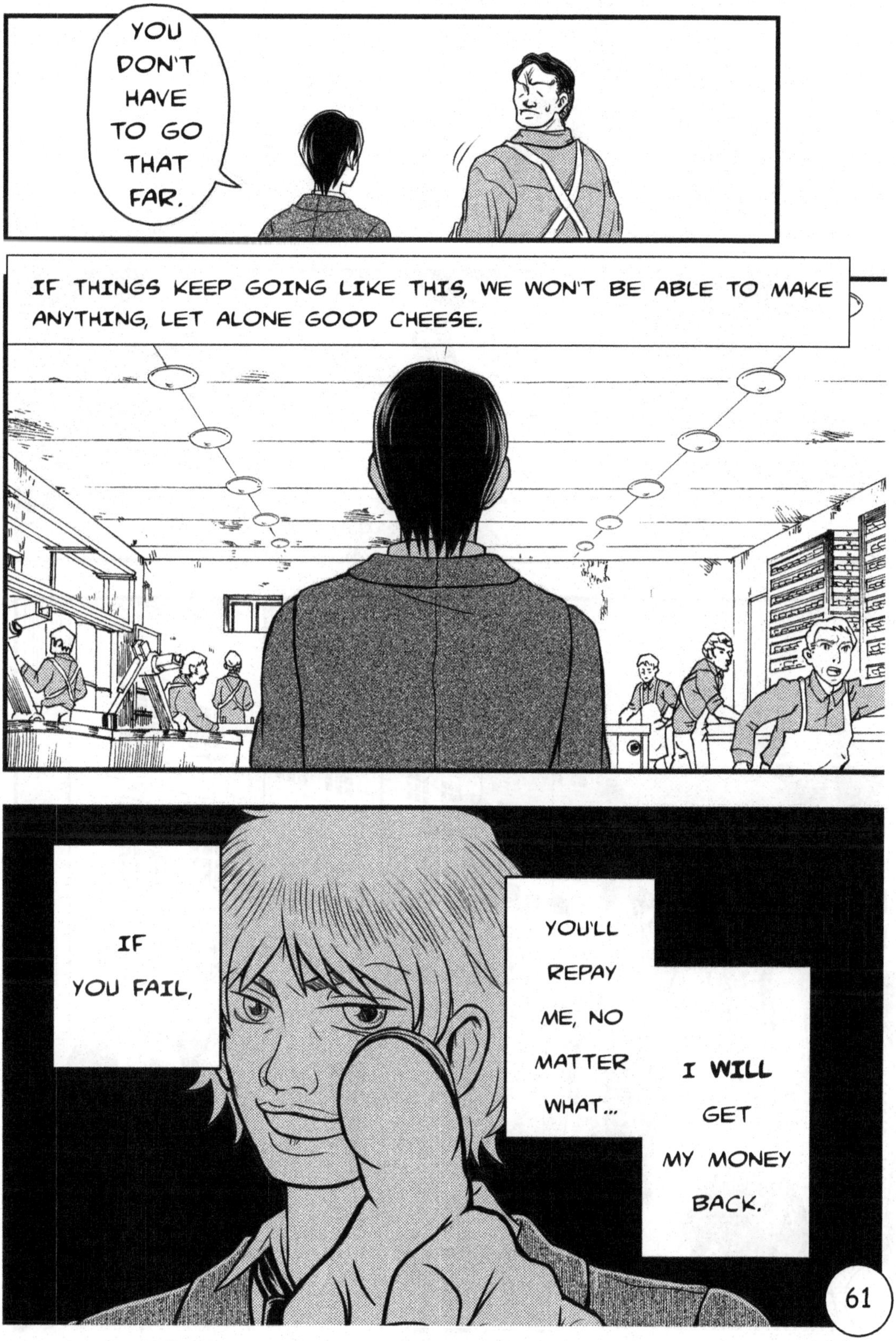
YOU DON'T HAVE TO GO THAT FAR.
IF THINGS KEEP GOING LIKE THIS, WE WON'T BE ABLE TO MAKE ANYTHING, LET ALONE GOOD CHEESE.
IF YOU FAIL,
YOU'LL REPAY ME, NO MATTER WHAT...
I **WILL** GET MY MONEY BACK.

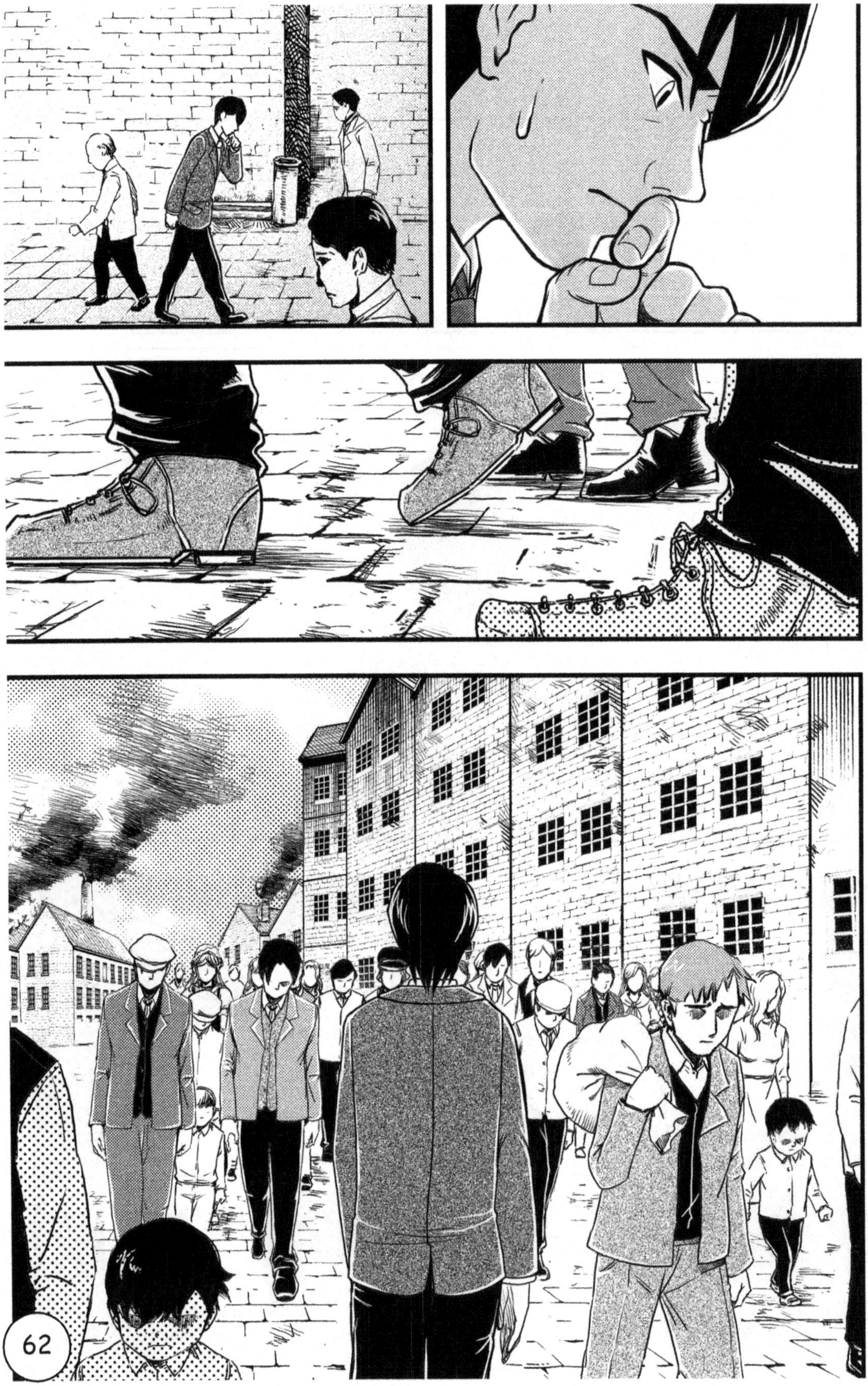
62

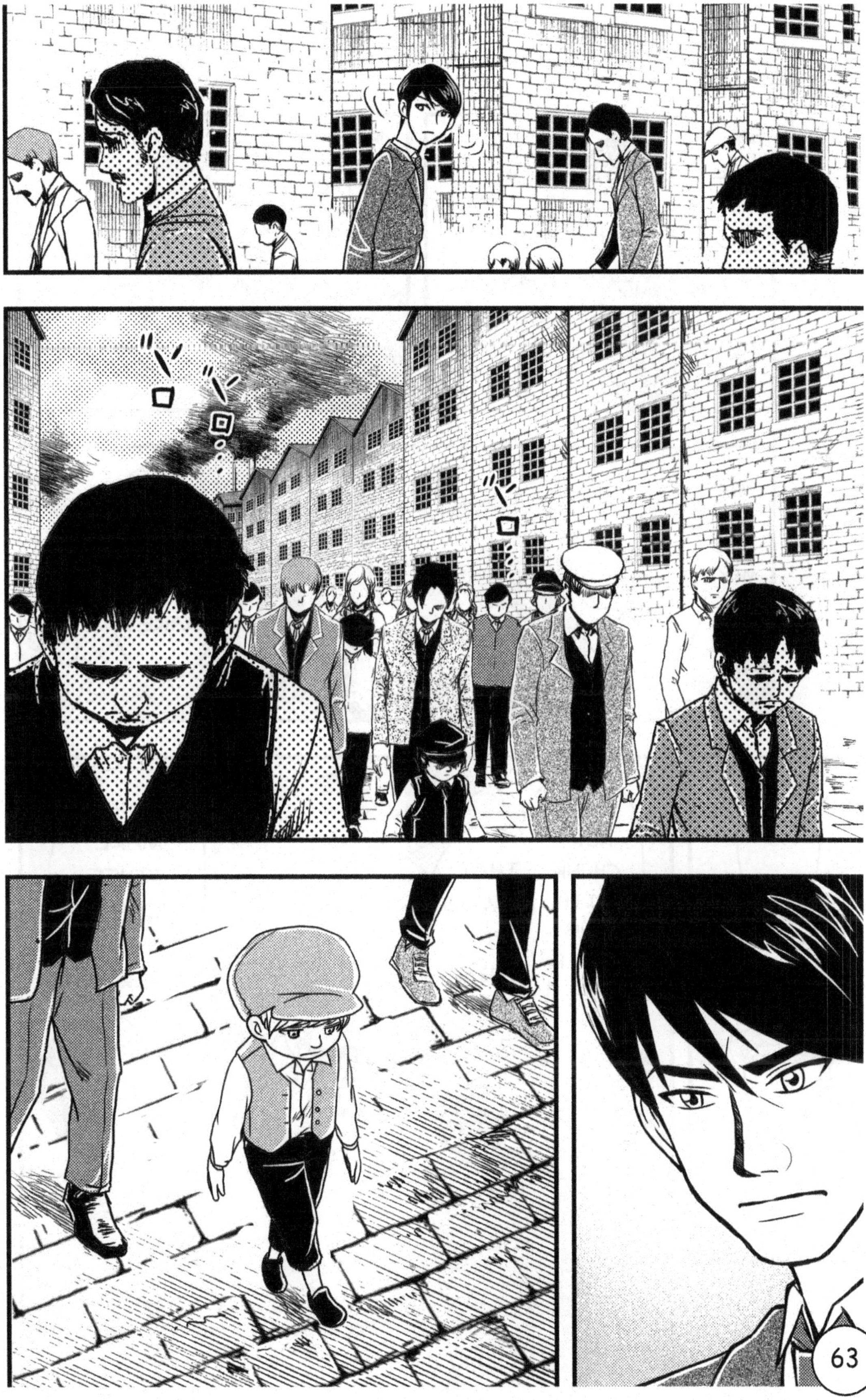
ブロ
ブロ…
ブロ…

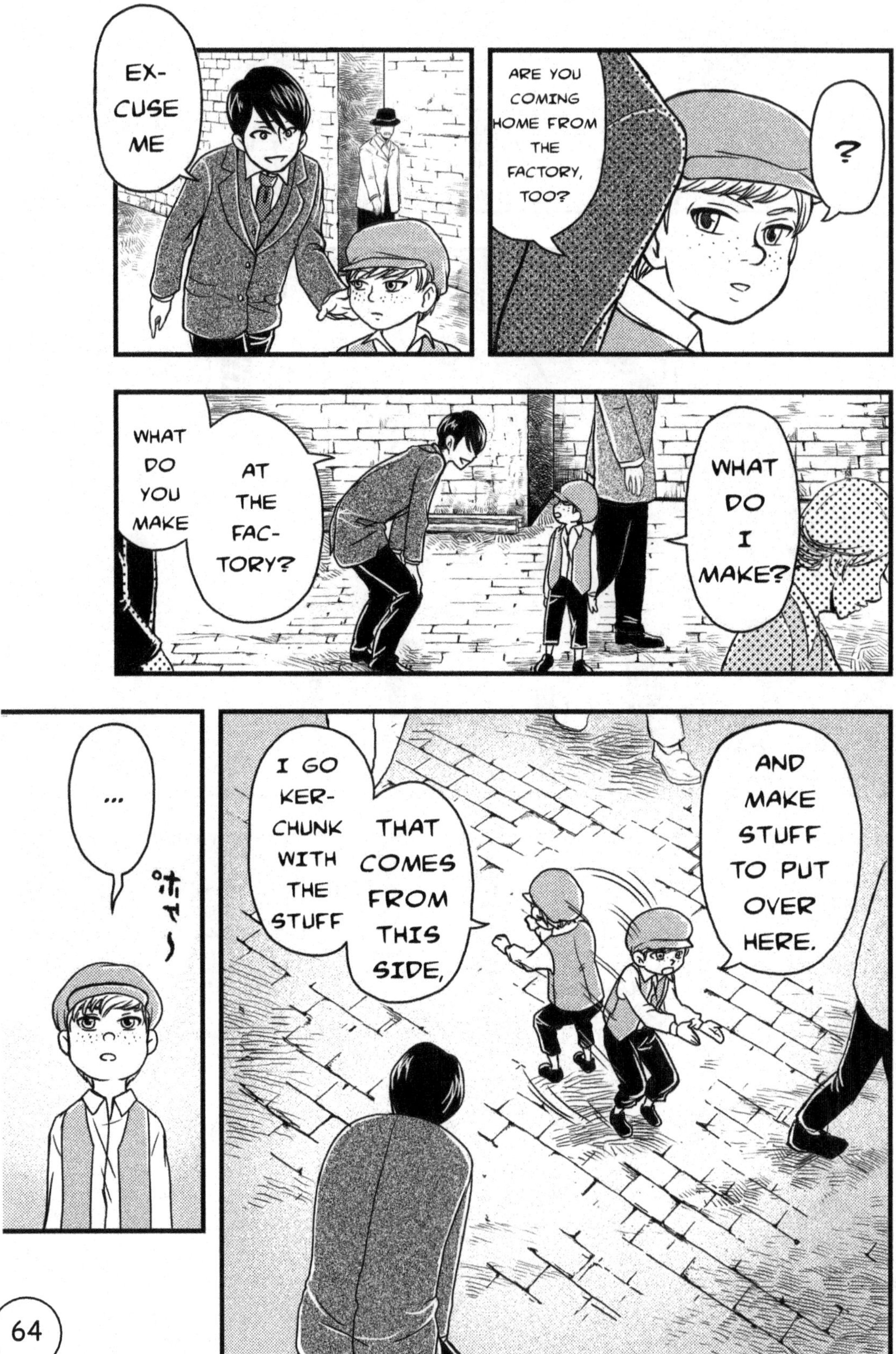
EX-CUSE ME
ARE YOU COMING HOME FROM THE FACTORY, TOO?
?
WHAT DO YOU MAKE AT THE FACTORY?
WHAT DO I MAKE?
...
I GO KER-CHUNK WITH THE STUFF THAT COMES FROM THIS SIDE,
AND MAKE STUFF TO PUT OVER HERE.

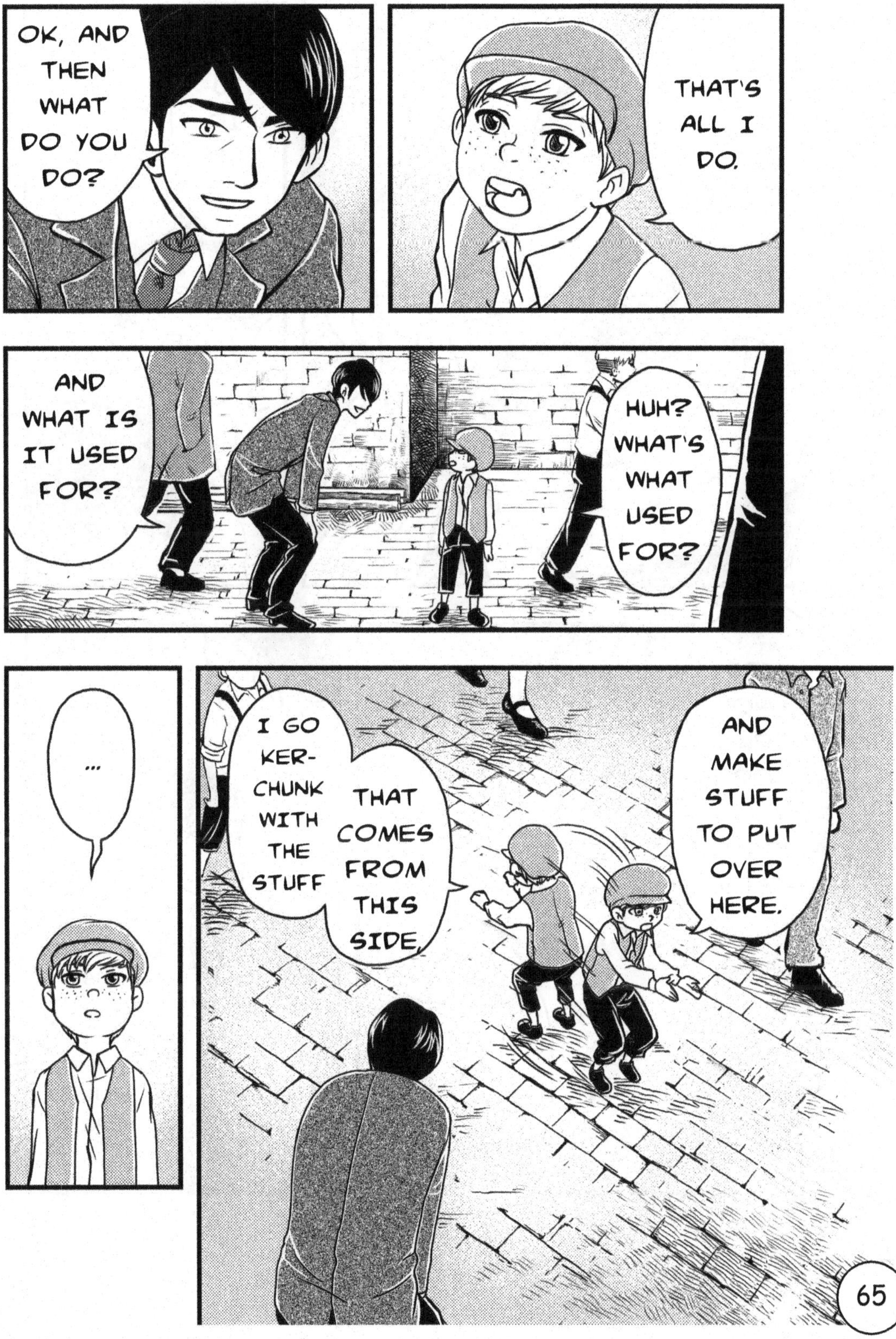

OK, AND THEN WHAT DO YOU DO?
THAT'S ALL I DO.
AND WHAT IS IT USED FOR?
HUH? WHAT'S WHAT USED FOR?
...
I GO KER-CHUNK WITH THE STUFF
THAT COMES FROM THIS SIDE,
AND MAKE STUFF TO PUT OVER HERE.

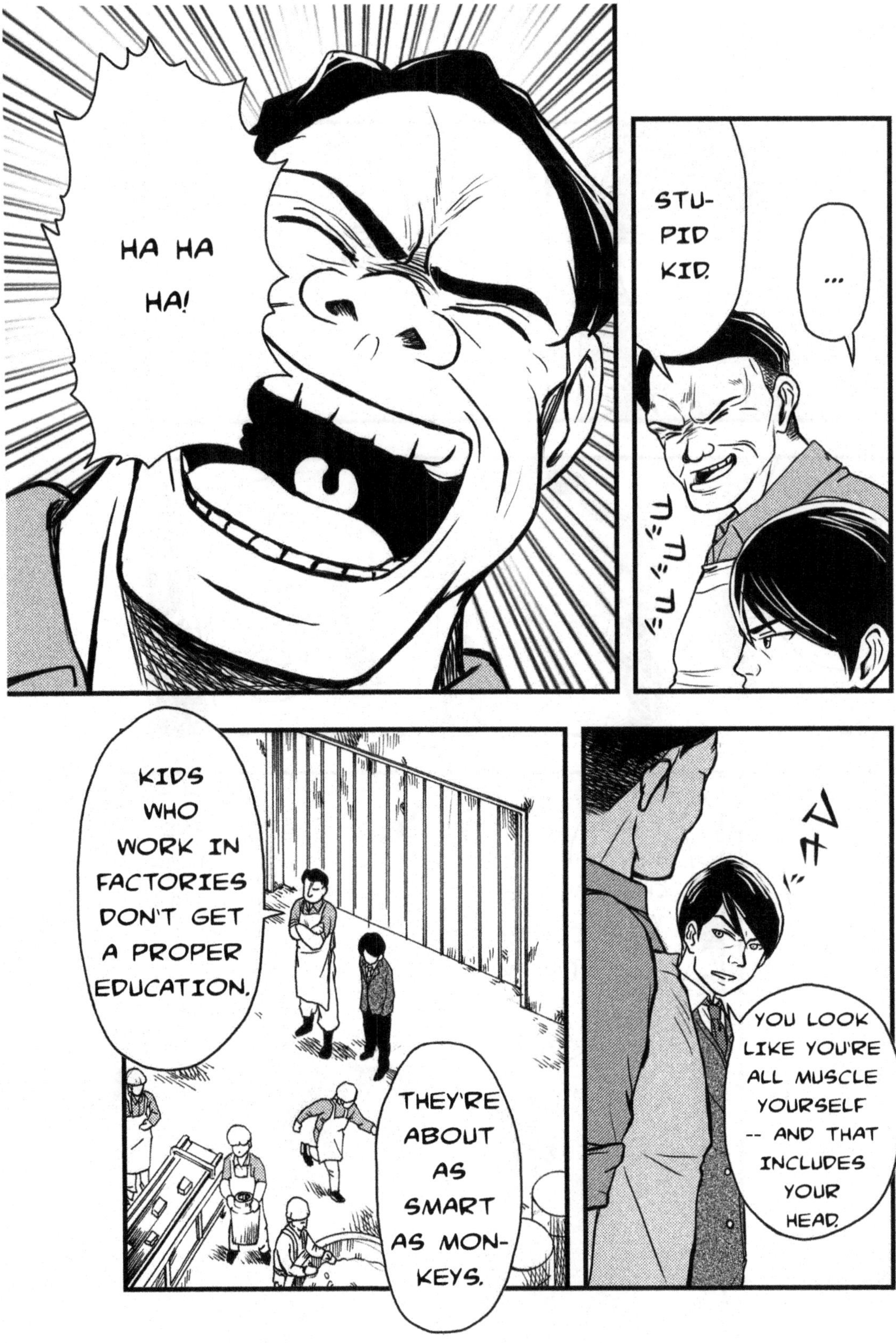
HA HA HA!
STUPID KID.
...
KIDS WHO WORK IN FACTORIES DON'T GET A PROPER EDUCATION.
THEY'RE ABOUT AS SMART AS MONKEYS.
YOU LOOK LIKE YOU'RE ALL MUSCLE YOURSELF -- AND THAT INCLUDES YOUR HEAD.

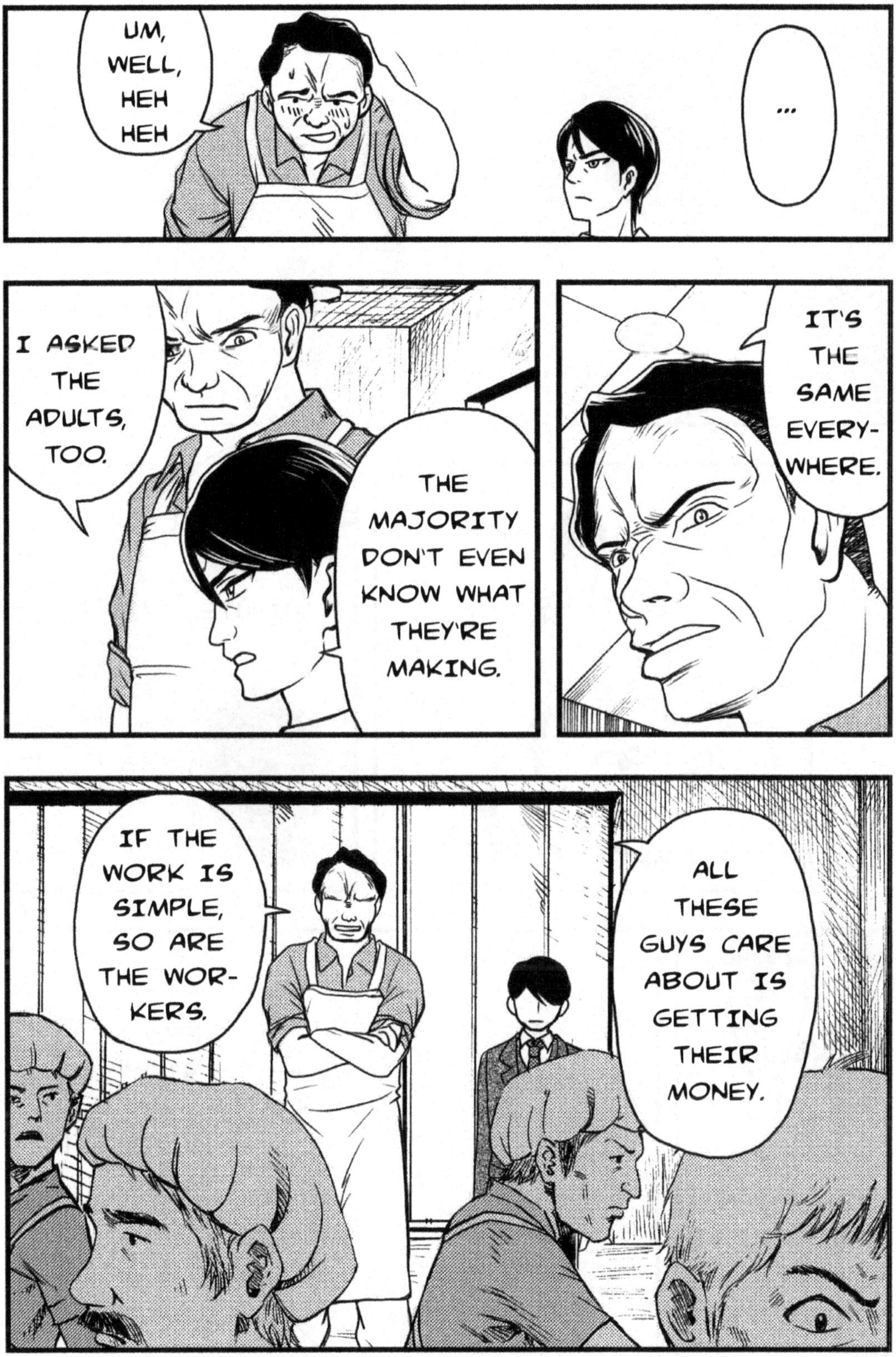
UM, WELL, HEH HEH
...
I ASKED THE ADULTS, TOO.
THE MAJORITY DON'T EVEN KNOW WHAT THEY'RE MAKING.
IT'S THE SAME EVERY-WHERE.
IF THE WORK IS SIMPLE, SO ARE THE WOR-KERS.
ALL THESE GUYS CARE ABOUT IS GETTING THEIR MONEY.

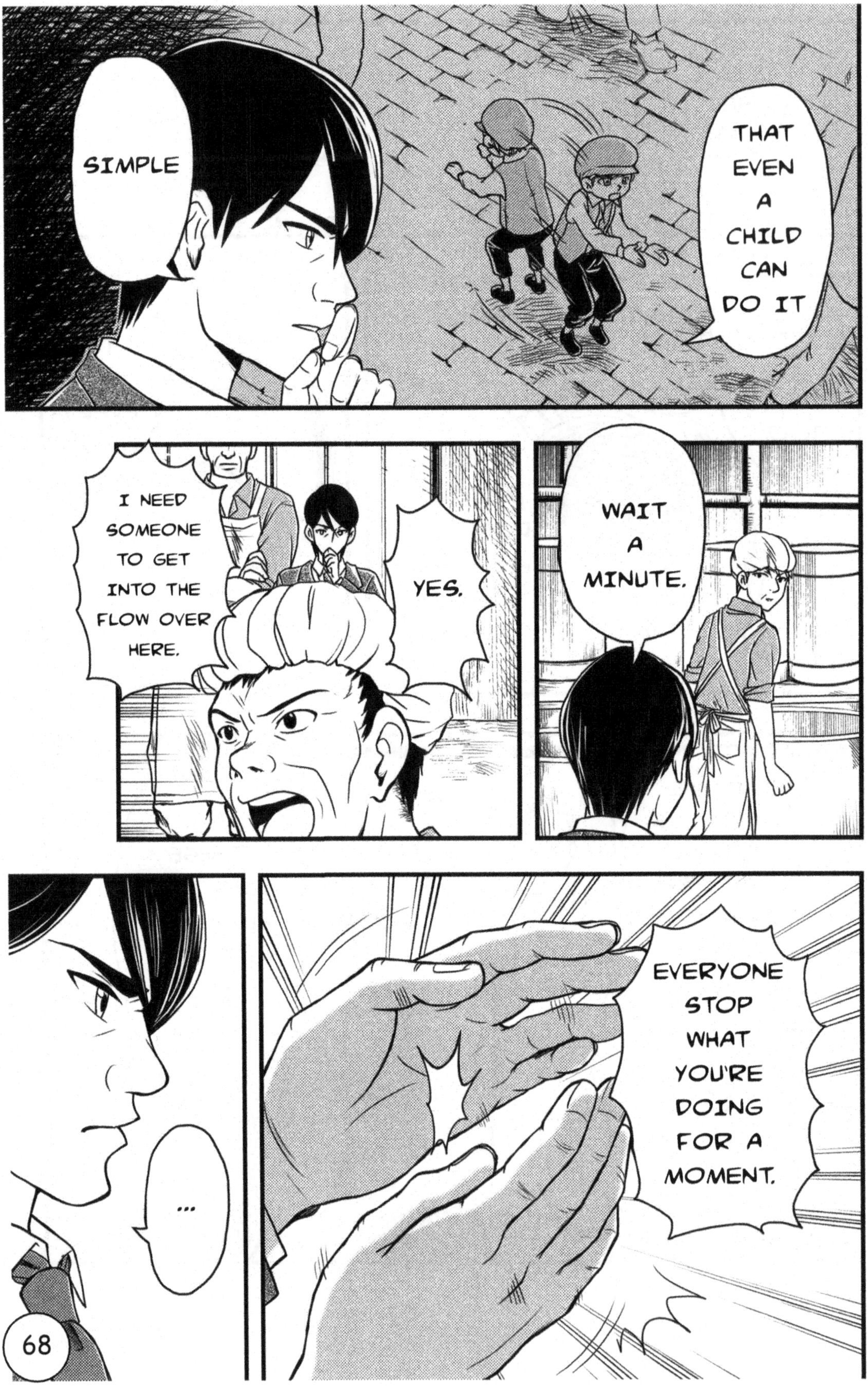
SIMPLE
THAT EVEN A CHILD CAN DO IT
I NEED SOMEONE TO GET INTO THE FLOW OVER HERE.
YES.
WAIT A MINUTE.
...
EVERYONE STOP WHAT YOU'RE DOING FOR A MOMENT.

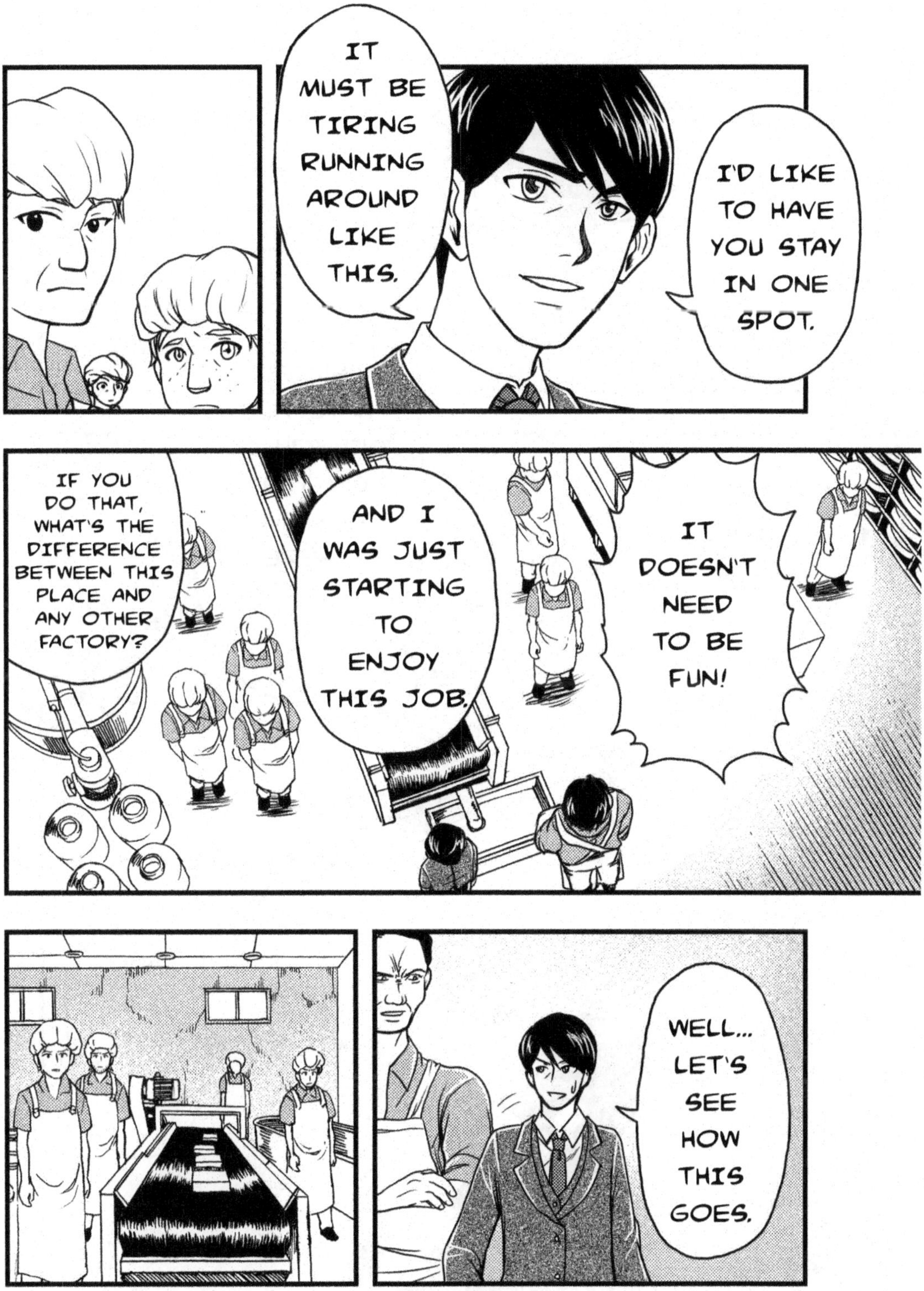
IT MUST BE TIRING RUNNING AROUND LIKE THIS.
I'D LIKE TO HAVE YOU STAY IN ONE SPOT.
IF YOU DO THAT, WHAT'S THE DIFFERENCE BETWEEN THIS PLACE AND ANY OTHER FACTORY?
AND I WAS JUST STARTING TO ENJOY THIS JOB.
IT DOESN'T NEED TO BE FUN!
WELL... LET'S SEE HOW THIS GOES.

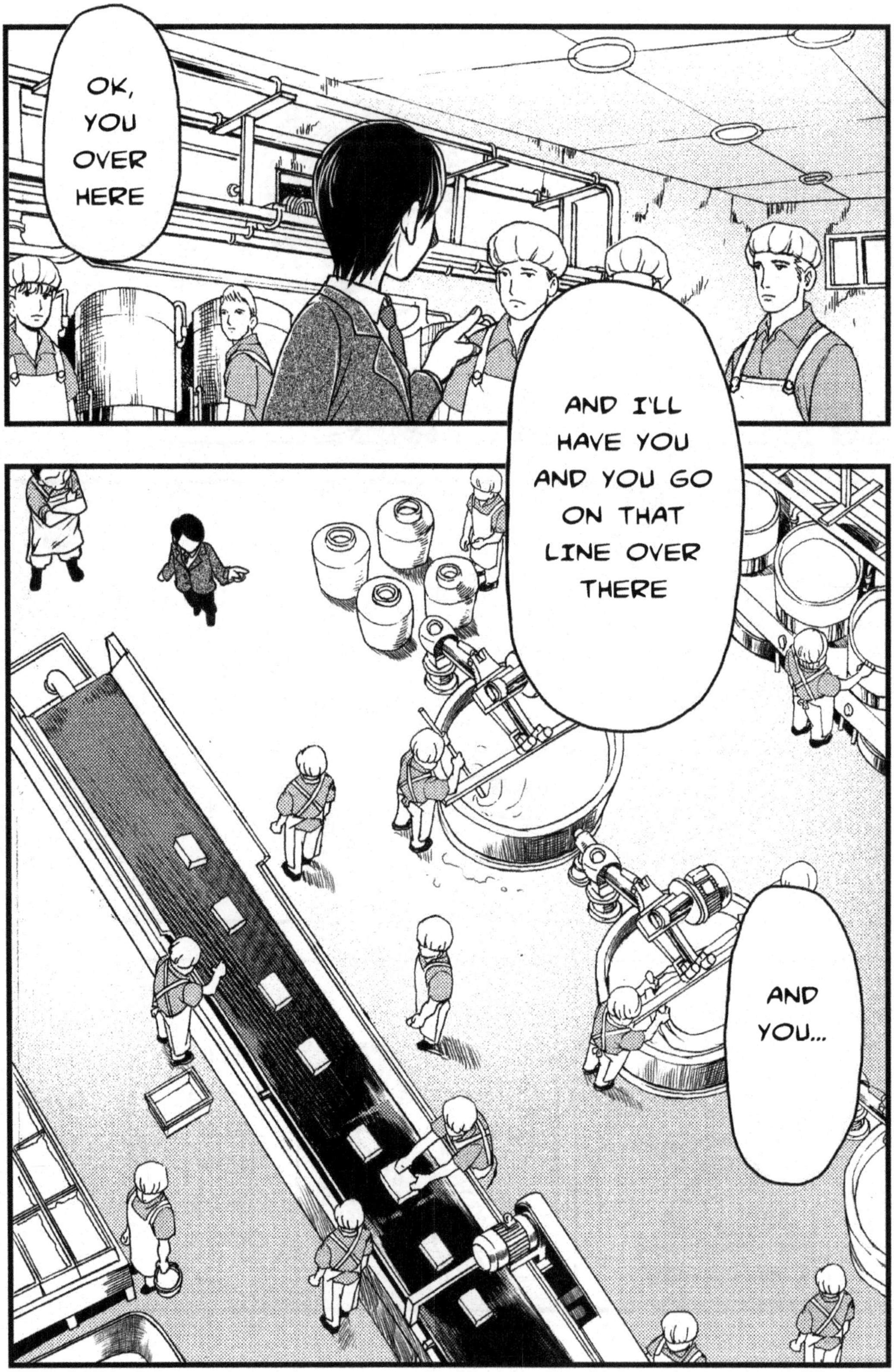
OK, YOU OVER HERE
AND I'LL HAVE YOU AND YOU GO ON THAT LINE OVER THERE
AND YOU...

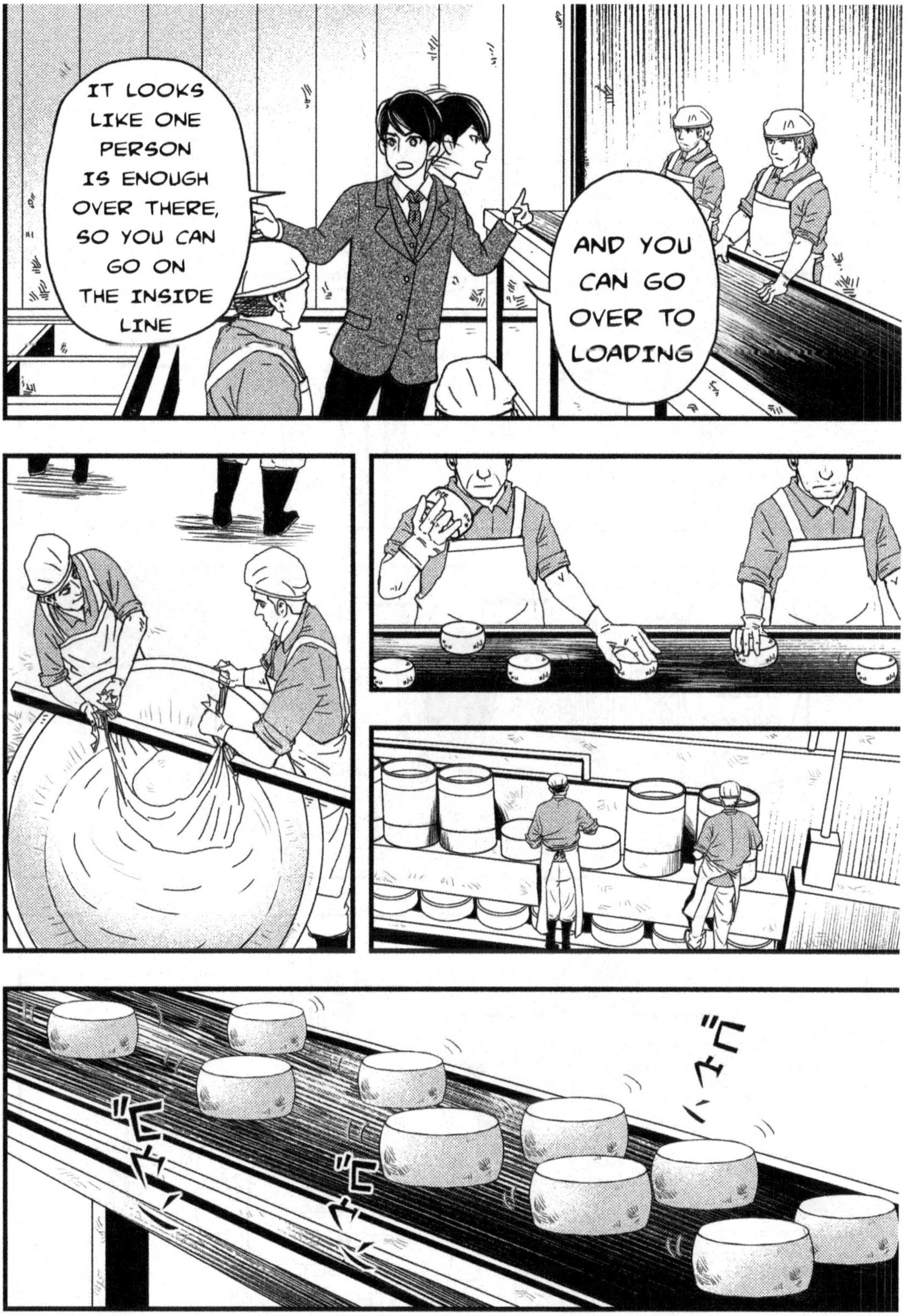
IT LOOKS LIKE ONE PERSON IS ENOUGH OVER THERE, SO YOU CAN GO ON THE INSIDE LINE
AND YOU CAN GO OVER TO LOADING

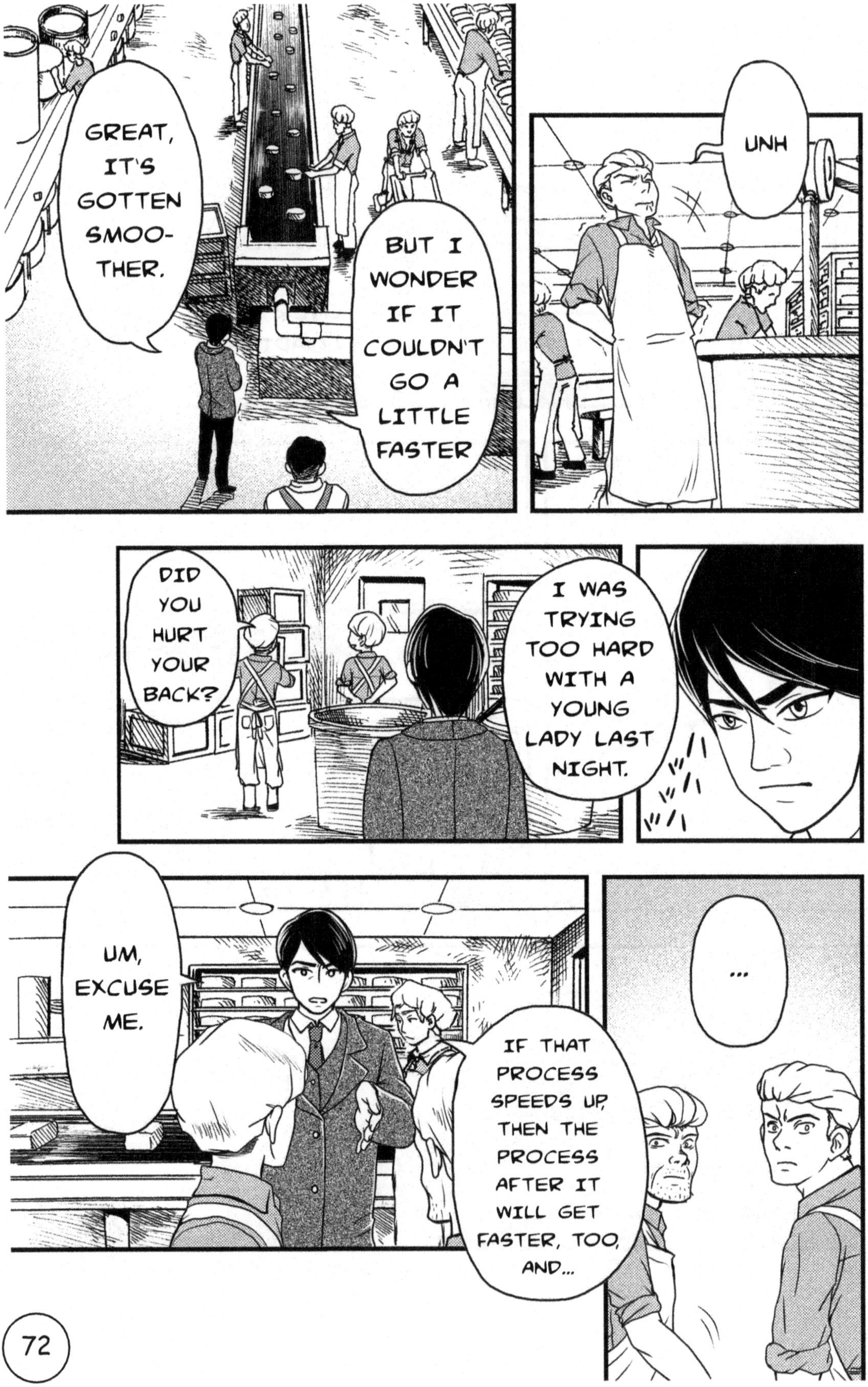
GREAT, IT'S GOTTEN SMOO-THER.
BUT I WONDER IF IT COULDN'T GO A LITTLE FASTER
UNH
DID YOU HURT YOUR BACK?
I WAS TRYING TOO HARD WITH A YOUNG LADY LAST NIGHT.
UM, EXCUSE ME.
IF THAT PROCESS SPEEDS UP, THEN THE PROCESS AFTER IT WILL GET FASTER, TOO, AND...
...

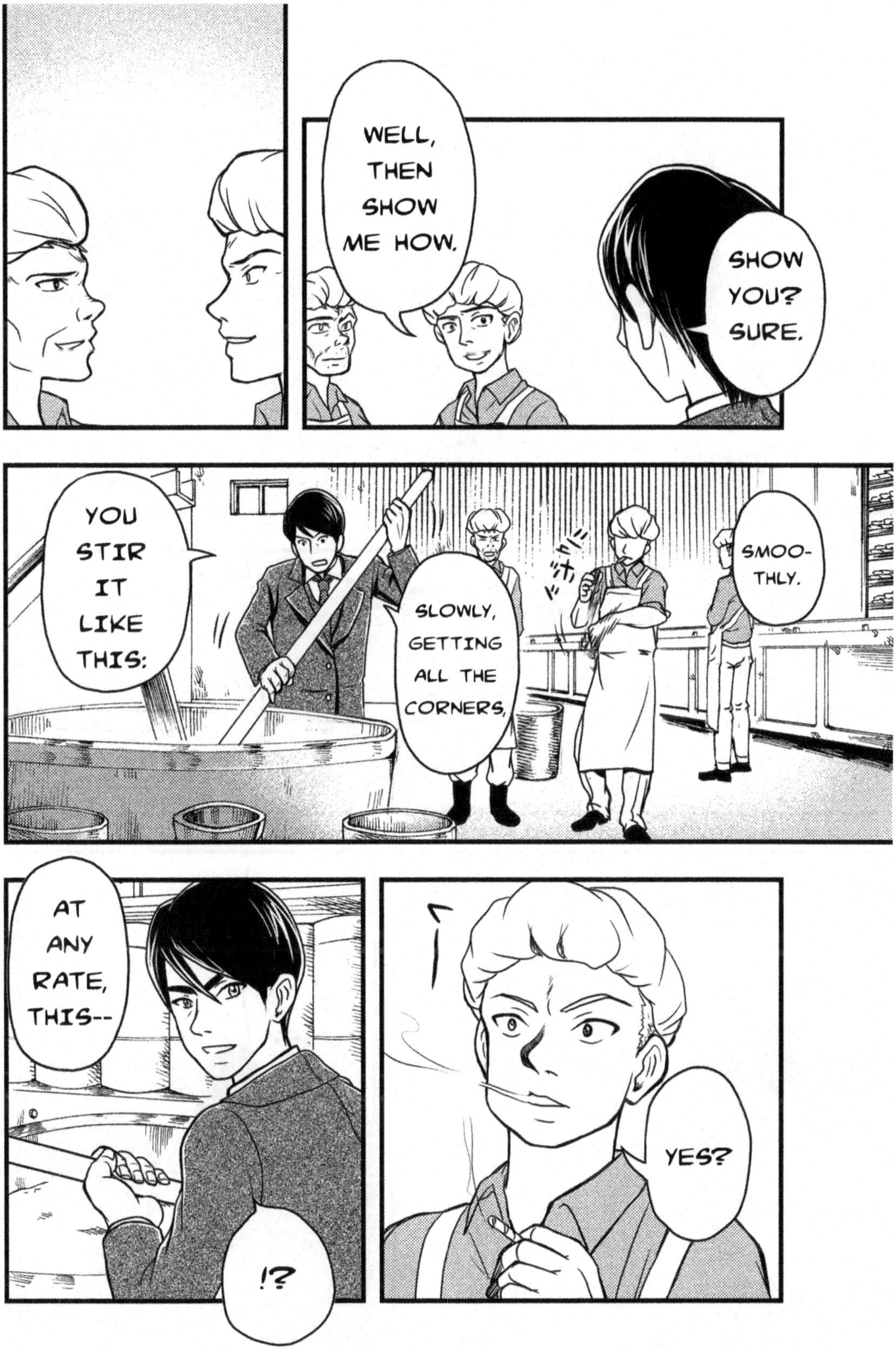
WELL, THEN SHOW ME HOW.
SHOW YOU? SURE.
YOU STIR IT LIKE THIS:
SLOWLY, GETTING ALL THE CORNERS,
SMOOTHLY.
AT ANY RATE, THIS--
!?
YES?

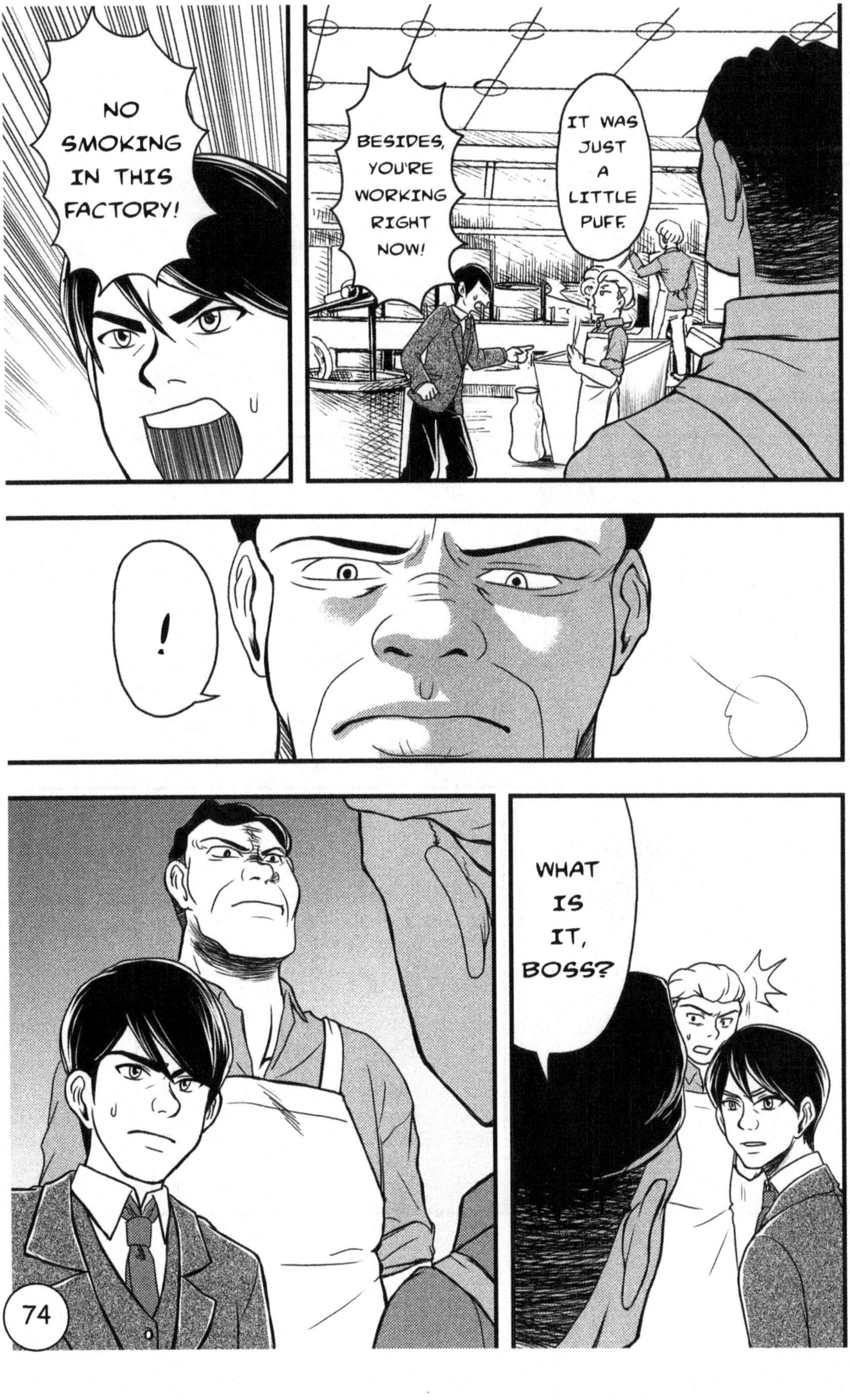
NO SMOKING IN THIS FACTORY!
BESIDES, YOU'RE WORKING RIGHT NOW!
IT WAS JUST A LITTLE PUFF.
!
WHAT IS IT, BOSS?

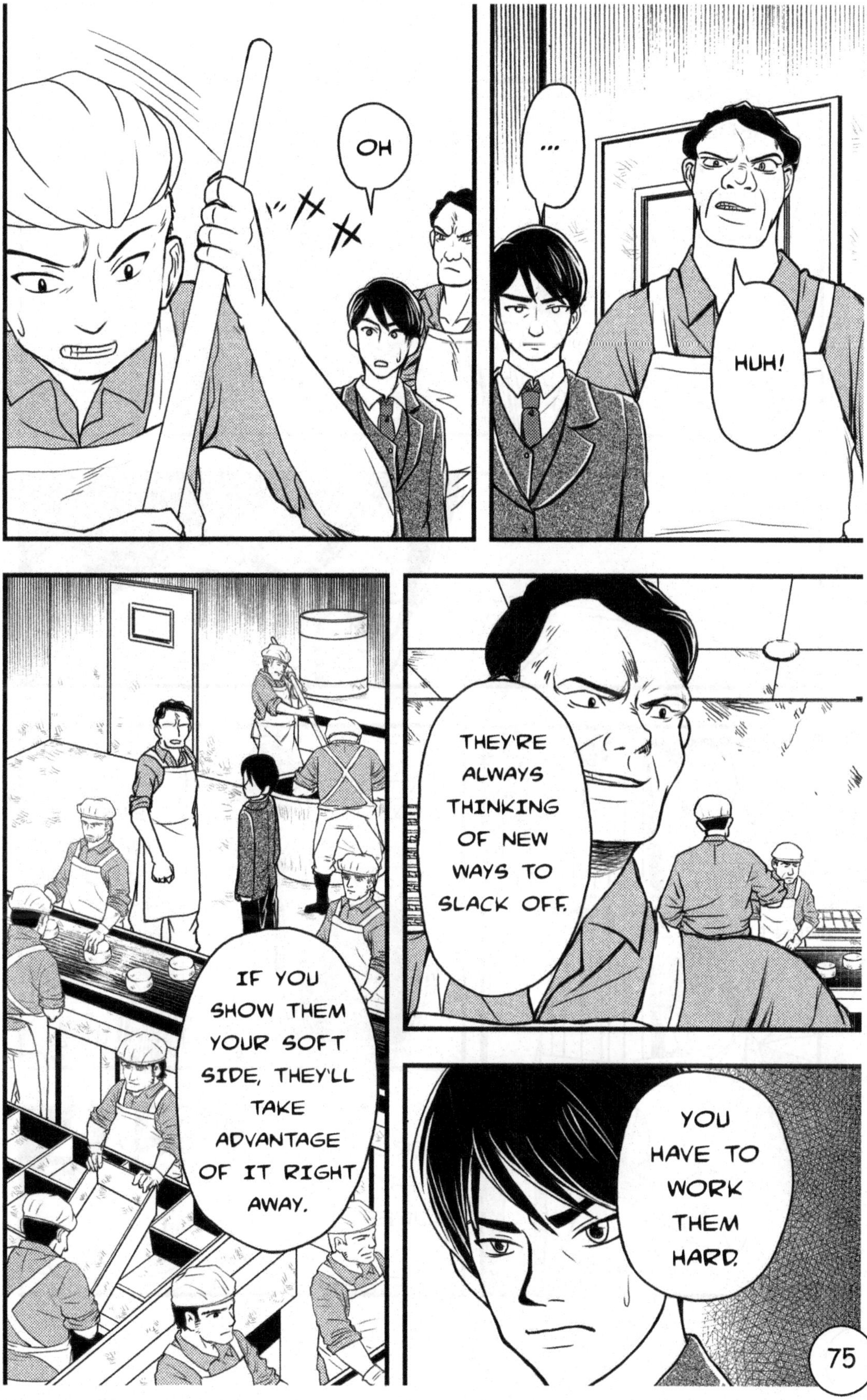
OH
...
HUH!
IF YOU SHOW THEM YOUR SOFT SIDE, THEY'LL TAKE ADVANTAGE OF IT RIGHT AWAY.
THEY'RE ALWAYS THINKING OF NEW WAYS TO SLACK OFF.
YOU HAVE TO WORK THEM HARD.

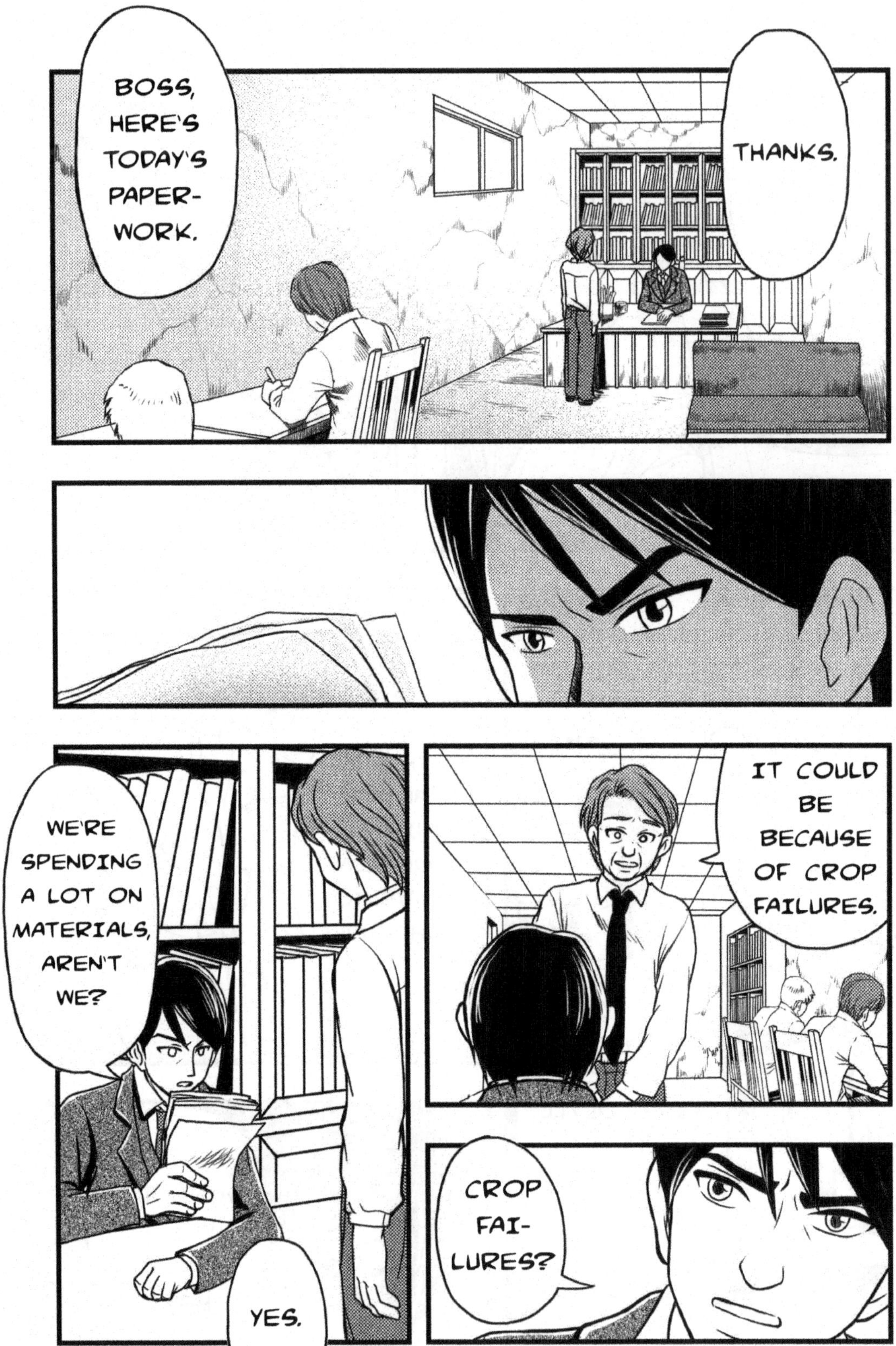
BOSS, HERE'S TODAY'S PAPER-WORK.
THANKS.
WE'RE SPENDING A LOT ON MATERIALS, AREN'T WE?
YES.
IT COULD BE BECAUSE OF CROP FAILURES.
CROP FAI-LURES?

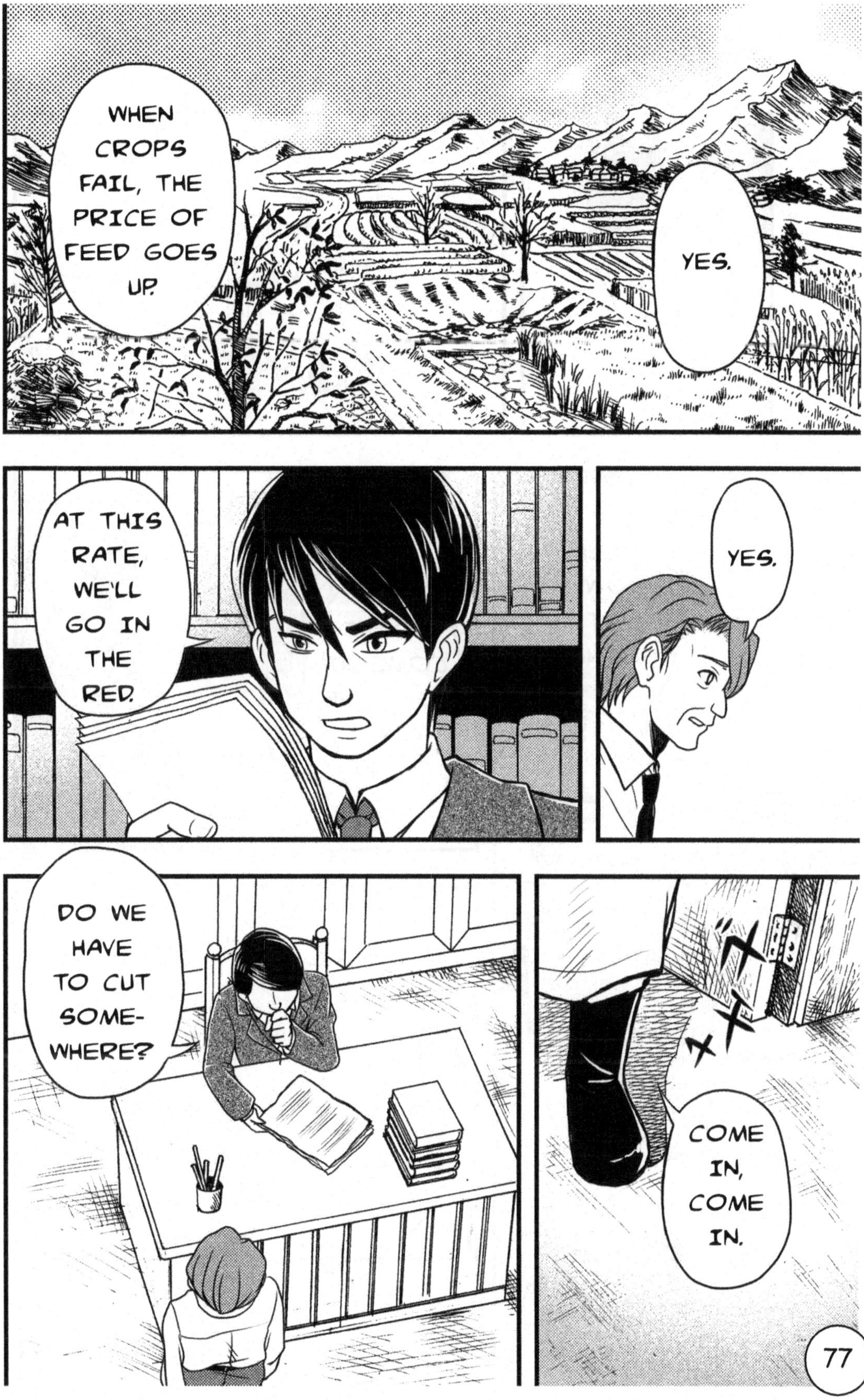
WHEN CROPS FAIL, THE PRICE OF FEED GOES UP.
YES.
AT THIS RATE, WE'LL GO IN THE RED.
YES.
DO WE HAVE TO CUT SOME-WHERE?
COME IN, COME IN.

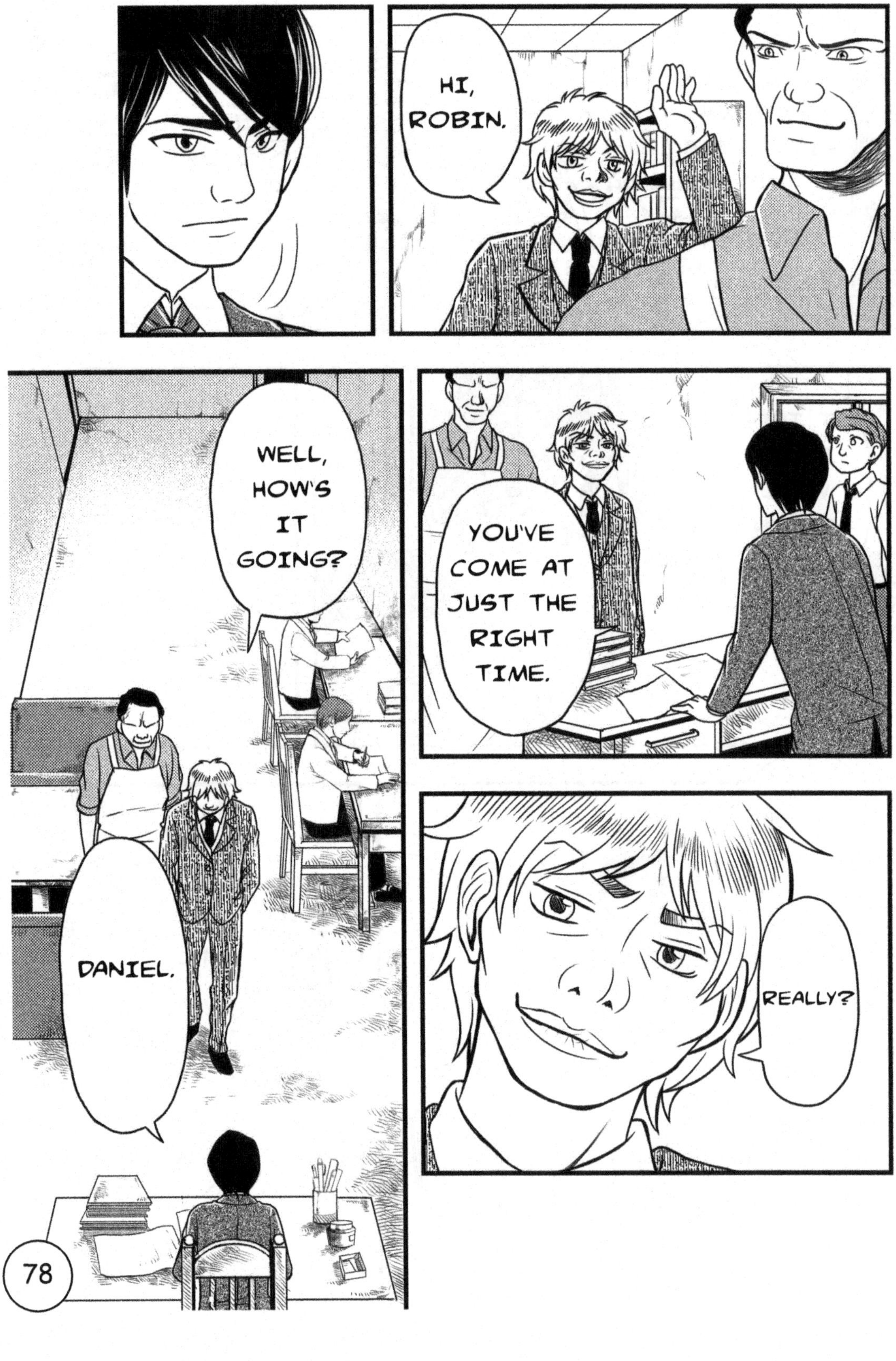
HI, ROBIN.
WELL, HOW'S IT GOING?
DANIEL.
YOU'VE COME AT JUST THE RIGHT TIME.
REALLY?

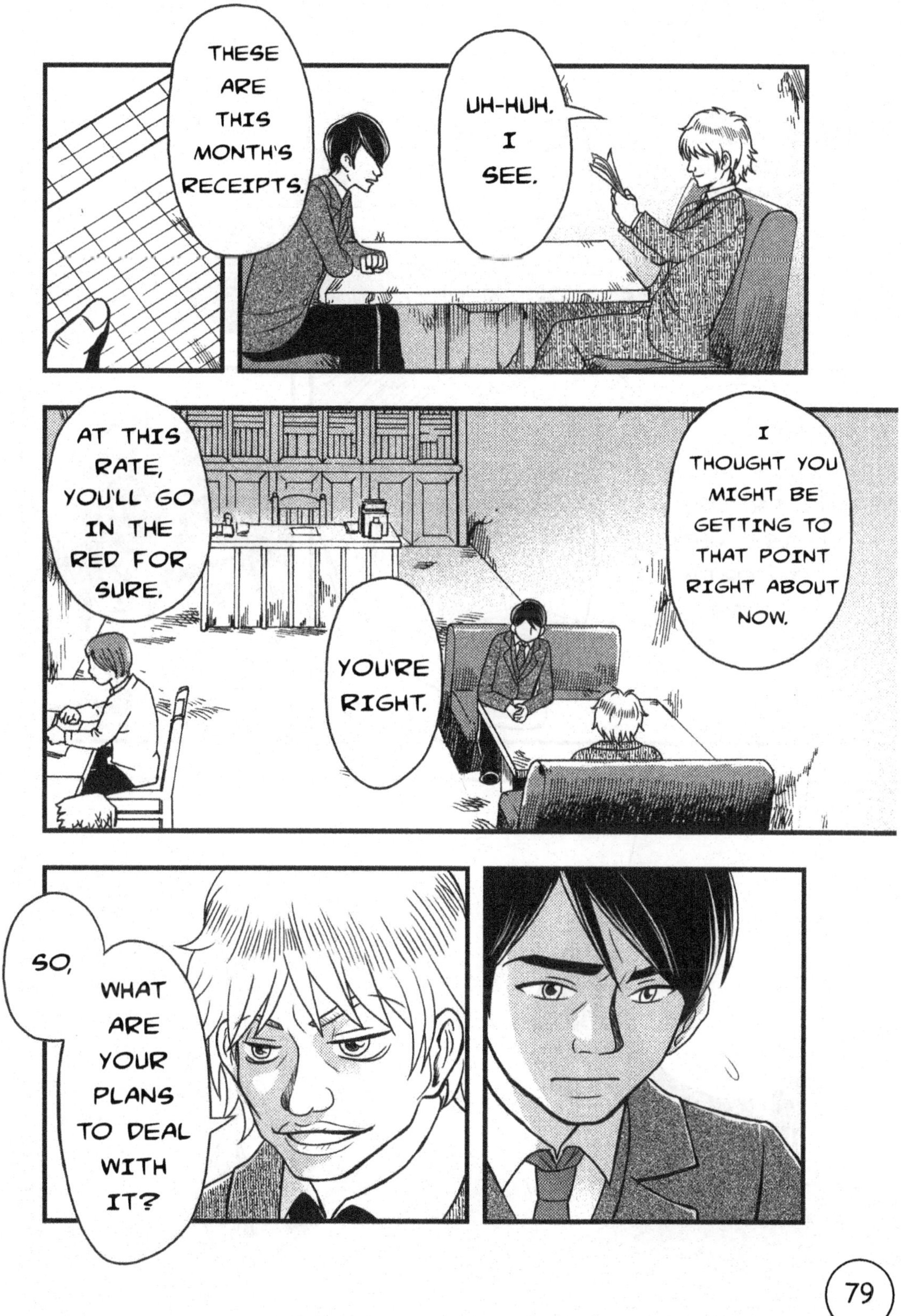
THESE ARE THIS MONTH'S RECEIPTS.
UH-HUH. I SEE.
AT THIS RATE, YOU'LL GO IN THE RED FOR SURE.
YOU'RE RIGHT.
I THOUGHT YOU MIGHT BE GETTING TO THAT POINT RIGHT ABOUT NOW.
SO, WHAT ARE YOUR PLANS TO DEAL WITH IT?

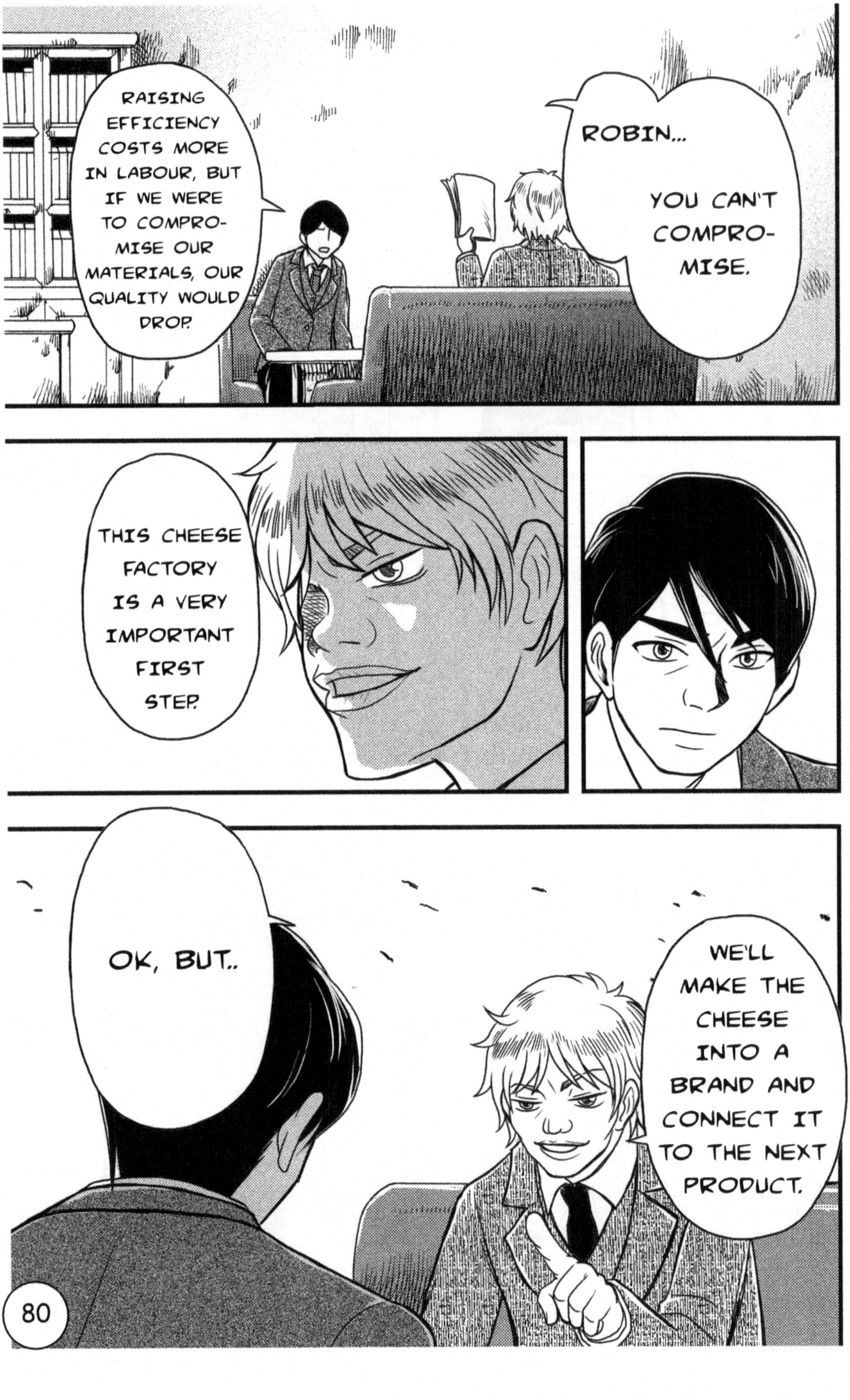
RAISING EFFICIENCY COSTS MORE IN LABOUR, BUT IF WE WERE TO COMPRO-MISE OUR MATERIALS, OUR QUALITY WOULD DROP.
ROBIN...
YOU CAN'T COMPRO-MISE.
THIS CHEESE FACTORY IS A VERY IMPORTANT FIRST STEP.
OK, BUT..
WE'LL MAKE THE CHEESE INTO A BRAND AND CONNECT IT TO THE NEXT PRODUCT.

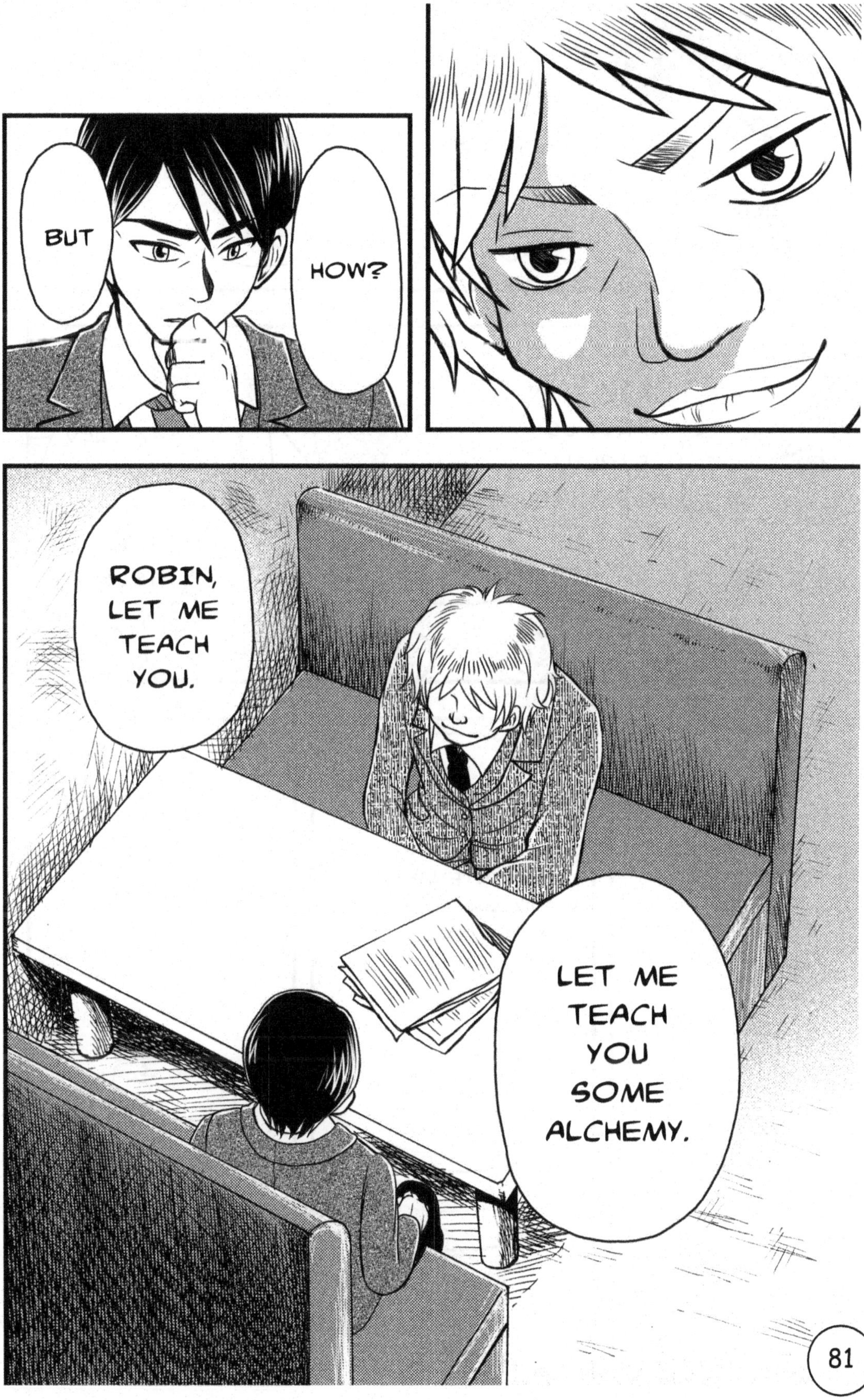
BUT
HOW?
ROBIN, LET ME TEACH YOU.
LET ME TEACH YOU SOME ALCHEMY.

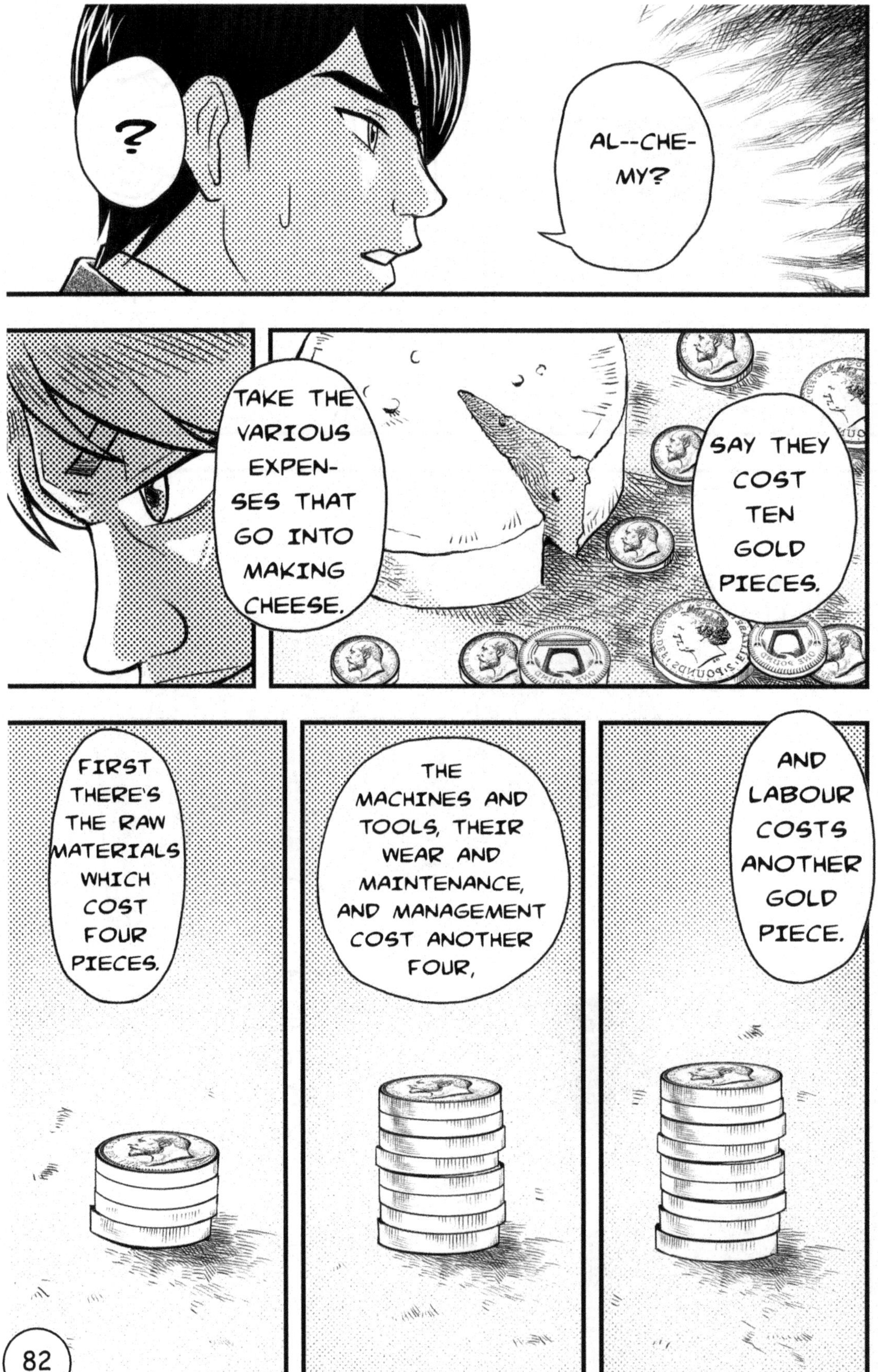
?
AL--CHE-MY?
TAKE THE VARIOUS EXPENSES THAT GO INTO MAKING CHEESE.
SAY THEY COST TEN GOLD PIECES.
FIRST THERE'S THE RAW MATERIALS WHICH COST FOUR PIECES.
THE MACHINES AND TOOLS, THEIR WEAR AND MAINTENANCE, AND MANAGEMENT COST ANOTHER FOUR,
AND LABOUR COSTS ANOTHER GOLD PIECE.

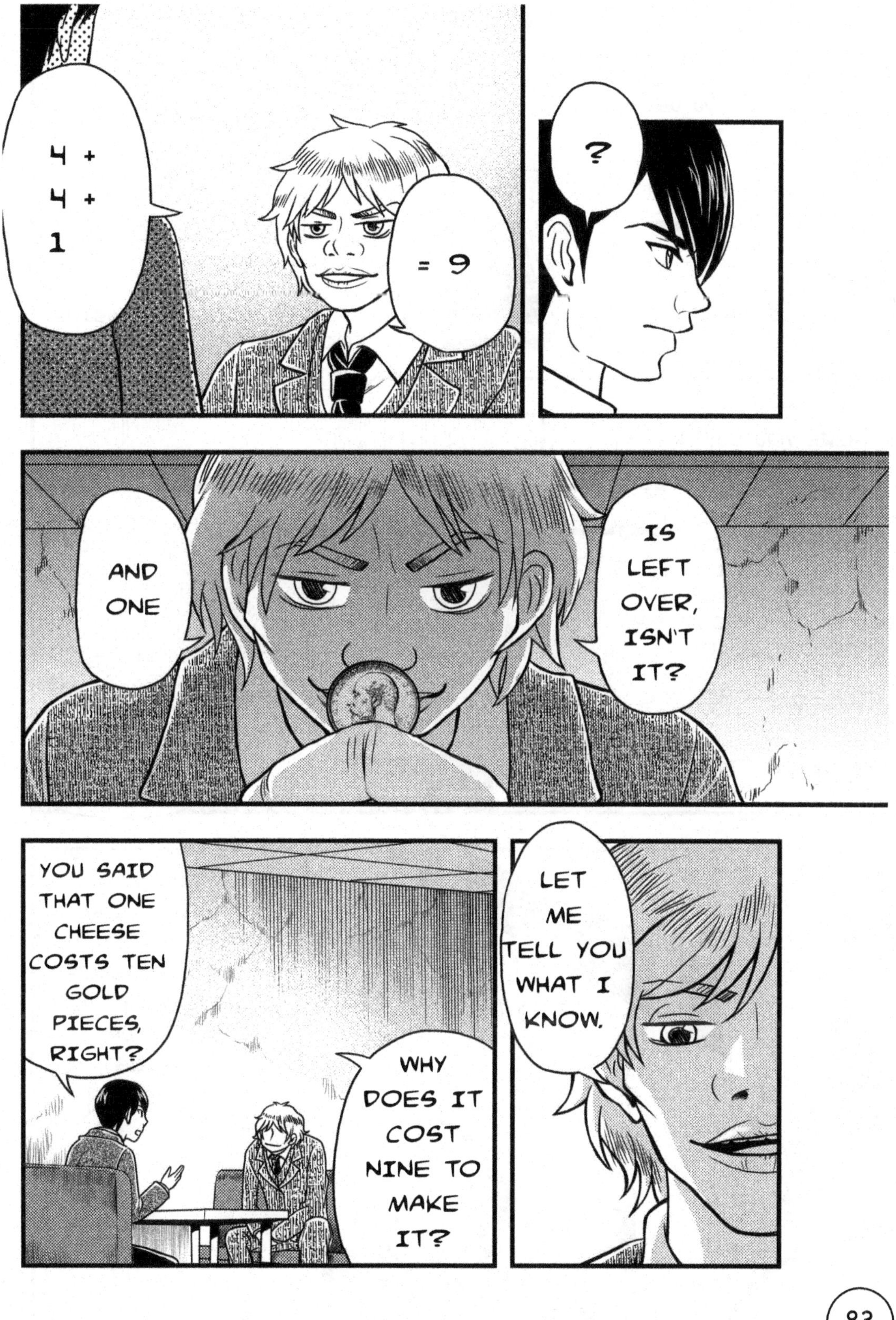
4 + 4 + 1
= 9
?
AND ONE
IS LEFT OVER, ISN'T IT?
YOU SAID THAT ONE CHEESE COSTS TEN GOLD PIECES, RIGHT?
WHY DOES IT COST NINE TO MAKE IT?
LET ME TELL YOU WHAT I KNOW.

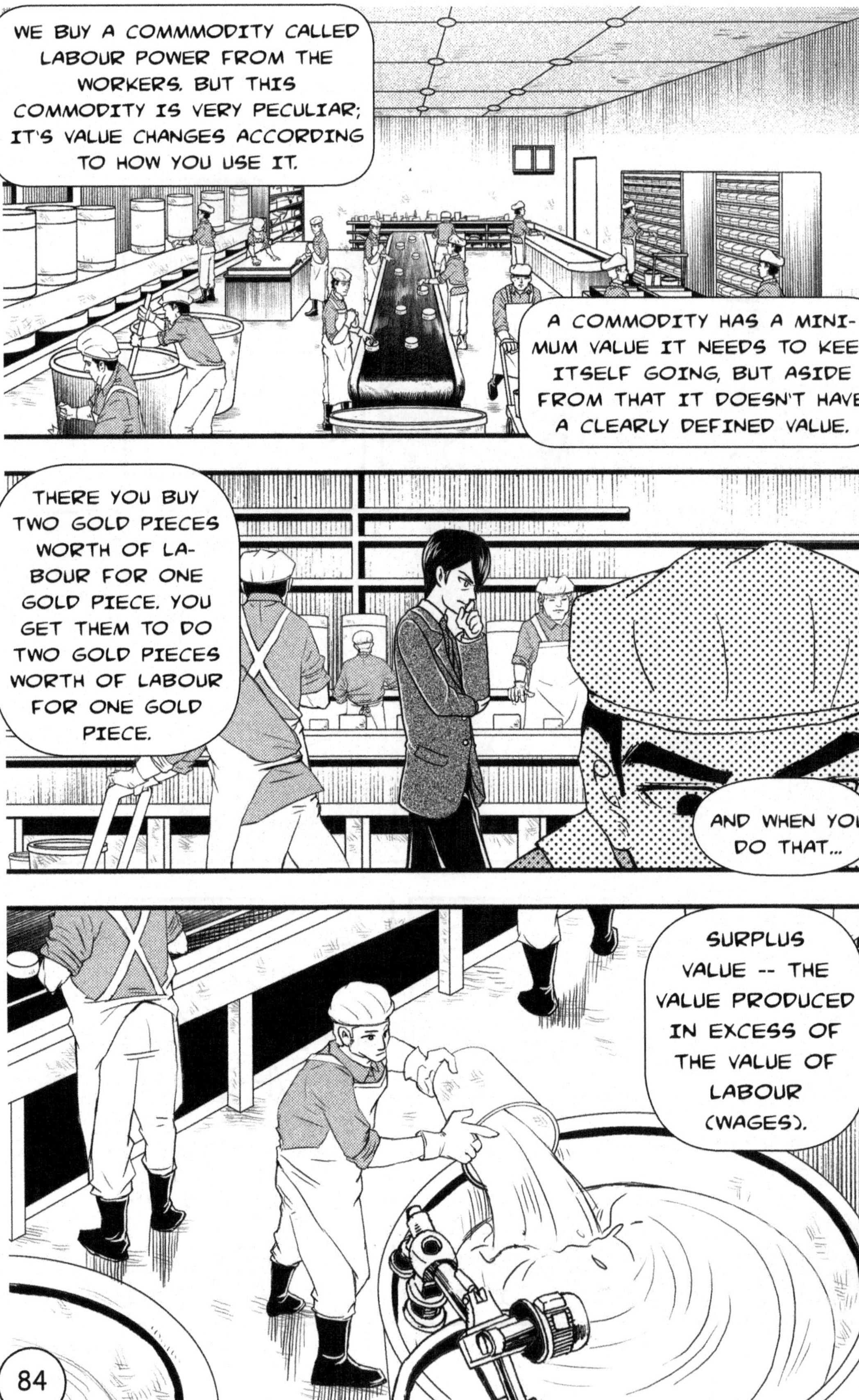
WE BUY A COMMMODITY CALLED LABOUR POWER FROM THE WORKERS. BUT THIS COMMODITY IS VERY PECULIAR; IT'S VALUE CHANGES ACCORDING TO HOW YOU USE IT.
A COMMODITY HAS A MINIMUM VALUE IT NEEDS TO KEEP ITSELF GOING, BUT ASIDE FROM THAT IT DOESN'T HAVE A CLEARLY DEFINED VALUE.
THERE YOU BUY TWO GOLD PIECES WORTH OF LABOUR FOR ONE GOLD PIECE. YOU GET THEM TO DO TWO GOLD PIECES WORTH OF LABOUR FOR ONE GOLD PIECE.
AND WHEN YOU DO THAT...
SURPLUS VALUE -- THE VALUE PRODUCED IN EXCESS OF THE VALUE OF LABOUR (WAGES).

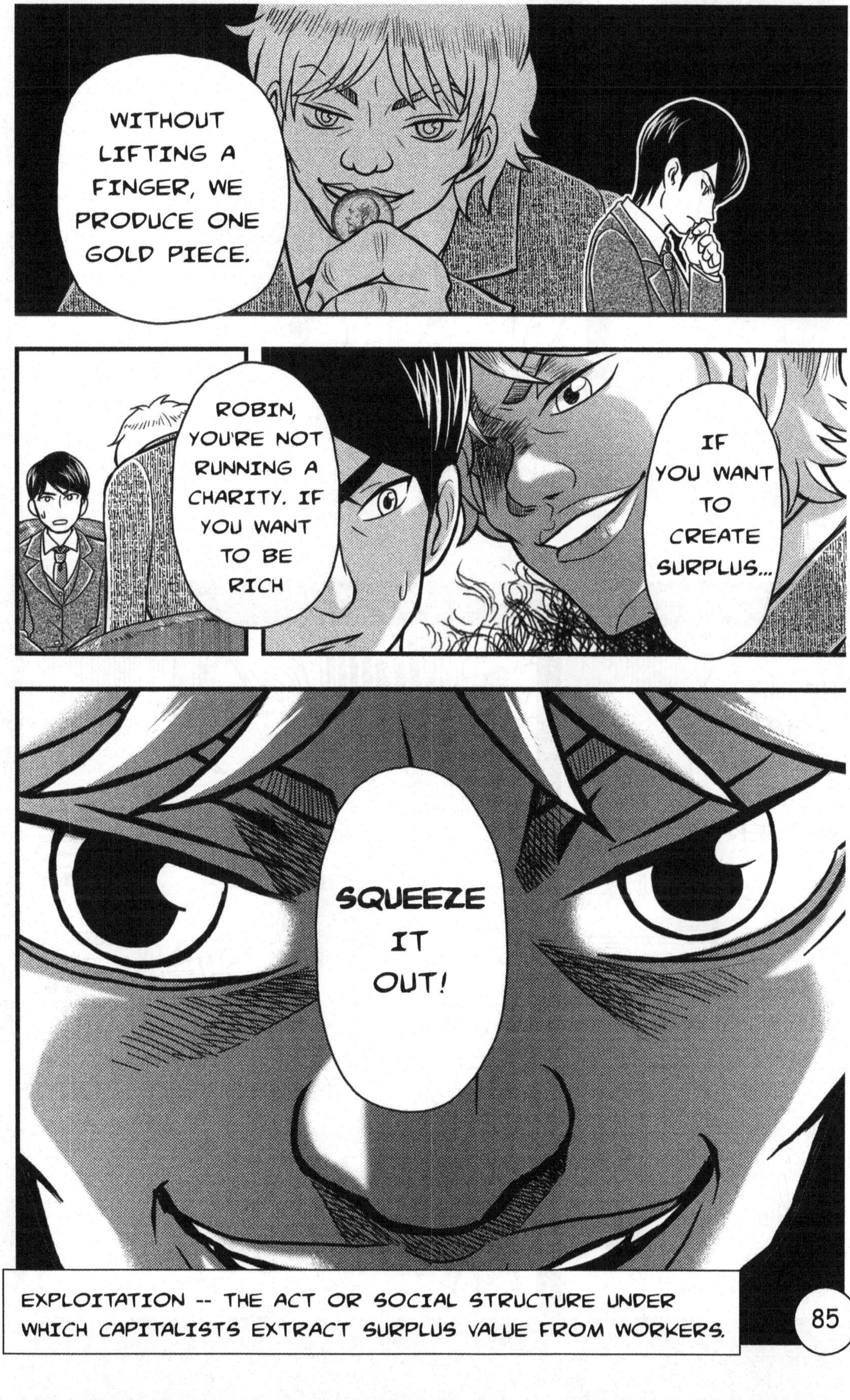
WITHOUT LIFTING A FINGER, WE PRODUCE ONE GOLD PIECE.
ROBIN, YOU'RE NOT RUNNING A CHARITY. IF YOU WANT TO BE RICH
IF YOU WANT TO CREATE SURPLUS...
SQUEEZE IT OUT!
EXPLOITATION -- THE ACT OR SOCIAL STRUCTURE UNDER WHICH CAPITALISTS EXTRACT SURPLUS VALUE FROM WORKERS.

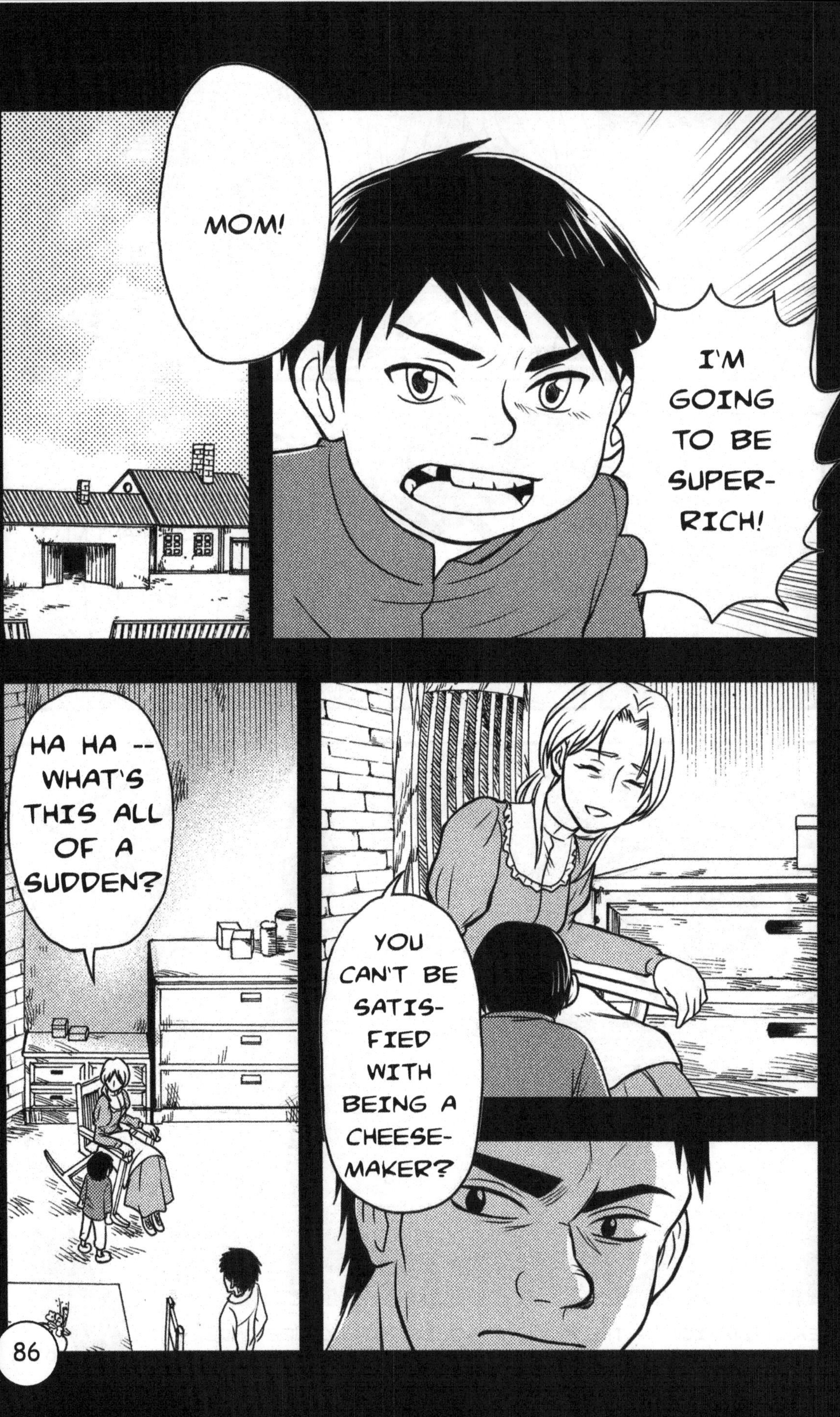
MOM!
I'M GOING TO BE SUPER-RICH!
HA HA -- WHAT'S THIS ALL OF A SUDDEN?
YOU CAN'T BE SATIS-FIED WITH BEING A CHEESE-MAKER?

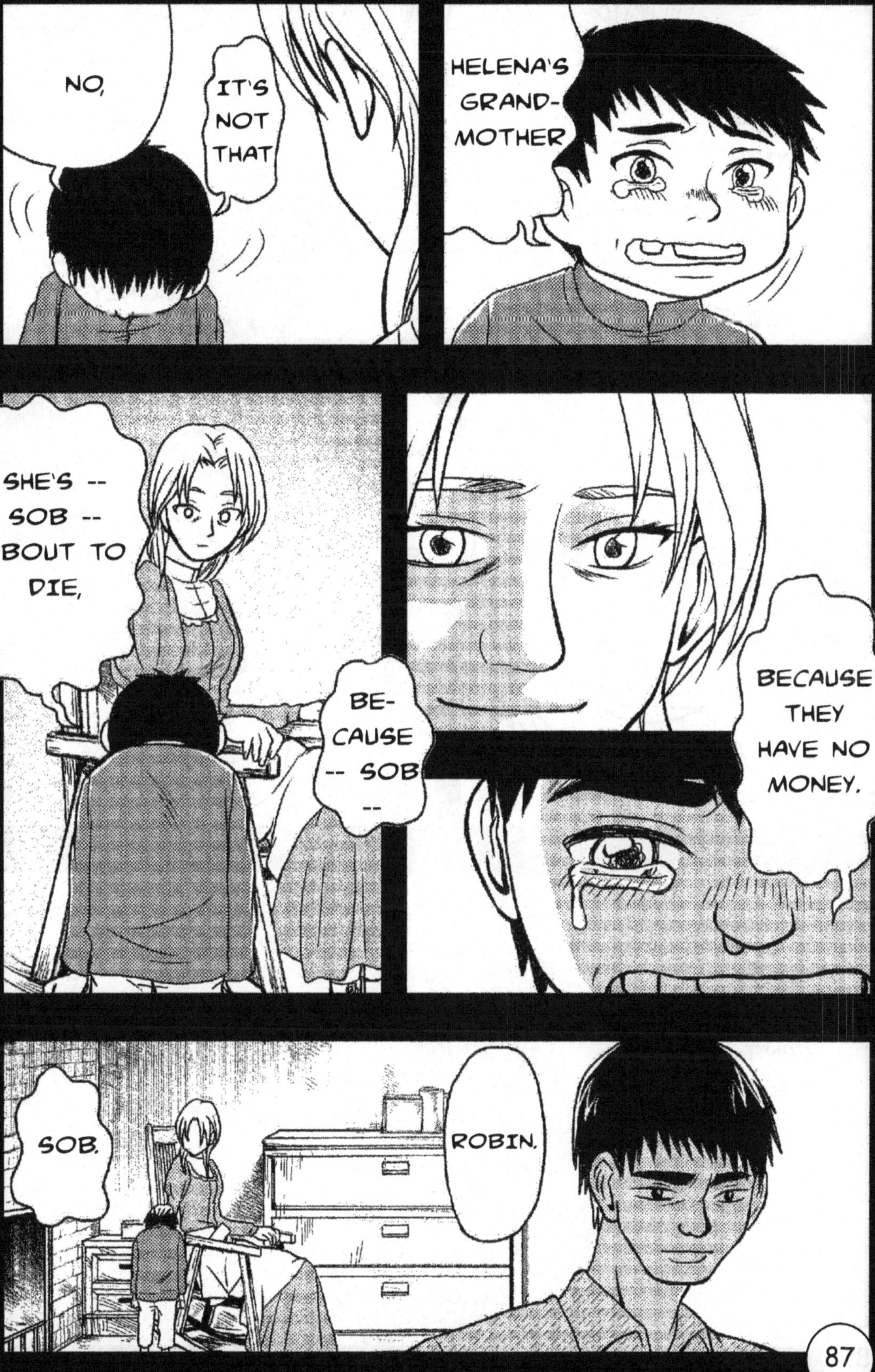
NO,
IT'S NOT THAT
HELENA'S GRAND-MOTHER
SHE'S -- SOB -- ABOUT TO DIE,
BE-CAUSE -- SOB --
BECAUSE THEY HAVE NO MONEY.
SOB.
ROBIN.

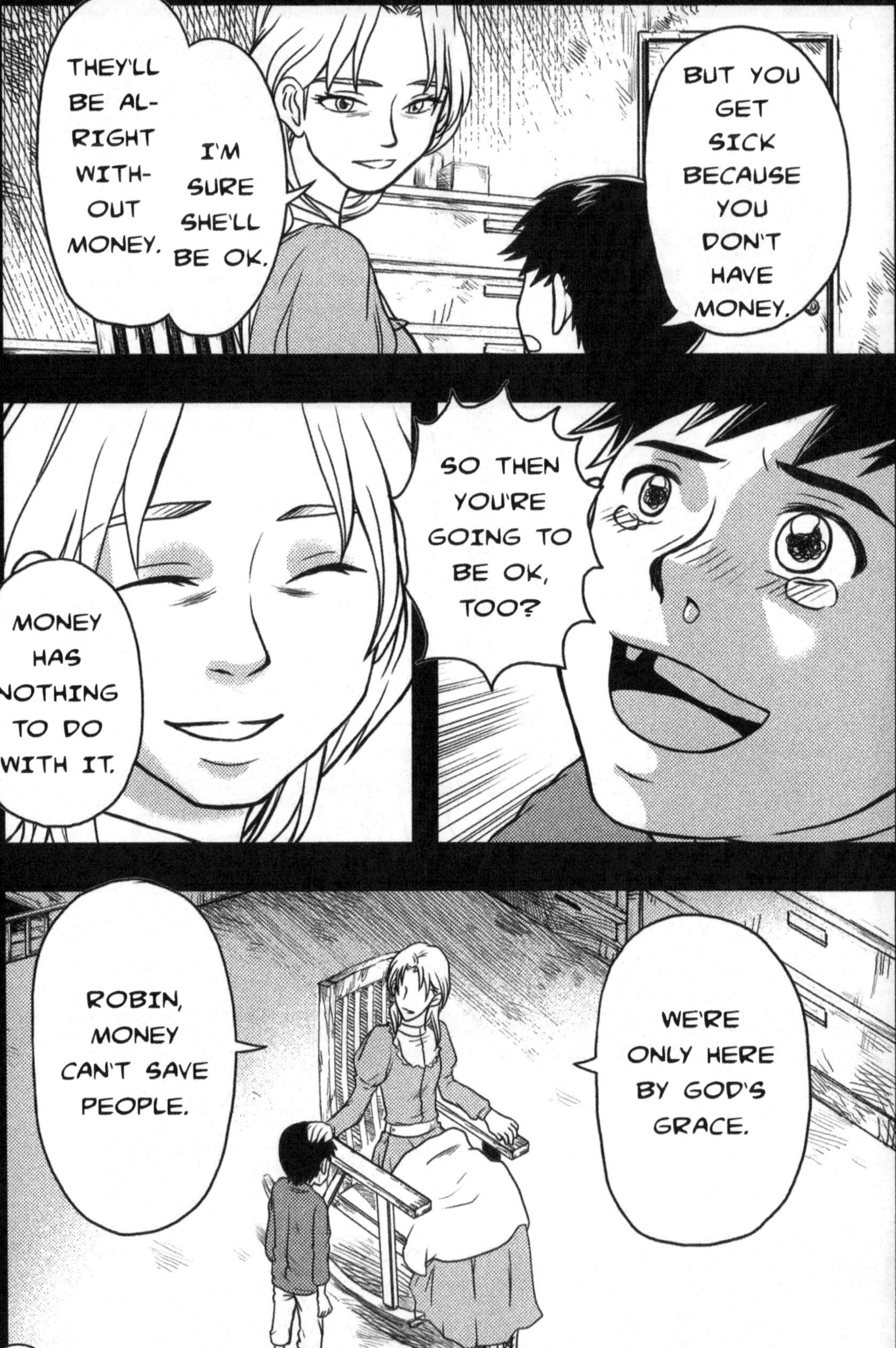
THEY'LL BE AL-RIGHT WITH-OUT MONEY.
I'M SURE SHE'LL BE OK.
BUT YOU GET SICK BECAUSE YOU DON'T HAVE MONEY.
MONEY HAS NOTHING TO DO WITH IT.
SO THEN YOU'RE GOING TO BE OK, TOO?
ROBIN, MONEY CAN'T SAVE PEOPLE.
WE'RE ONLY HERE BY GOD'S GRACE.

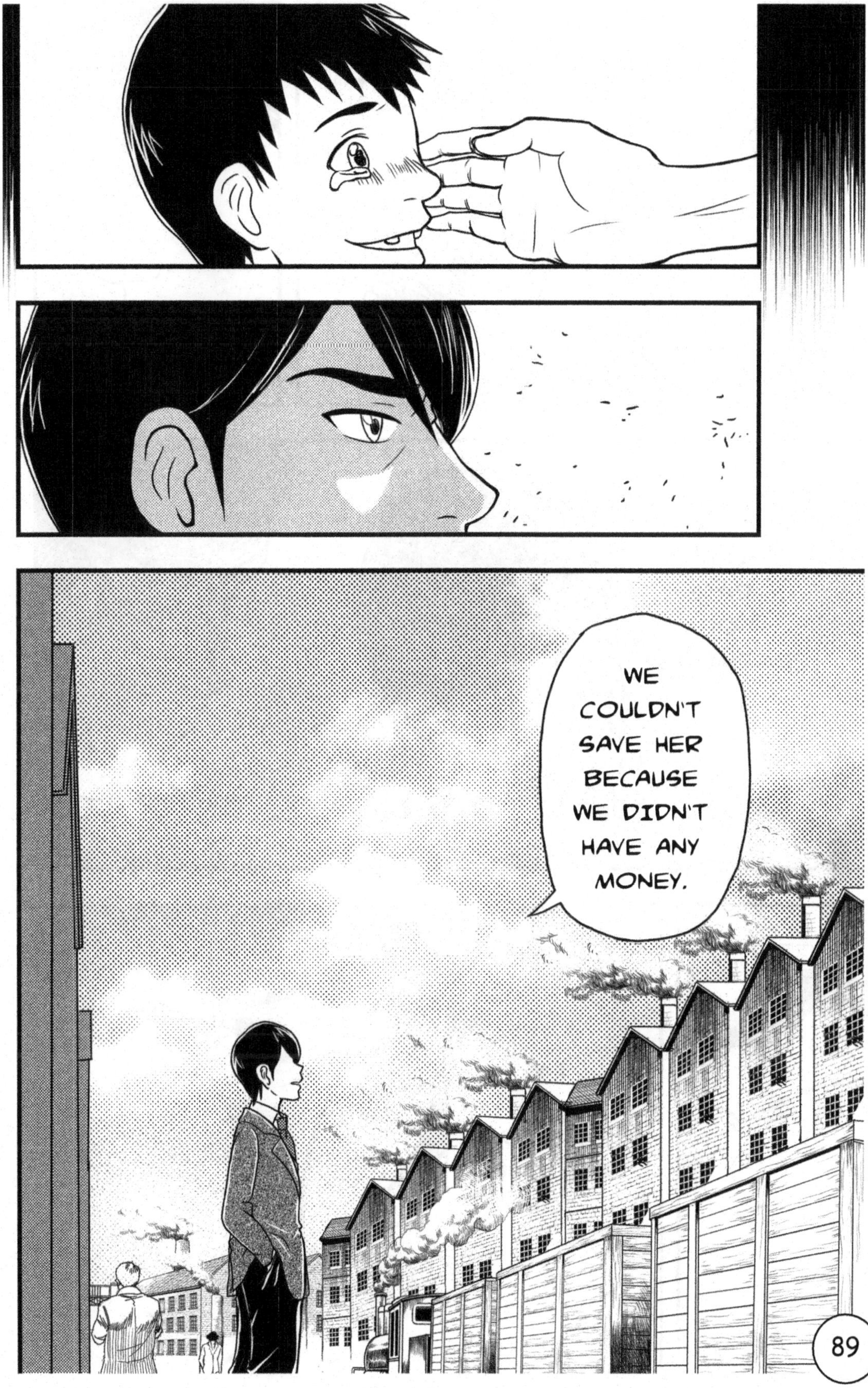
WE COULDN'T SAVE HER BECAUSE WE DIDN'T HAVE ANY MONEY.

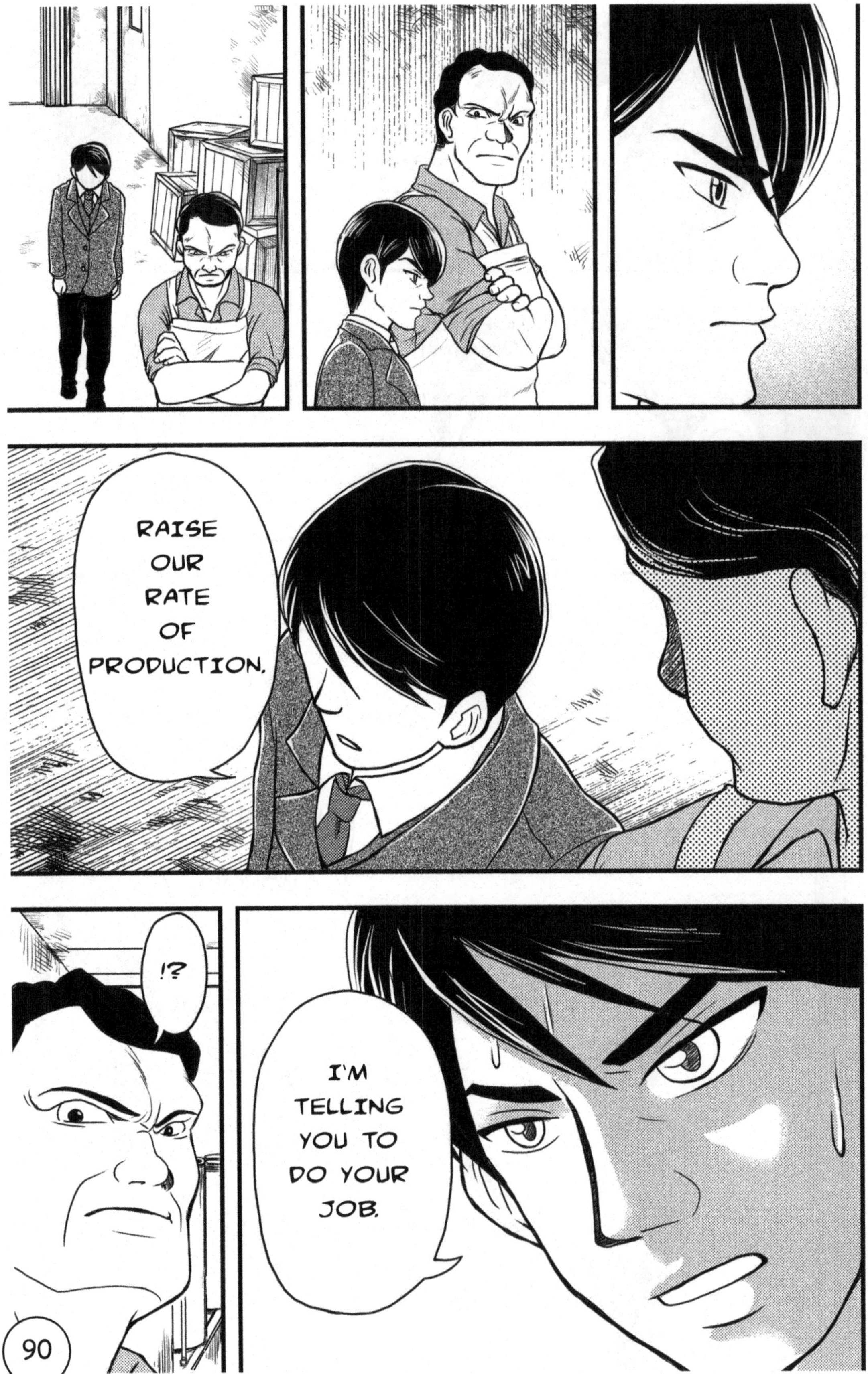
RAISE OUR RATE OF PRODUCTION.
!?
I'M TELLING YOU TO DO YOUR JOB.

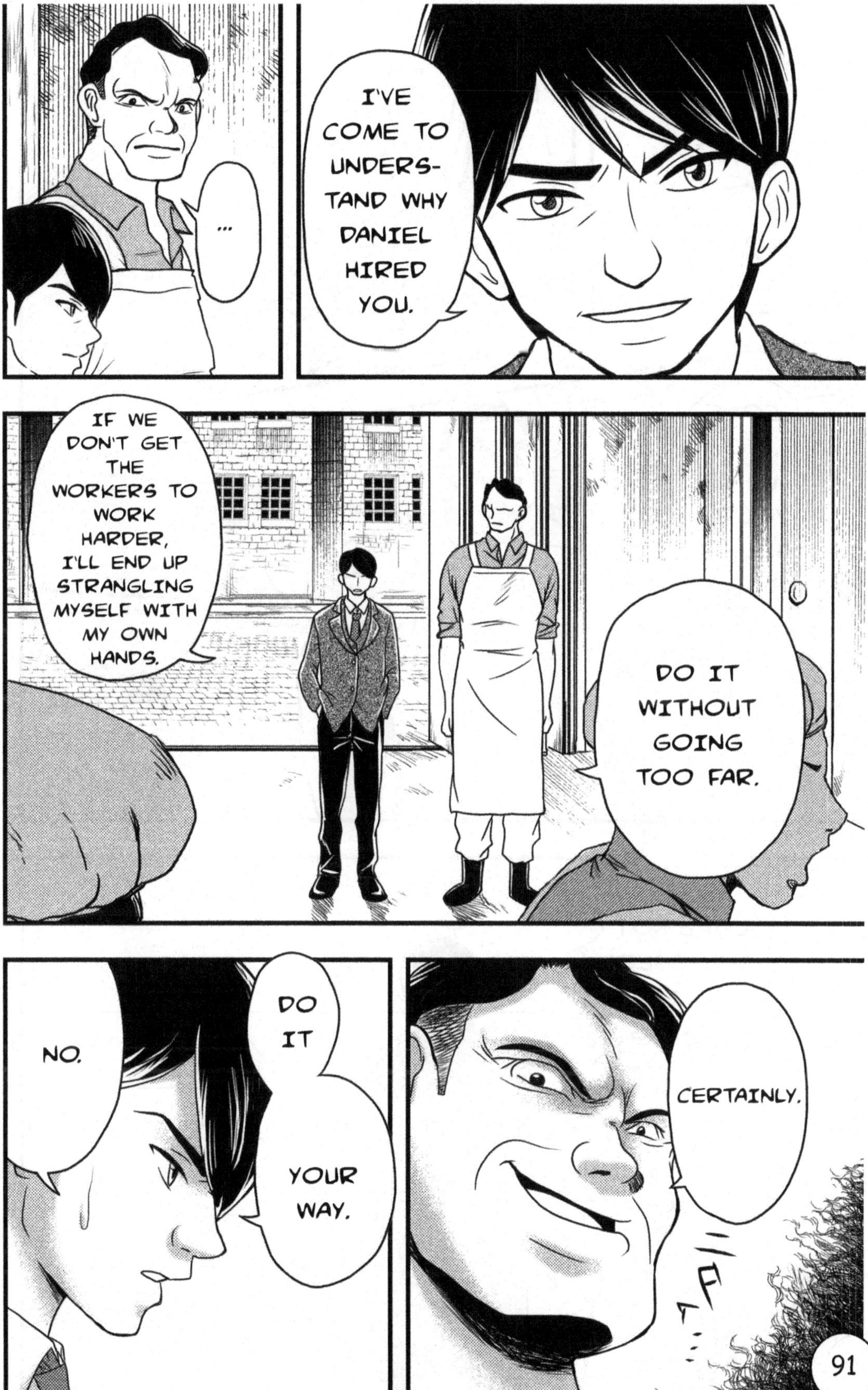
...
I'VE COME TO UNDERS- TAND WHY DANIEL HIRED YOU.
IF WE DON'T GET THE WORKERS TO WORK HARDER, I'LL END UP STRANGLING MYSELF WITH MY OWN HANDS.
DO IT WITHOUT GOING TOO FAR.
NO.
DO IT YOUR WAY.
CERTAINLY.

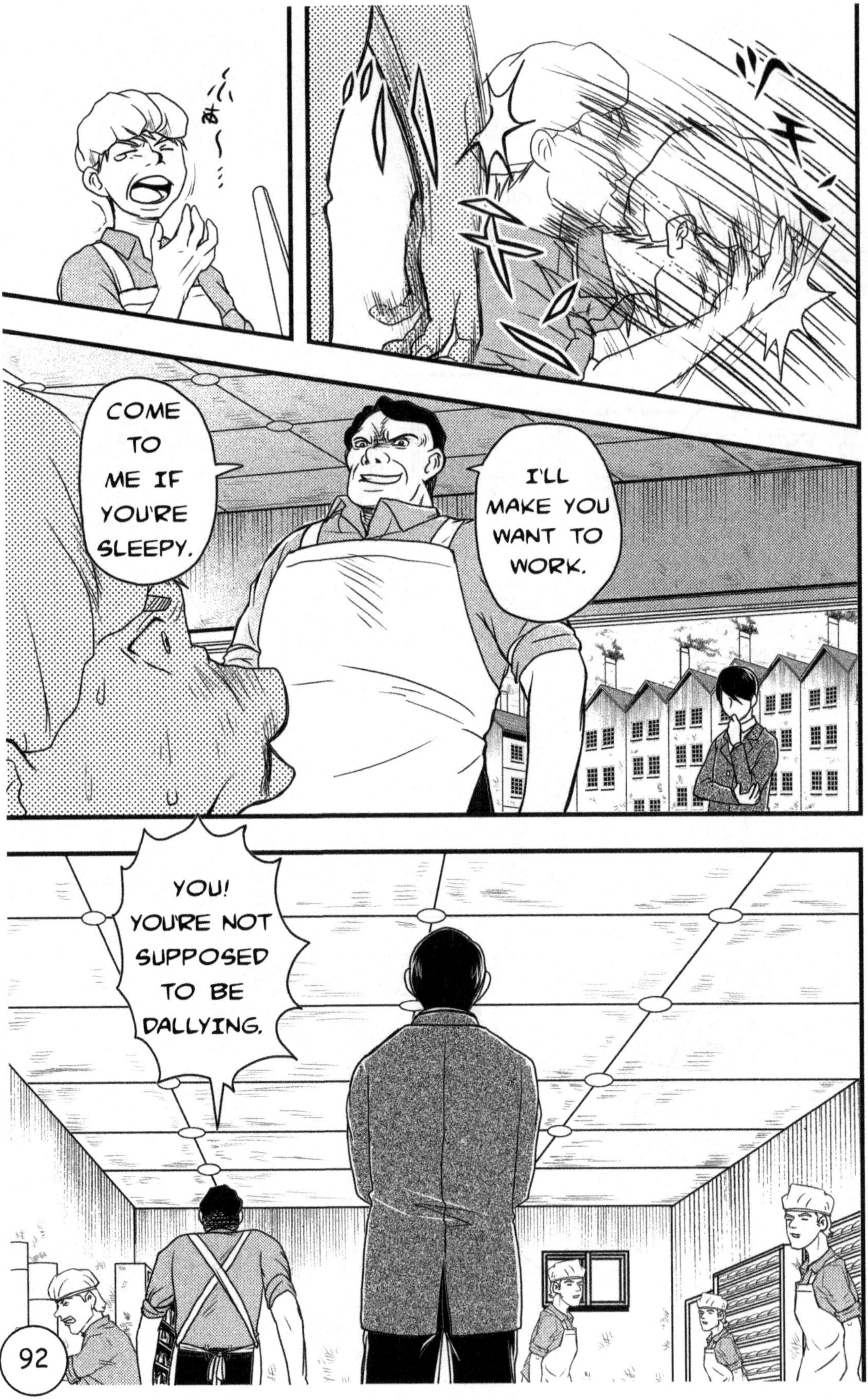
ふぁ〜…
バチーン
COME TO ME IF YOU'RE SLEEPY.
I'LL MAKE YOU WANT TO WORK.
YOU! YOU'RE NOT SUPPOSED TO BE DALLYING.

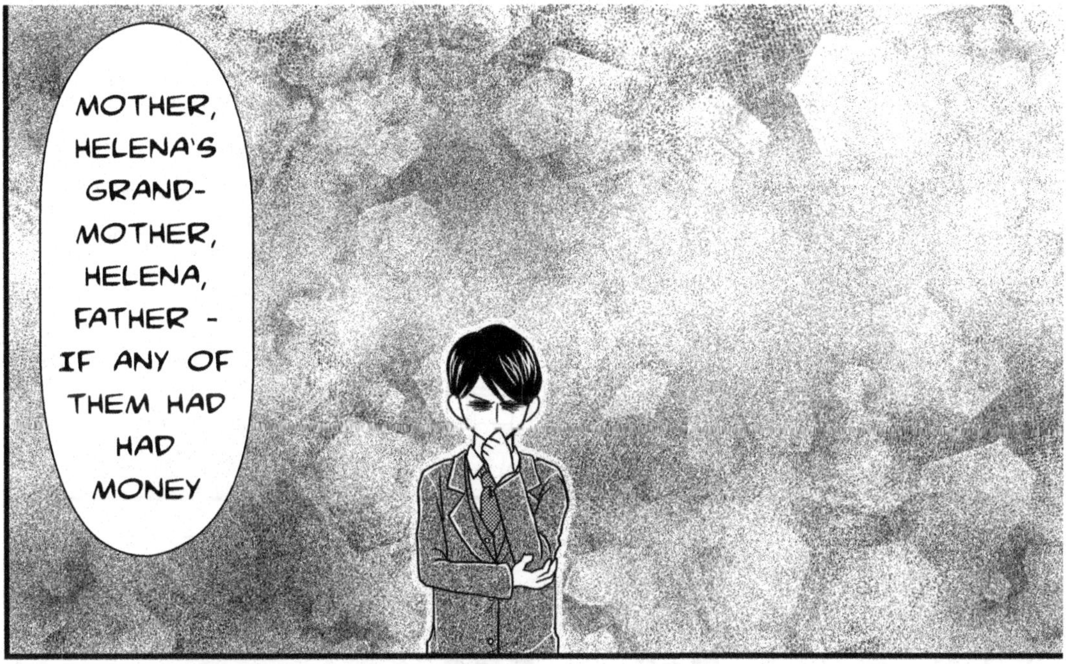
MOTHER, HELENA'S GRAND-MOTHER, HELENA, FATHER - IF ANY OF THEM HAD HAD MONEY
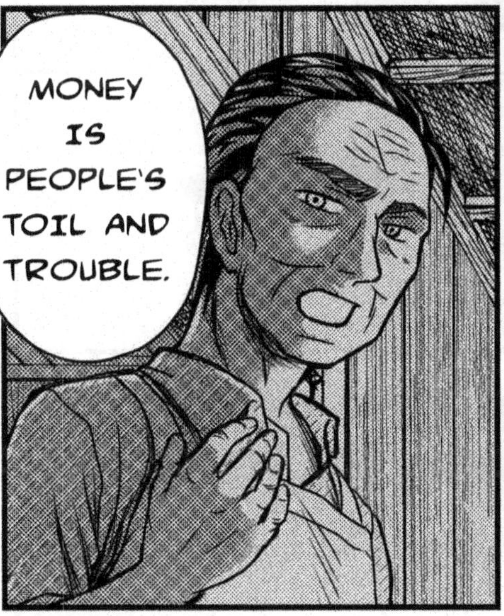
MONEY IS PEOPLE'S TOIL AND TROUBLE.
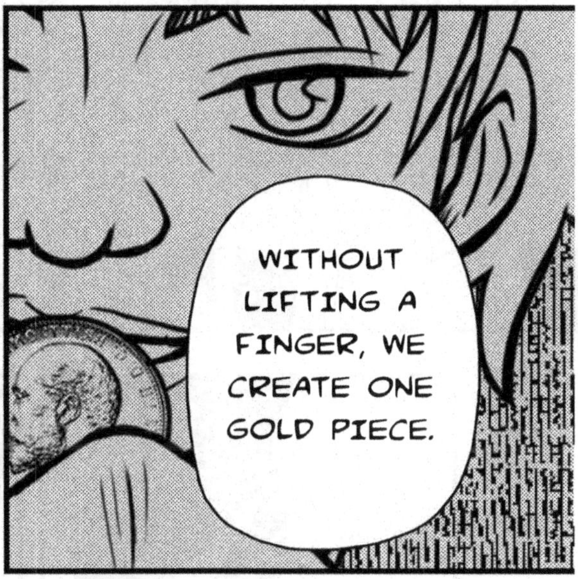
WITHOUT LIFTING A FINGER, WE CREATE ONE GOLD PIECE.
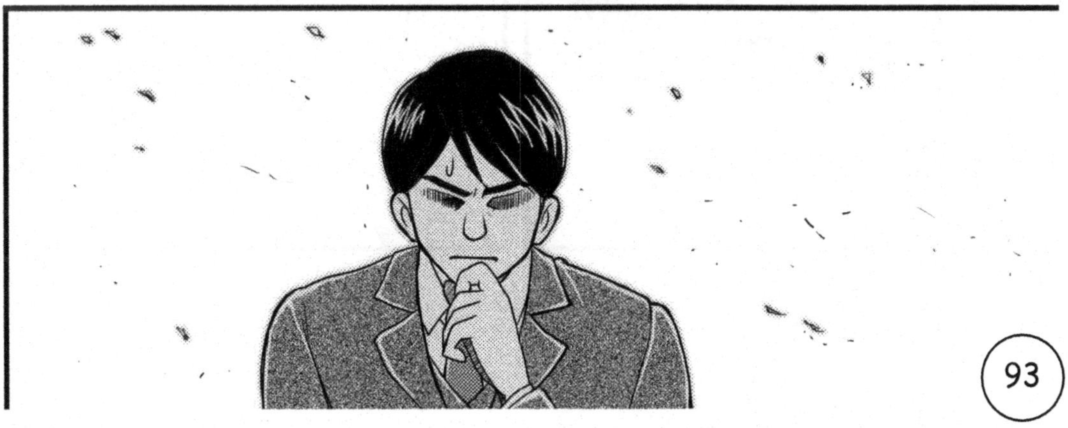

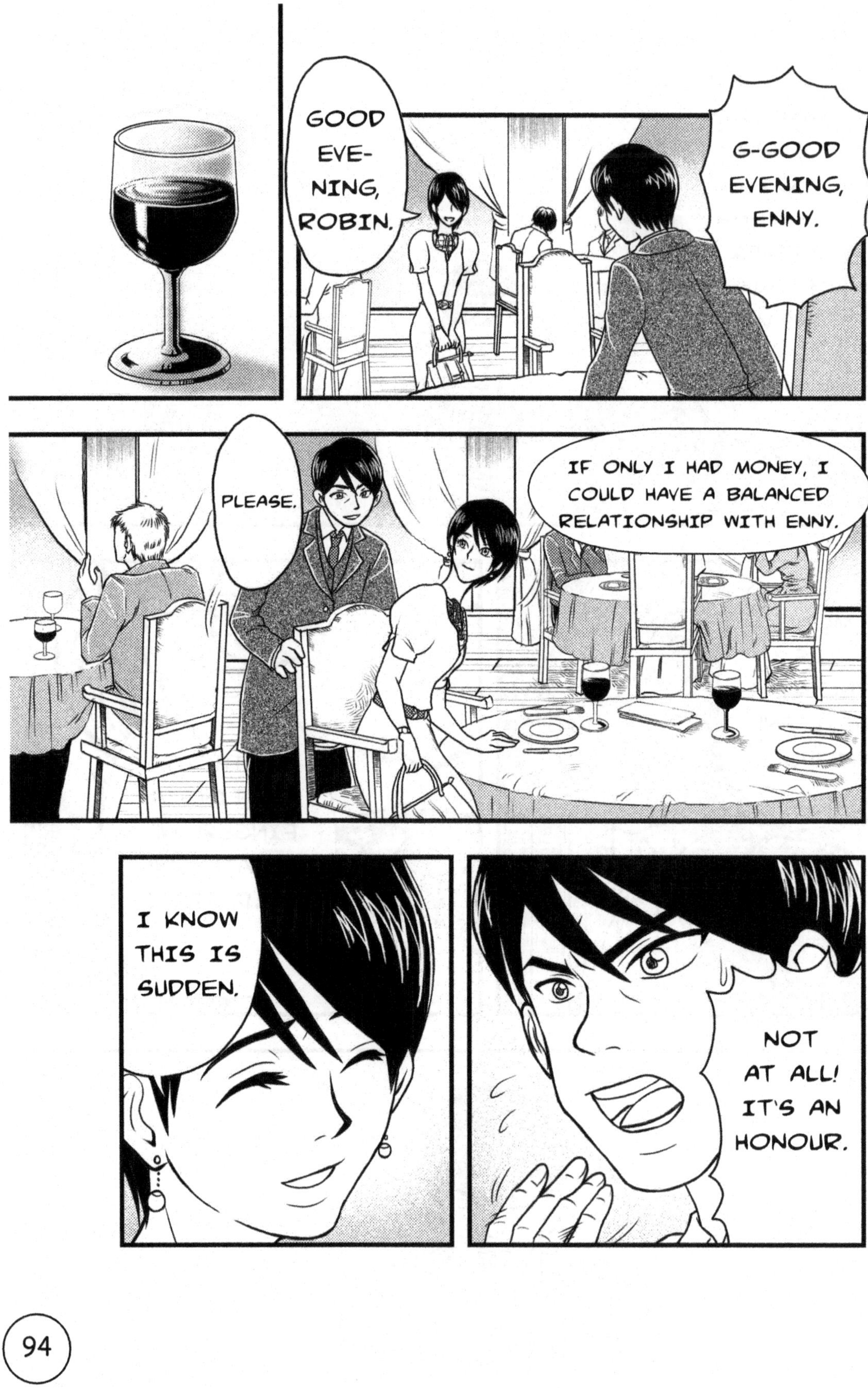
GOOD EVE-NING, ROBIN.
G-GOOD EVENING, ENNY.
PLEASE.
IF ONLY I HAD MONEY, I COULD HAVE A BALANCED RELATIONSHIP WITH ENNY.
I KNOW THIS IS SUDDEN.
NOT AT ALL! IT'S AN HONOUR.

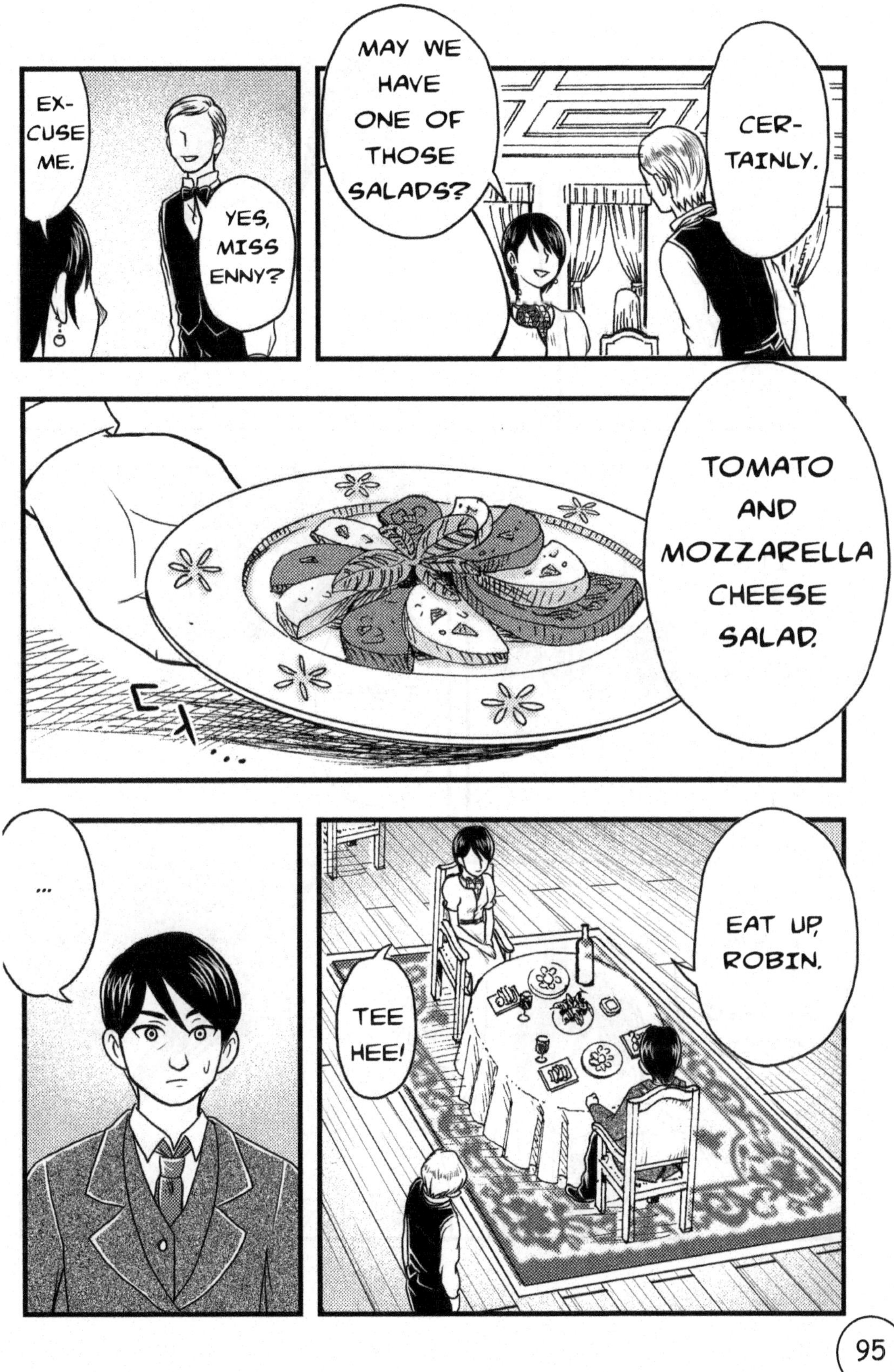
EX-CUSE ME.
YES, MISS ENNY?
MAY WE HAVE ONE OF THOSE SALADS?
CER-TAINLY.
TOMATO AND MOZZARELLA CHEESE SALAD.
...
TEE HEE!
EAT UP, ROBIN.

UM, NICE.

THE CHEESE IS PRETTY GOOD.

IT'S FROM YOUR FACTORY.

RE-ALLY?

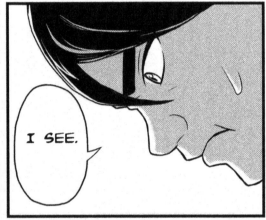

I SEE.

MY FATHER OWNS STOCK IN THIS RESTAU-RANT.

I ASKED HIM TO HAVE IT PUT ON THE MENU.

COULD THE TASTE BE OFF?

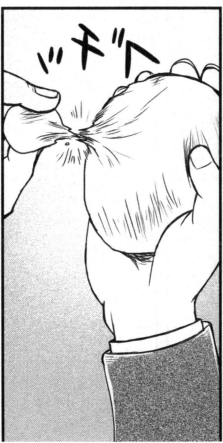

WHAT?

97

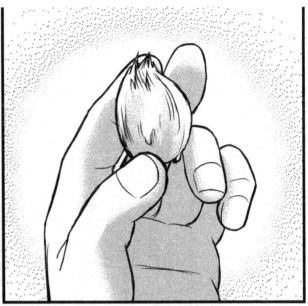

BOSS, WHY SO SMALL?

DON'T WORRY ABOUT IT.

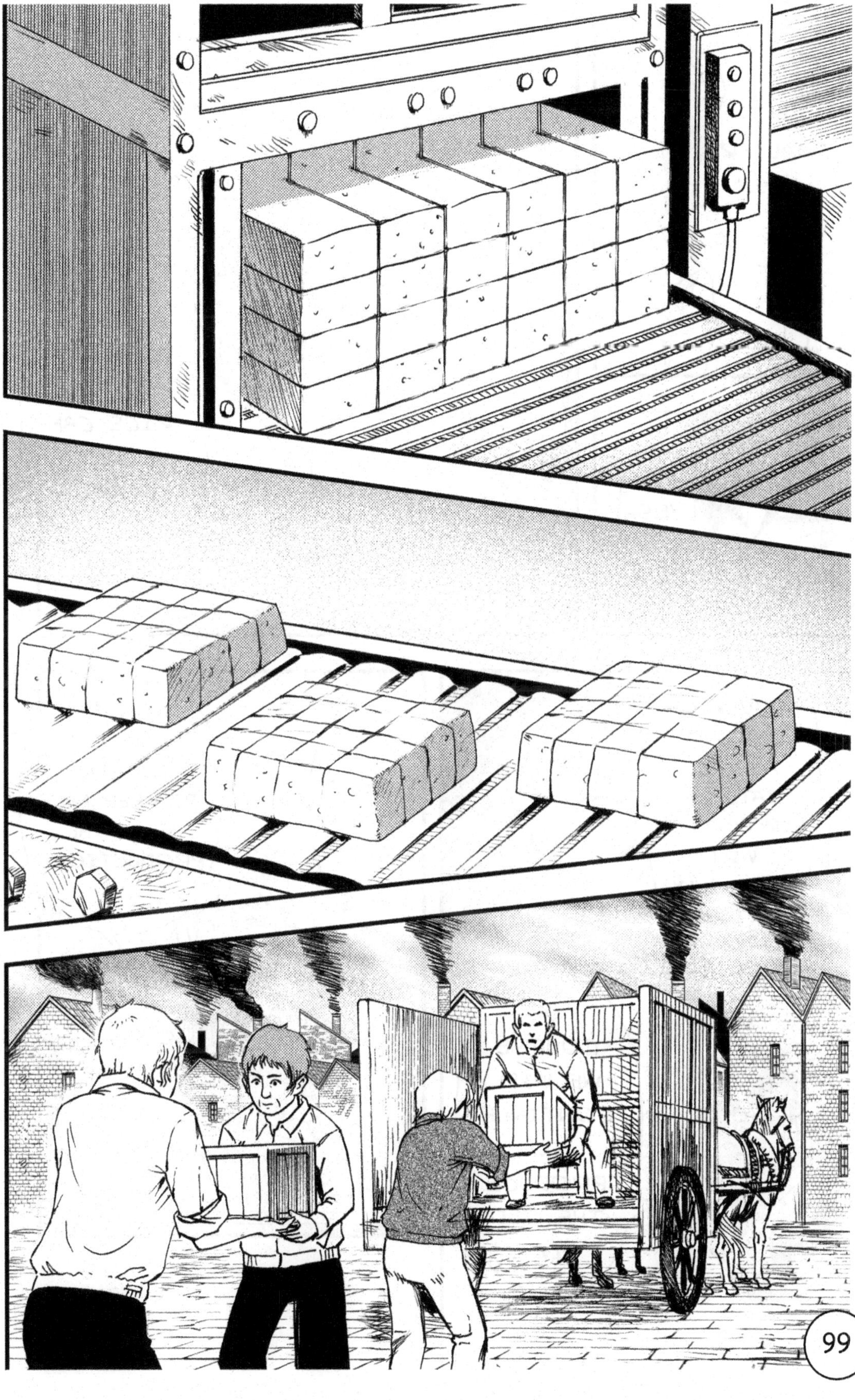

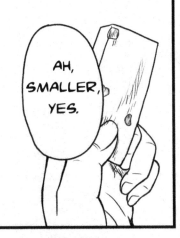

AH, SMALLER, YES.

SMALL, EASY TO EAT, CONVENIENT SIZE FOR COOKING

EASY TO CONSUME AND THE PRICE CAN BE KEPT DOWN.

YES.

THE NUMBER OF CUSTOMERS AND THE RATE OF CIRCULATION WILL CERTAINLY RISE.

OF COURSE WE WILL CONTINUE TO PRODUCE THE OLD SIZE.

GOOD IDEA.

WILL THE QUALITY BE ABLE TO KEEP PACE WITH THE PRODUCTION?

100

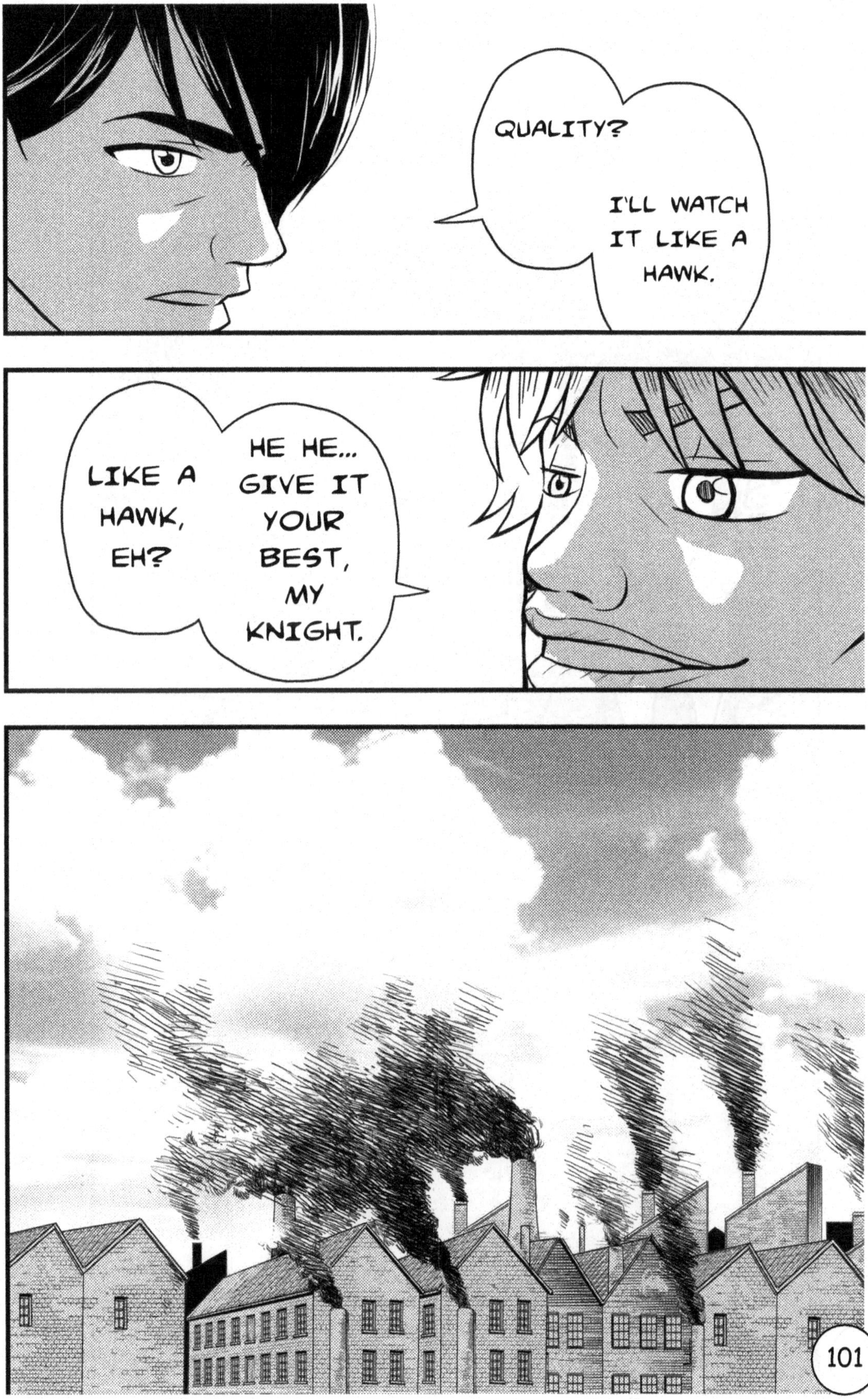
QUALITY?
I'LL WATCH IT LIKE A HAWK.
LIKE A HAWK, EH?
HE HE... GIVE IT YOUR BEST, MY KNIGHT.

THE SALE AND PURCHASE OF LABOUR

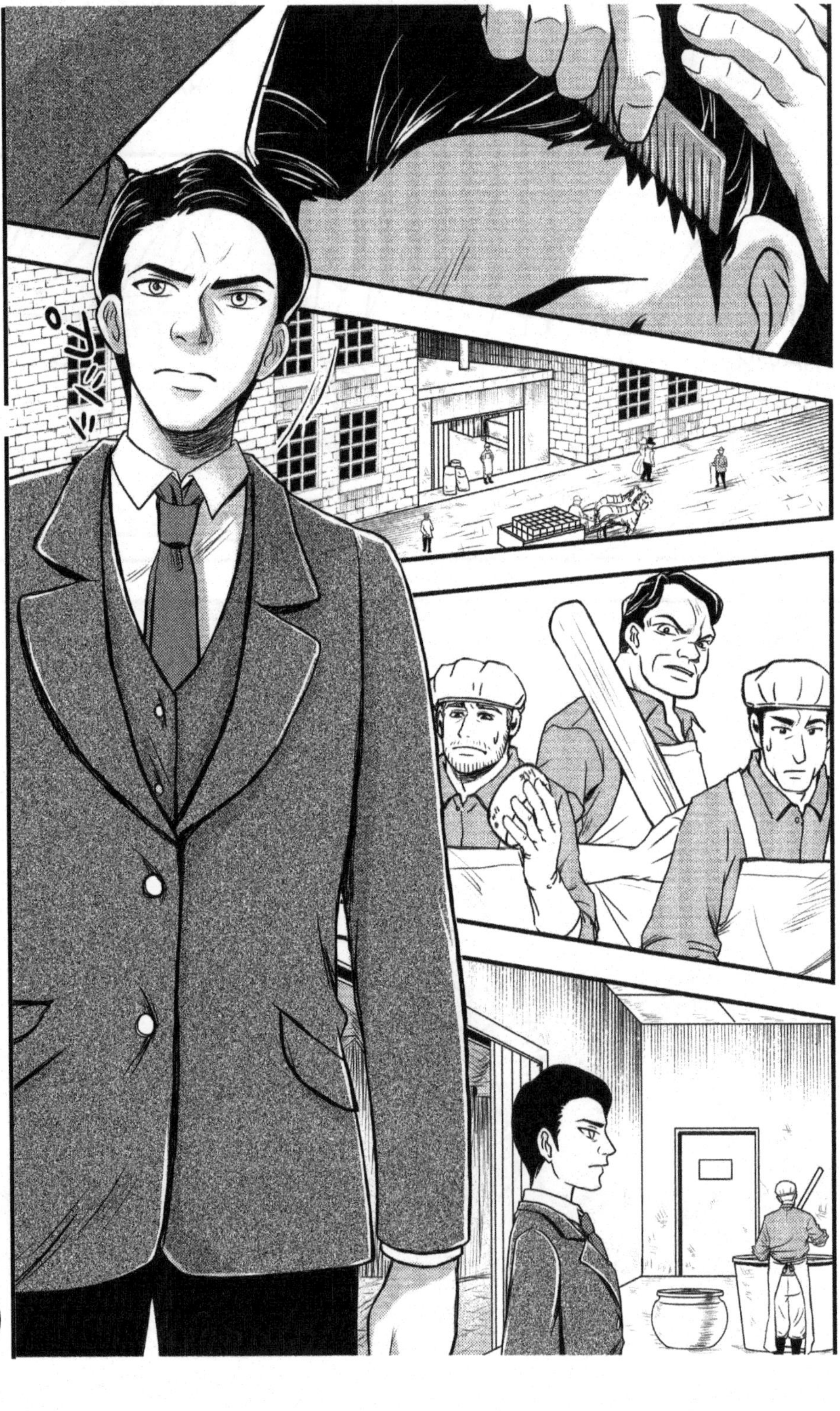

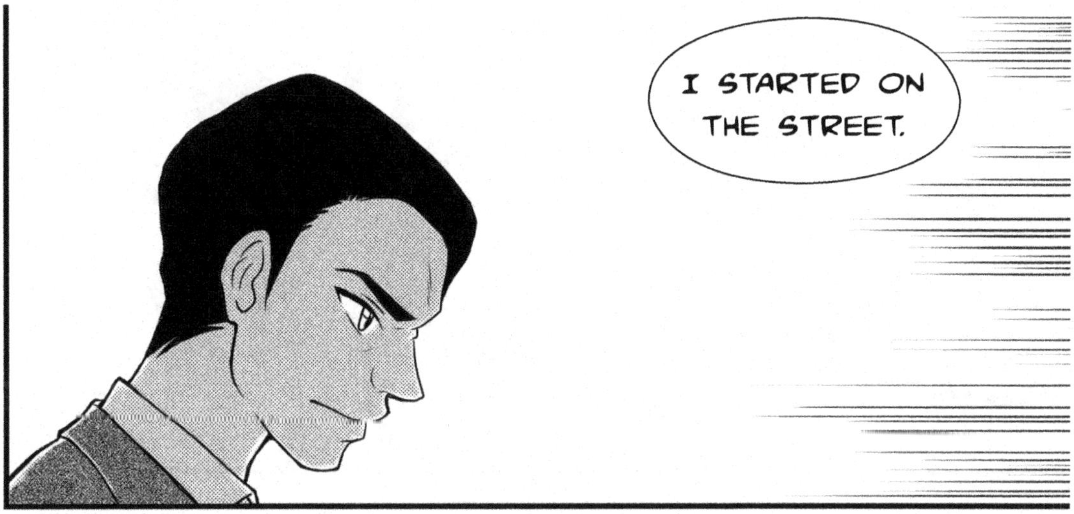
I STARTED ON THE STREET.
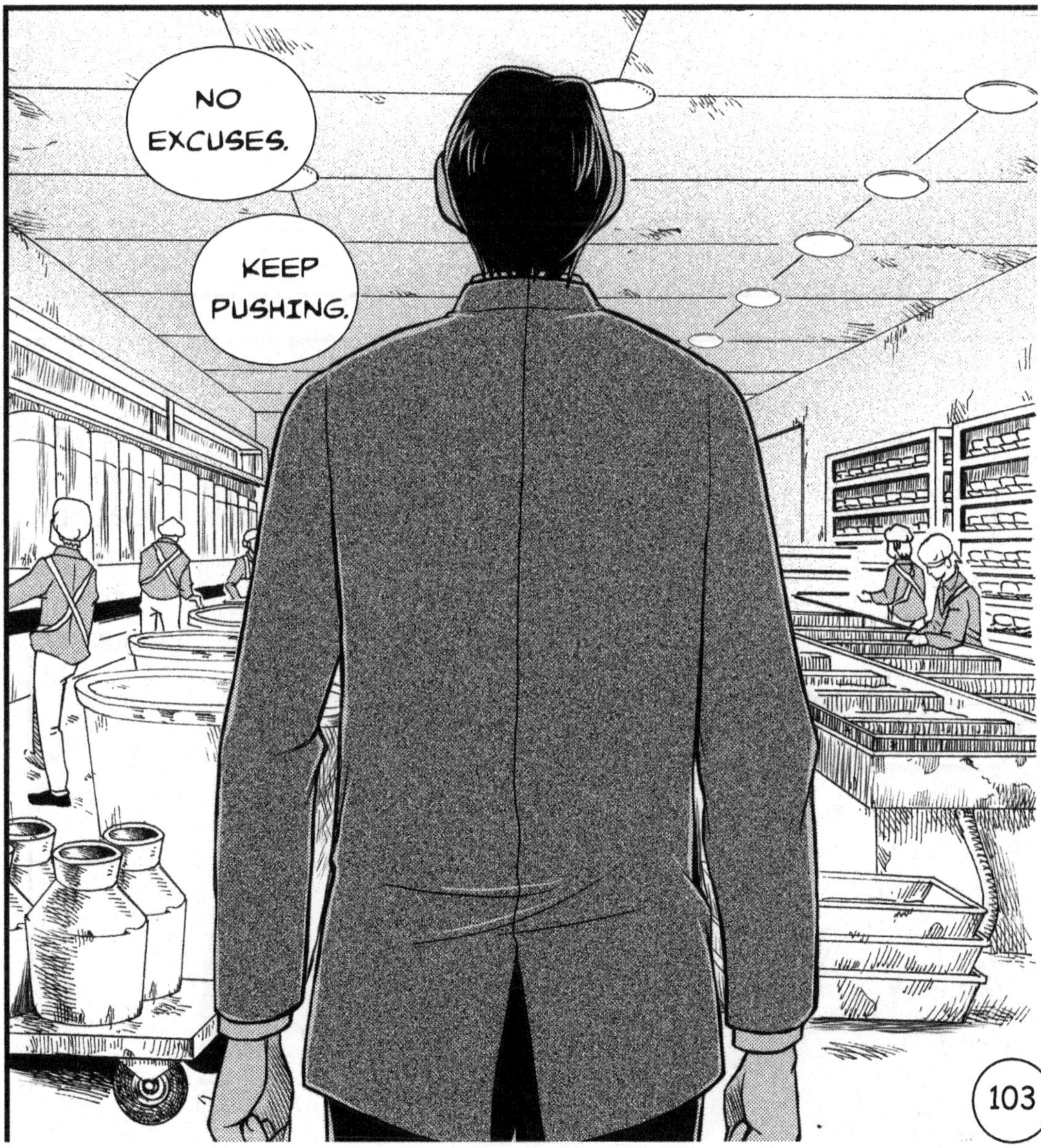
NO EXCUSES.
KEEP PUSHING.

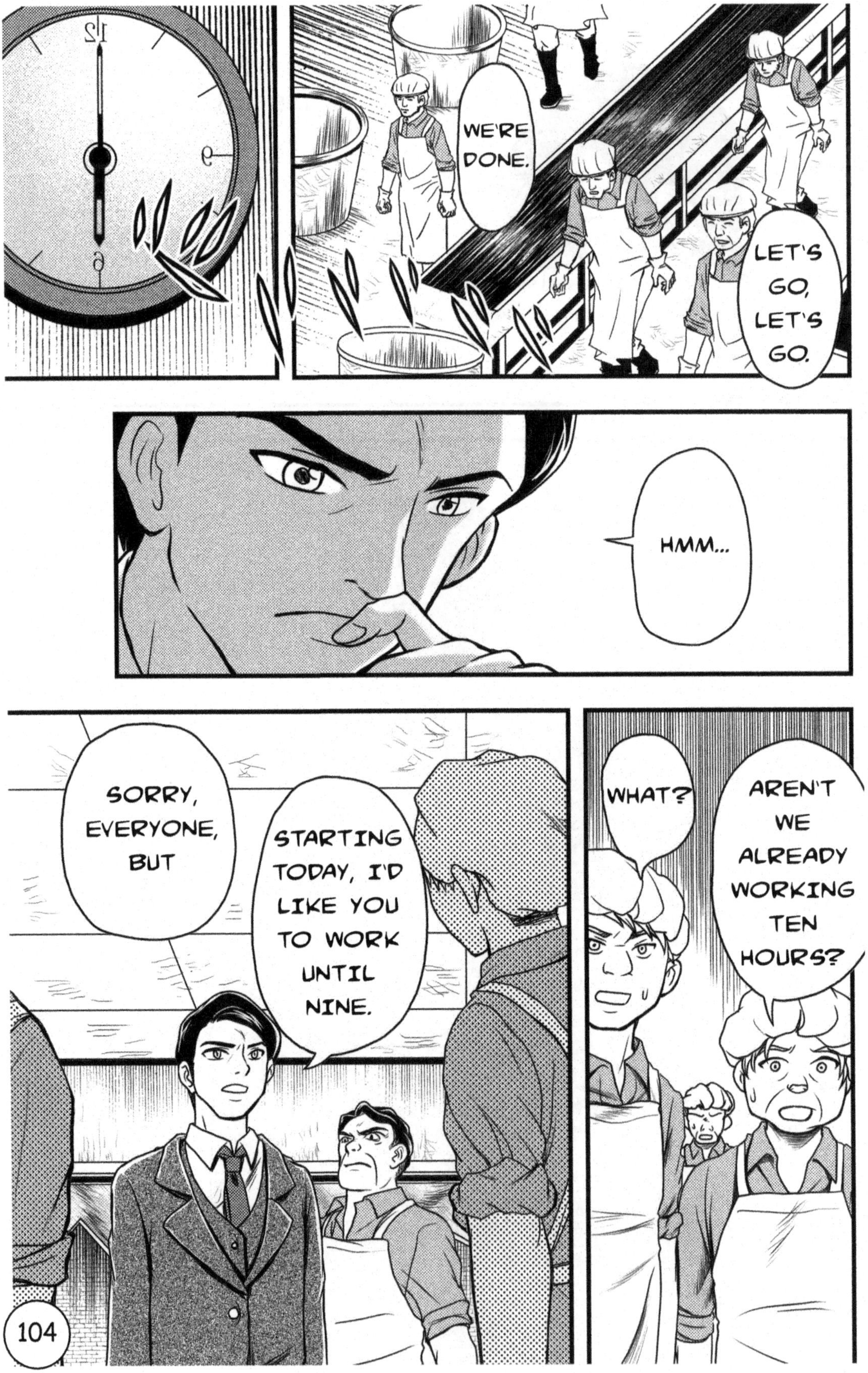
WE'RE DONE.
LET'S GO, LET'S GO.
HMM...
SORRY, EVERYONE, BUT
STARTING TODAY, I'D LIKE YOU TO WORK UNTIL NINE.
WHAT?
AREN'T WE ALREADY WORKING TEN HOURS?

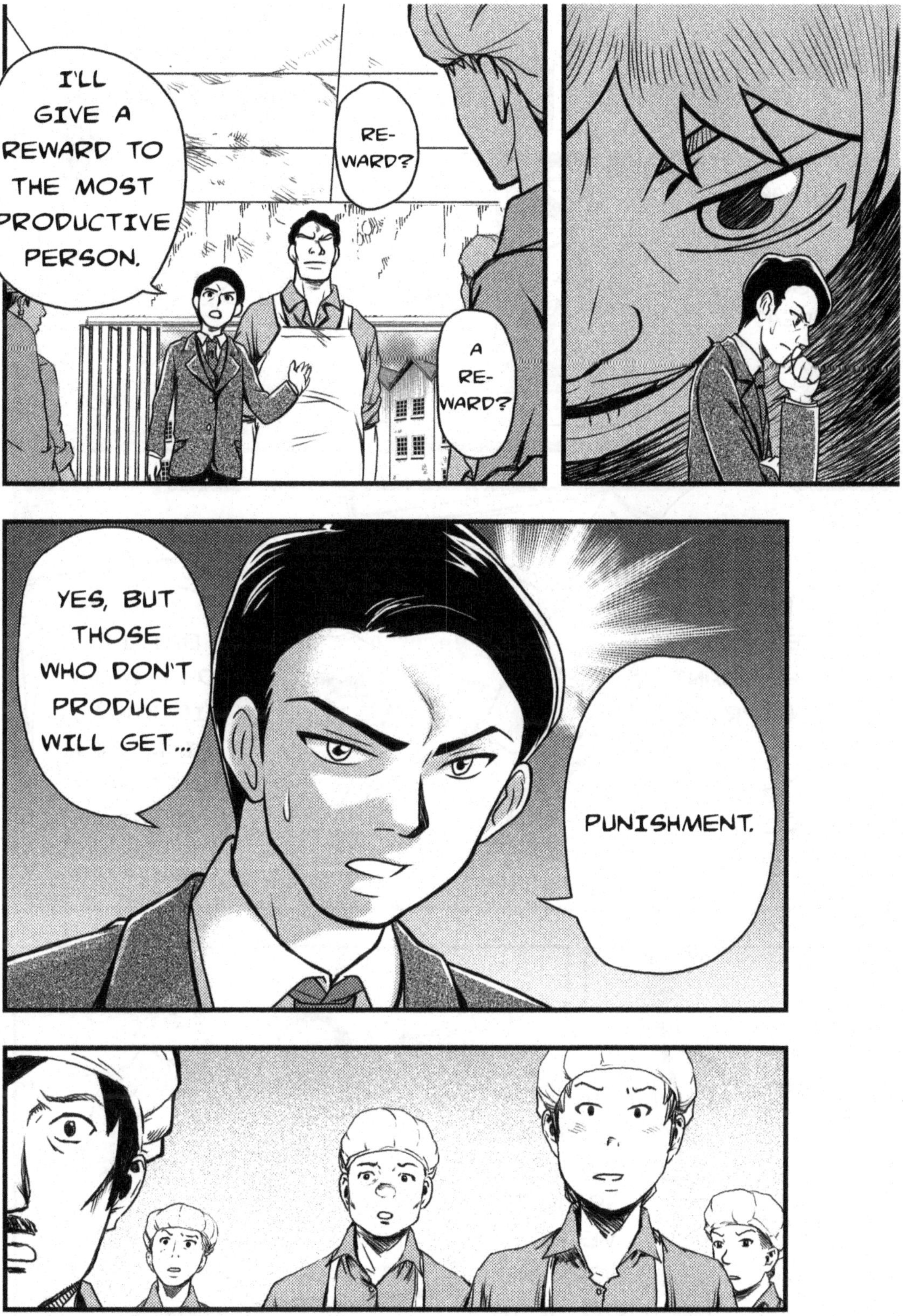
I'LL GIVE A REWARD TO THE MOST PRODUCTIVE PERSON.
RE-WARD?
A RE-WARD?
YES, BUT THOSE WHO DON'T PRODUCE WILL GET...
PUNISHMENT.

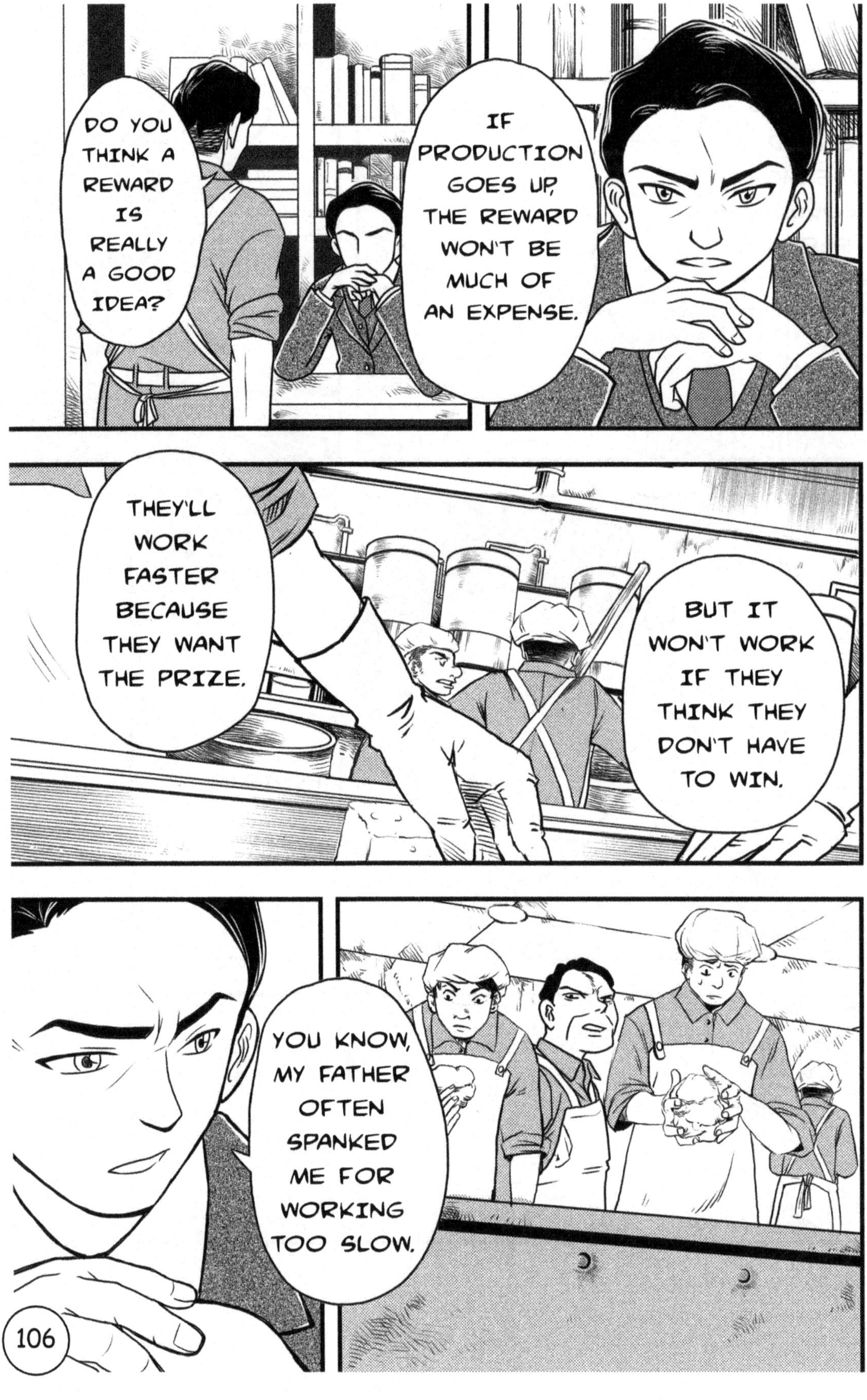
DO YOU THINK A REWARD IS REALLY A GOOD IDEA?
IF PRODUCTION GOES UP, THE REWARD WON'T BE MUCH OF AN EXPENSE.
THEY'LL WORK FASTER BECAUSE THEY WANT THE PRIZE.
BUT IT WON'T WORK IF THEY THINK THEY DON'T HAVE TO WIN.
YOU KNOW, MY FATHER OFTEN SPANKED ME FOR WORKING TOO SLOW.

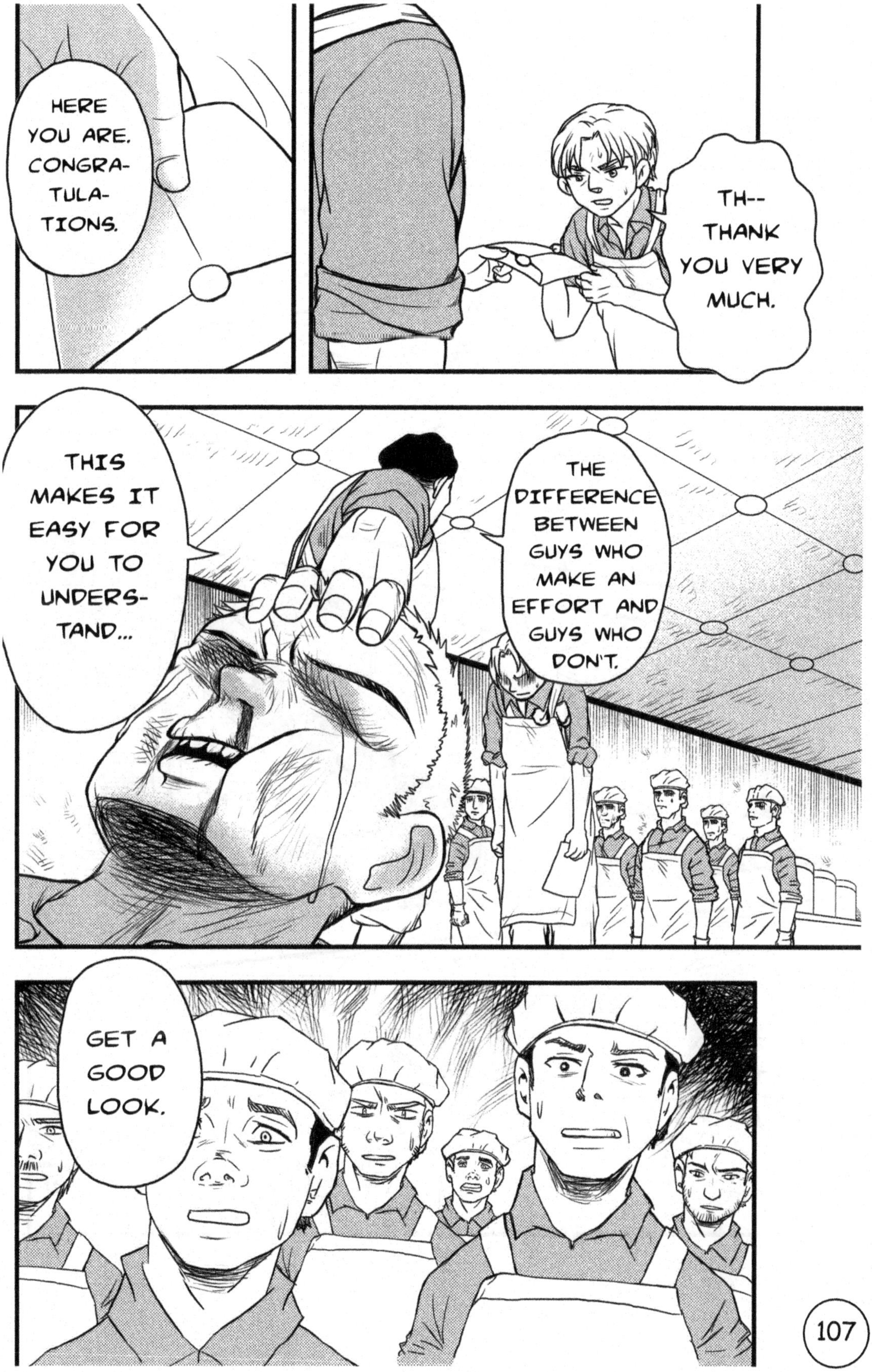
HERE YOU ARE. CONGRATULATIONS.
TH-- THANK YOU VERY MUCH.
THIS MAKES IT EASY FOR YOU TO UNDERSTAND...
THE DIFFERENCE BETWEEN GUYS WHO MAKE AN EFFORT AND GUYS WHO DON'T.
GET A GOOD LOOK.

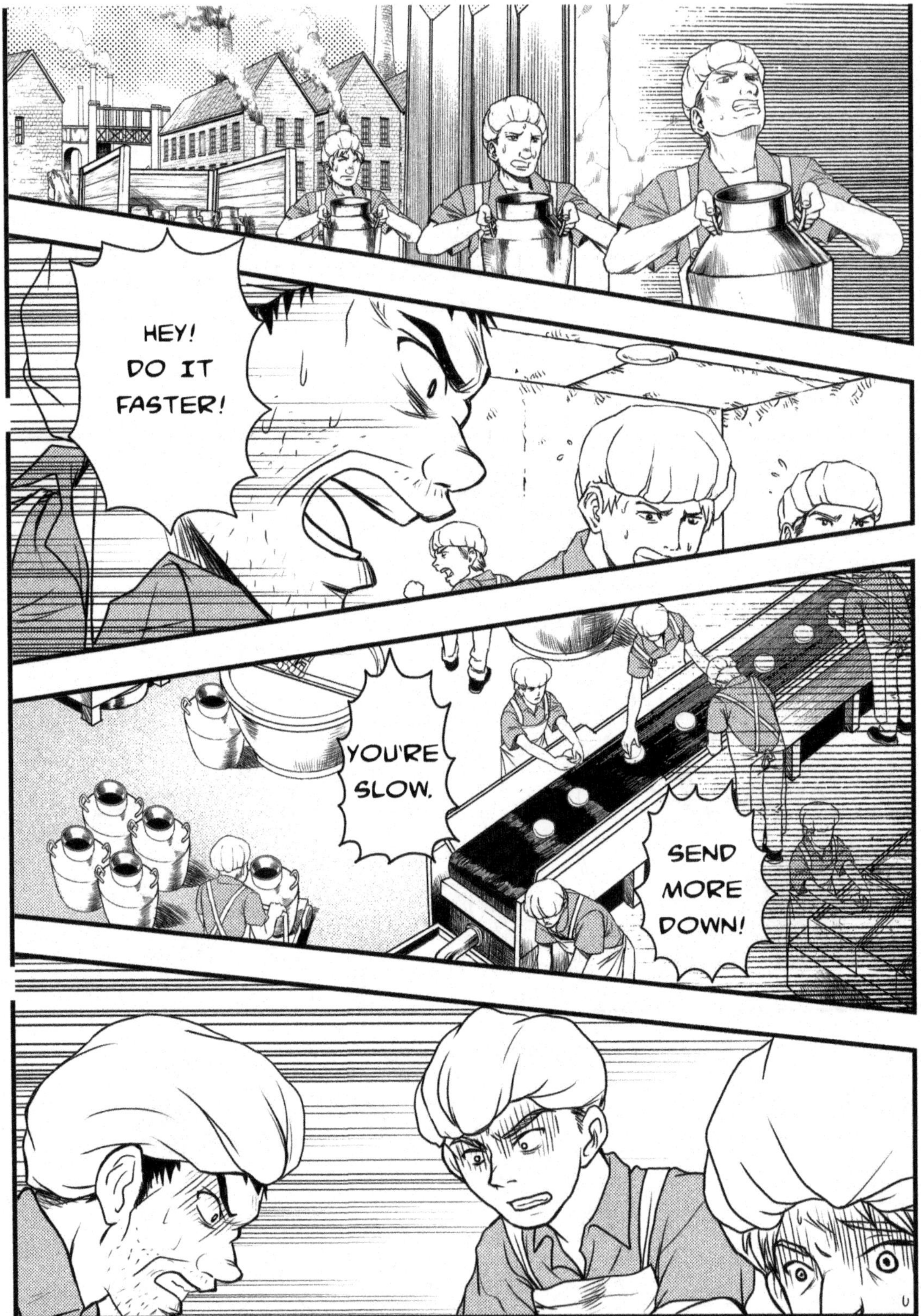
HEY! DO IT FASTER!
YOU'RE SLOW.
SEND MORE DOWN!

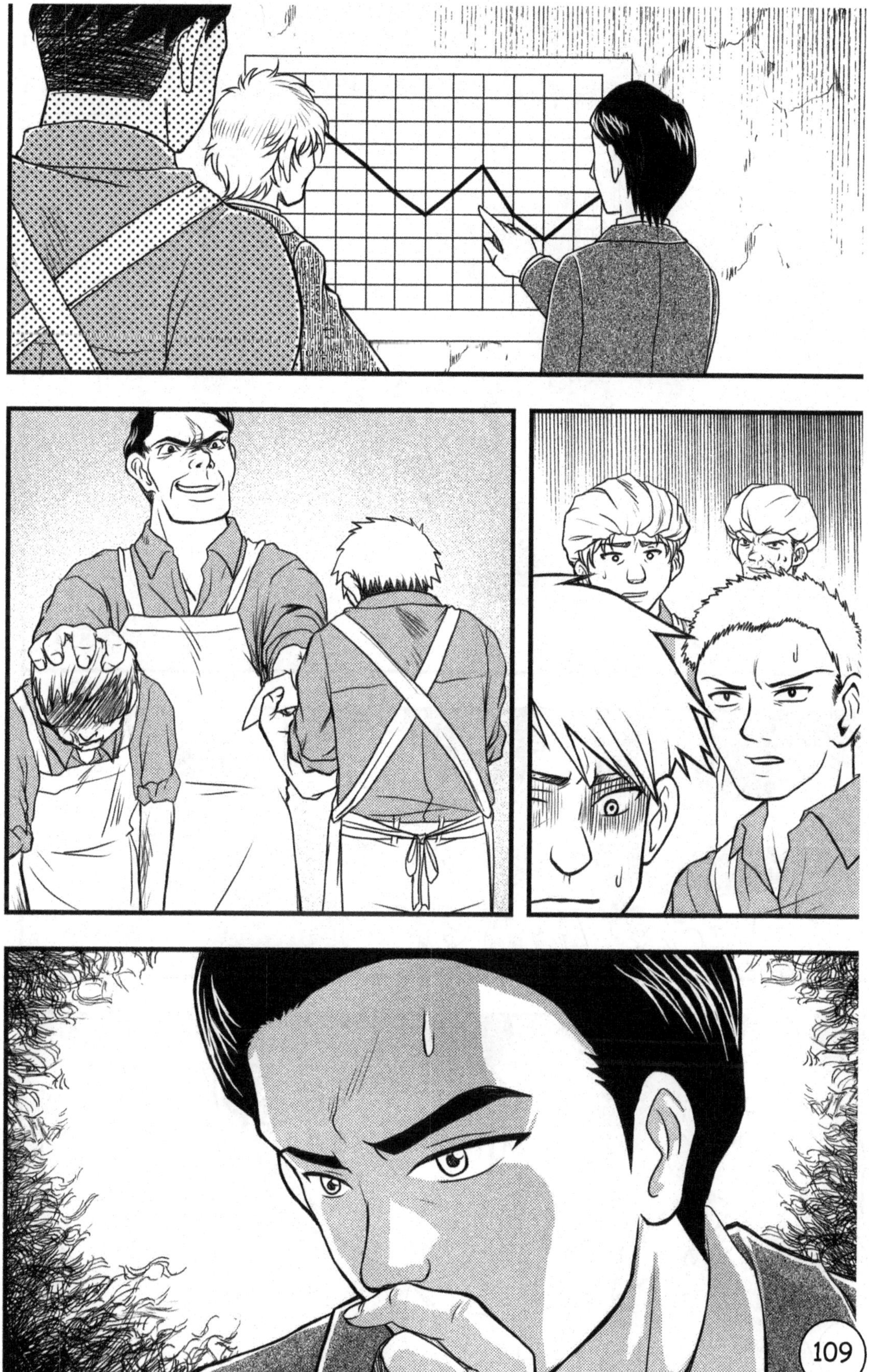

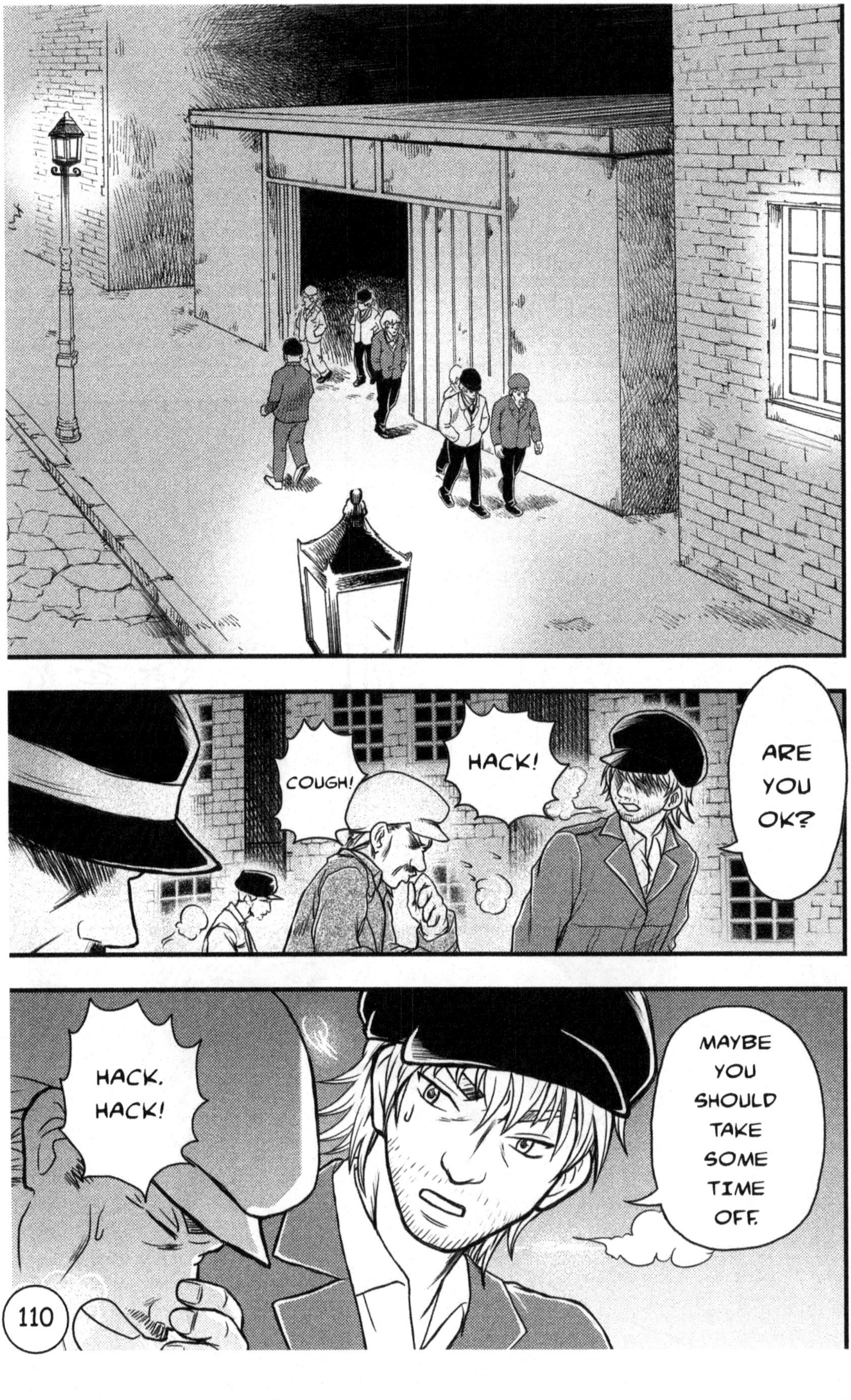
COUGH!
HACK!
ARE YOU OK?
HACK. HACK!
MAYBE YOU SHOULD TAKE SOME TIME OFF.

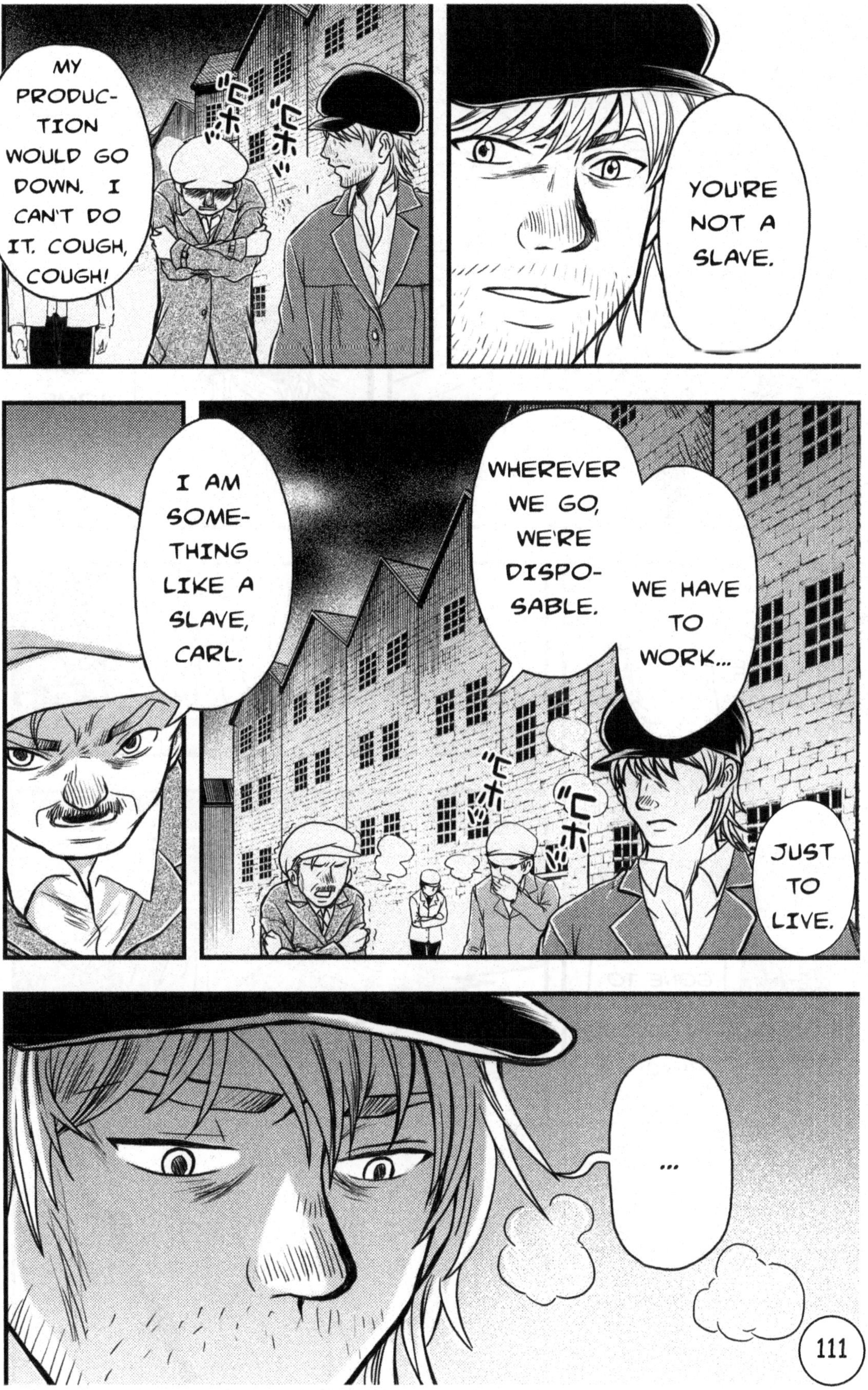
MY PRODUCTION WOULD GO DOWN. I CAN'T DO IT. COUGH, COUGH!
YOU'RE NOT A SLAVE.
I AM SOMETHING LIKE A SLAVE, CARL.
WHEREVER WE GO, WE'RE DISPOSABLE.
WE HAVE TO WORK...
JUST TO LIVE.
...

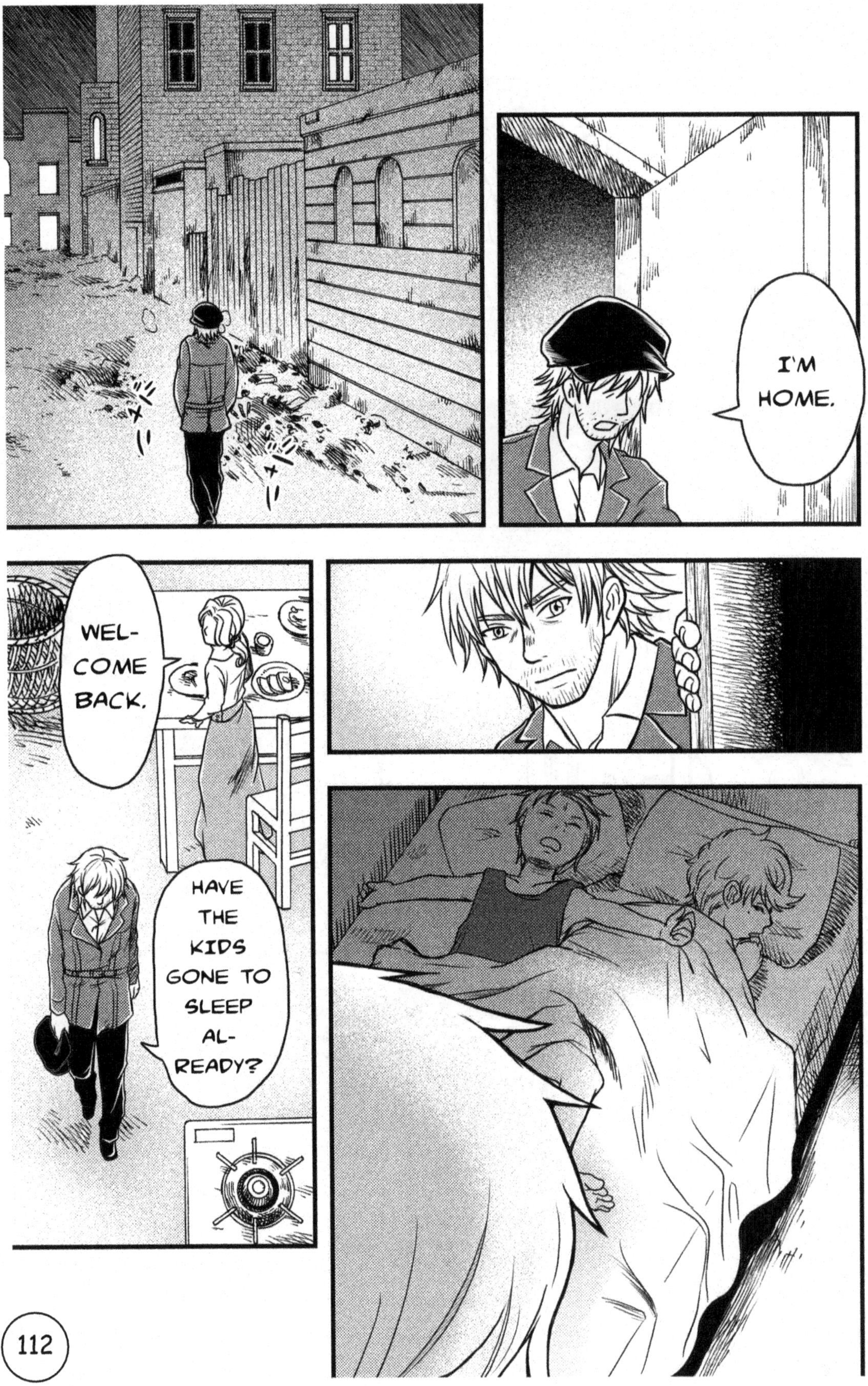
I'M HOME.
WEL-COME BACK.
HAVE THE KIDS GONE TO SLEEP AL-READY?

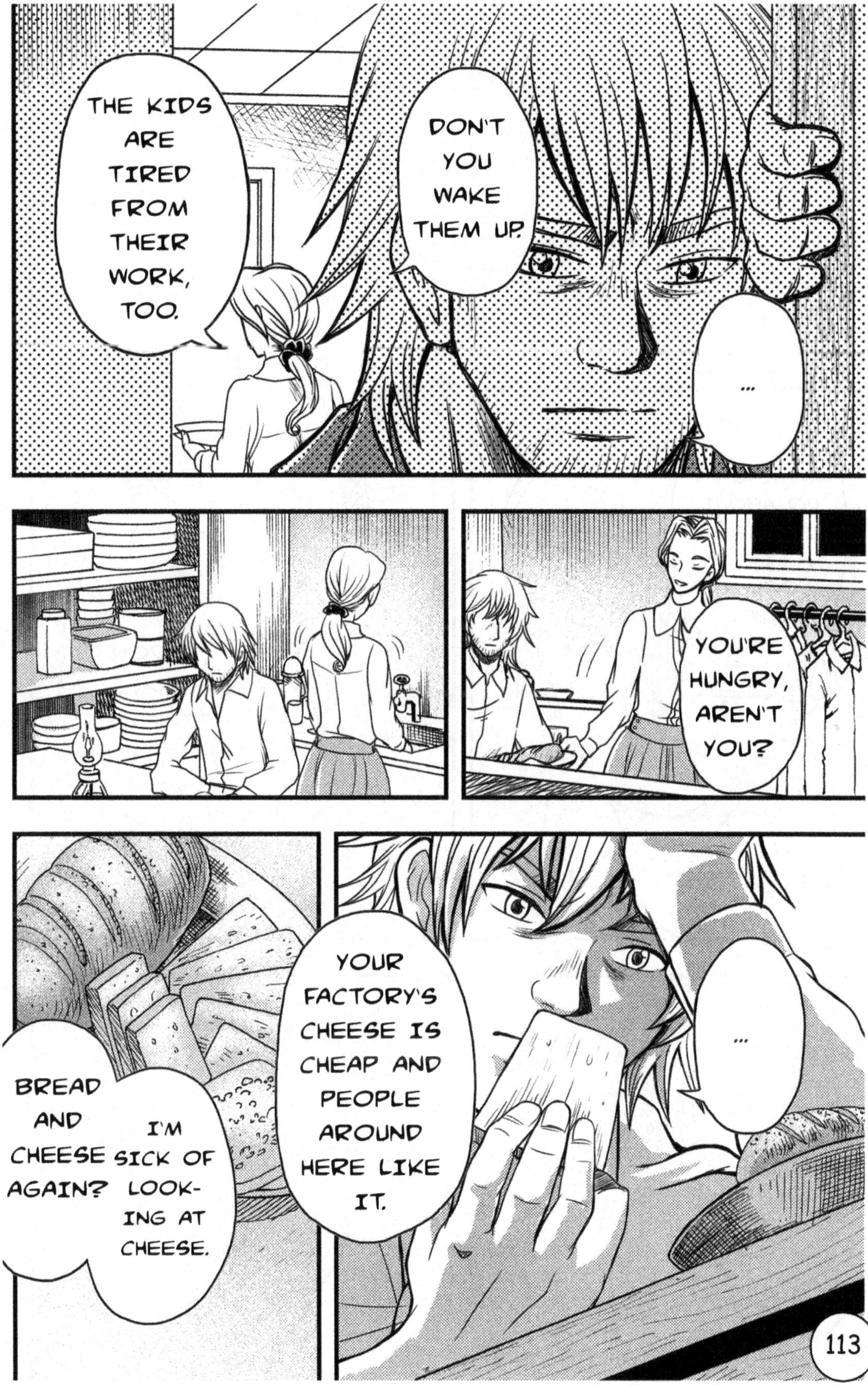
THE KIDS ARE TIRED FROM THEIR WORK, TOO.
DON'T YOU WAKE THEM UP.
...
YOU'RE HUNGRY, AREN'T YOU?
BREAD AND CHEESE AGAIN?
I'M SICK OF LOOKING AT CHEESE.
YOUR FACTORY'S CHEESE IS CHEAP AND PEOPLE AROUND HERE LIKE IT.
...

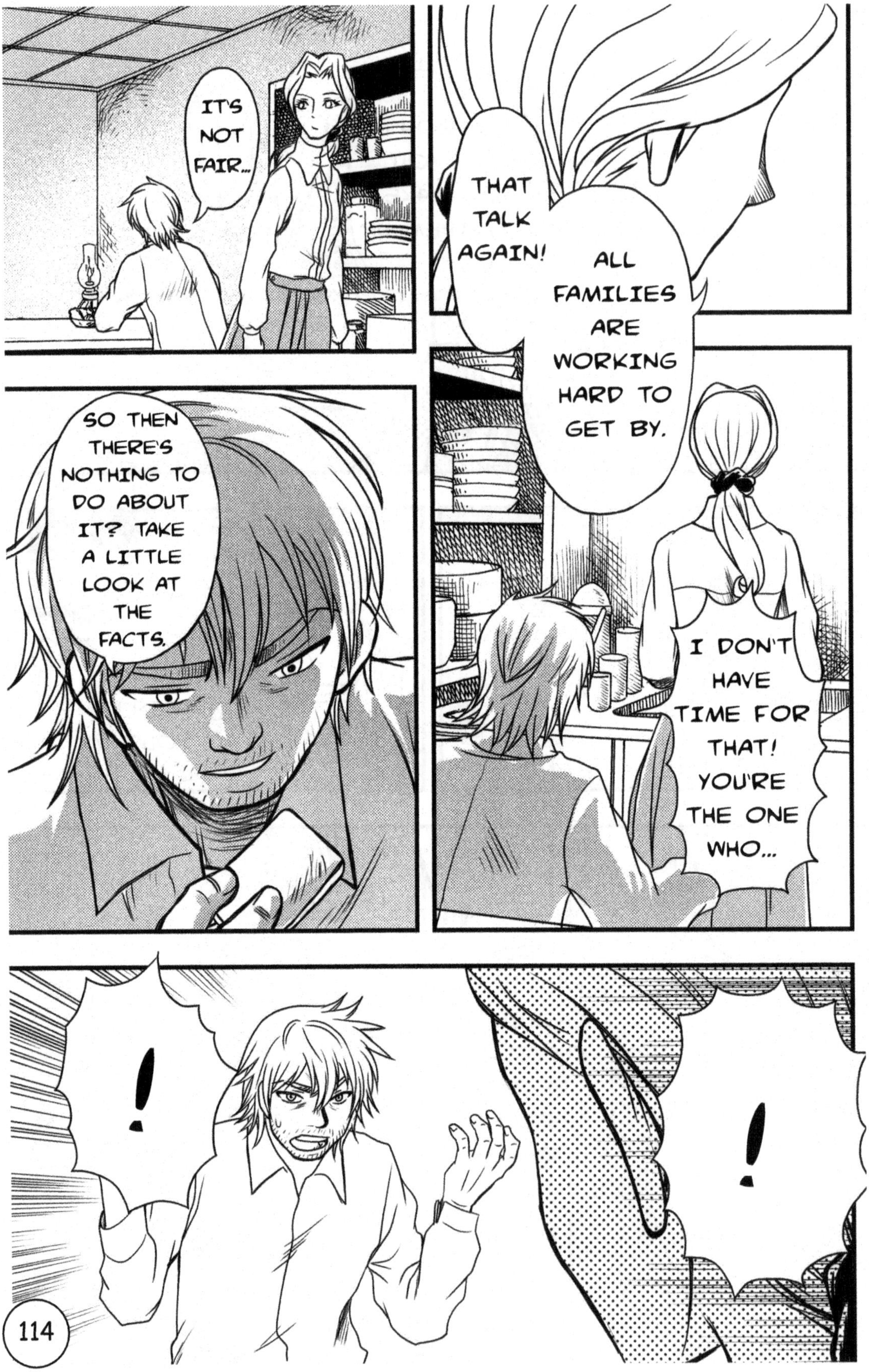
IT'S NOT FAIR...
THAT TALK AGAIN!
ALL FAMILIES ARE WORKING HARD TO GET BY.
SO THEN THERE'S NOTHING TO DO ABOUT IT? TAKE A LITTLE LOOK AT THE FACTS.
I DON'T HAVE TIME FOR THAT! YOU'RE THE ONE WHO...
!
!

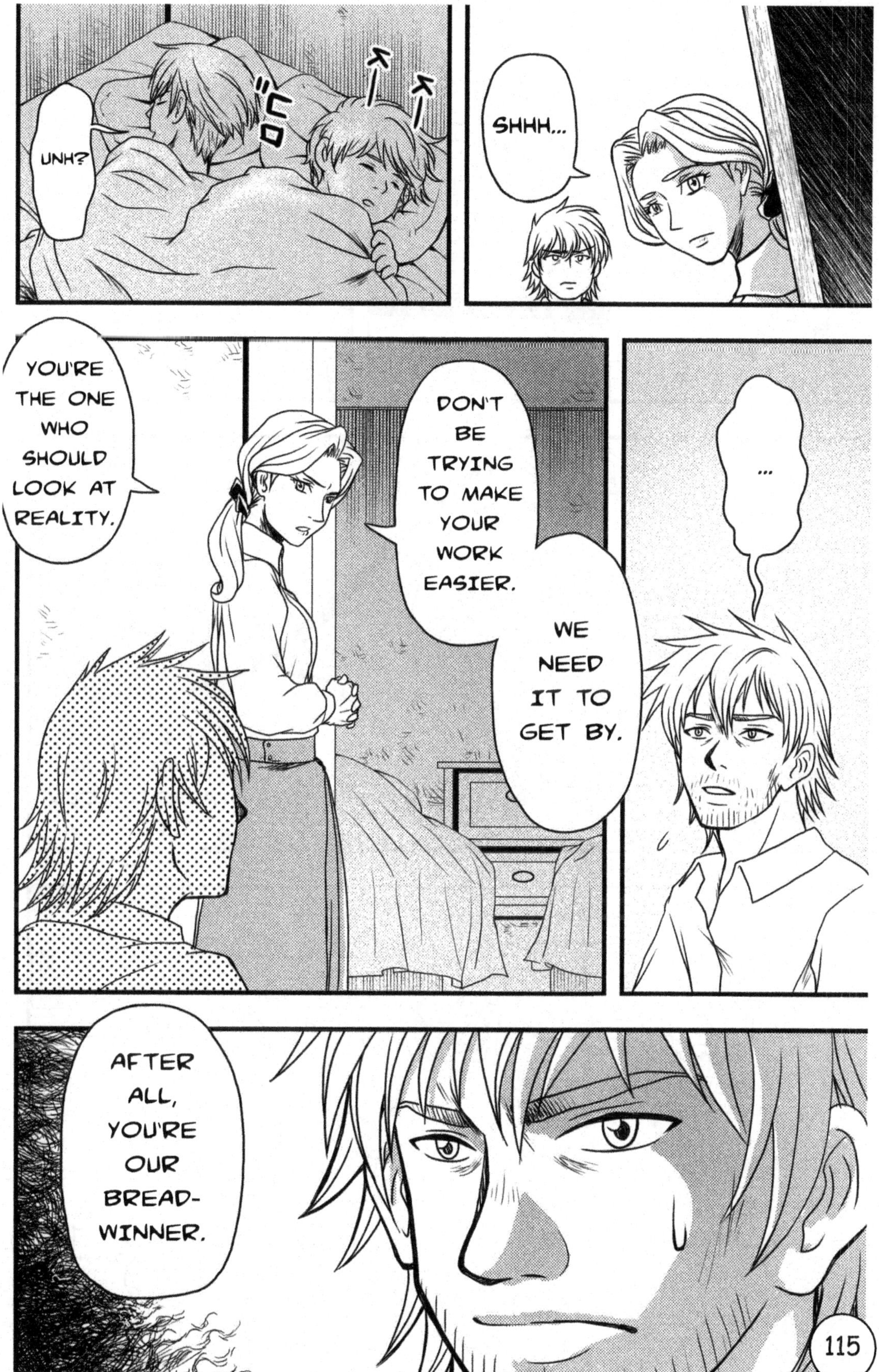
UNH?
ゴロ
スー
スー
SHHH...
YOU'RE THE ONE WHO SHOULD LOOK AT REALITY.
DON'T BE TRYING TO MAKE YOUR WORK EASIER.
WE NEED IT TO GET BY.
...
AFTER ALL, YOU'RE OUR BREAD-WINNER.

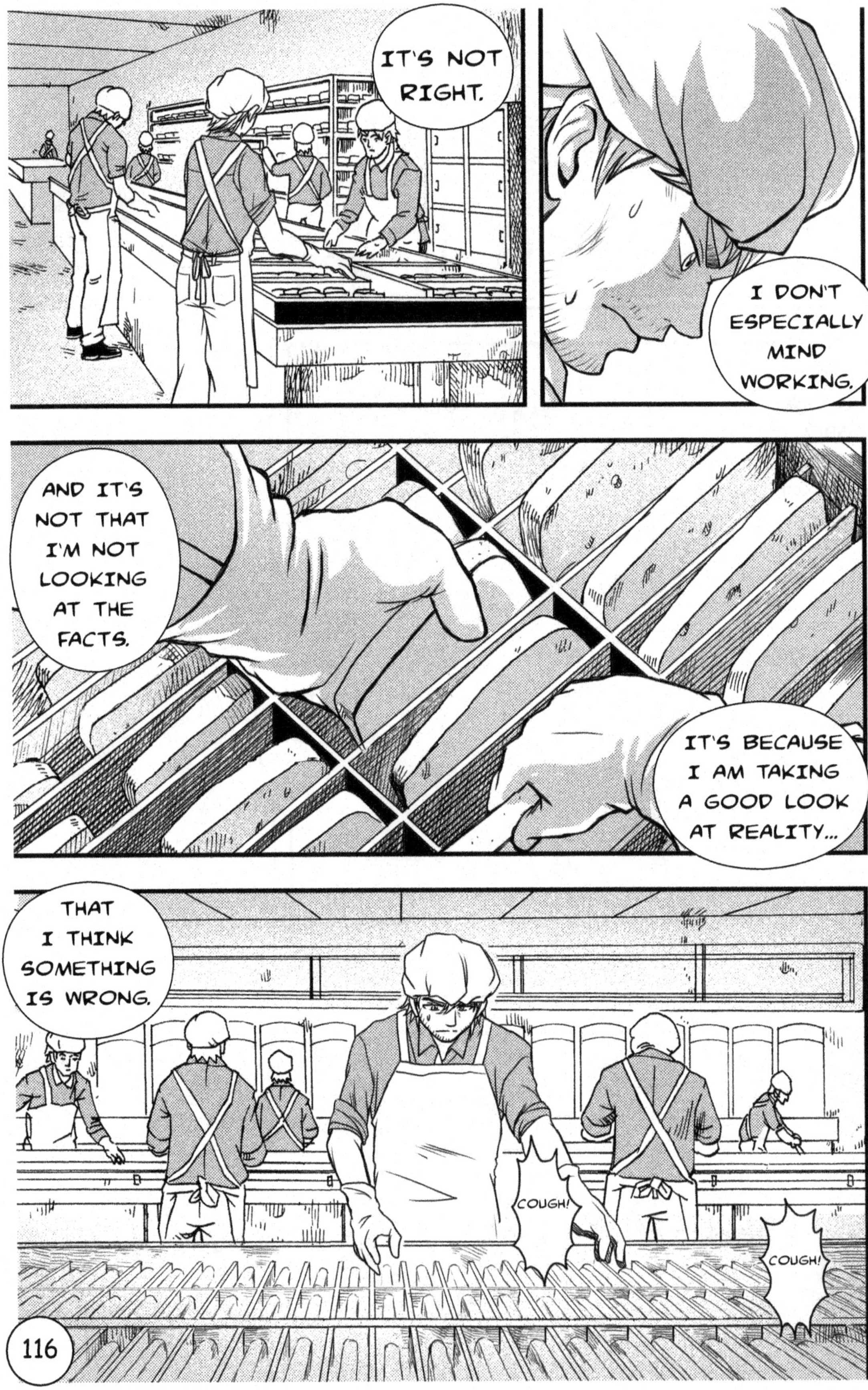
IT'S NOT RIGHT.
I DON'T ESPECIALLY MIND WORKING.
AND IT'S NOT THAT I'M NOT LOOKING AT THE FACTS.
IT'S BECAUSE I AM TAKING A GOOD LOOK AT REALITY...
THAT I THINK SOMETHING IS WRONG.
COUGH!
COUGH!

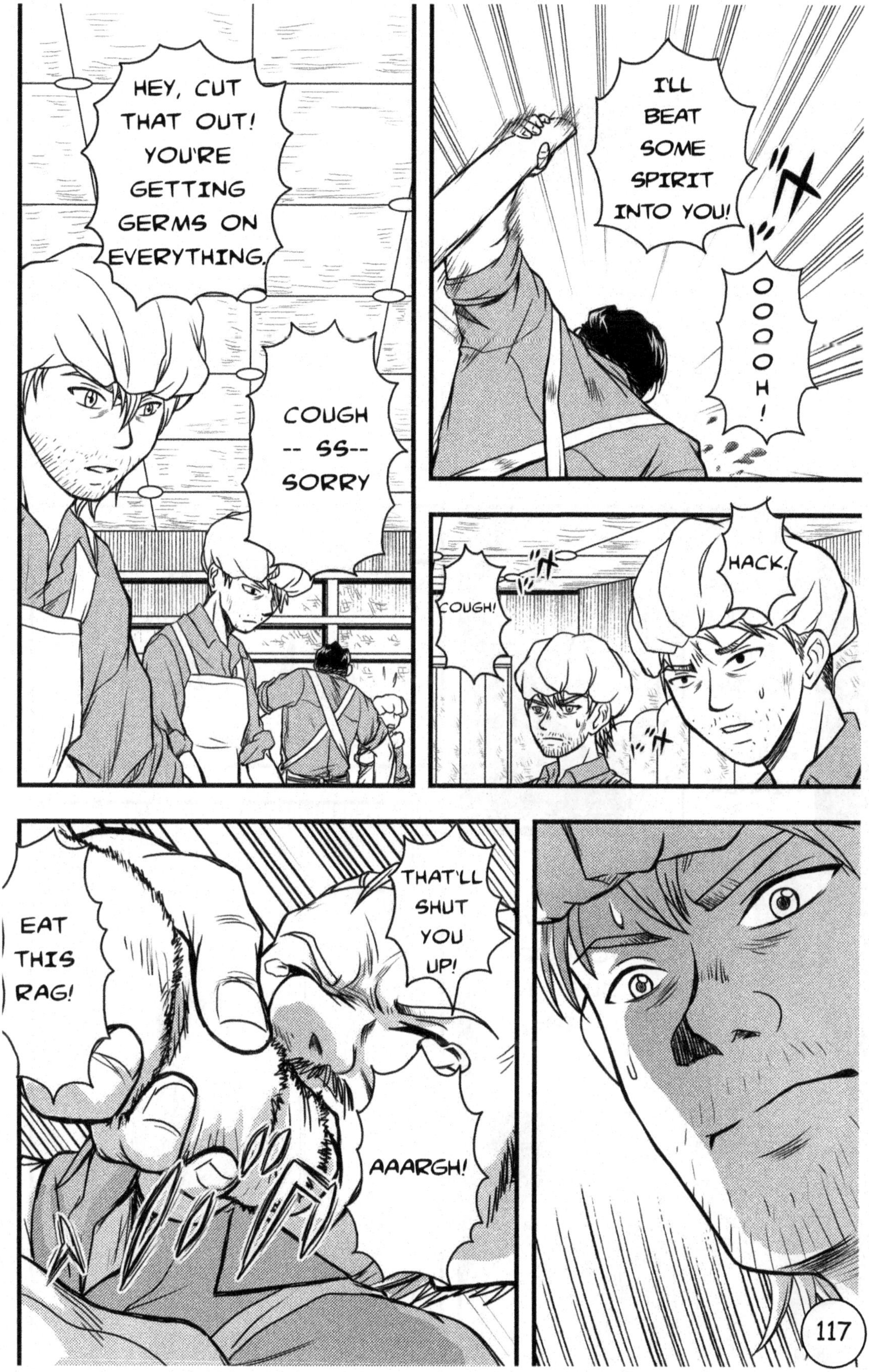
HEY, CUT THAT OUT! YOU'RE GETTING GERMS ON EVERYTHING.
COUGH -- SS-- SORRY
I'LL BEAT SOME SPIRIT INTO YOU!
OOOOOH!
COUGH!
HACK.
EAT THIS RAG!
THAT'LL SHUT YOU UP!
AAARGH!

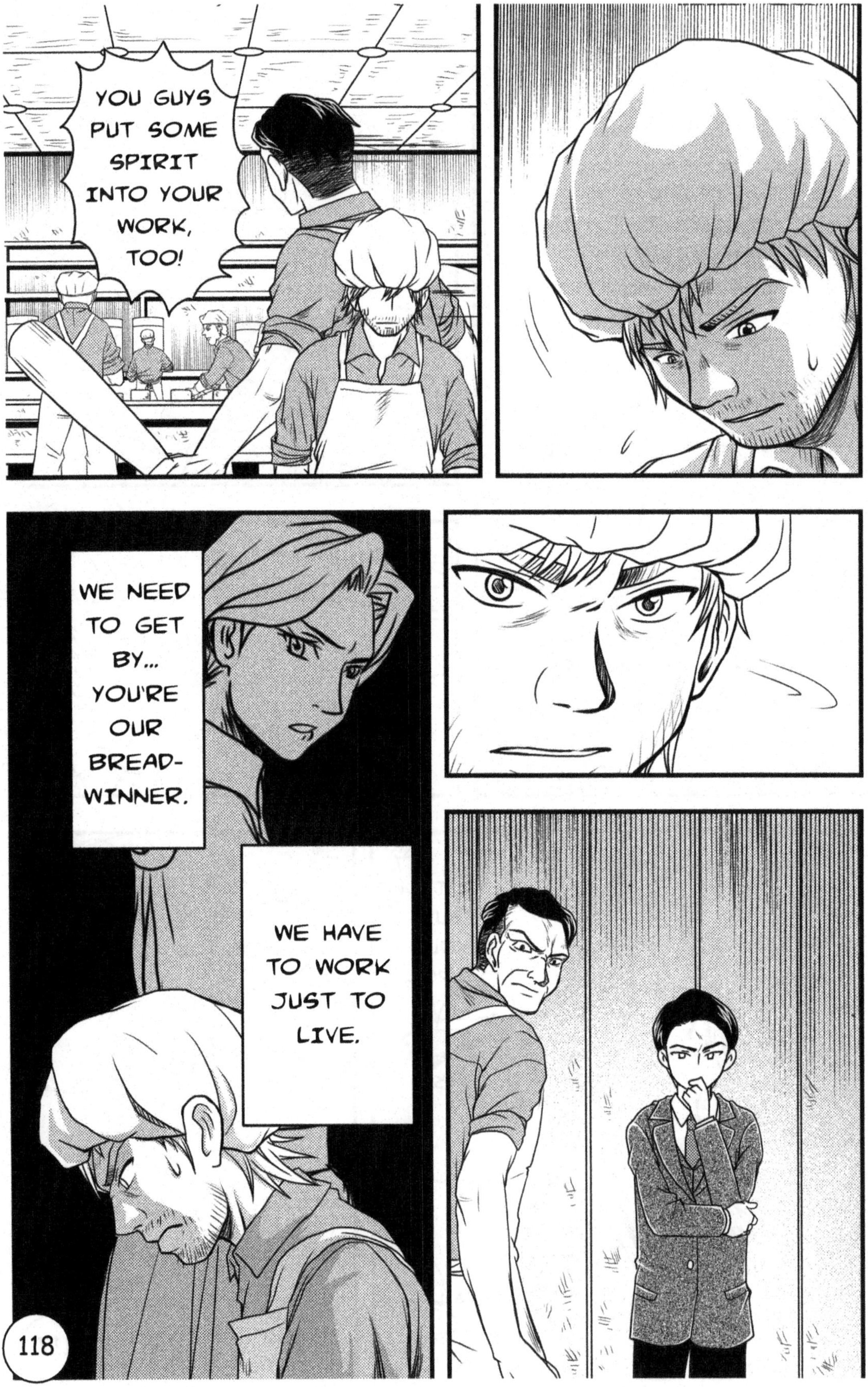
YOU GUYS PUT SOME SPIRIT INTO YOUR WORK, TOO!
WE NEED TO GET BY... YOU'RE OUR BREAD-WINNER.
WE HAVE TO WORK JUST TO LIVE.

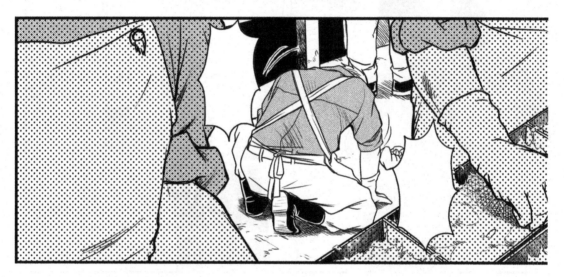

...

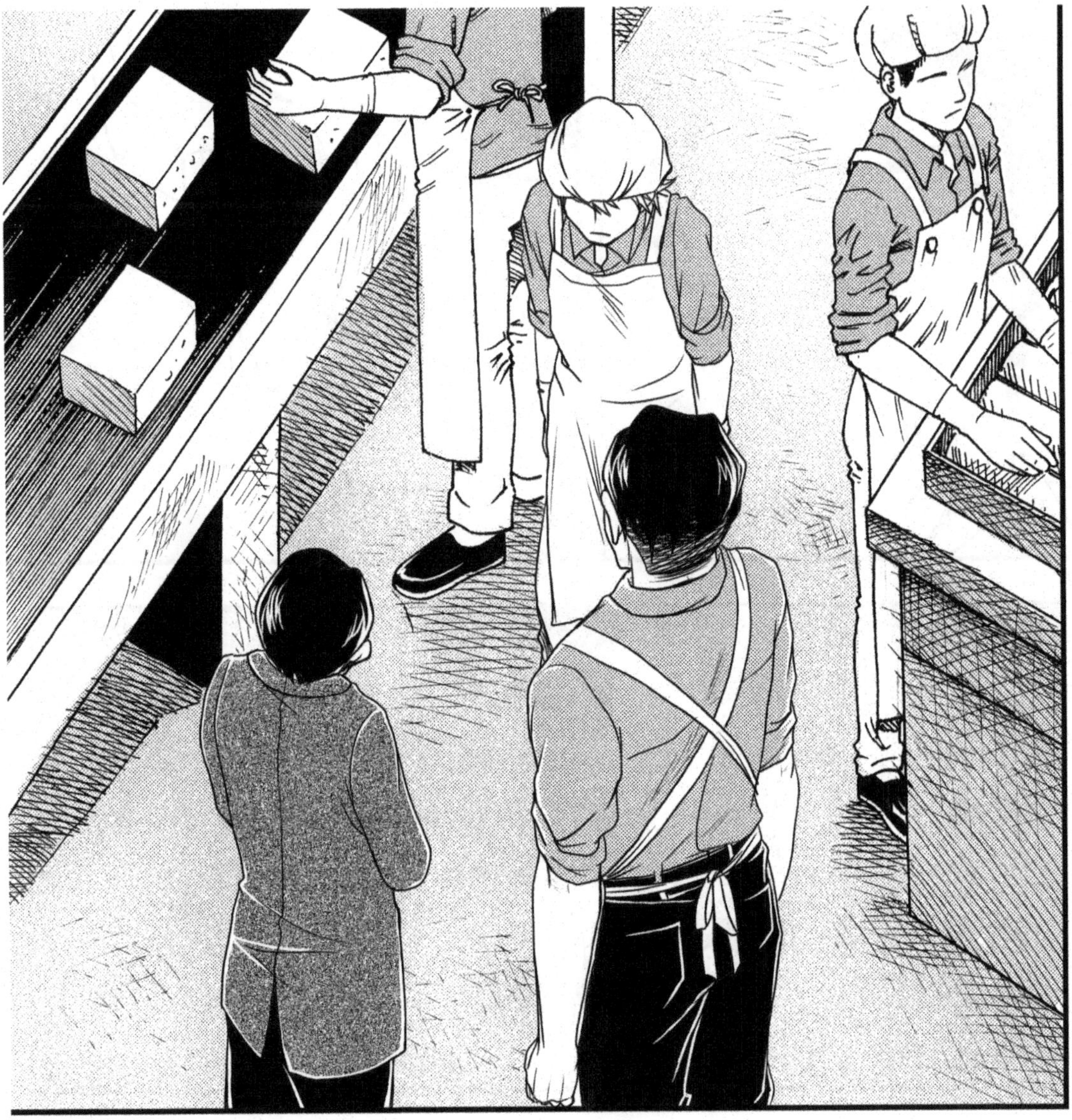

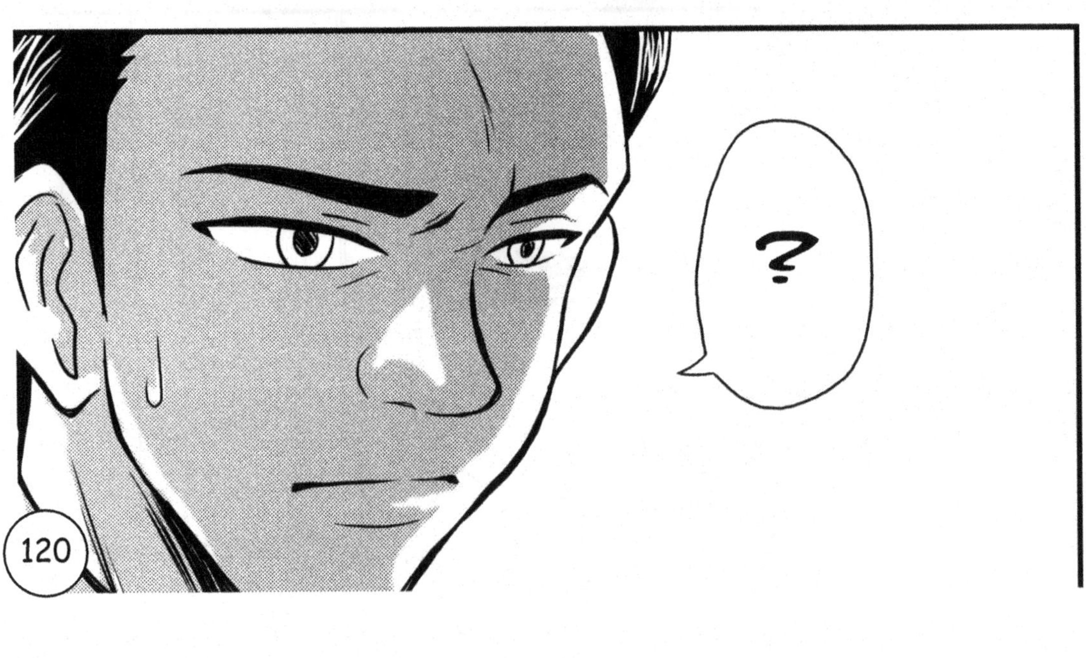
?

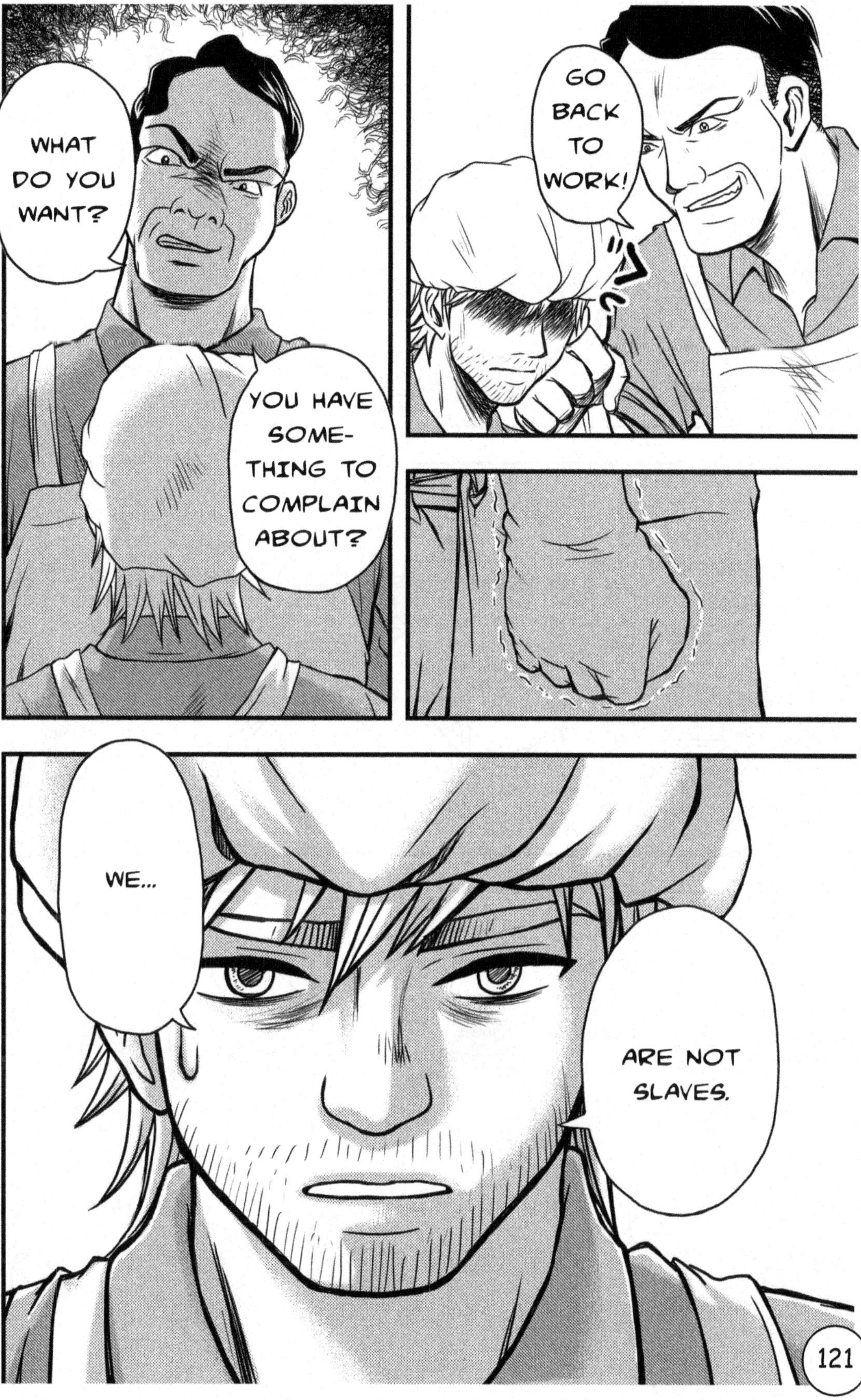
WHAT DO YOU WANT?
YOU HAVE SOME-THING TO COMPLAIN ABOUT?
GO BACK TO WORK!
WE...
ARE NOT SLAVES.

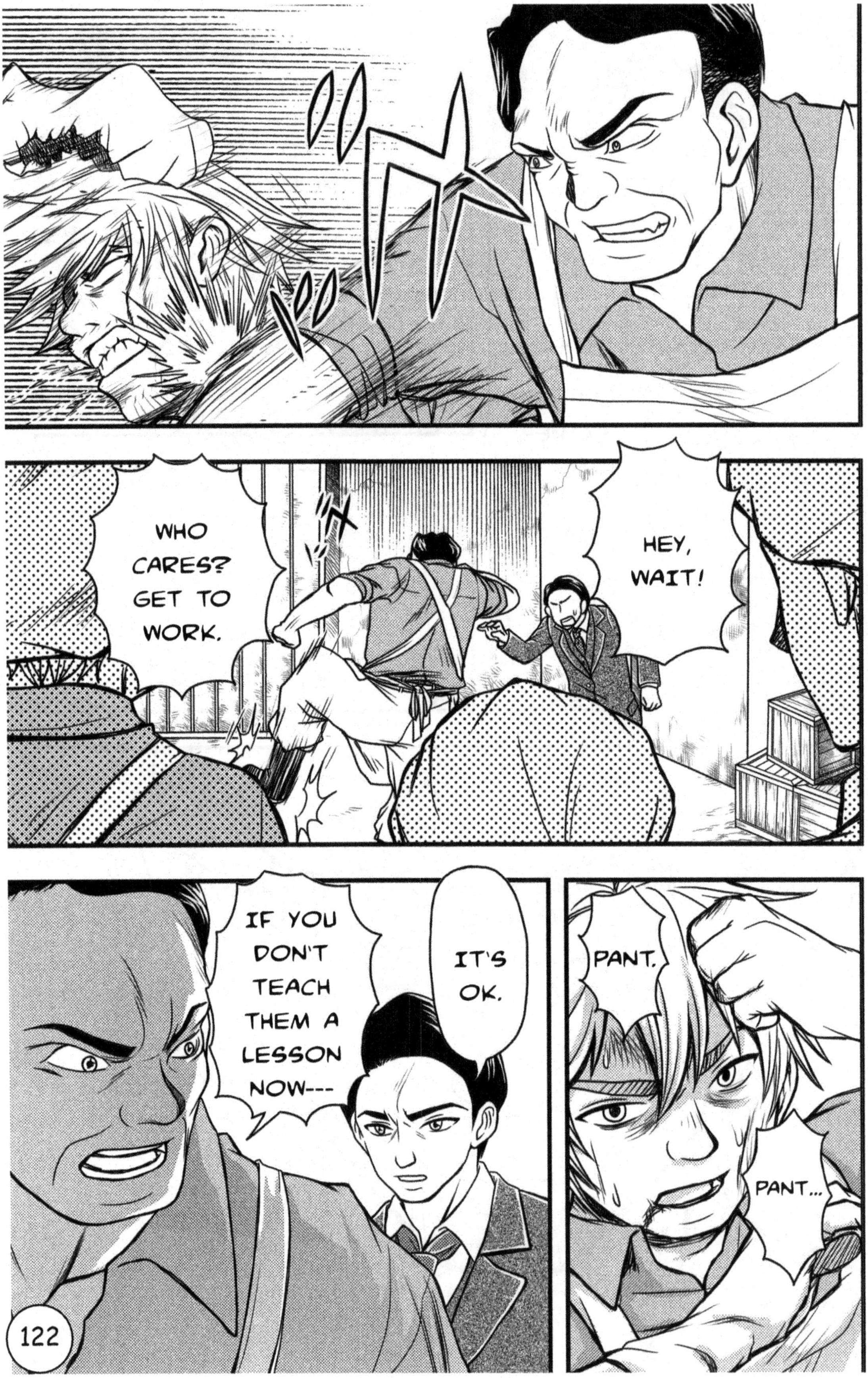
WHO CARES? GET TO WORK.
HEY, WAIT!
IF YOU DON'T TEACH THEM A LESSON NOW---
IT'S OK.
PANT.
PANT...

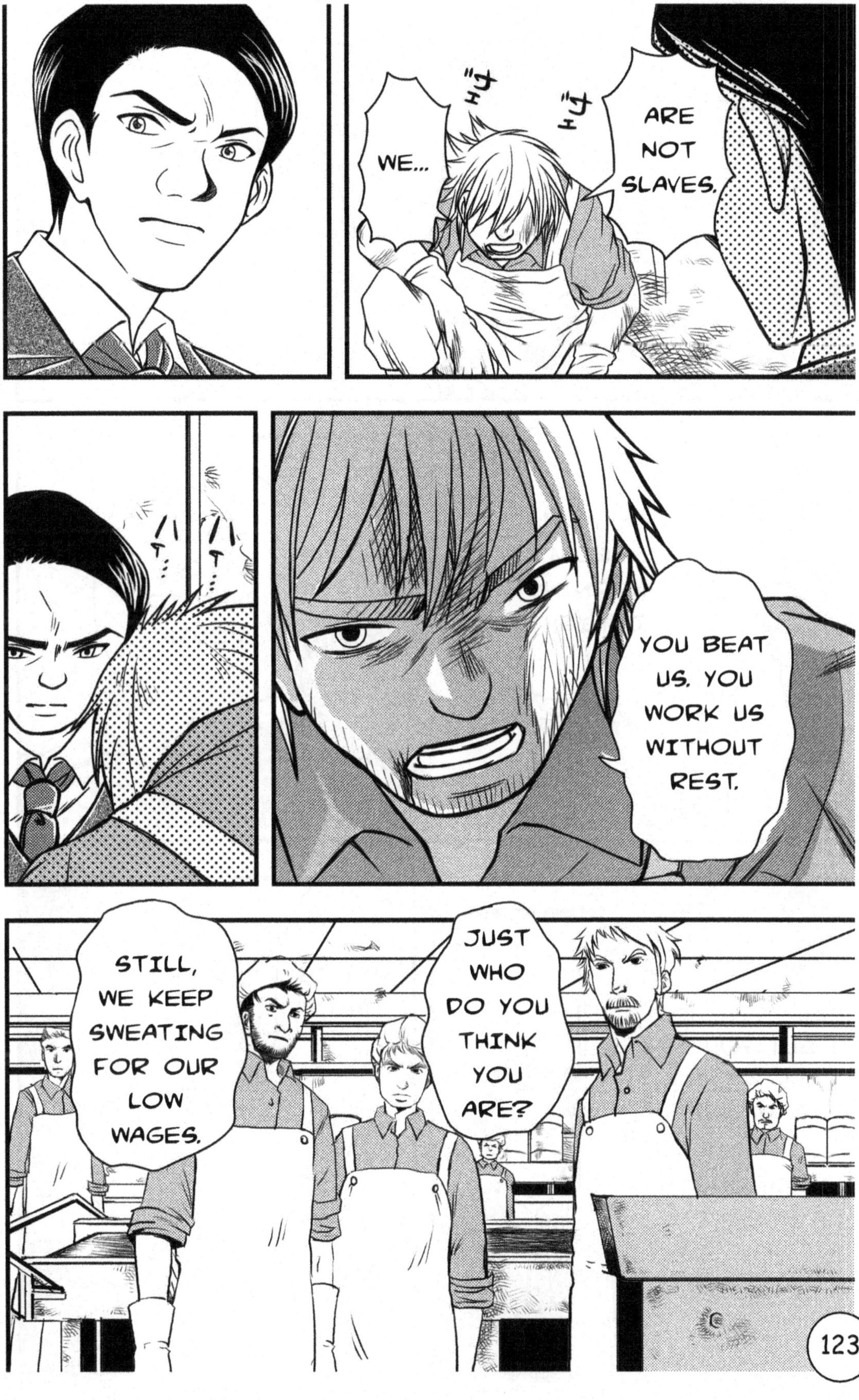
WE...
ARE NOT SLAVES.
YOU BEAT US. YOU WORK US WITHOUT REST.
STILL, WE KEEP SWEATING FOR OUR LOW WAGES.
JUST WHO DO YOU THINK YOU ARE?

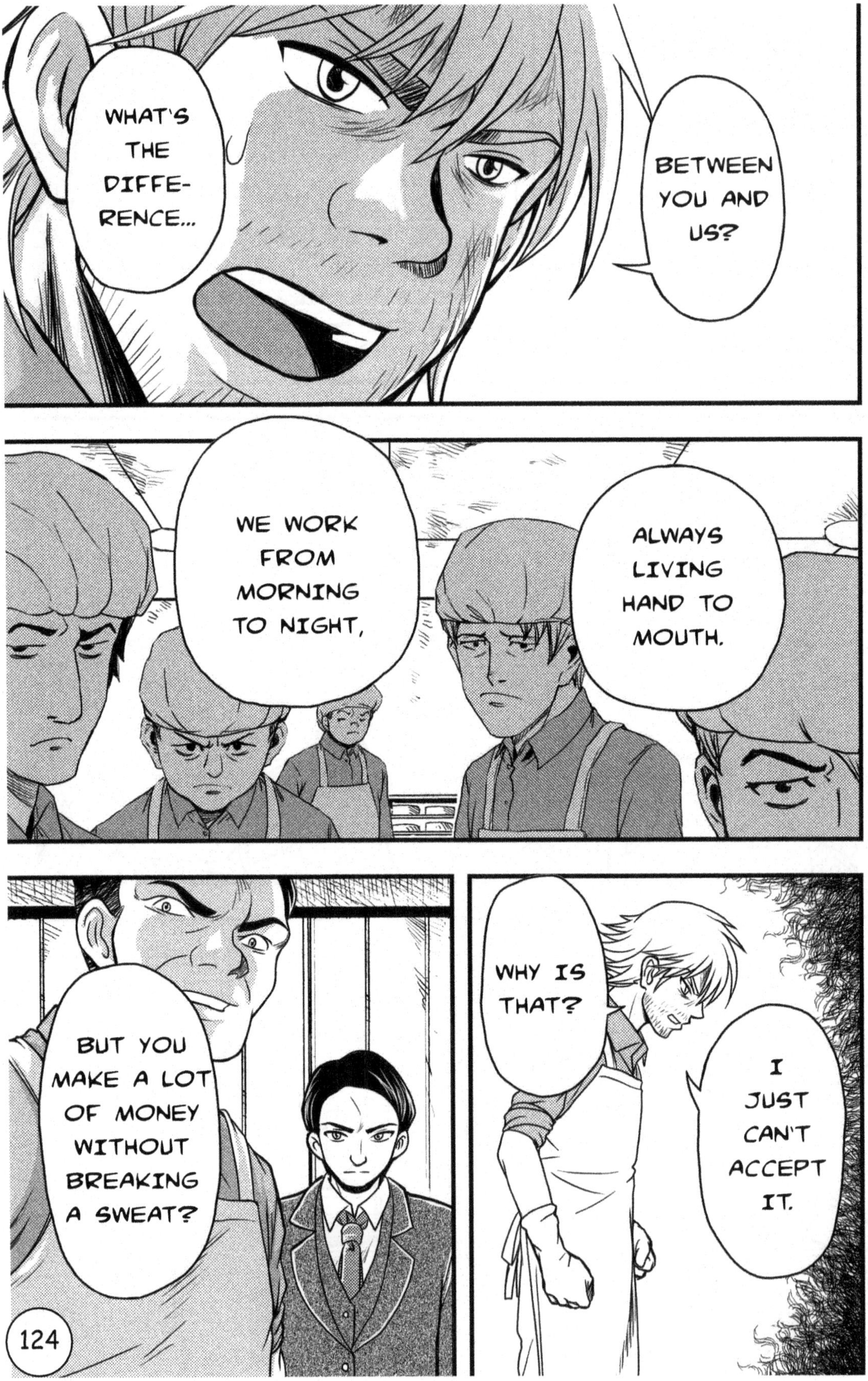
WHAT'S THE DIFFE-RENCE...
BETWEEN YOU AND US?
WE WORK FROM MORNING TO NIGHT,
ALWAYS LIVING HAND TO MOUTH.
BUT YOU MAKE A LOT OF MONEY WITHOUT BREAKING A SWEAT?
WHY IS THAT?
I JUST CAN'T ACCEPT IT.

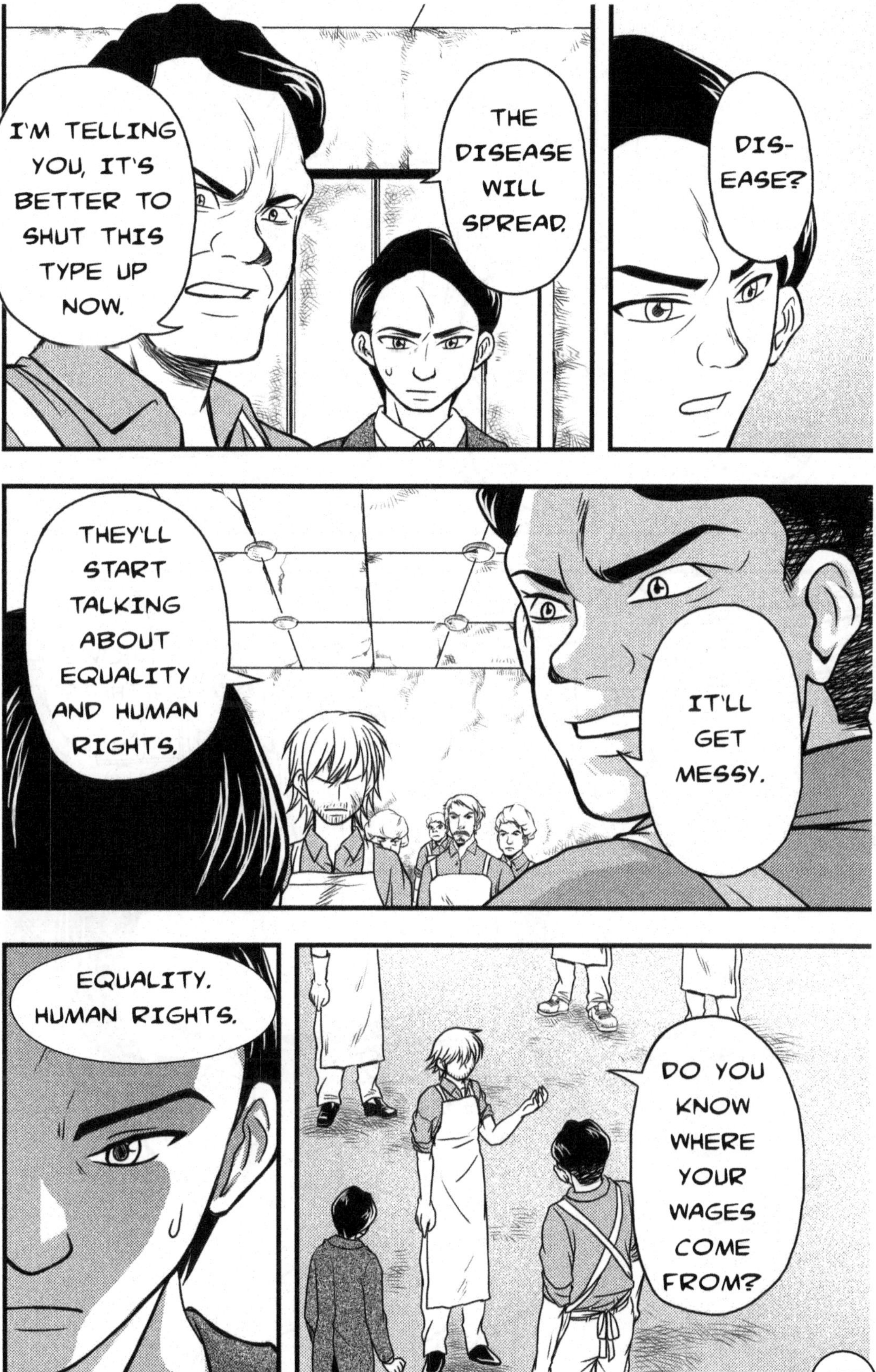
I'M TELLING YOU, IT'S BETTER TO SHUT THIS TYPE UP NOW.
THE DISEASE WILL SPREAD.
DIS-EASE?
THEY'LL START TALKING ABOUT EQUALITY AND HUMAN RIGHTS.
IT'LL GET MESSY.
EQUALITY. HUMAN RIGHTS.
DO YOU KNOW WHERE YOUR WAGES COME FROM?

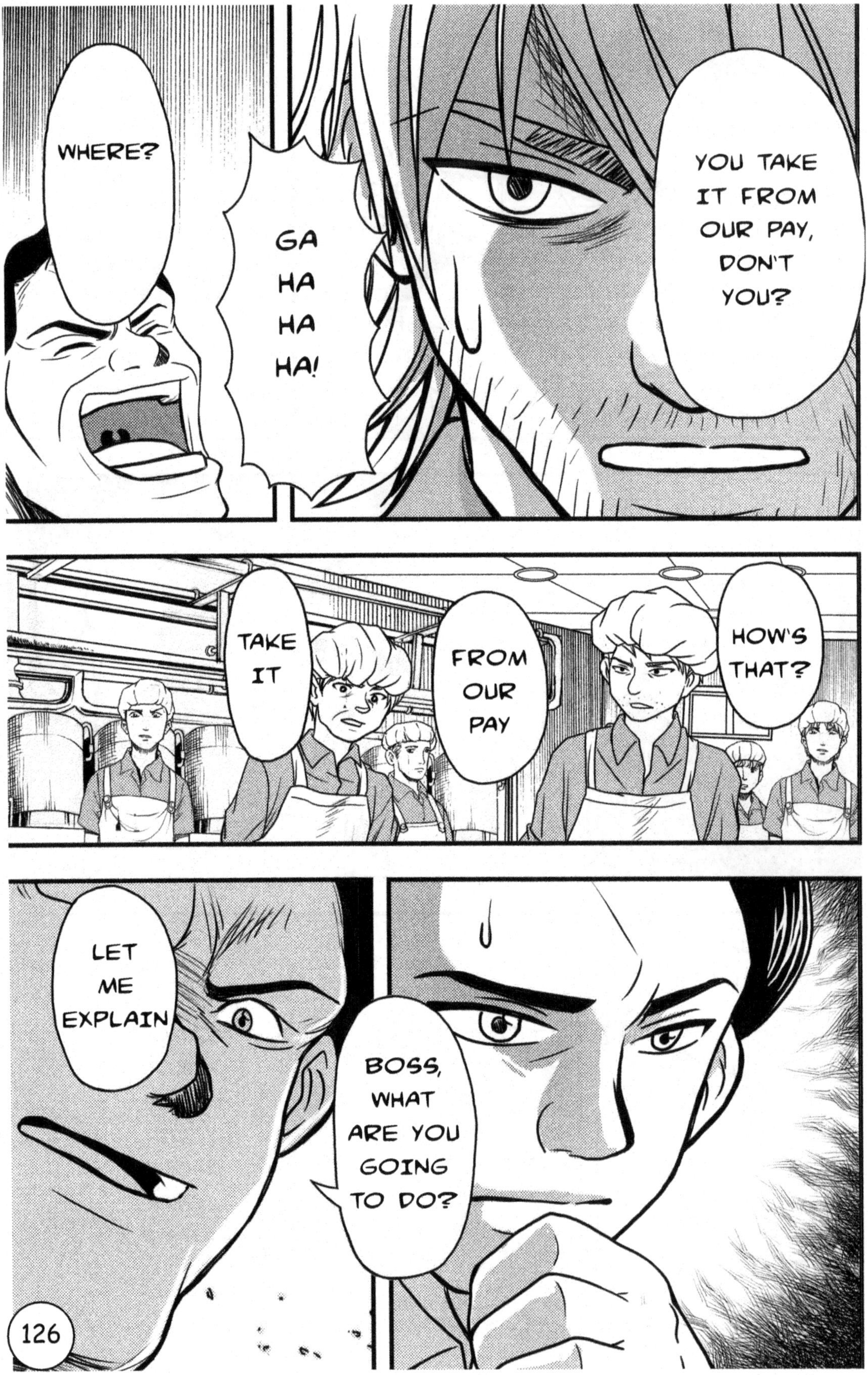
WHERE?
GA HA HA HA!
YOU TAKE IT FROM OUR PAY, DON'T YOU?
TAKE IT
FROM OUR PAY
HOW'S THAT?
LET ME EXPLAIN
BOSS, WHAT ARE YOU GOING TO DO?

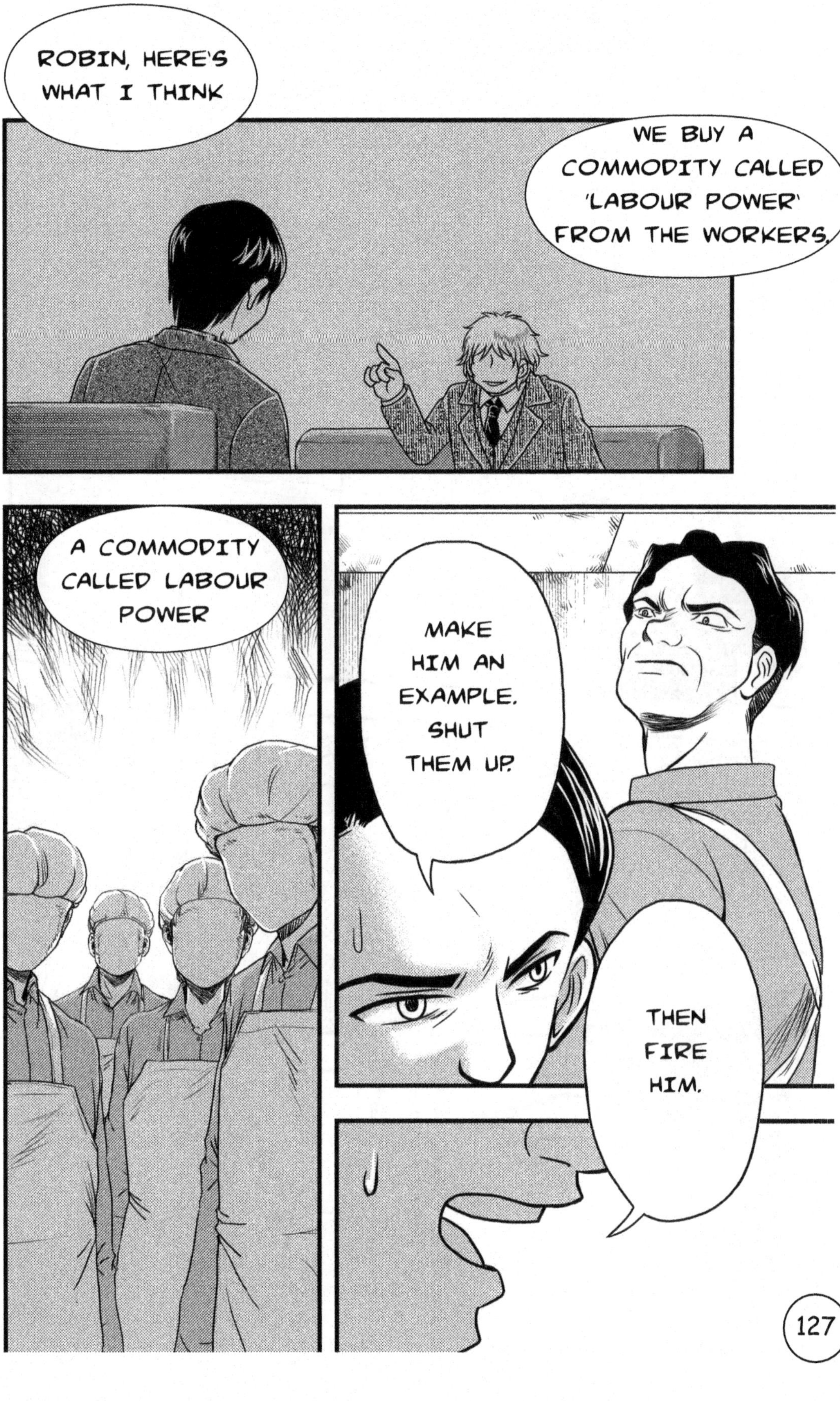
ROBIN, HERE'S WHAT I THINK
WE BUY A COMMODITY CALLED 'LABOUR POWER' FROM THE WORKERS.
A COMMODITY CALLED LABOUR POWER
MAKE HIM AN EXAMPLE. SHUT THEM UP.
THEN FIRE HIM.

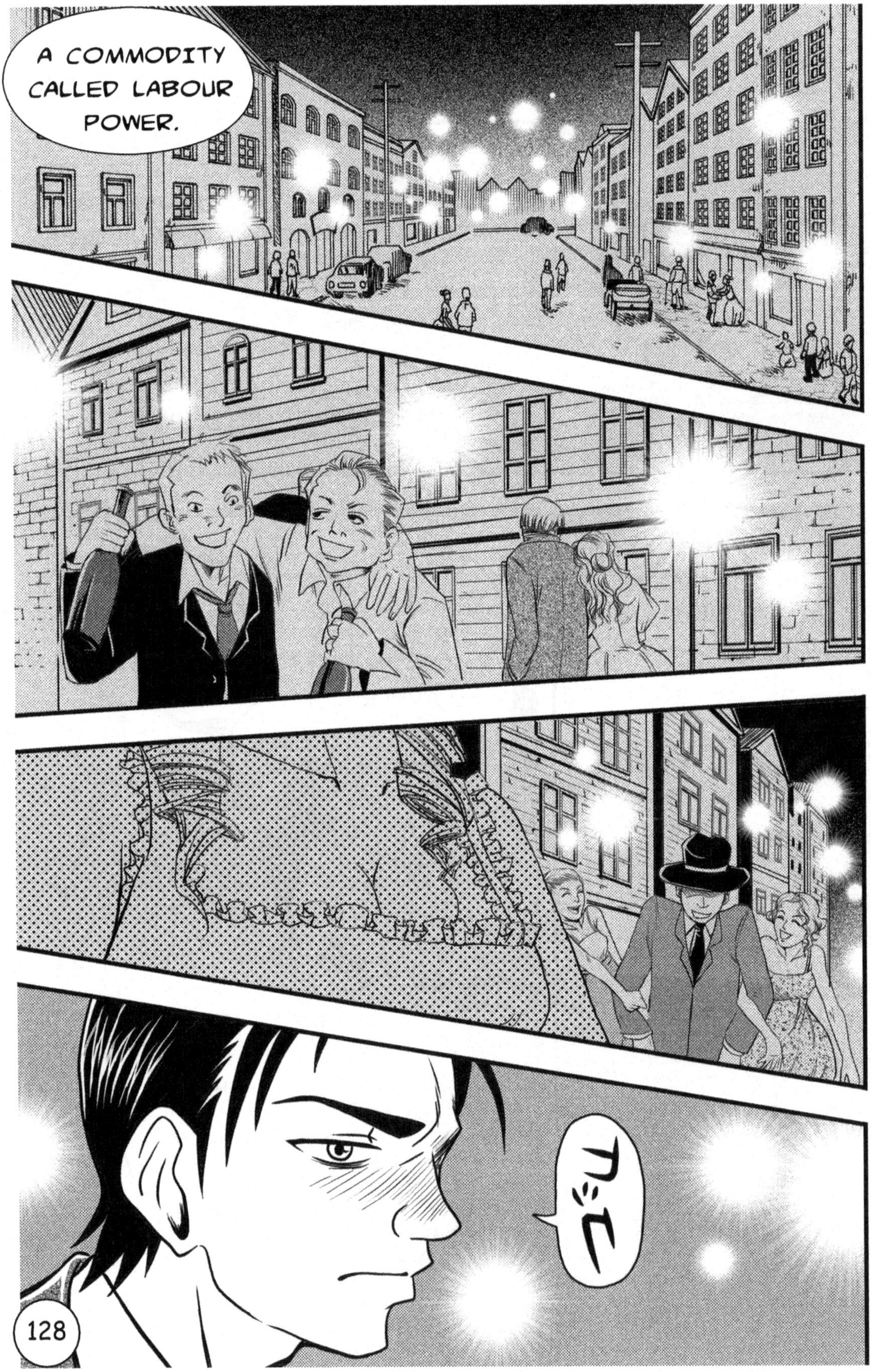
A COMMODITY CALLED LABOUR POWER.

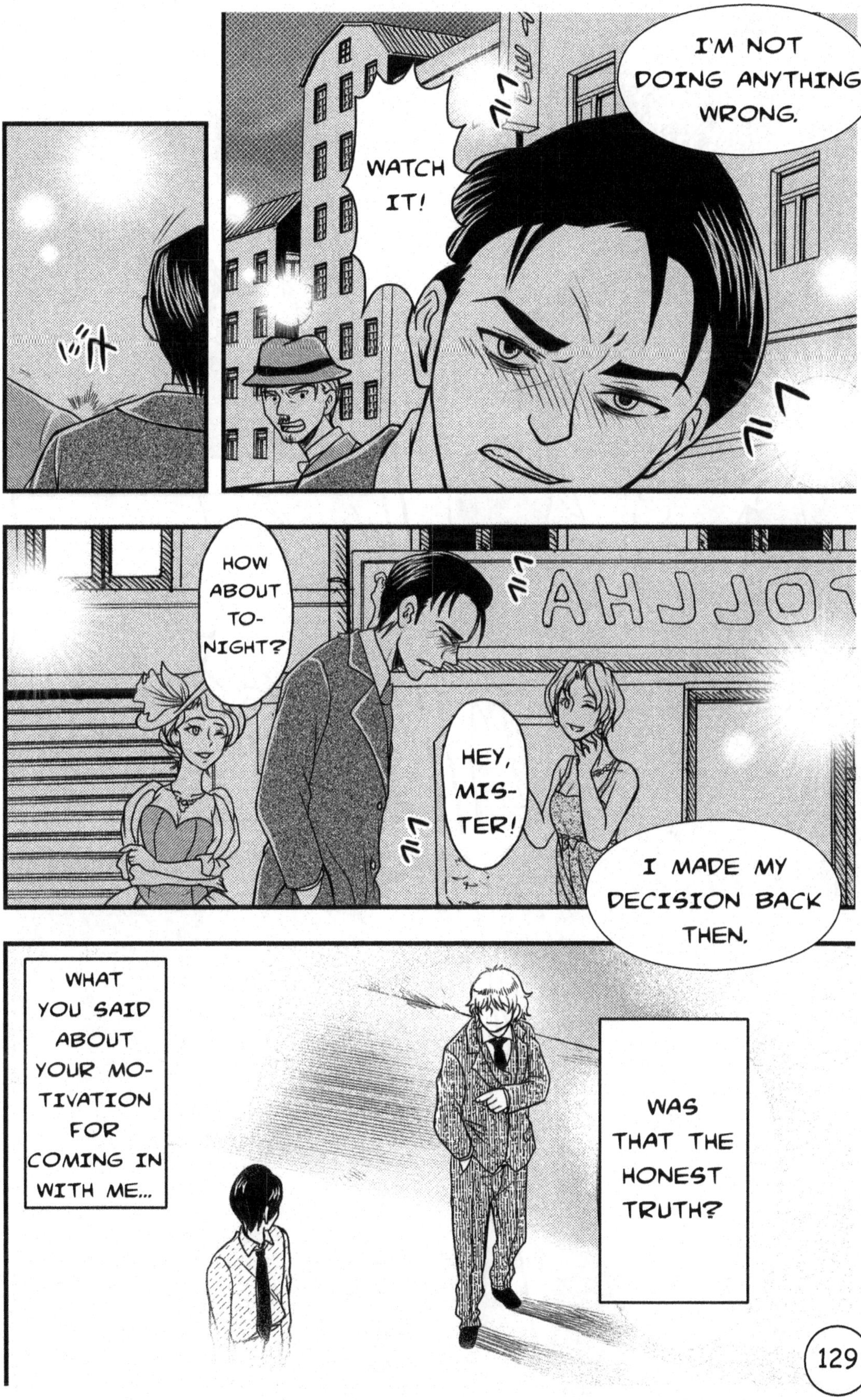
WATCH IT!
I'M NOT DOING ANYTHING WRONG.
HOW ABOUT TO-NIGHT?
HEY, MIS-TER!
I MADE MY DECISION BACK THEN.
WHAT YOU SAID ABOUT YOUR MO-TIVATION FOR COMING IN WITH ME...
WAS THAT THE HONEST TRUTH?

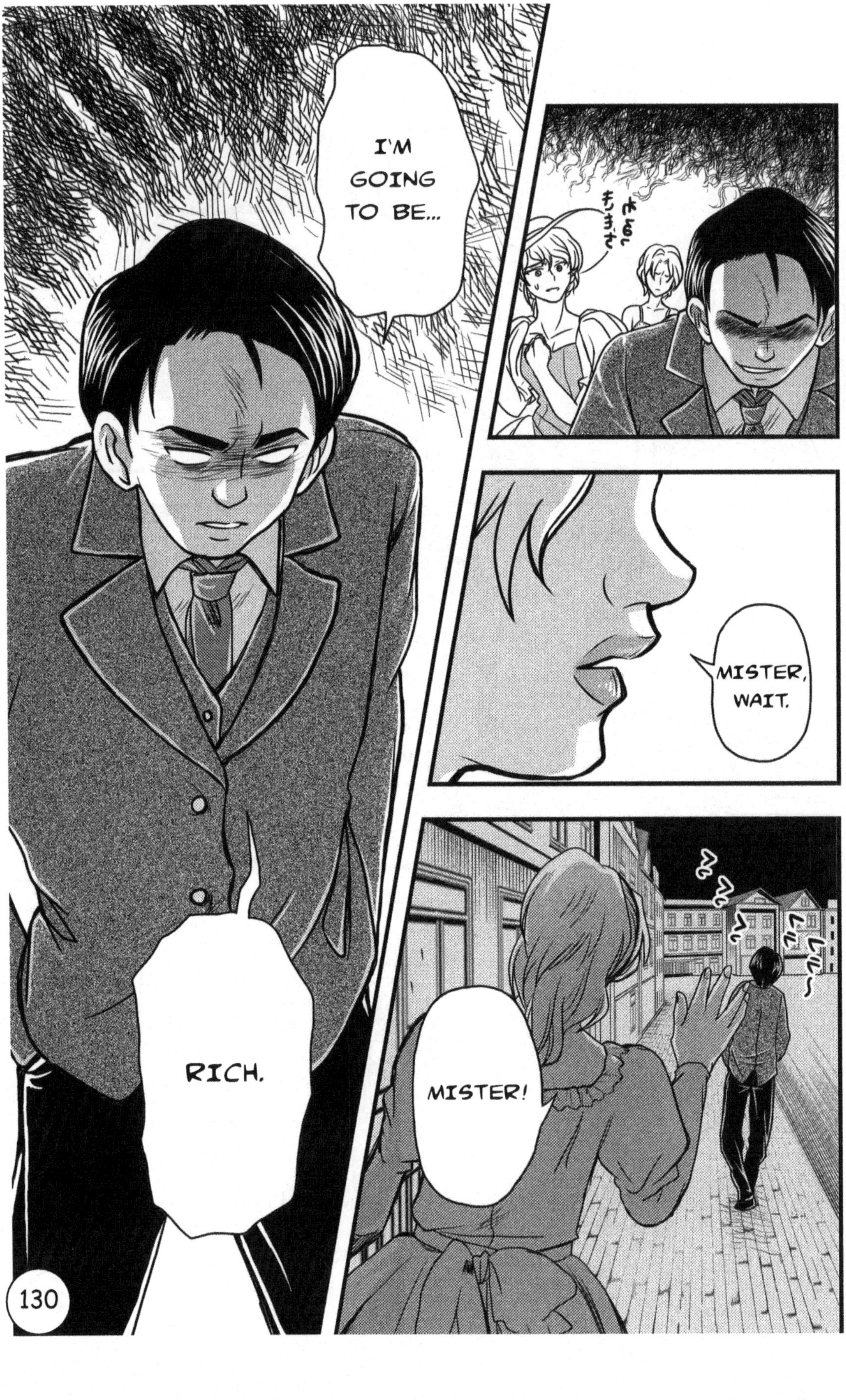
I'M GOING TO BE...
RICH.
MISTER, WAIT.
MISTER!

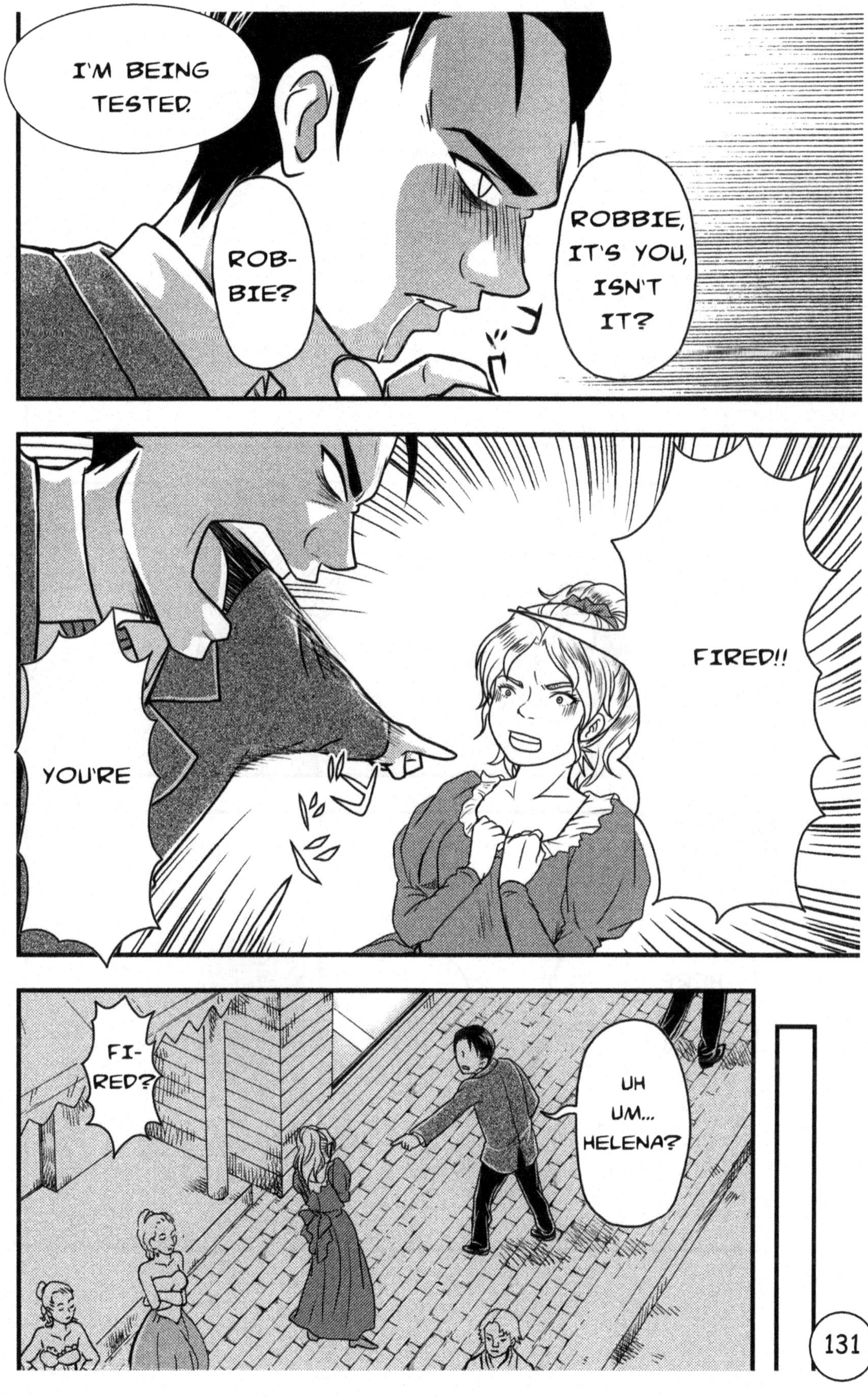
I'M BEING TESTED.
ROB-BIE?
ROBBIE, IT'S YOU, ISN'T IT?
YOU'RE
FIRED!!
FI-RED?
UH UM... HELENA?

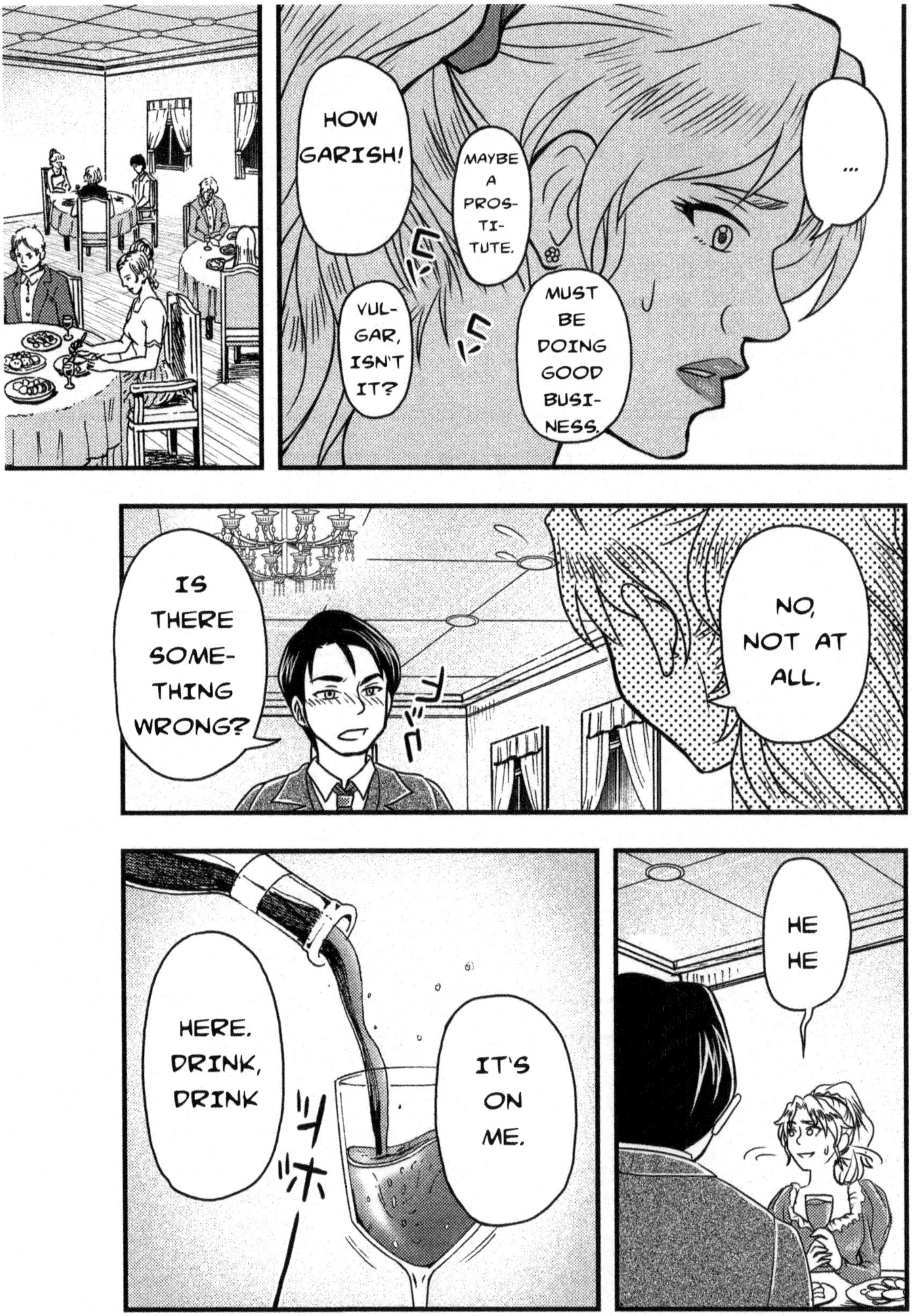
HOW GARISH!
MAYBE A PROSTITUTE.
VULGAR, ISN'T IT?
MUST BE DOING GOOD BUSINESS.
...
IS THERE SOMETHING WRONG?
NO, NOT AT ALL.
HERE. DRINK, DRINK
IT'S ON ME.
HE HE

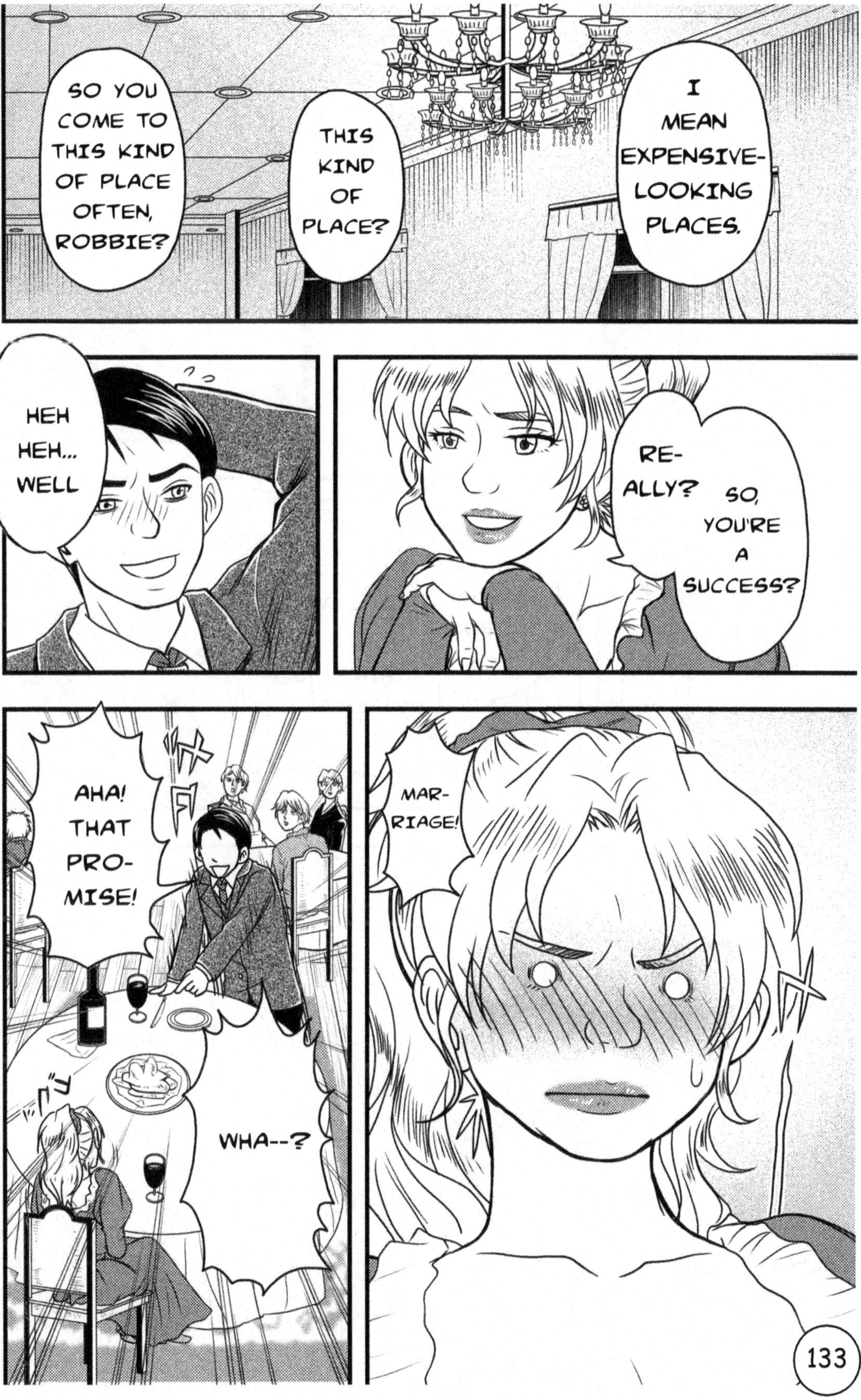
SO YOU COME TO THIS KIND OF PLACE OFTEN, ROBBIE?
THIS KIND OF PLACE?
I MEAN EXPENSIVE-LOOKING PLACES.
HEH HEH... WELL
RE-ALLY?
SO, YOU'RE A SUCCESS?
AHA! THAT PRO-MISE!
WHA--?
MAR-RIAGE!

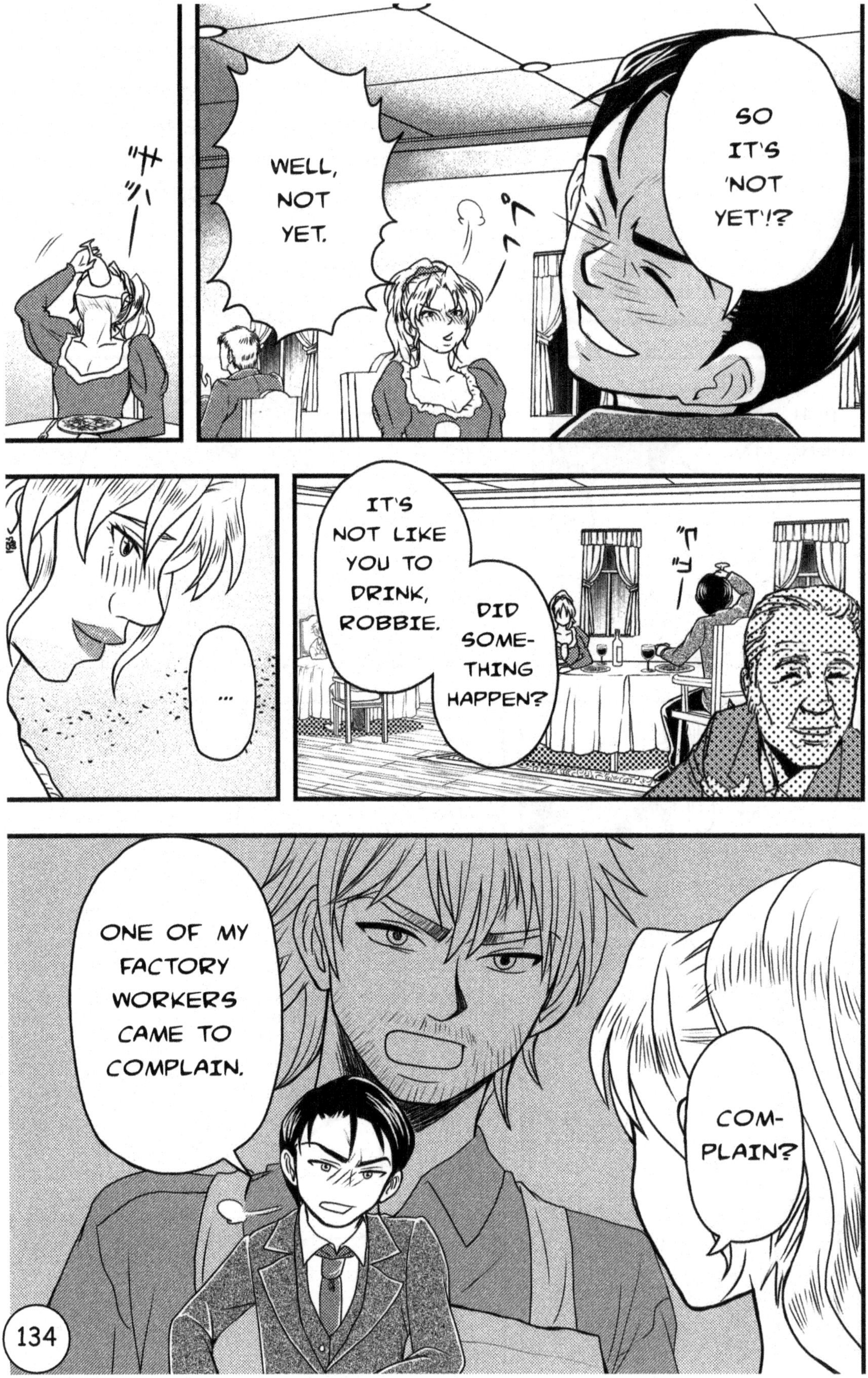
WELL, NOT YET.
SO IT'S 'NOT YET'!?
...
IT'S NOT LIKE YOU TO DRINK, ROBBIE.
DID SOMETHING HAPPEN?
ONE OF MY FACTORY WORKERS CAME TO COMPLAIN.
COM-PLAIN?

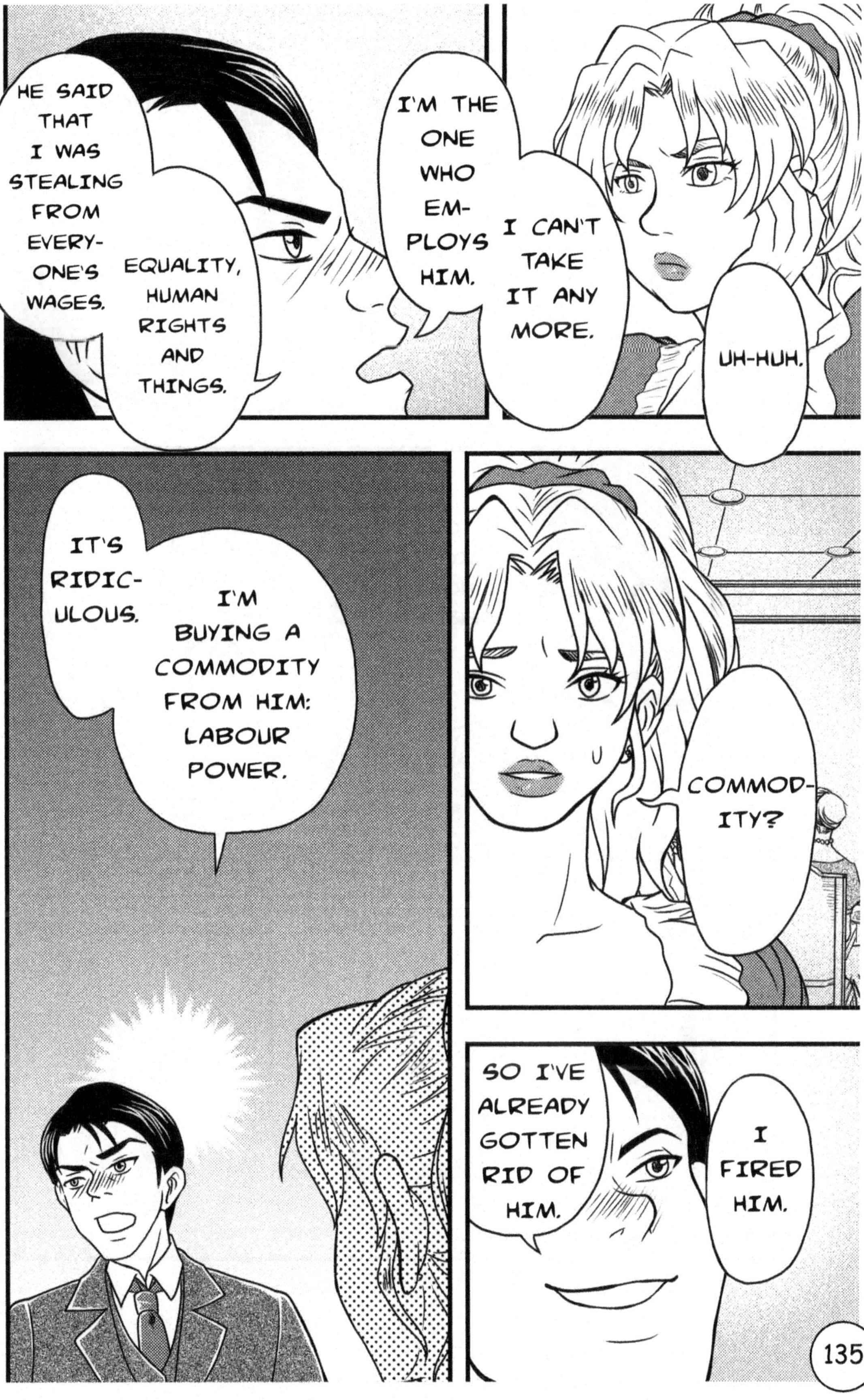
HE SAID THAT I WAS STEALING FROM EVERYONE'S WAGES.
EQUALITY, HUMAN RIGHTS AND THINGS.
I'M THE ONE WHO EMPLOYS HIM.
I CAN'T TAKE IT ANY MORE.
UH-HUH.
IT'S RIDICULOUS.
I'M BUYING A COMMODITY FROM HIM: LABOUR POWER.
COMMODITY?
SO I'VE ALREADY GOTTEN RID OF HIM.
I FIRED HIM.

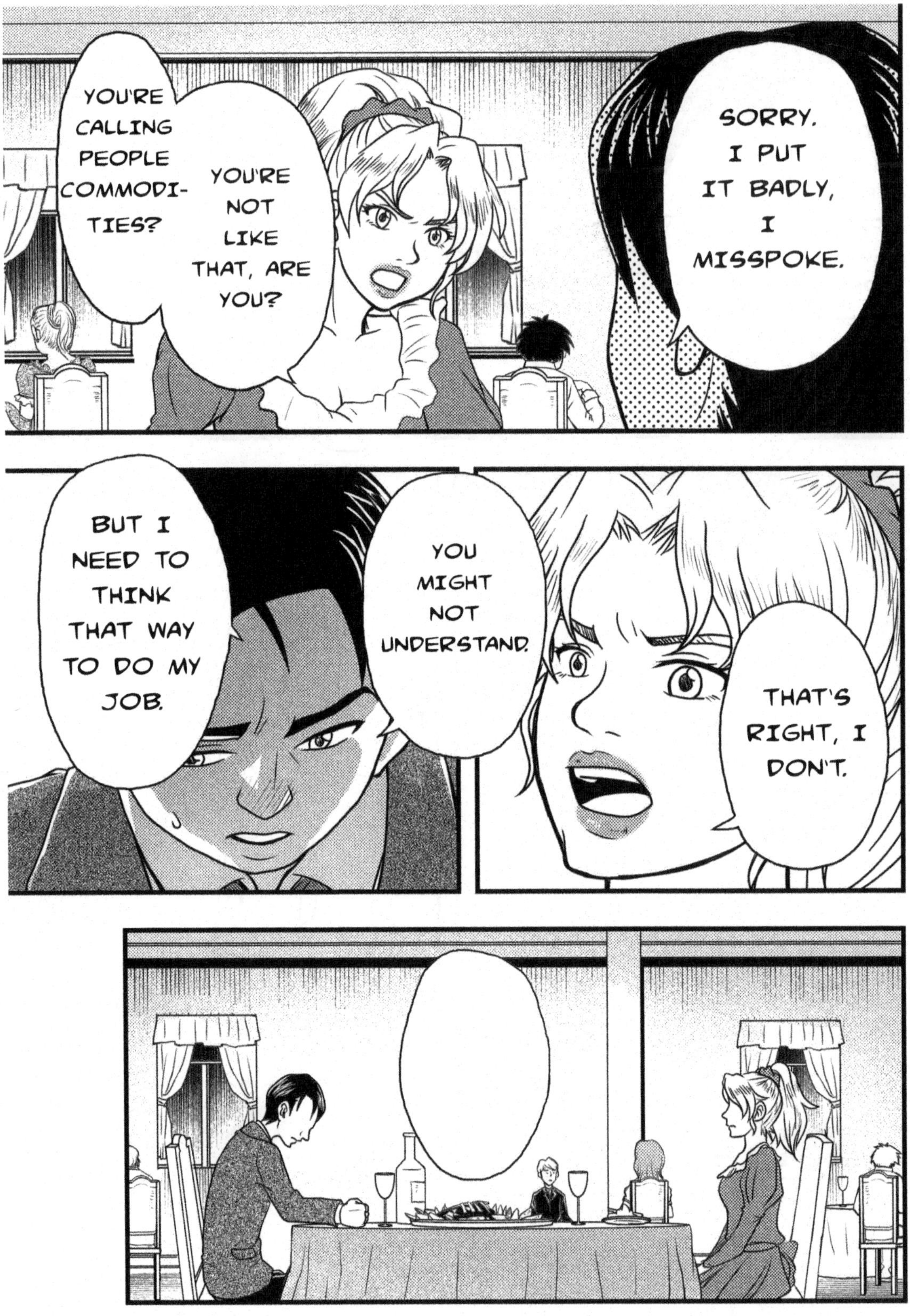
YOU'RE CALLING PEOPLE COMMODI-TIES?
YOU'RE NOT LIKE THAT, ARE YOU?
SORRY. I PUT IT BADLY, I MISSPOKE.
BUT I NEED TO THINK THAT WAY TO DO MY JOB.
YOU MIGHT NOT UNDERSTAND.
THAT'S RIGHT, I DON'T.

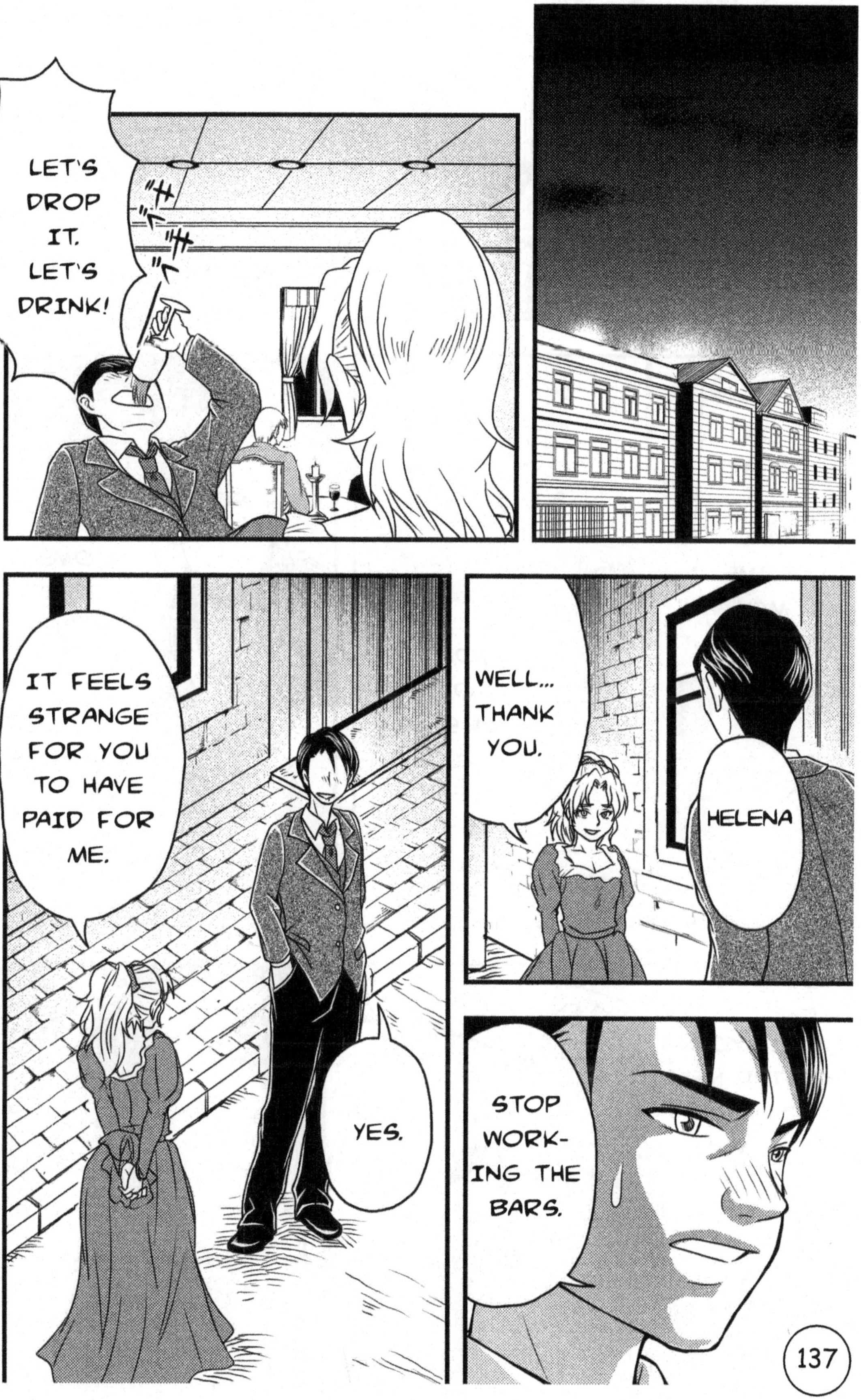

LET'S DROP IT. LET'S DRINK!
IT FEELS STRANGE FOR YOU TO HAVE PAID FOR ME.
YES.
WELL... THANK YOU.
HELENA
STOP WORKING THE BARS.

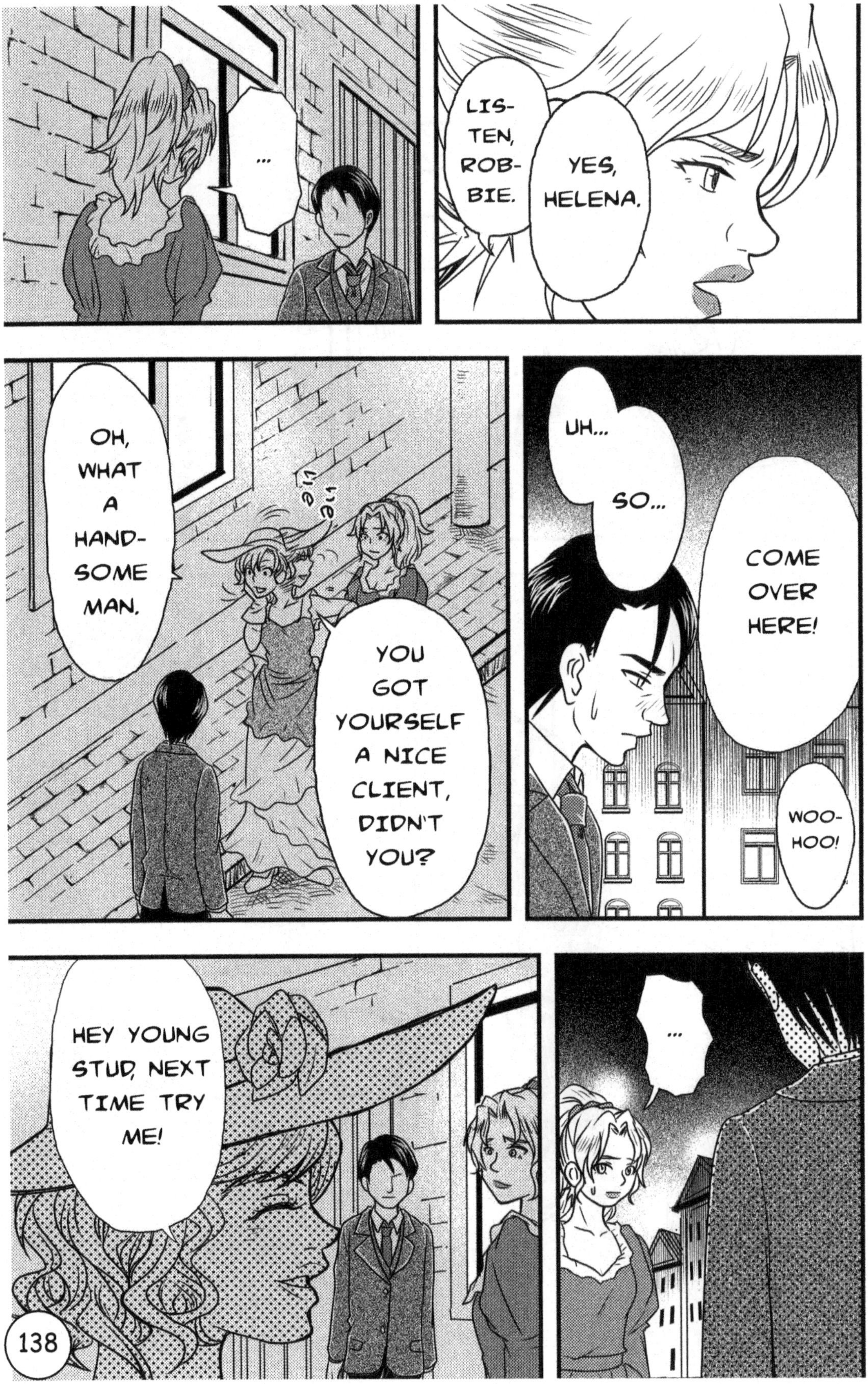
...
LIS-TEN, ROB-BIE.
YES, HELENA.
OH, WHAT A HAND-SOME MAN.
YOU GOT YOURSELF A NICE CLIENT, DIDN'T YOU?
UH...
SO...
COME OVER HERE!
WOO-HOO!
HEY YOUNG STUD, NEXT TIME TRY ME!
...

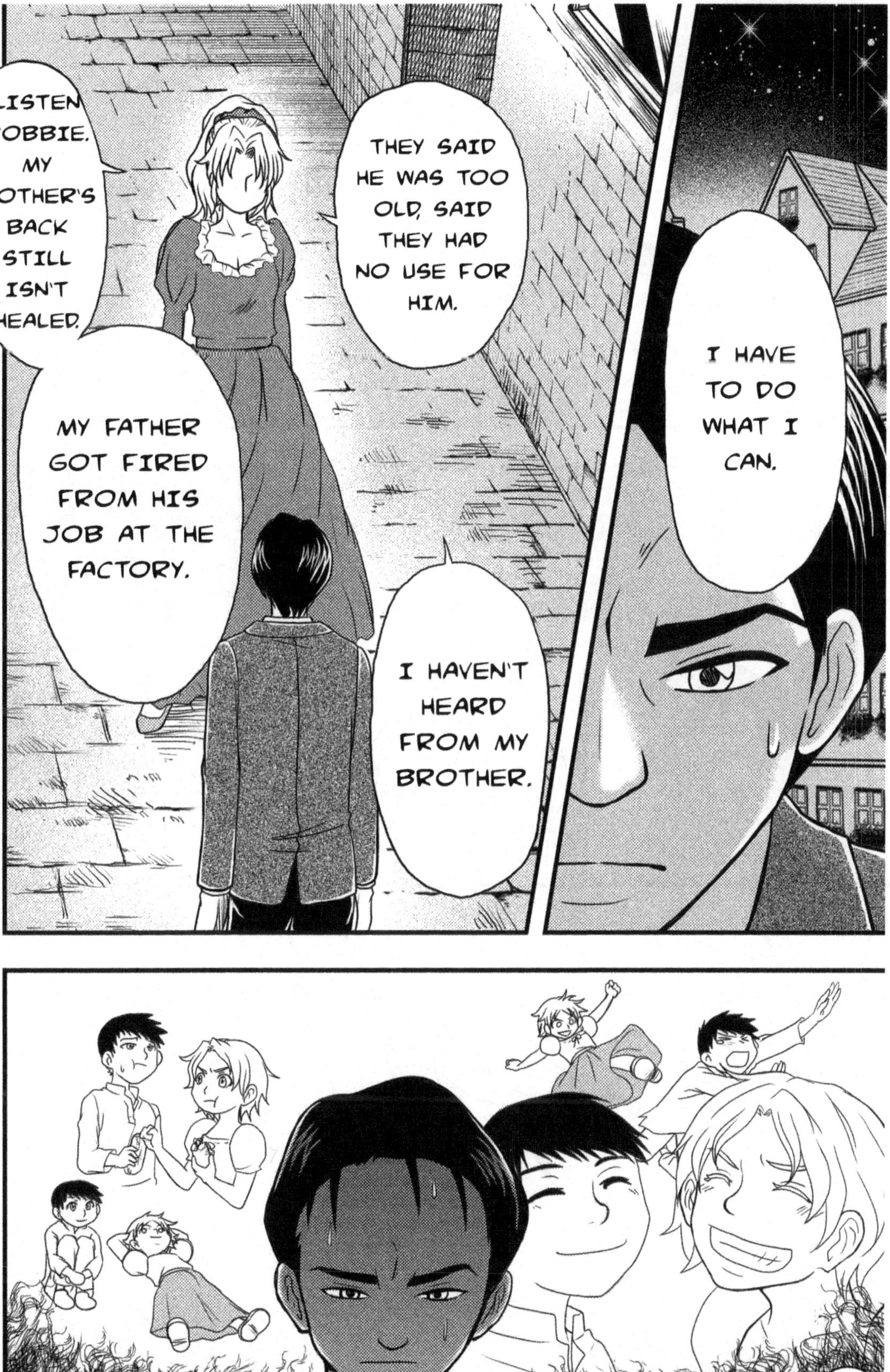
LISTEN ROBBIE. MY MOTHER'S BACK STILL ISN'T HEALED.
MY FATHER GOT FIRED FROM HIS JOB AT THE FACTORY.
THEY SAID HE WAS TOO OLD, SAID THEY HAD NO USE FOR HIM.
I HAVEN'T HEARD FROM MY BROTHER.
I HAVE TO DO WHAT I CAN.

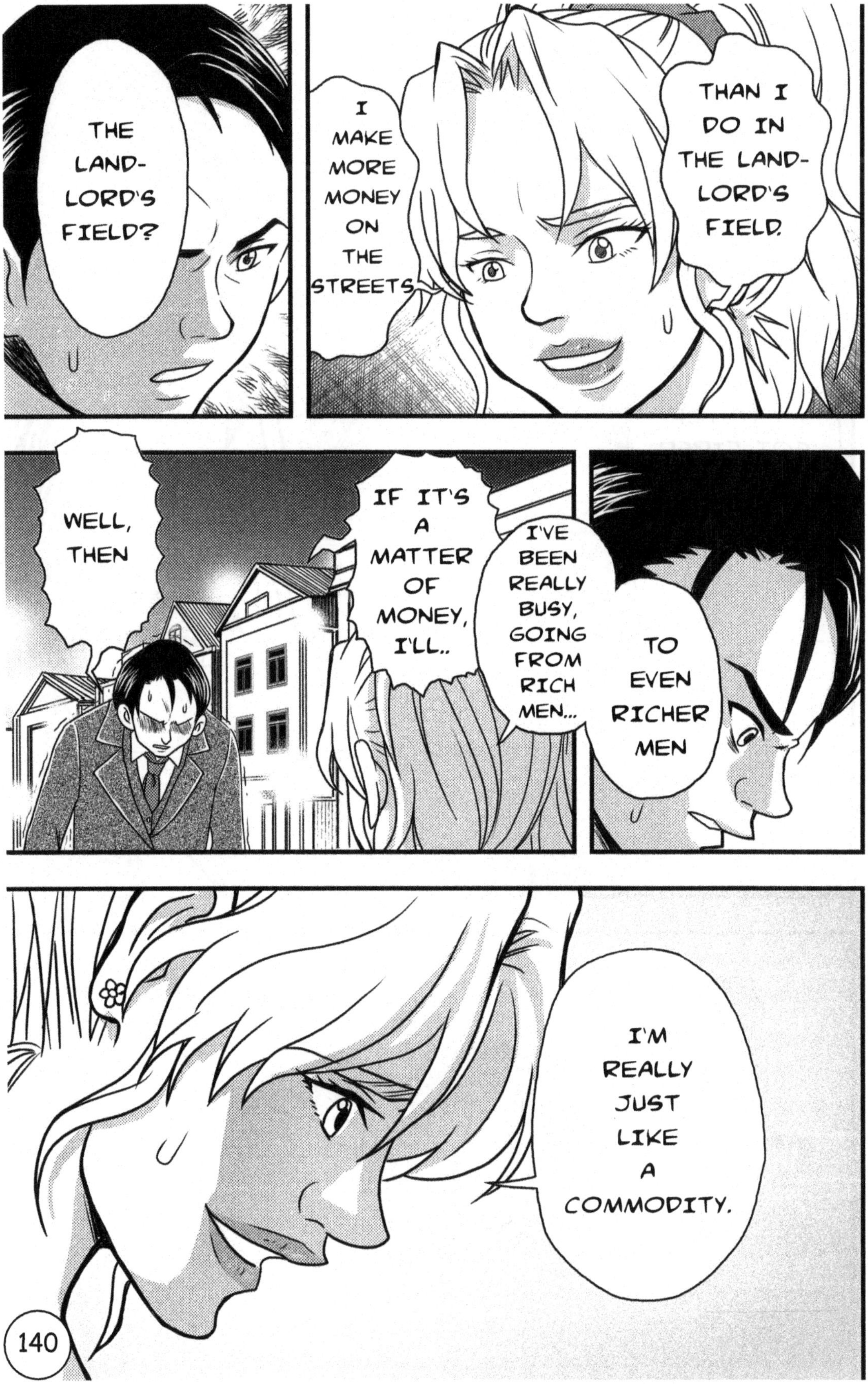
THE LAND-LORD'S FIELD?
I MAKE MORE MONEY ON THE STREETS
THAN I DO IN THE LAND-LORD'S FIELD.
WELL, THEN
IF IT'S A MATTER OF MONEY, I'LL..
I'VE BEEN REALLY BUSY, GOING FROM RICH MEN...
TO EVEN RICHER MEN
I'M REALLY JUST LIKE A COMMODITY.

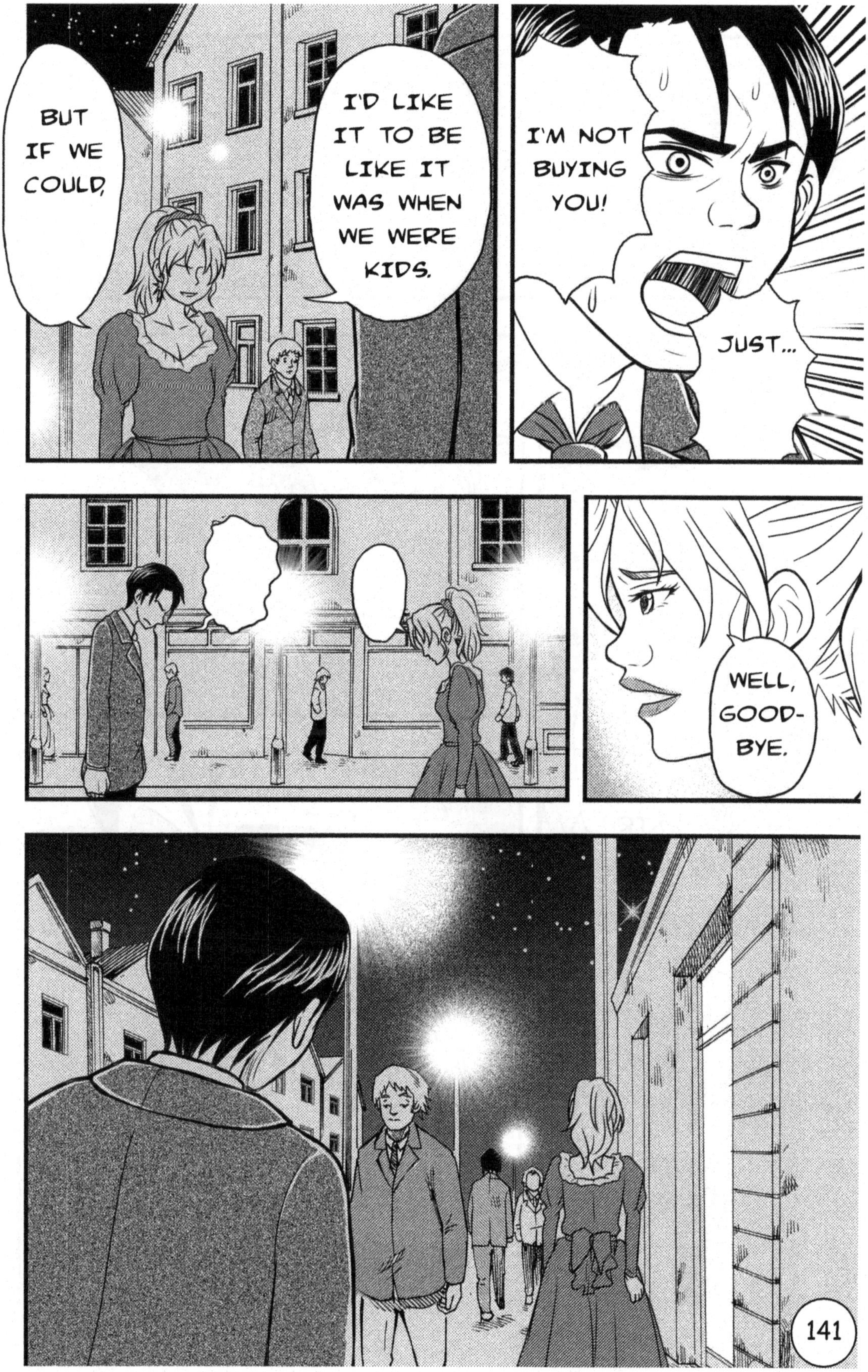
BUT IF WE COULD,
I'D LIKE IT TO BE LIKE IT WAS WHEN WE WERE KIDS.
I'M NOT BUYING YOU!
JUST...
WELL, GOOD-BYE.

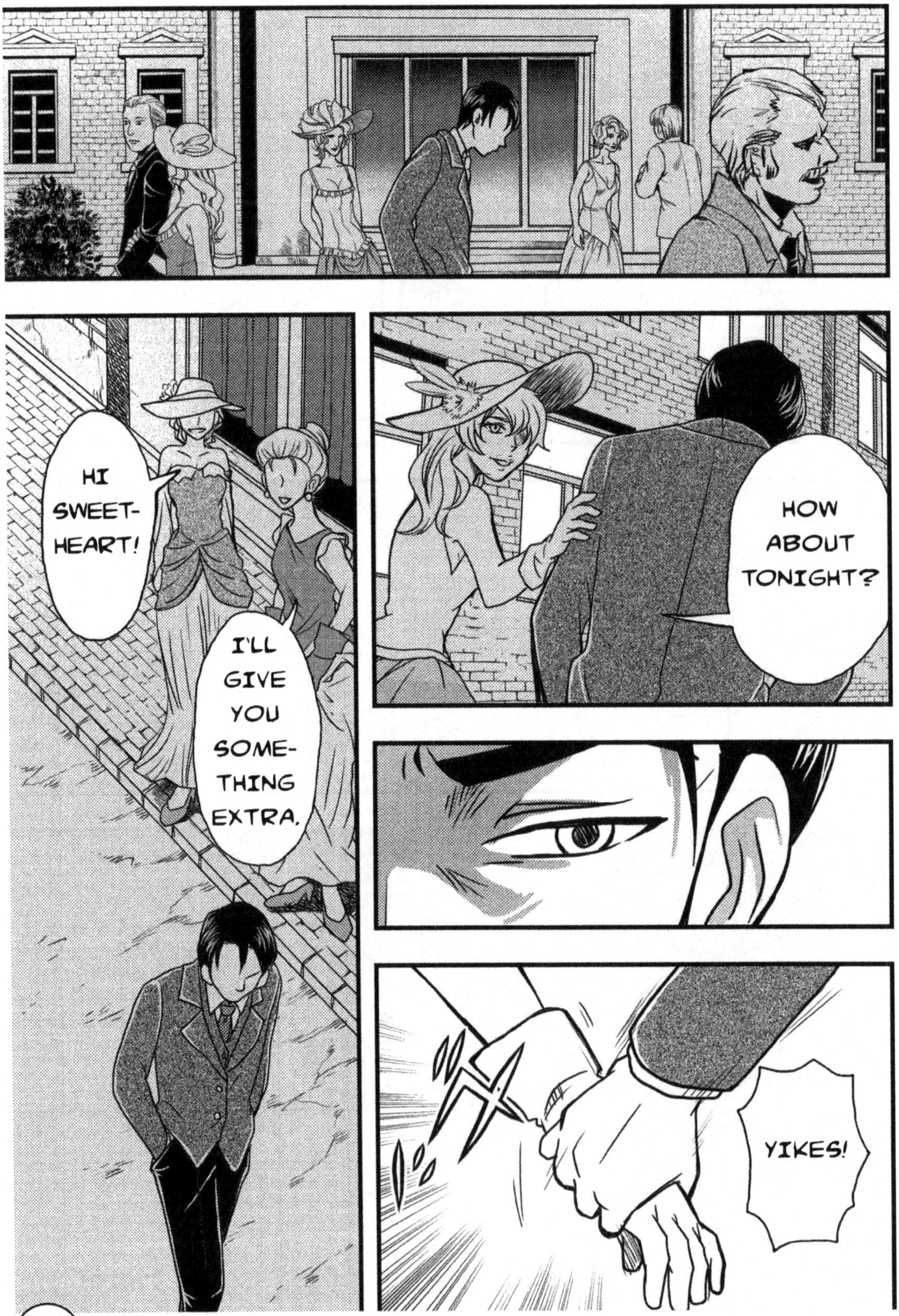
HI SWEET-HEART!
I'LL GIVE YOU SOME-THING EXTRA.
HOW ABOUT TONIGHT?
YIKES!

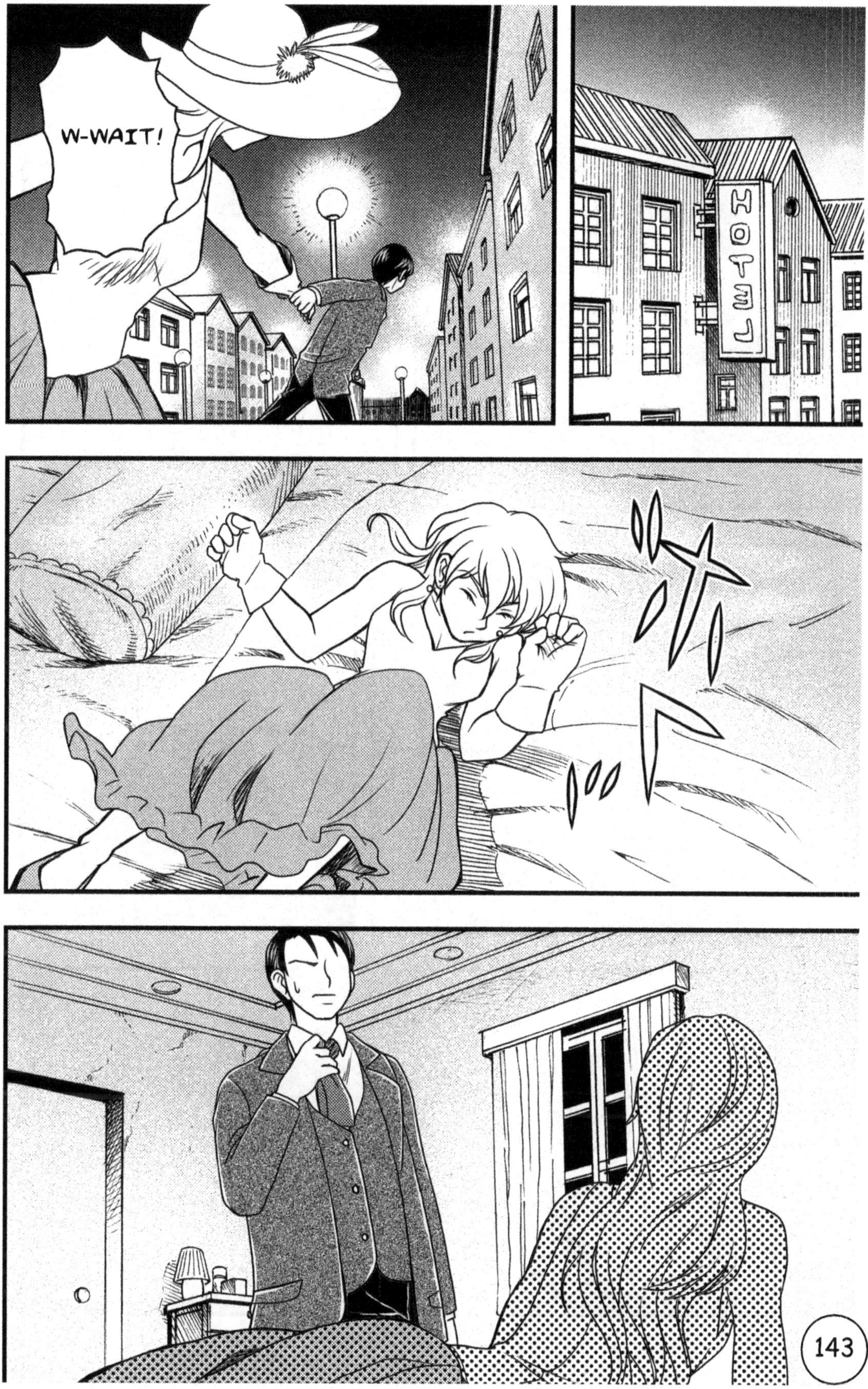
W-WAIT!
HOTEL

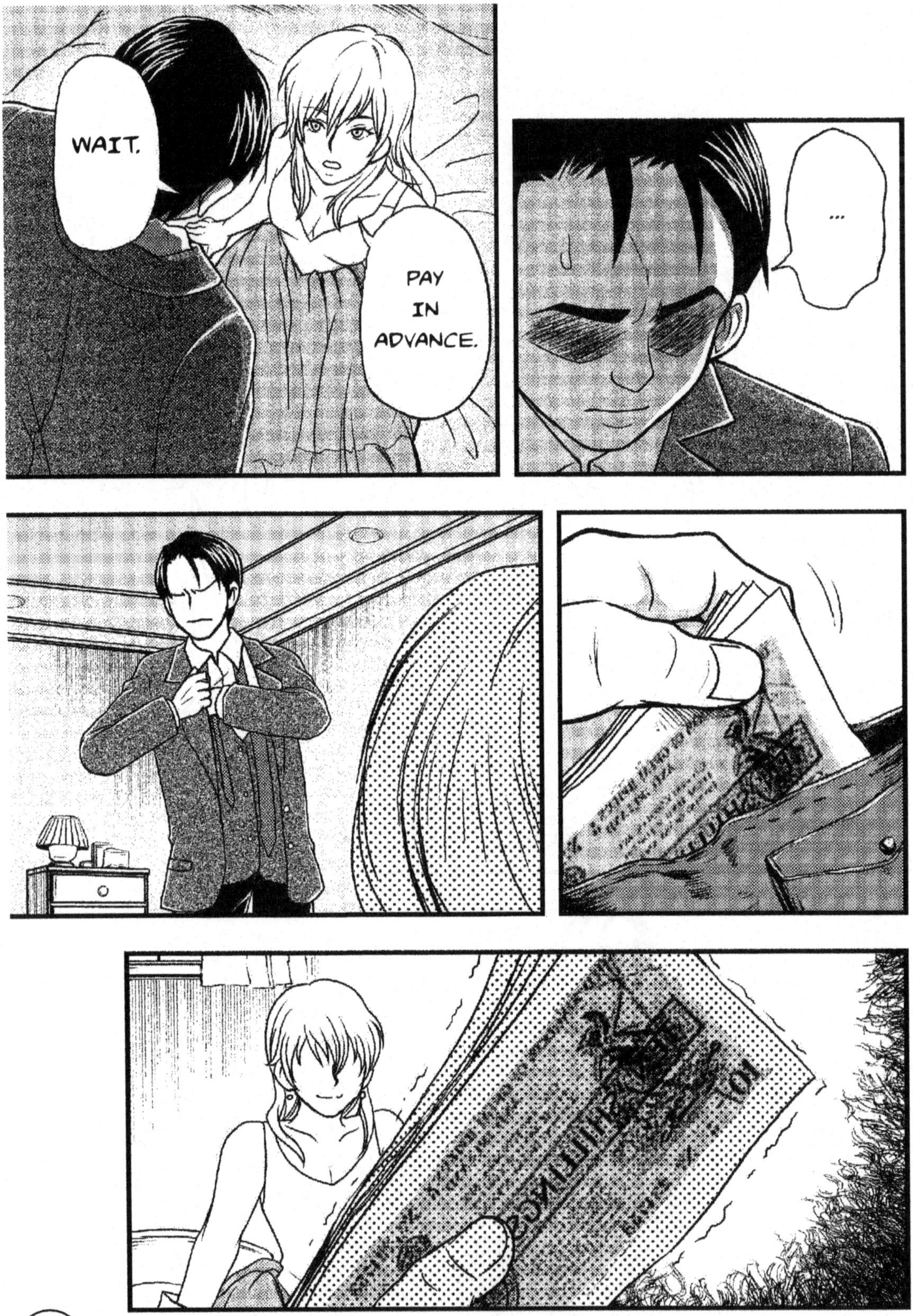
WAIT.
PAY IN ADVANCE.
...

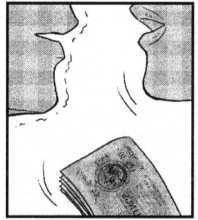

WHAT'S THIS? YOU'RE TREM-BLING?

!

WHAT HAPPENED TO ALL THAT ENERGY?

AYEE!

VALUE

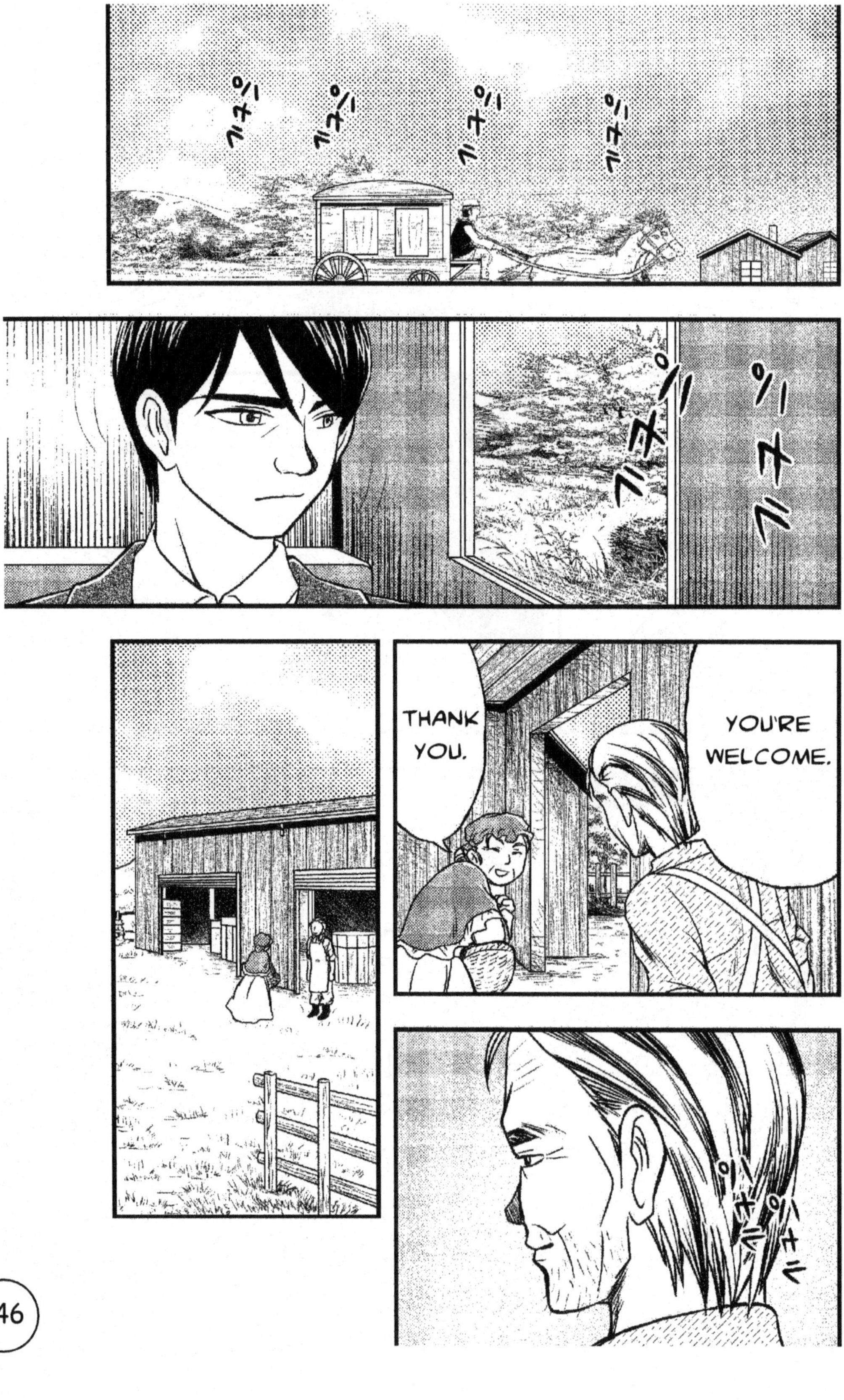
THANK YOU.
YOU'RE WELCOME.

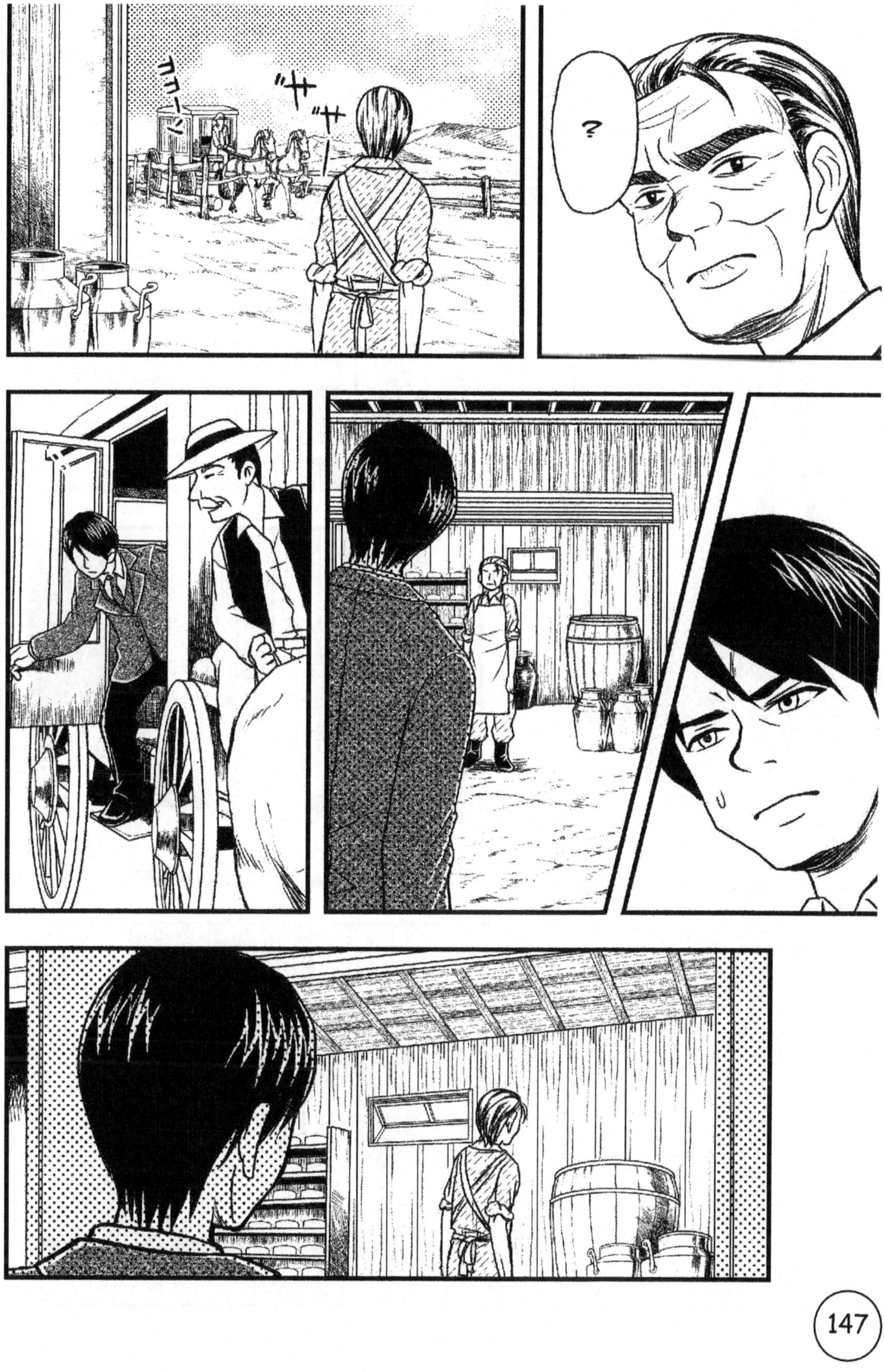
ザッ
ザッ
?

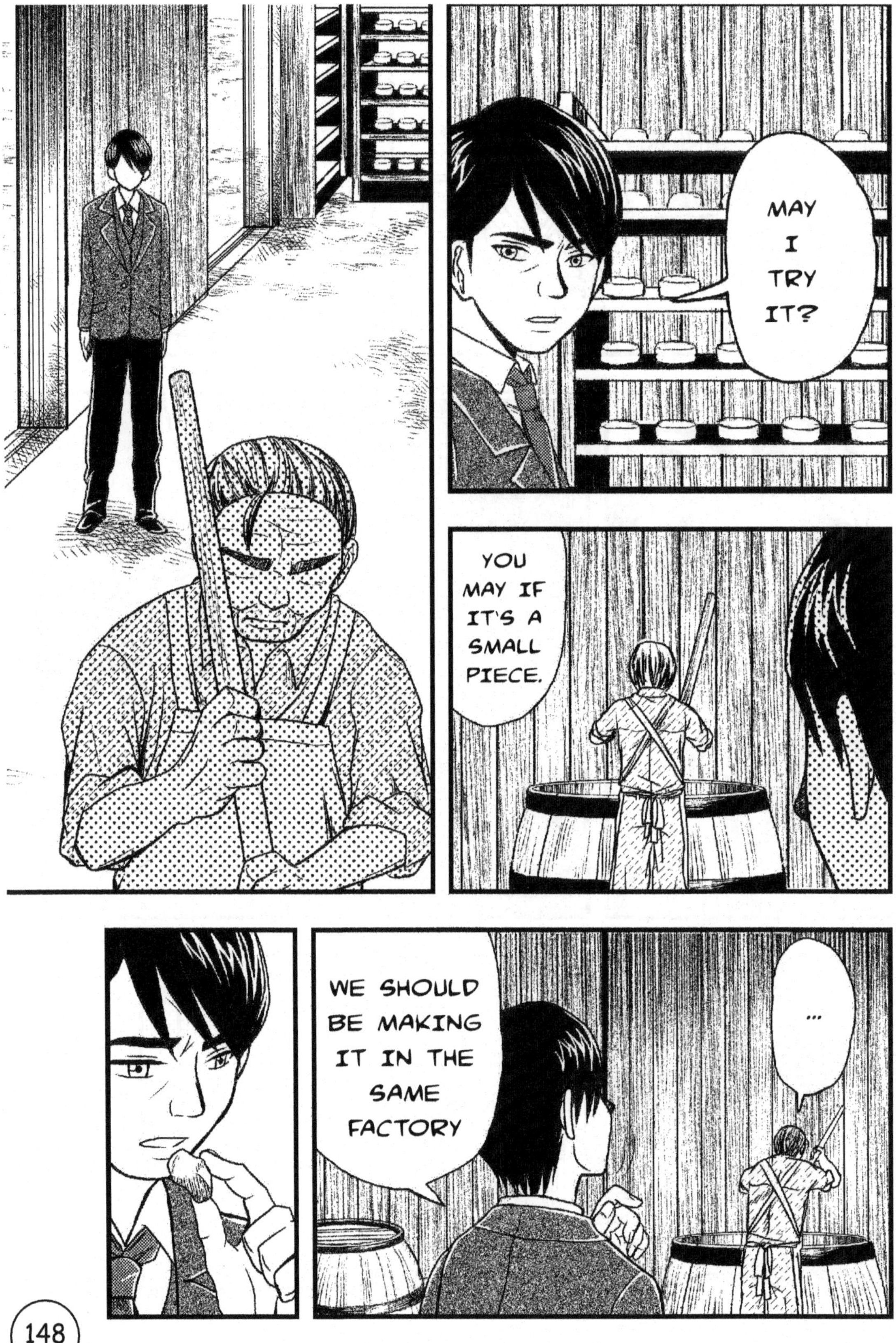
MAY I TRY IT?
YOU MAY IF IT'S A SMALL PIECE.
WE SHOULD BE MAKING IT IN THE SAME FACTORY
...

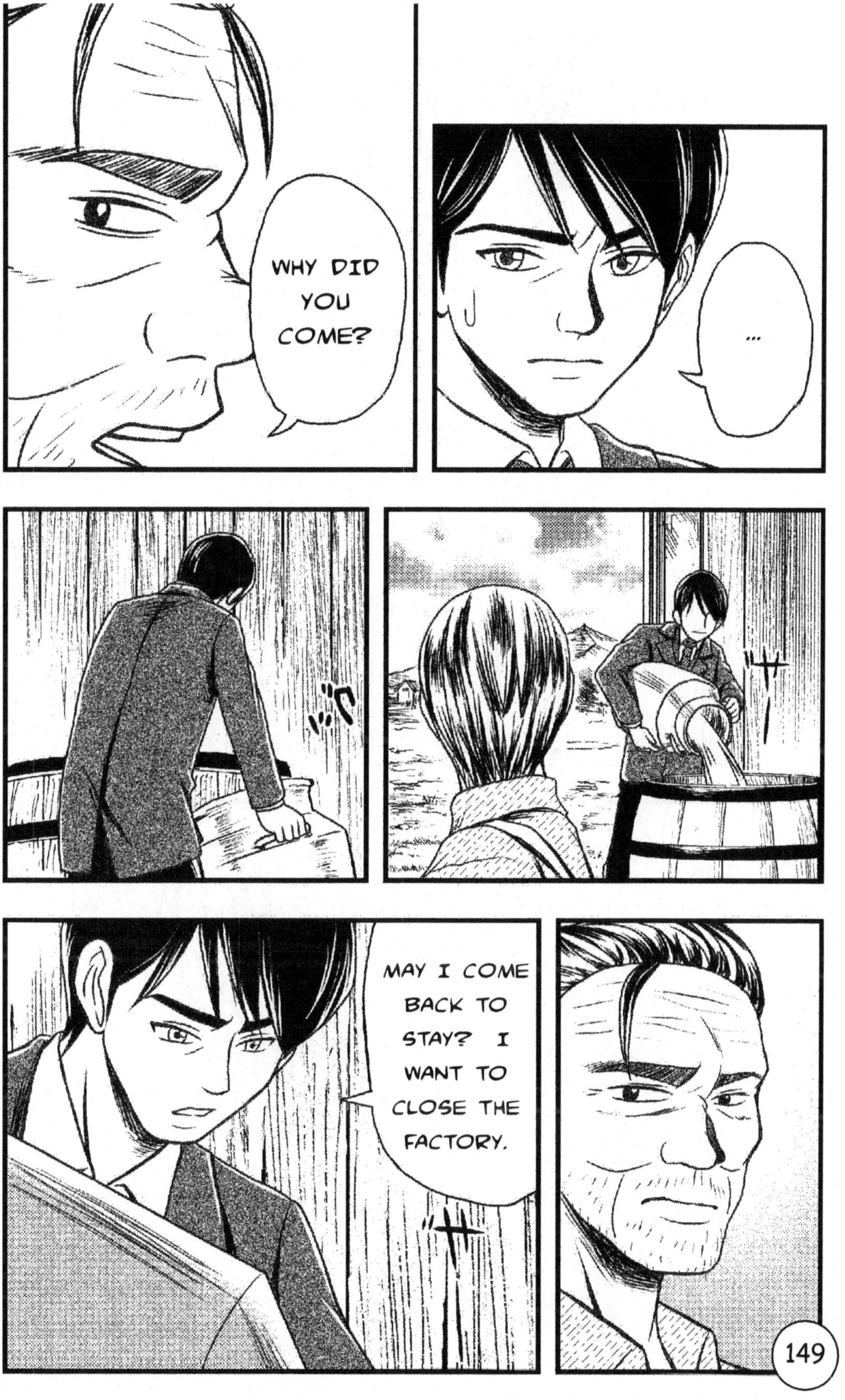
WHY DID YOU COME?
...
MAY I COME BACK TO STAY? I WANT TO CLOSE THE FACTORY.

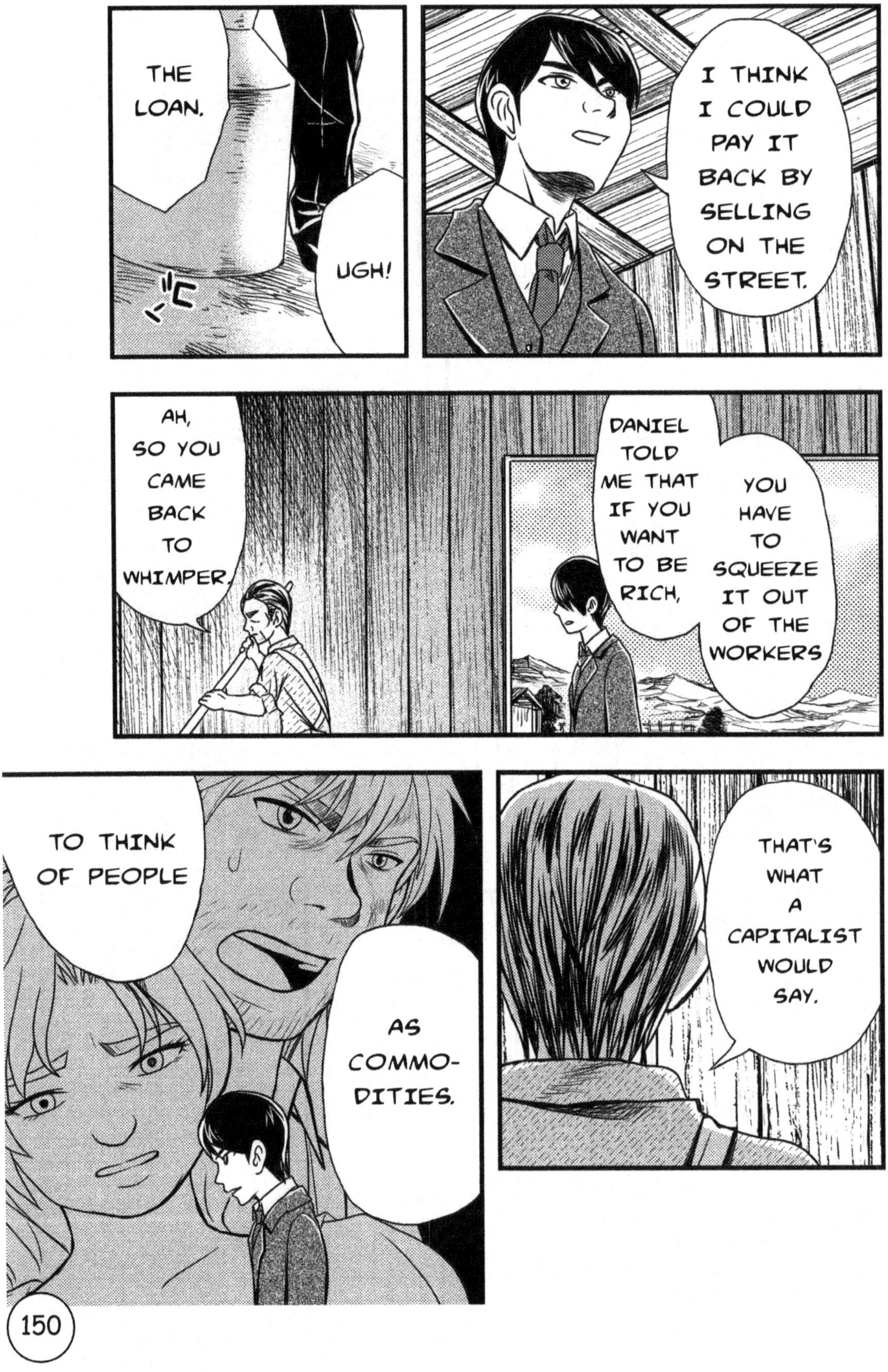
THE LOAN.
UGH!
I THINK I COULD PAY IT BACK BY SELLING ON THE STREET.
AH, SO YOU CAME BACK TO WHIMPER.
DANIEL TOLD ME THAT IF YOU WANT TO BE RICH,
YOU HAVE TO SQUEEZE IT OUT OF THE WORKERS
TO THINK OF PEOPLE
AS COMMODITIES.
THAT'S WHAT A CAPITALIST WOULD SAY.

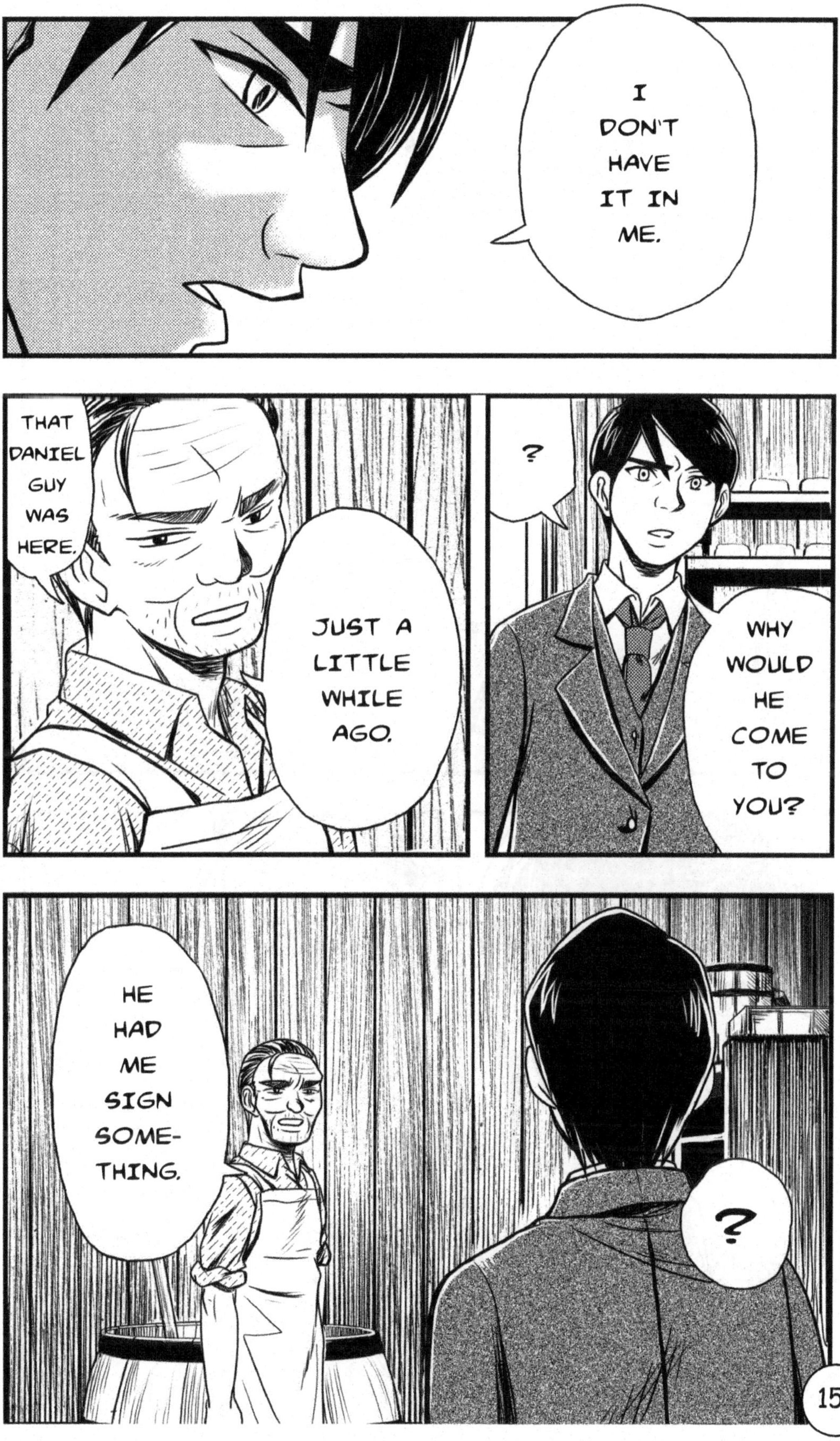
I DON'T HAVE IT IN ME.
THAT DANIEL GUY WAS HERE.
JUST A LITTLE WHILE AGO.
?
WHY WOULD HE COME TO YOU?
HE HAD ME SIGN SOME-THING.
?

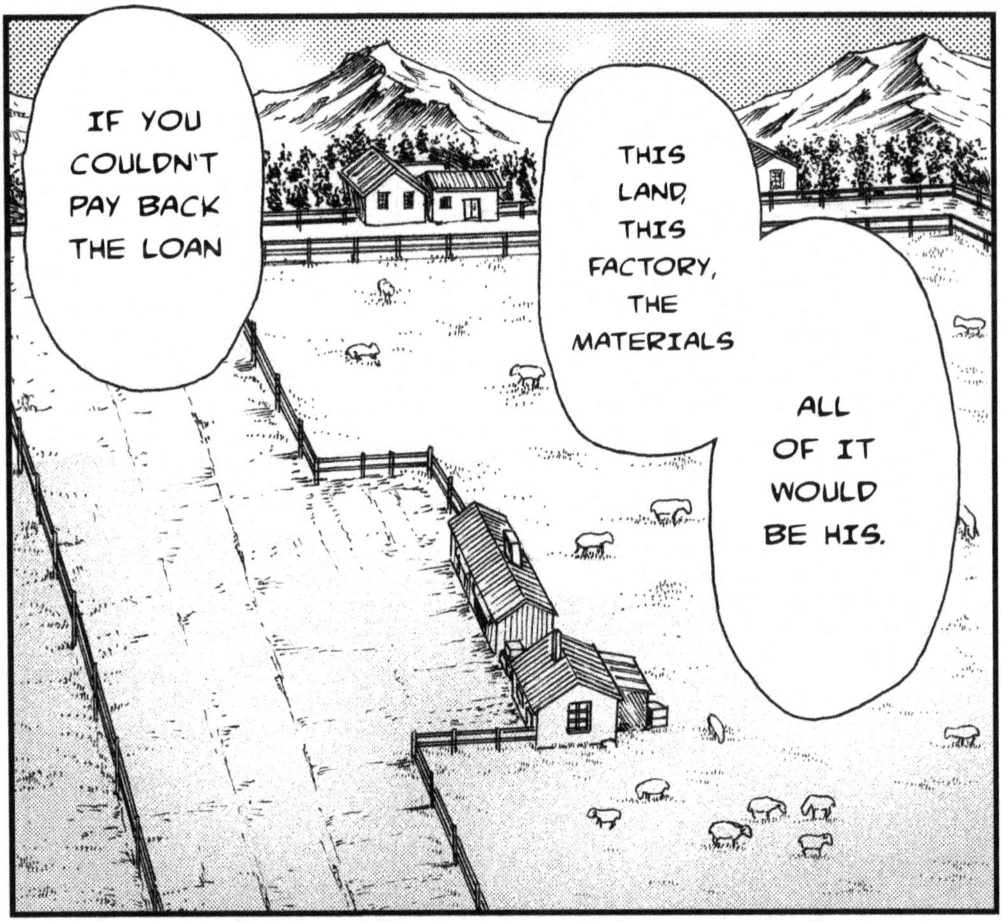
IF YOU COULDN'T PAY BACK THE LOAN
THIS LAND, THIS FACTORY, THE MATERIALS
ALL OF IT WOULD BE HIS.

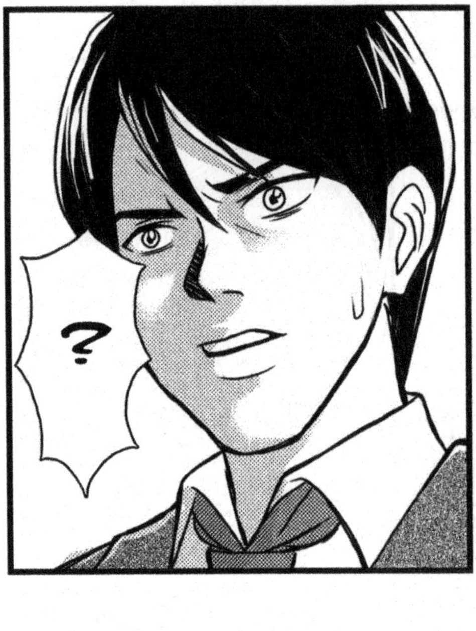
?

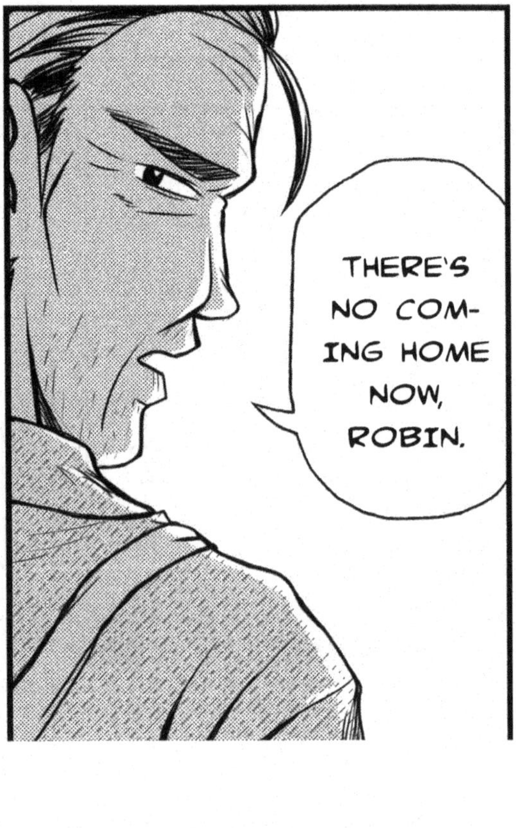
THERE'S NO COM-ING HOME NOW, ROBIN.

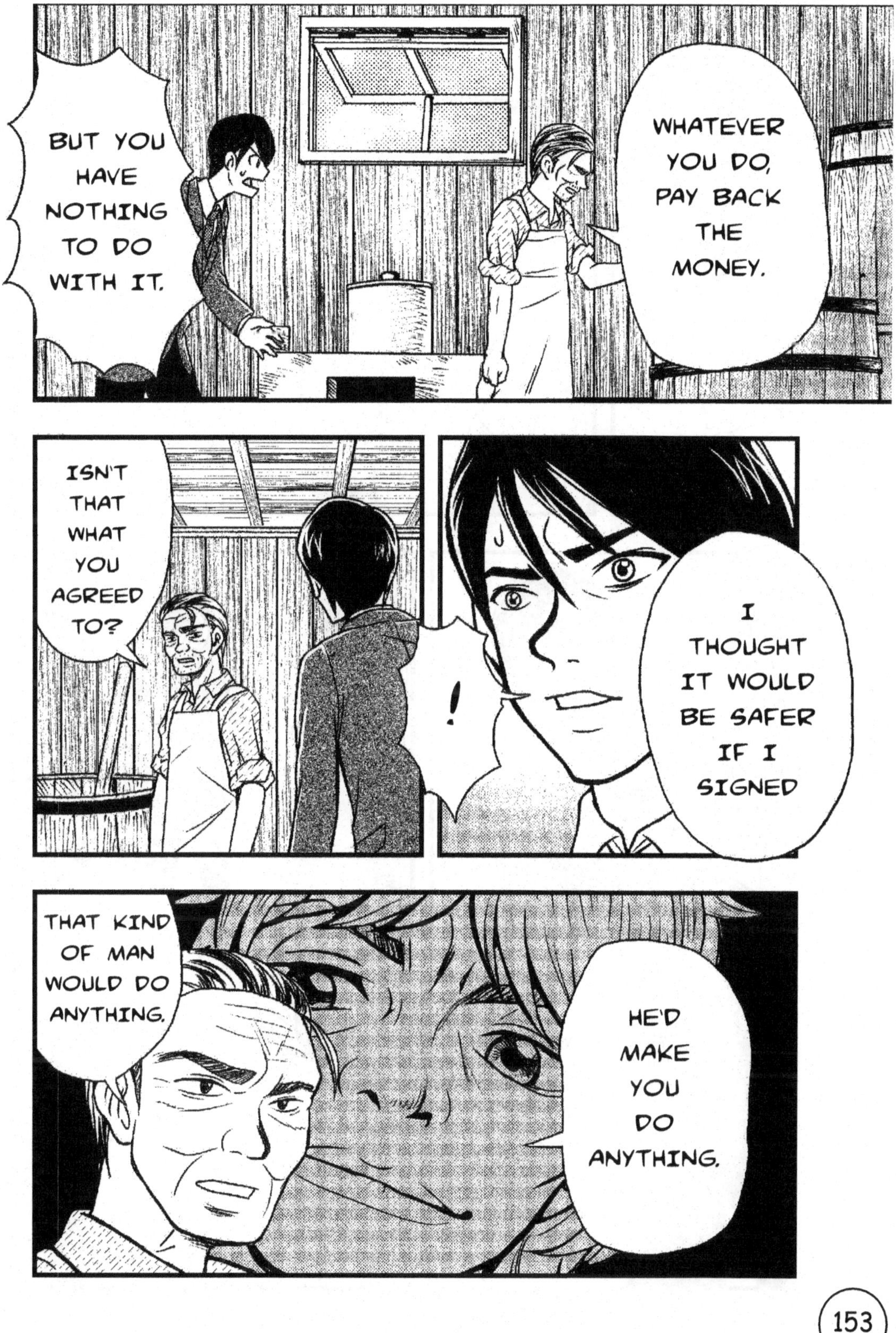
BUT YOU HAVE NOTHING TO DO WITH IT.
WHATEVER YOU DO, PAY BACK THE MONEY.
ISN'T THAT WHAT YOU AGREED TO?
!
I THOUGHT IT WOULD BE SAFER IF I SIGNED
THAT KIND OF MAN WOULD DO ANYTHING.
HE'D MAKE YOU DO ANYTHING.

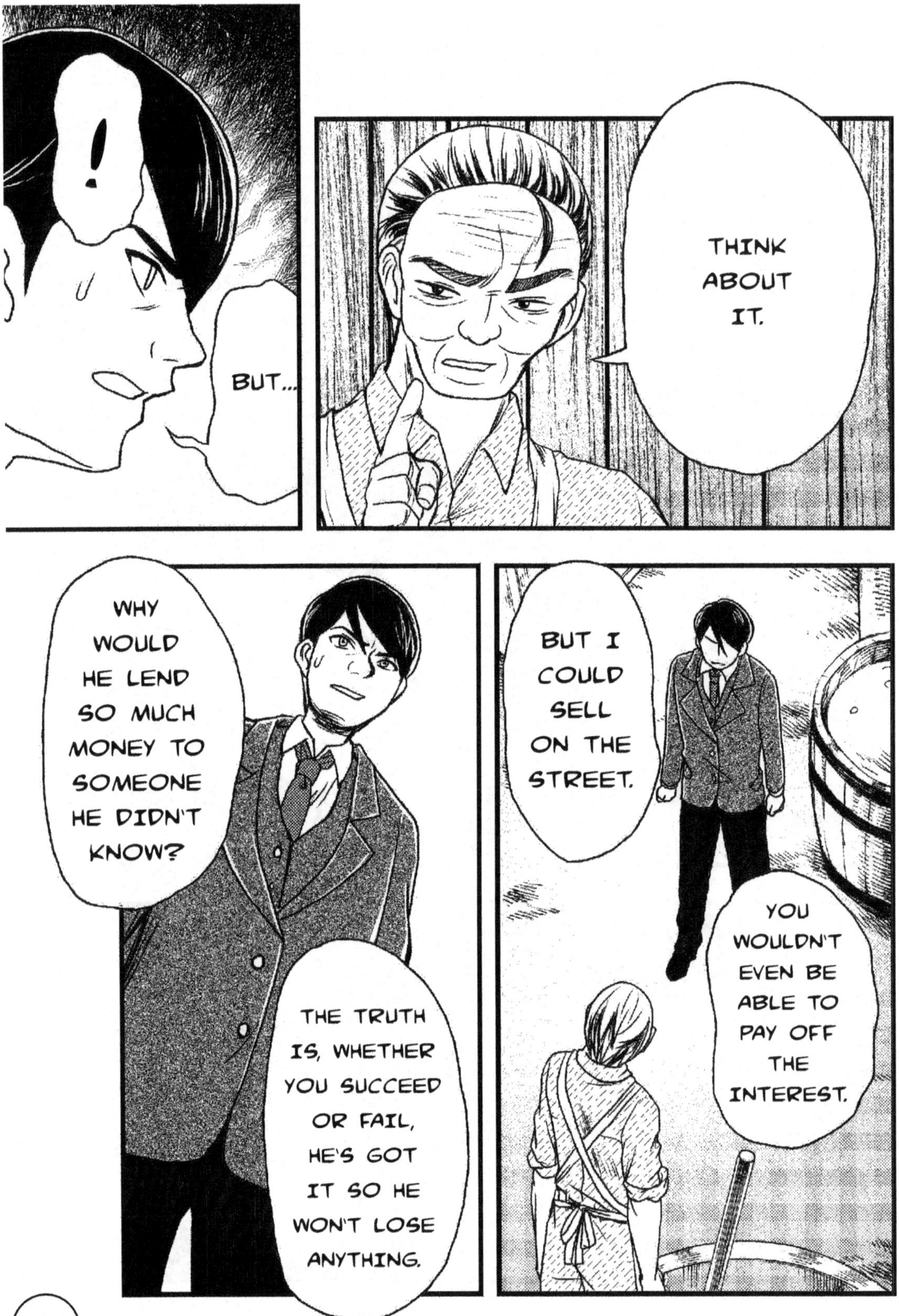
!
BUT...
THINK ABOUT IT.
WHY WOULD HE LEND SO MUCH MONEY TO SOMEONE HE DIDN'T KNOW?
THE TRUTH IS, WHETHER YOU SUCCEED OR FAIL, HE'S GOT IT SO HE WON'T LOSE ANYTHING.
BUT I COULD SELL ON THE STREET.
YOU WOULDN'T EVEN BE ABLE TO PAY OFF THE INTEREST.

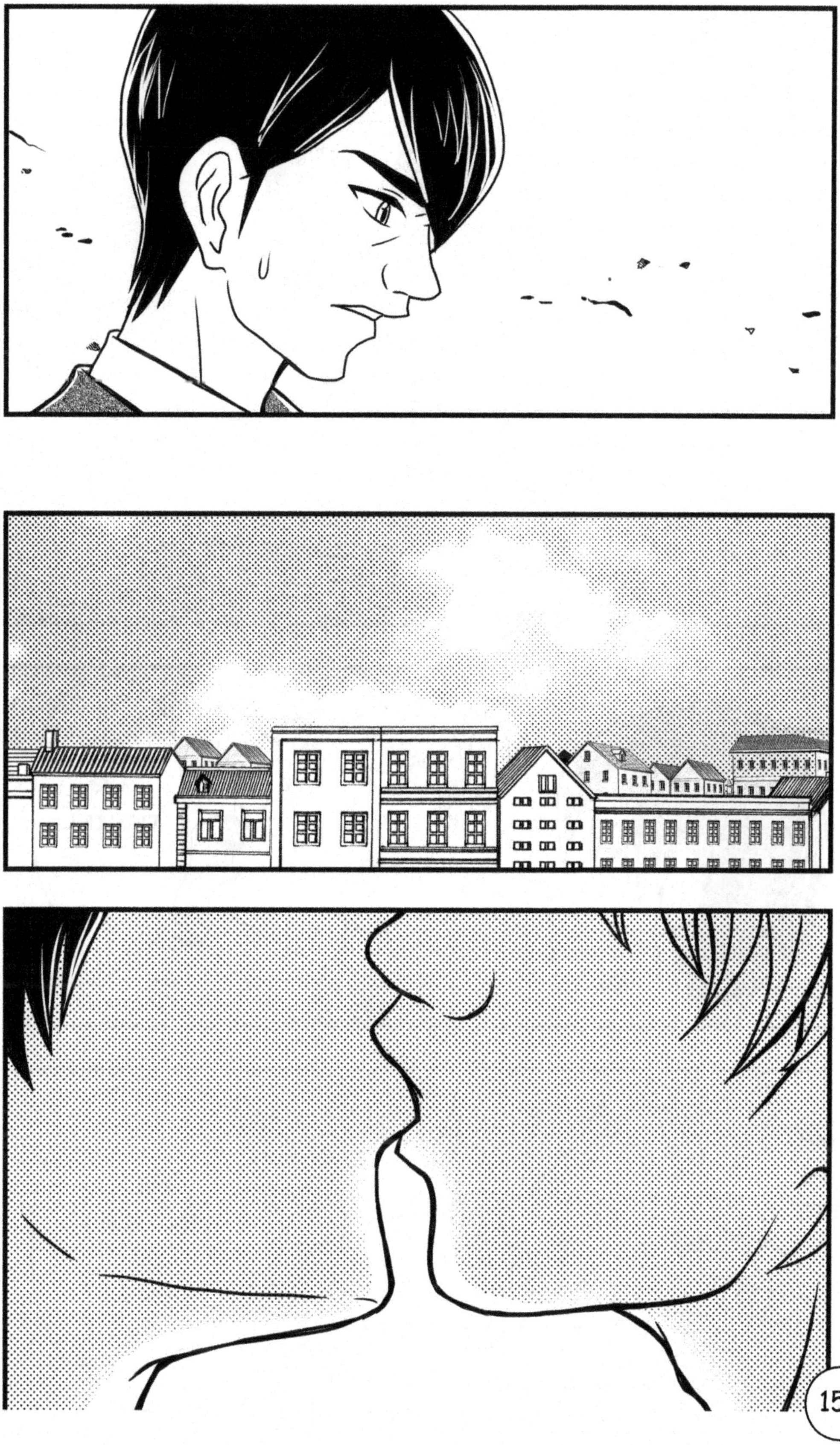

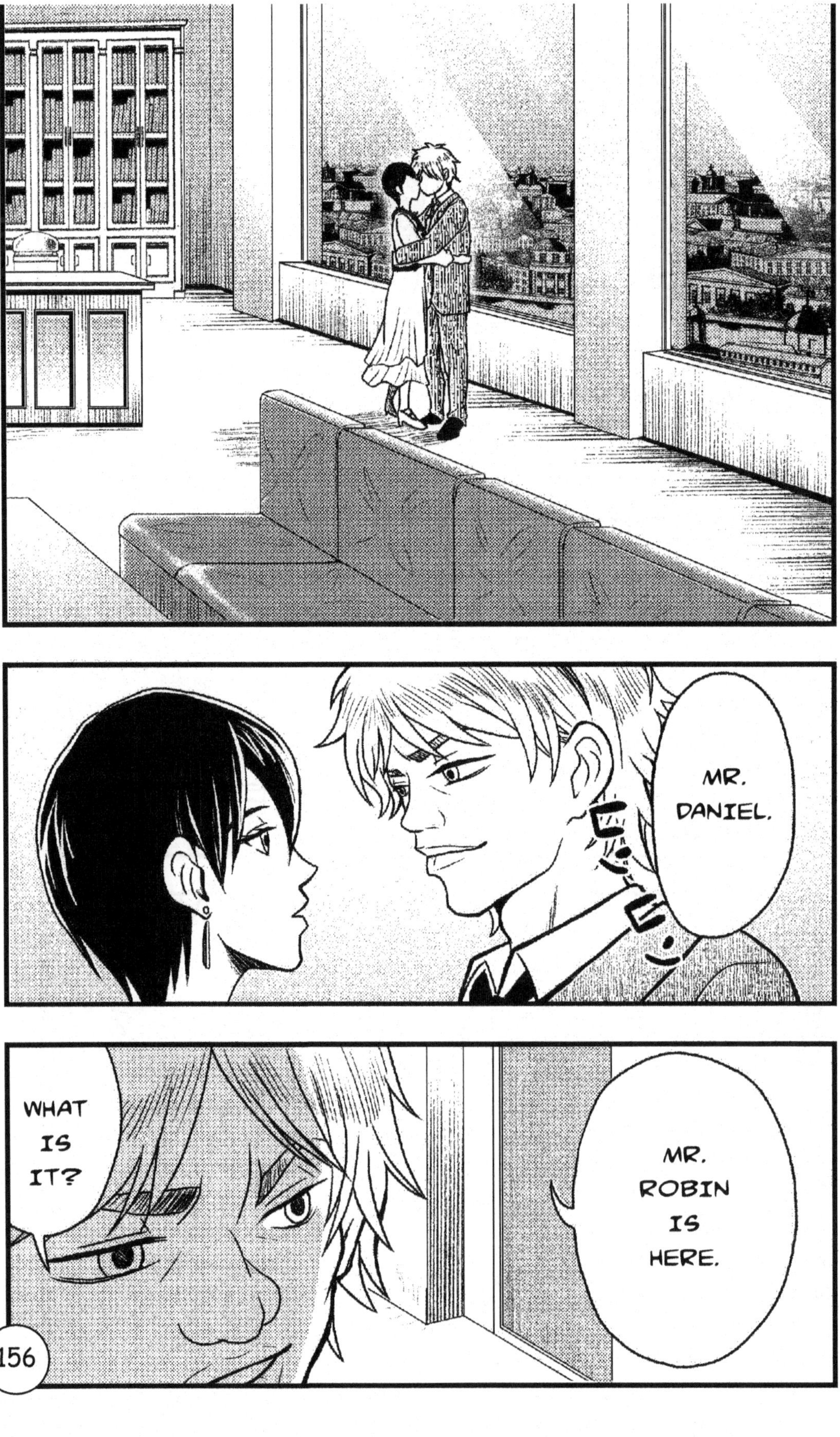
MR. DANIEL.
WHAT IS IT?
MR. ROBIN IS HERE.

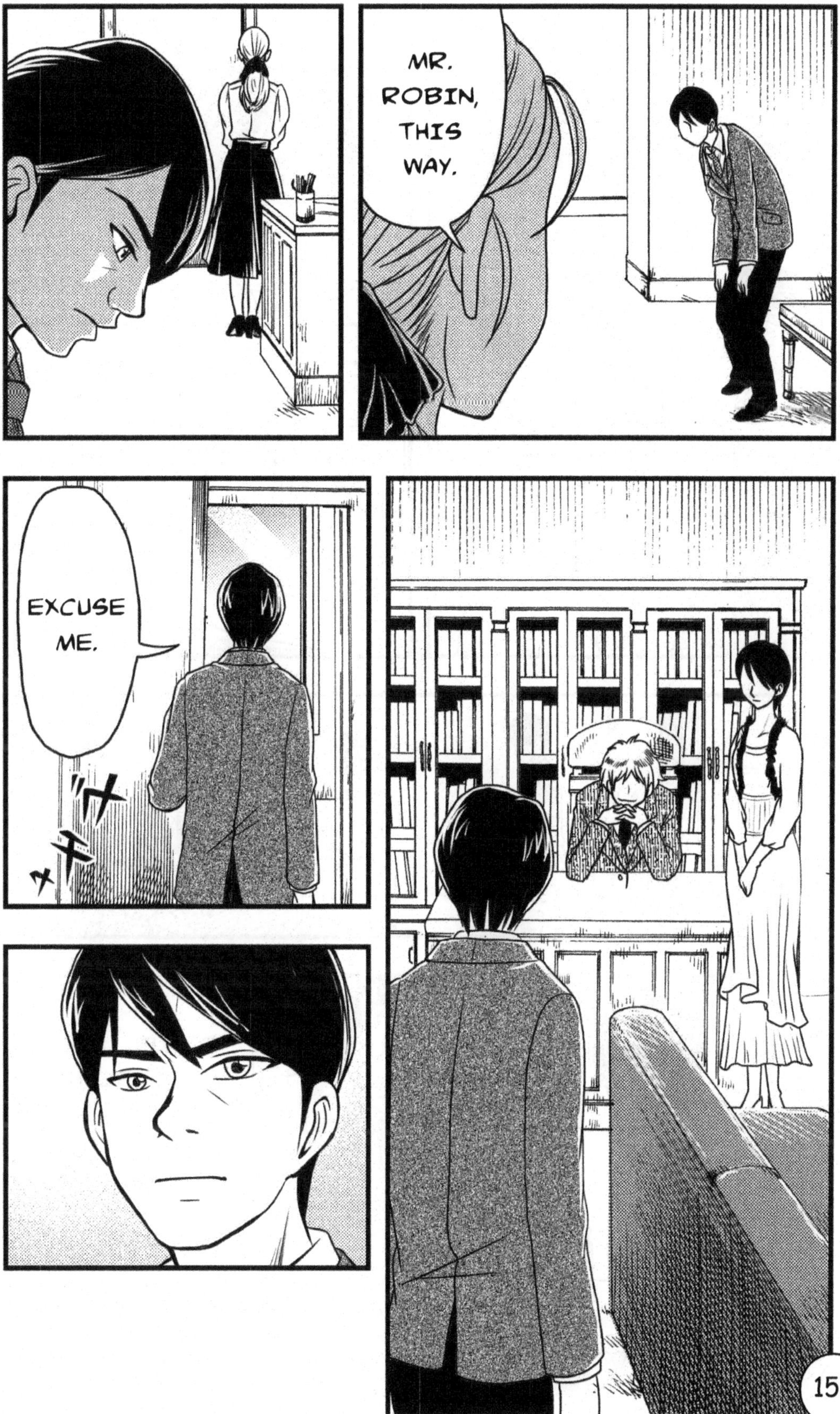
MR. ROBIN, THIS WAY.
EXCUSE ME.

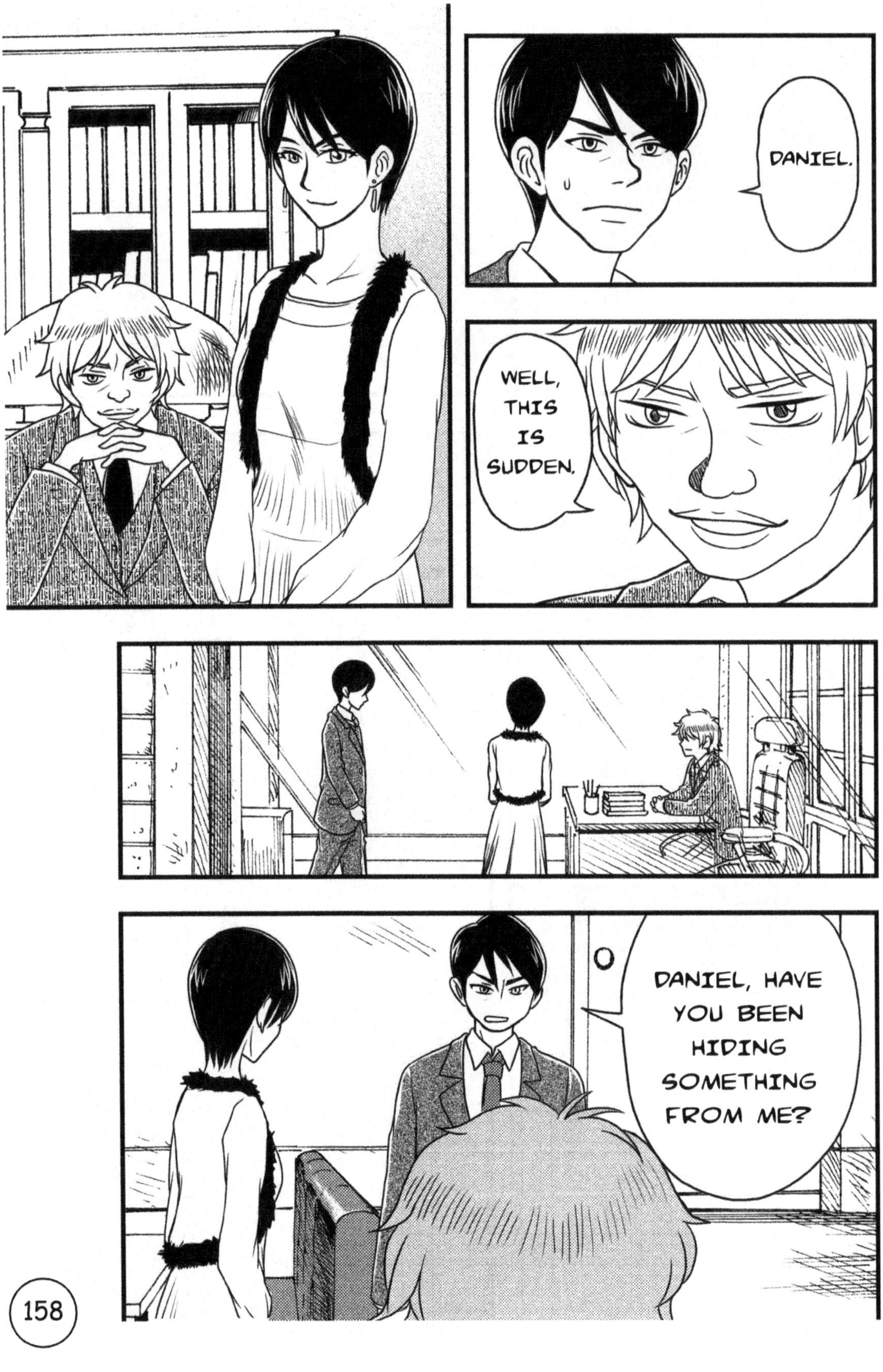
DANIEL.
WELL, THIS IS SUDDEN.
DANIEL, HAVE YOU BEEN HIDING SOMETHING FROM ME?

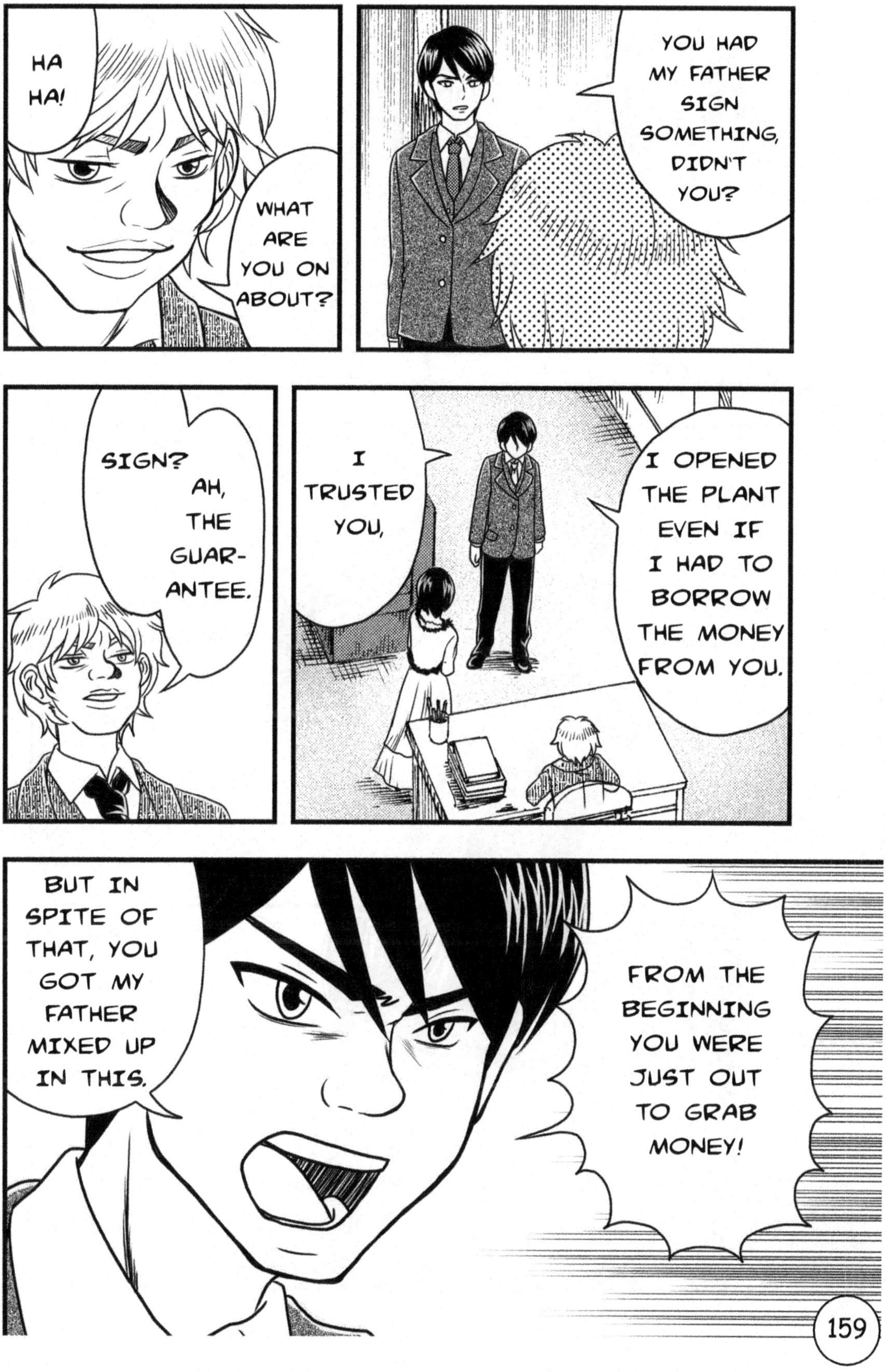
HA HA!
WHAT ARE YOU ON ABOUT?
YOU HAD MY FATHER SIGN SOMETHING, DIDN'T YOU?
SIGN? AH, THE GUAR-ANTEE.
I TRUSTED YOU,
I OPENED THE PLANT EVEN IF I HAD TO BORROW THE MONEY FROM YOU.
BUT IN SPITE OF THAT, YOU GOT MY FATHER MIXED UP IN THIS.
FROM THE BEGINNING YOU WERE JUST OUT TO GRAB MONEY!

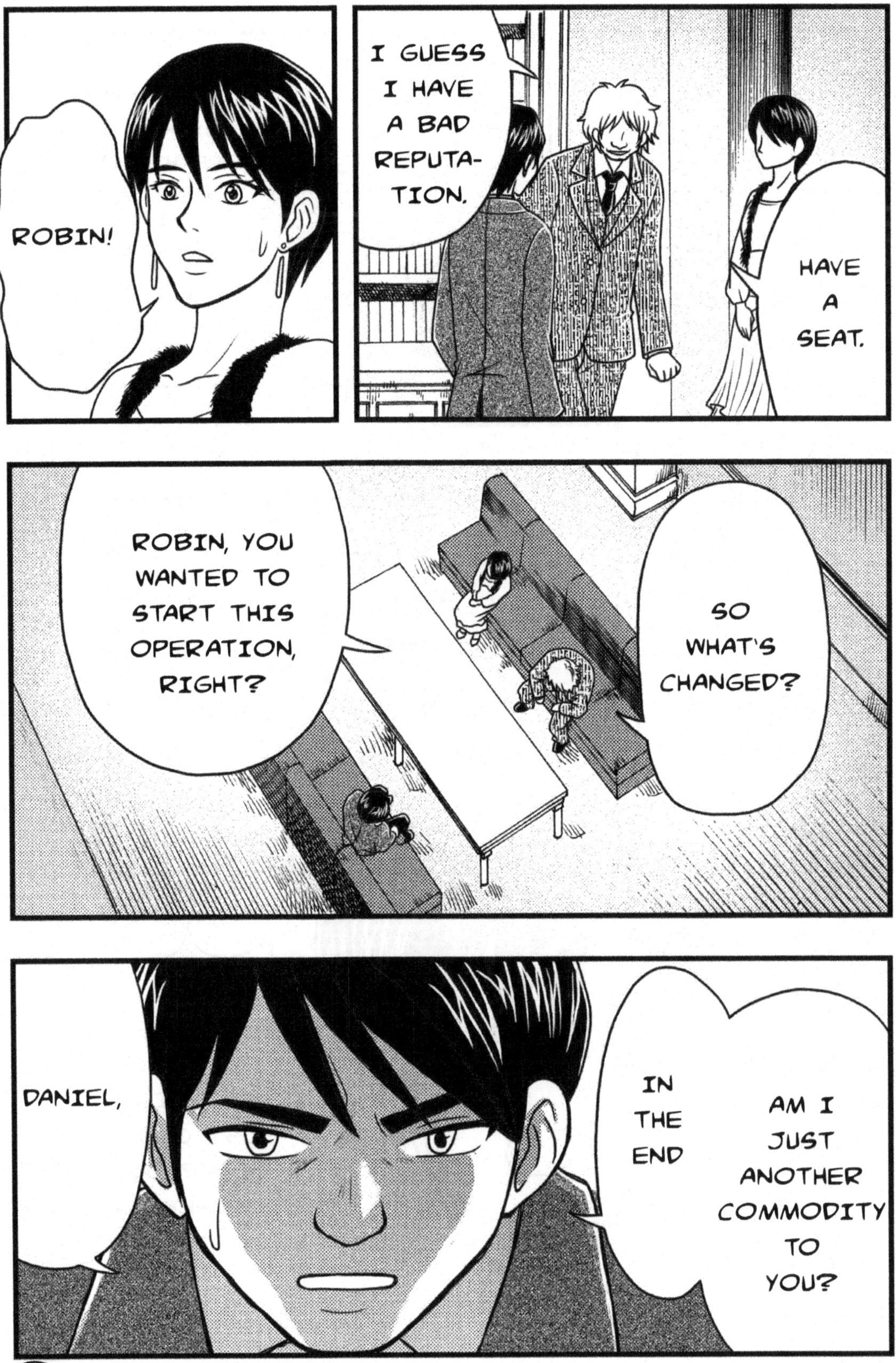
ROBIN!
I GUESS I HAVE A BAD REPUTATION.
HAVE A SEAT.
ROBIN, YOU WANTED TO START THIS OPERATION, RIGHT?
SO WHAT'S CHANGED?
DANIEL,
IN THE END
AM I JUST ANOTHER COMMODITY TO YOU?

... C-COMMODI-TY?

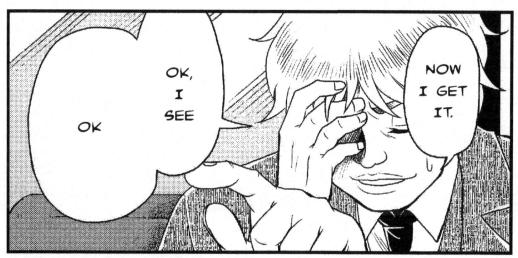

OK

OK, I SEE

NOW I GET IT.

THERE'S SOMETHING BASIC YOU DON'T UNDERSTAND.

I INVESTED IN YOU, SO YOU HAVE TO PRODUCE RESULTS.

IF YOU CAN'T DO THAT...

161

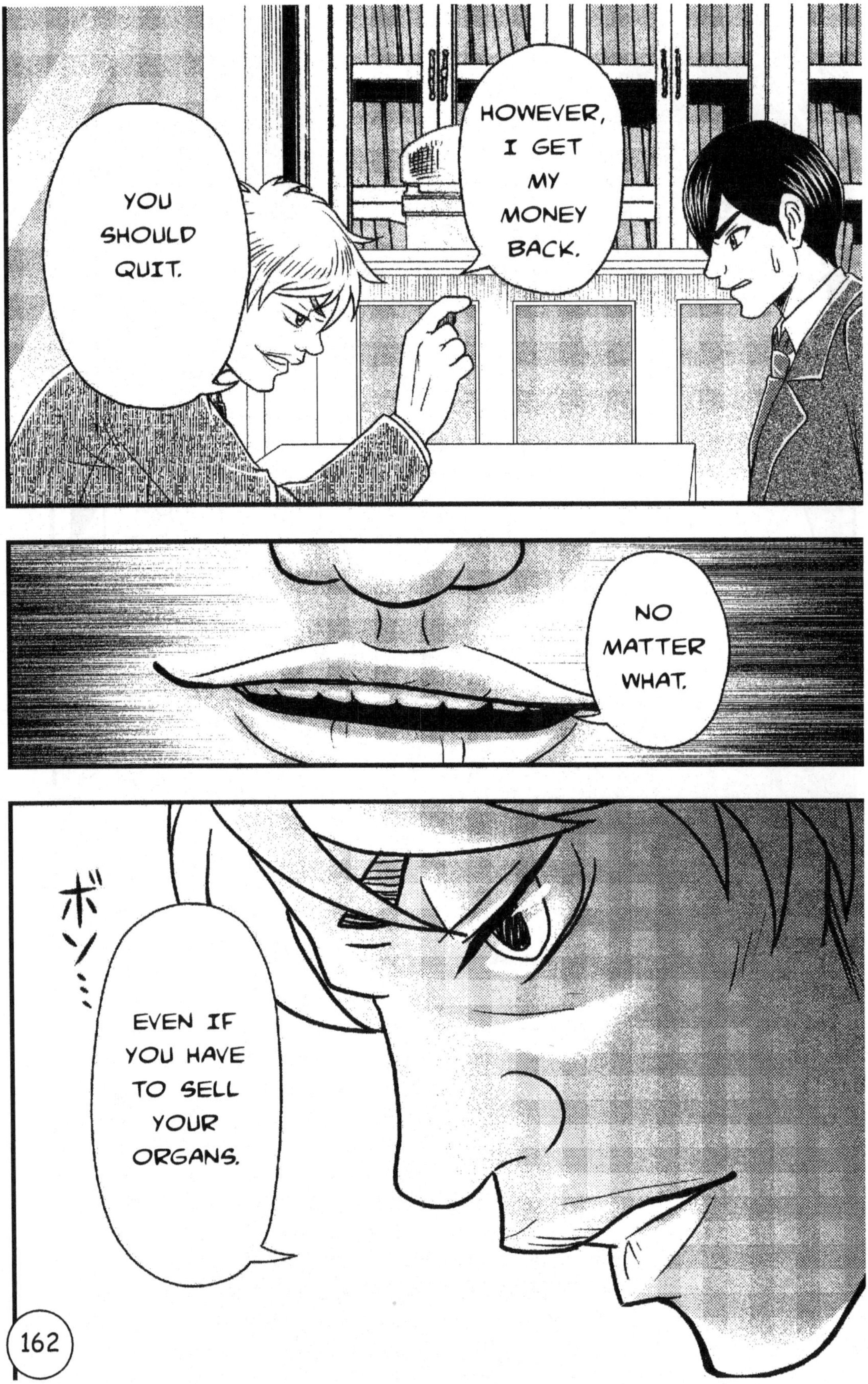
YOU SHOULD QUIT.
HOWEVER, I GET MY MONEY BACK.
NO MATTER WHAT.
ボン…
EVEN IF YOU HAVE TO SELL YOUR ORGANS.

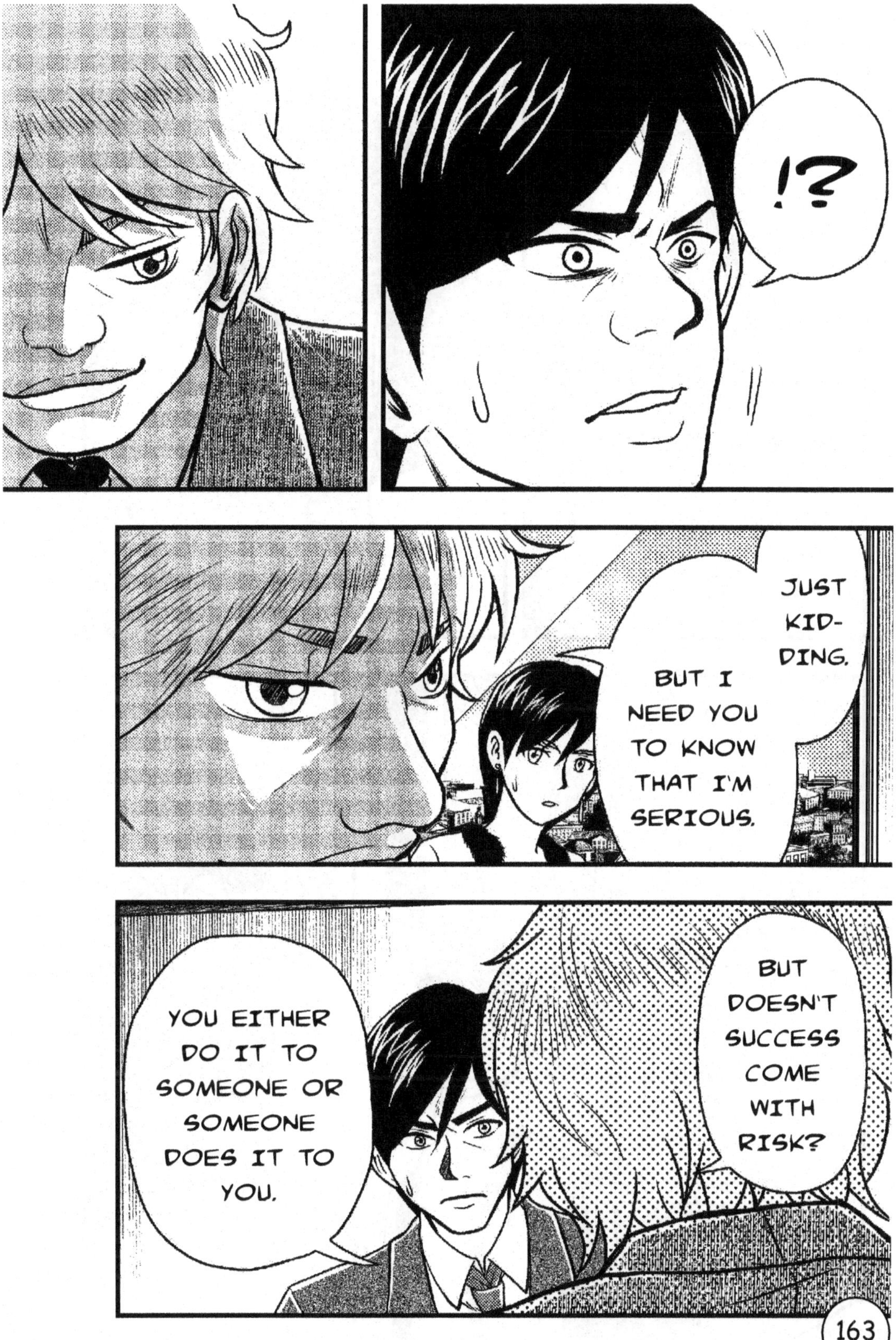
!?
JUST KID-DING.
BUT I NEED YOU TO KNOW THAT I'M SERIOUS.
YOU EITHER DO IT TO SOMEONE OR SOMEONE DOES IT TO YOU.
BUT DOESN'T SUCCESS COME WITH RISK?

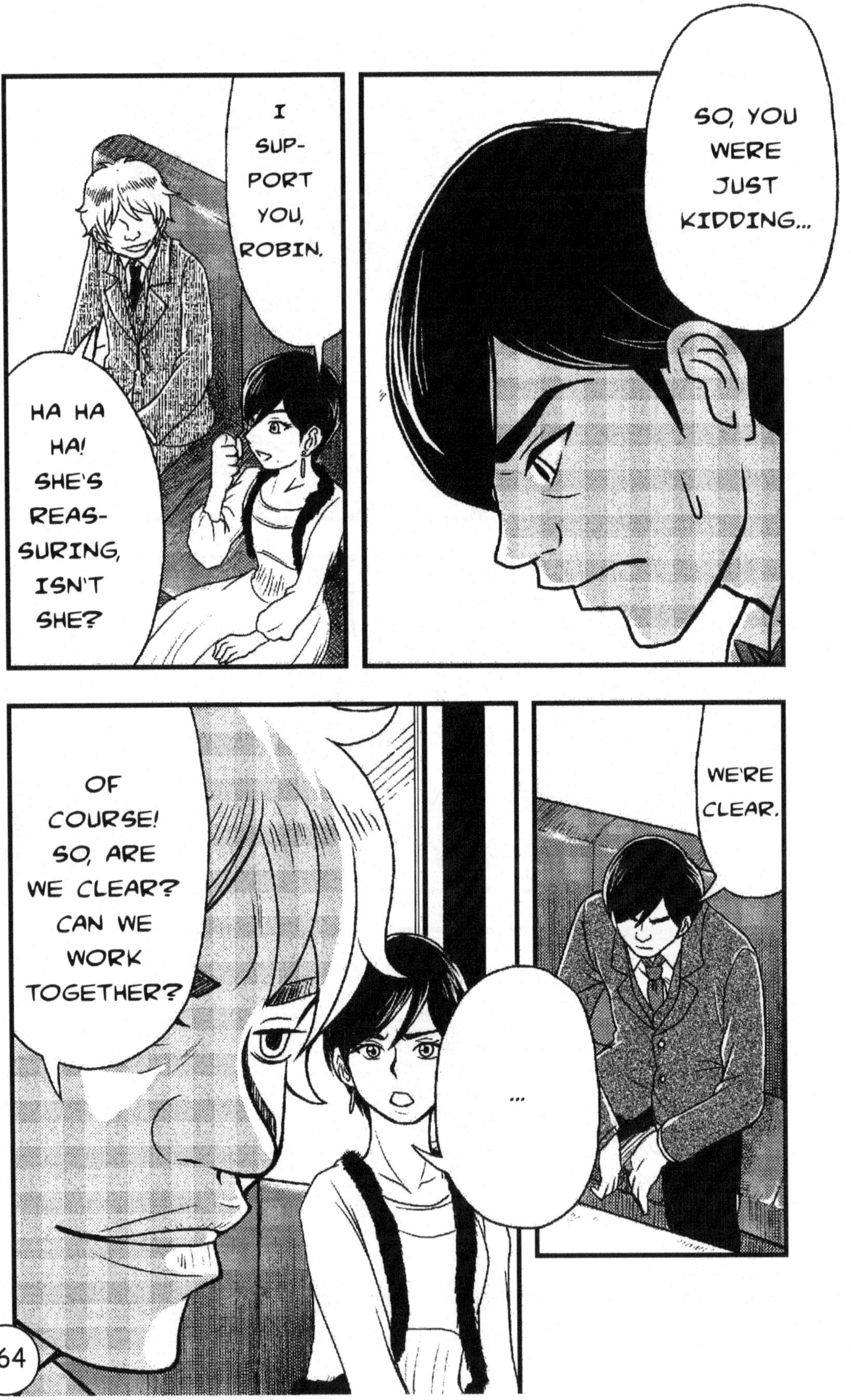
I SUP-PORT YOU, ROBIN.
HA HA HA! SHE'S REAS-SURING, ISN'T SHE?
SO, YOU WERE JUST KIDDING...
OF COURSE! SO, ARE WE CLEAR? CAN WE WORK TOGETHER?
...
WE'RE CLEAR.

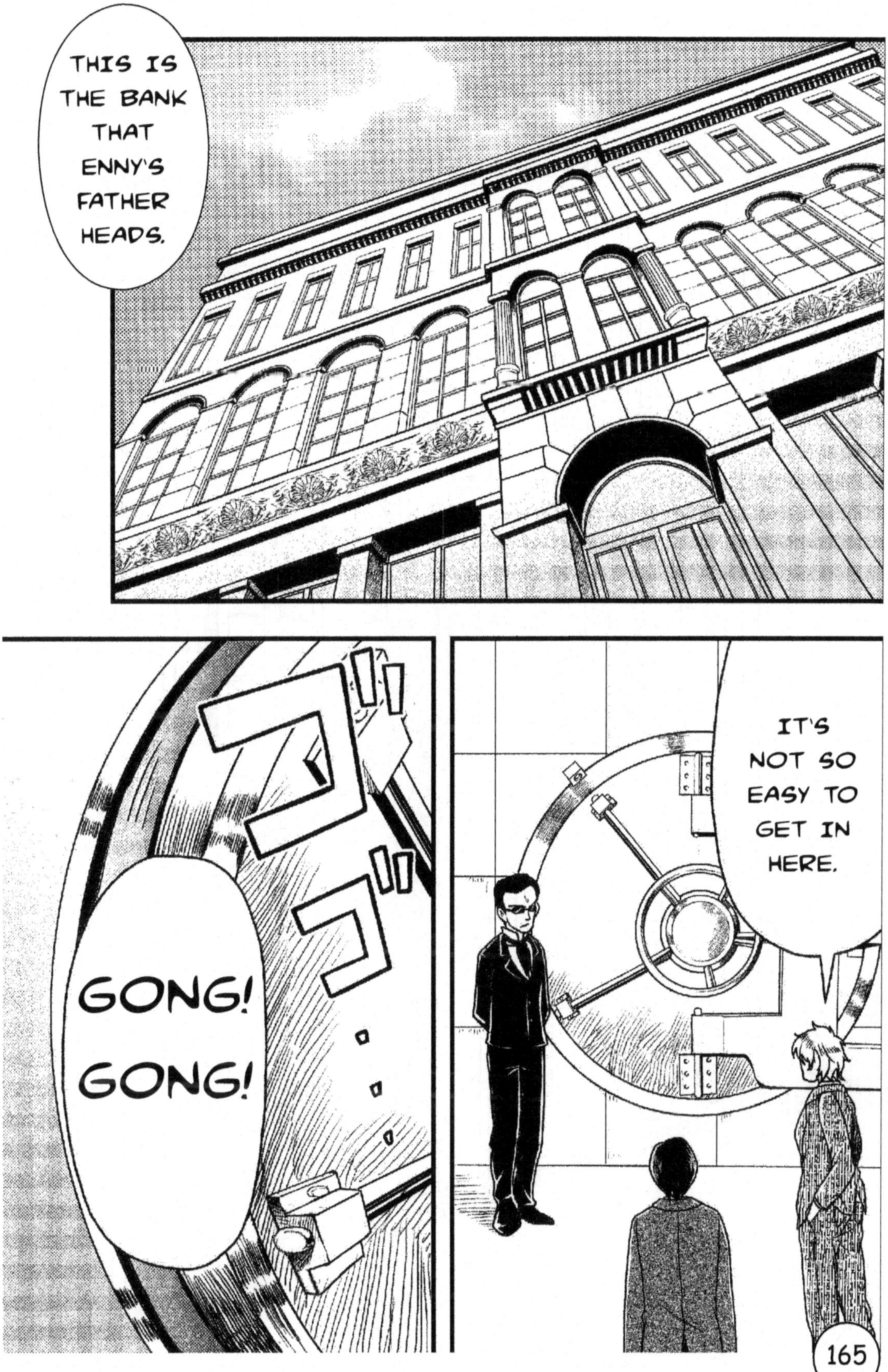
THIS IS THE BANK THAT ENNY'S FATHER HEADS.
GONG! GONG!
IT'S NOT SO EASY TO GET IN HERE.

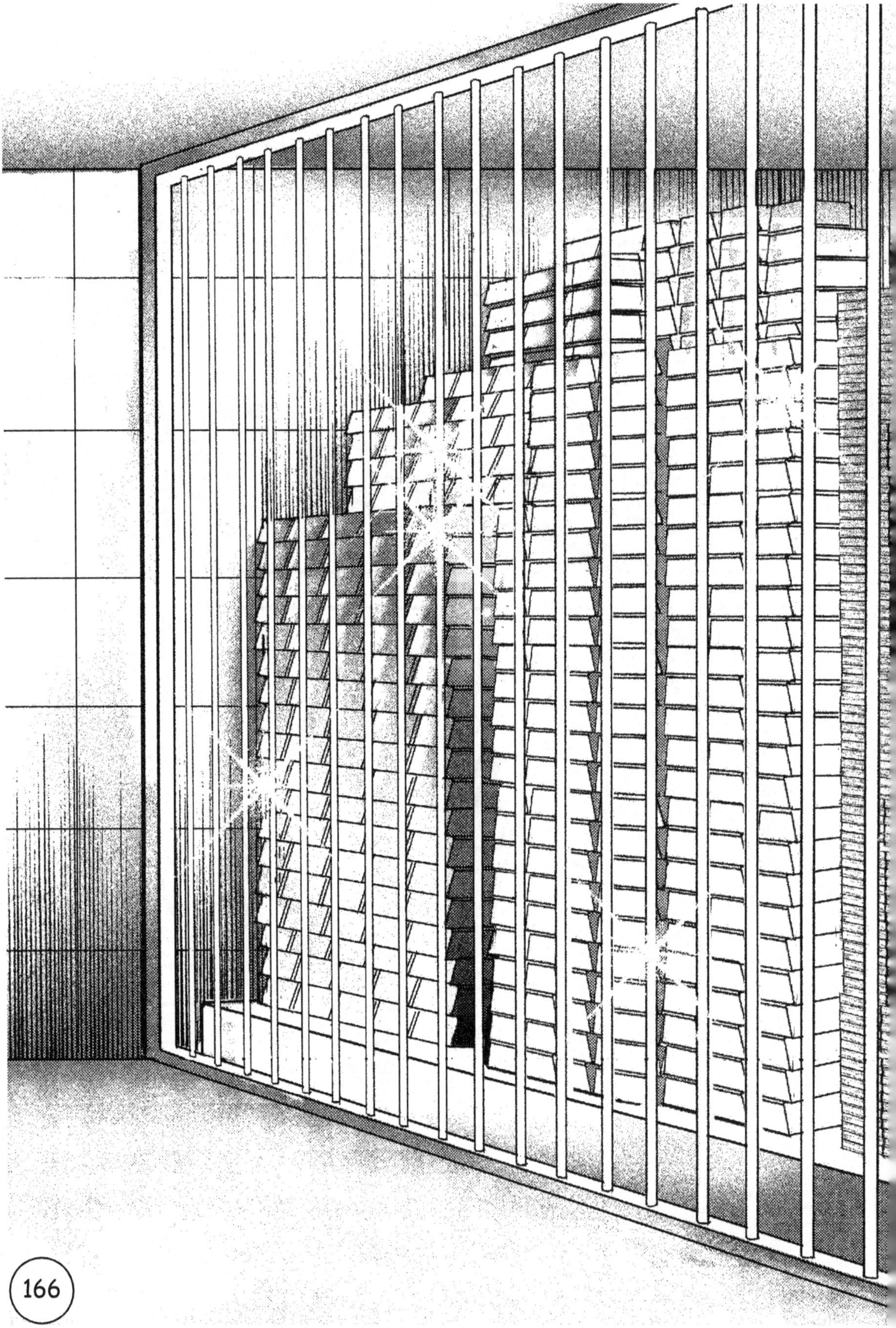

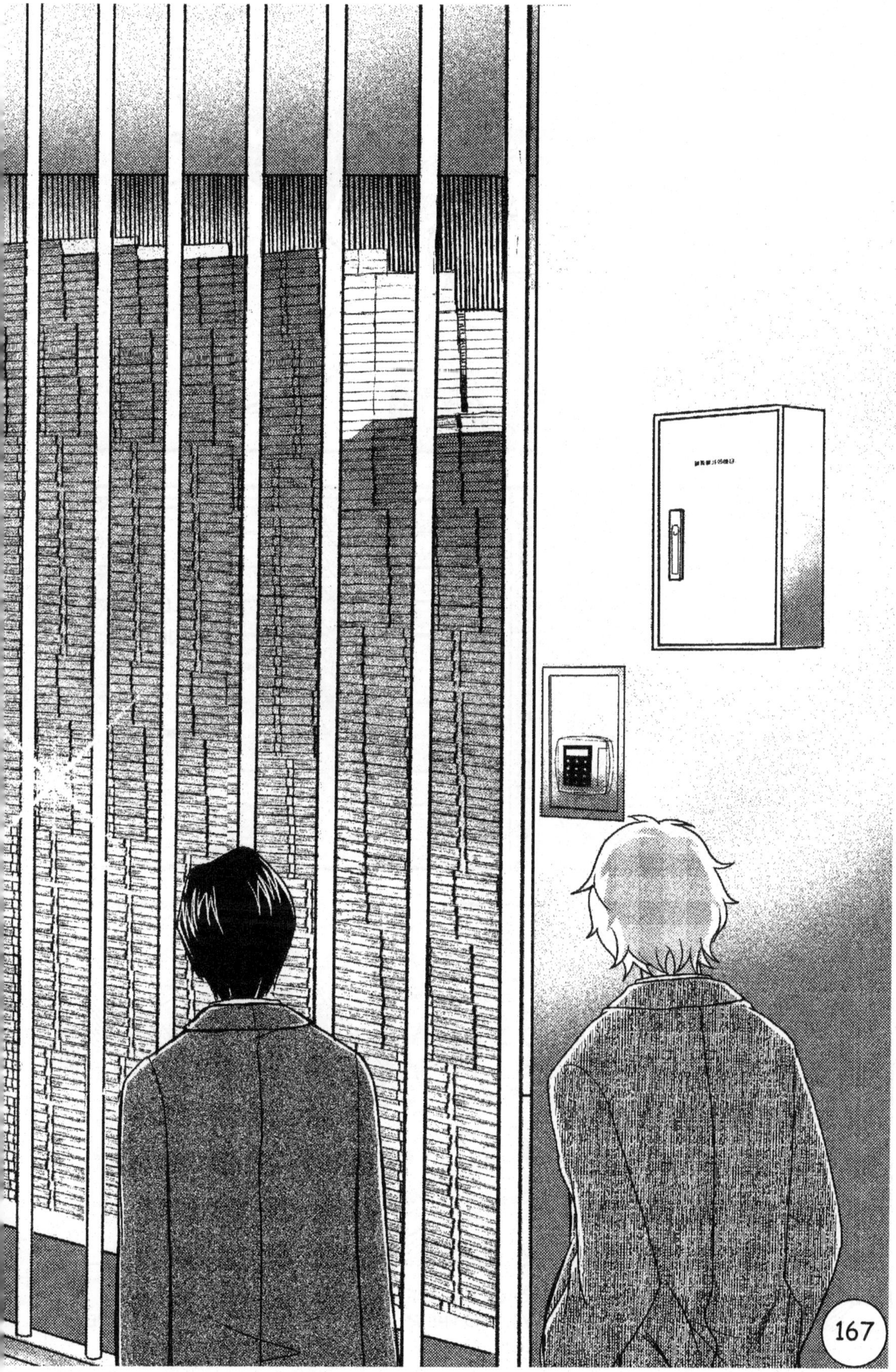

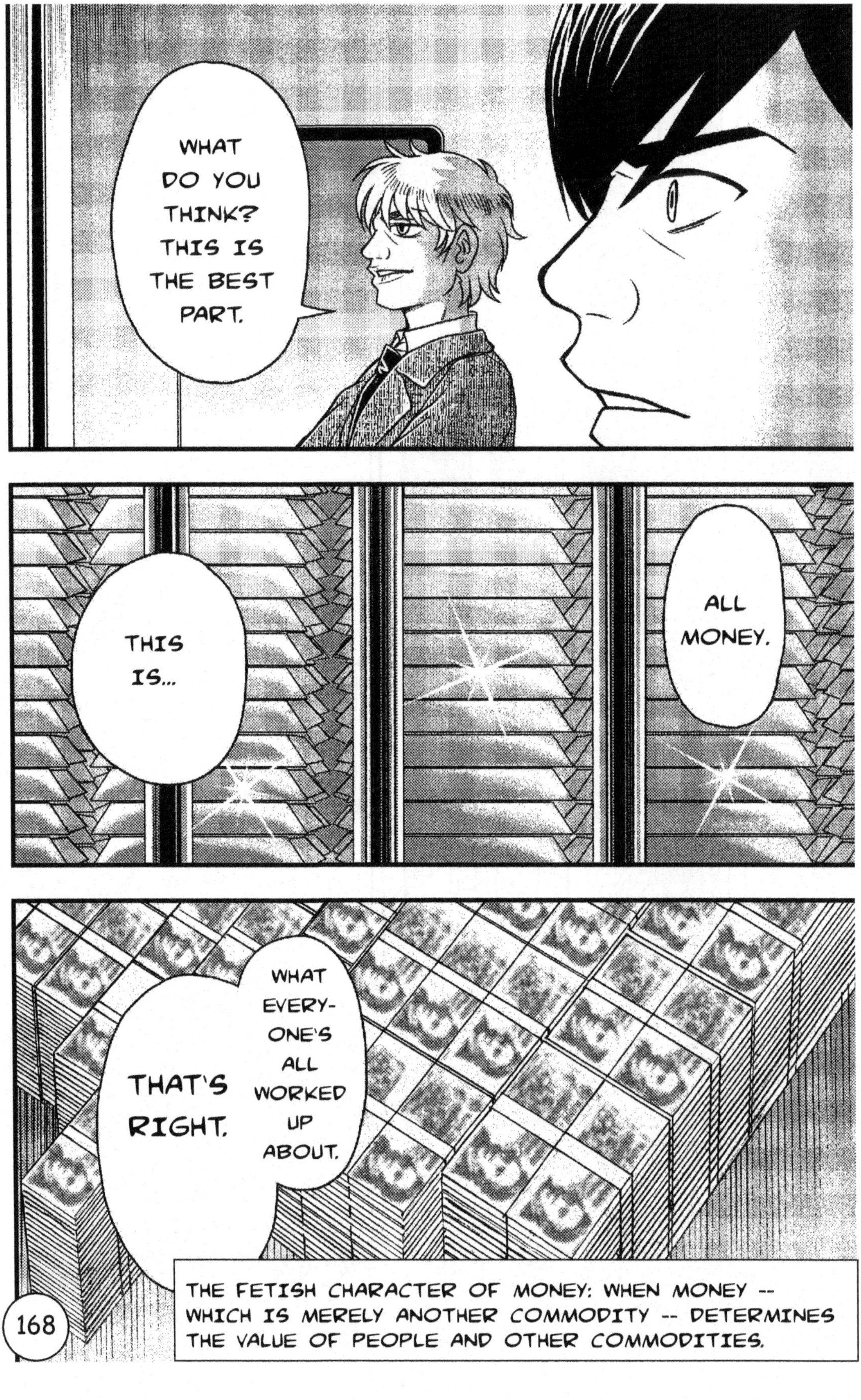
WHAT DO YOU THINK? THIS IS THE BEST PART.
THIS IS...
ALL MONEY.
THAT'S RIGHT.
WHAT EVERY-ONE'S ALL WORKED UP ABOUT.
THE FETISH CHARACTER OF MONEY: WHEN MONEY -- WHICH IS MERELY ANOTHER COMMODITY -- DETERMINES THE VALUE OF PEOPLE AND OTHER COMMODITIES.

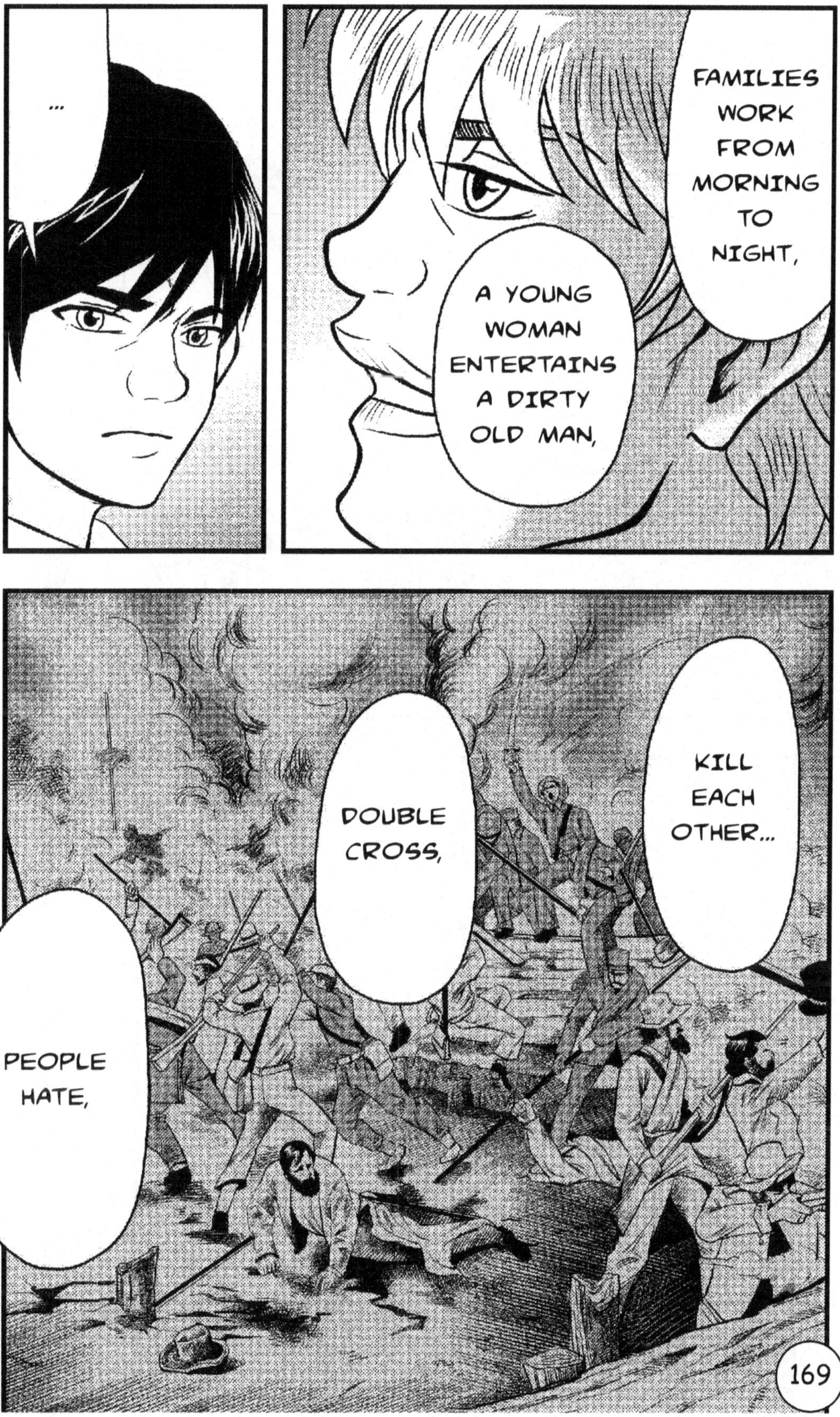
...
FAMILIES WORK FROM MORNING TO NIGHT,
A YOUNG WOMAN ENTERTAINS A DIRTY OLD MAN,
PEOPLE HATE,
DOUBLE CROSS,
KILL EACH OTHER...

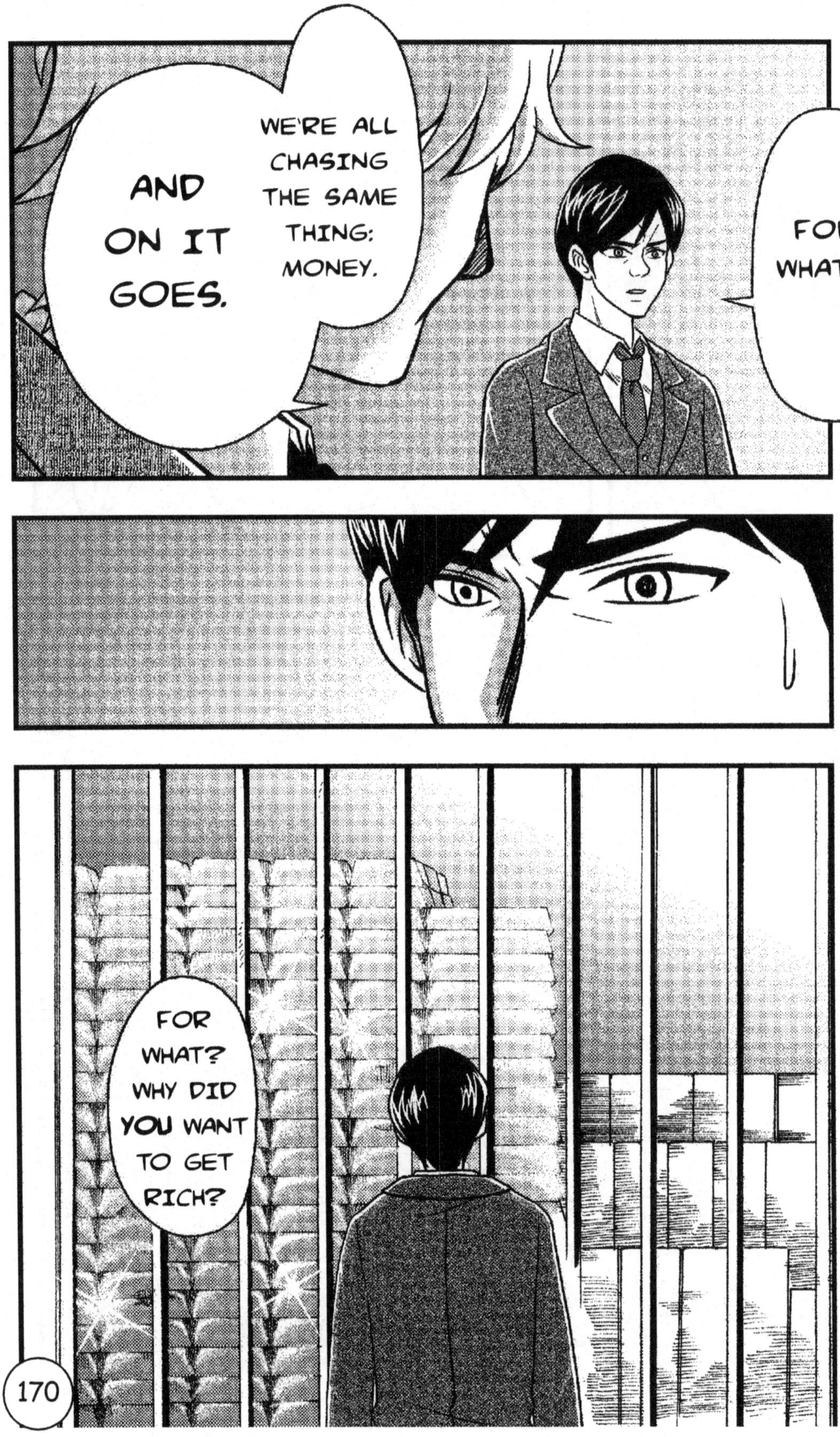
WE'RE ALL CHASING THE SAME THING: MONEY.
AND ON IT GOES.
FOR WHAT?
FOR WHAT? WHY DID YOU WANT TO GET RICH?

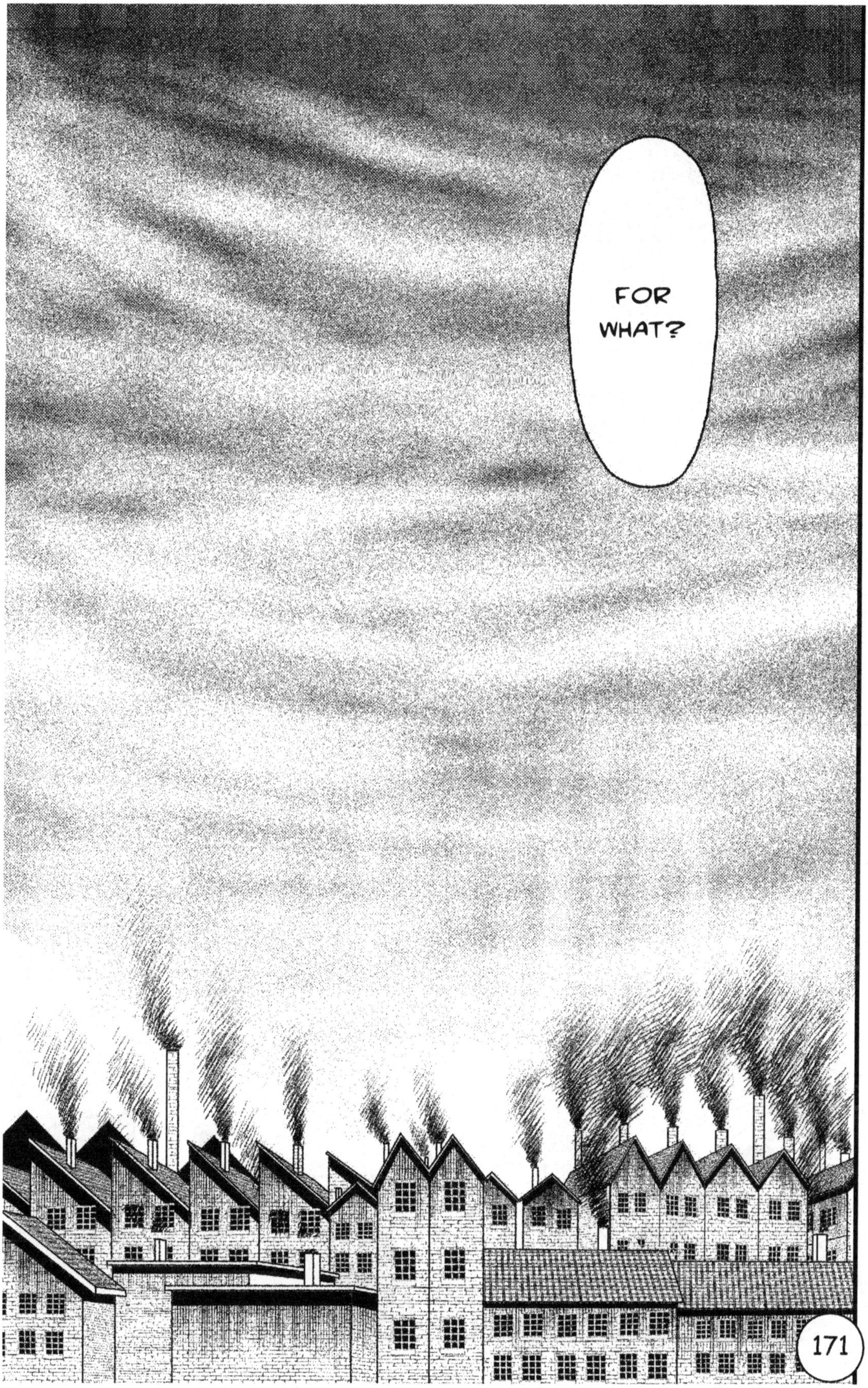
FOR WHAT?

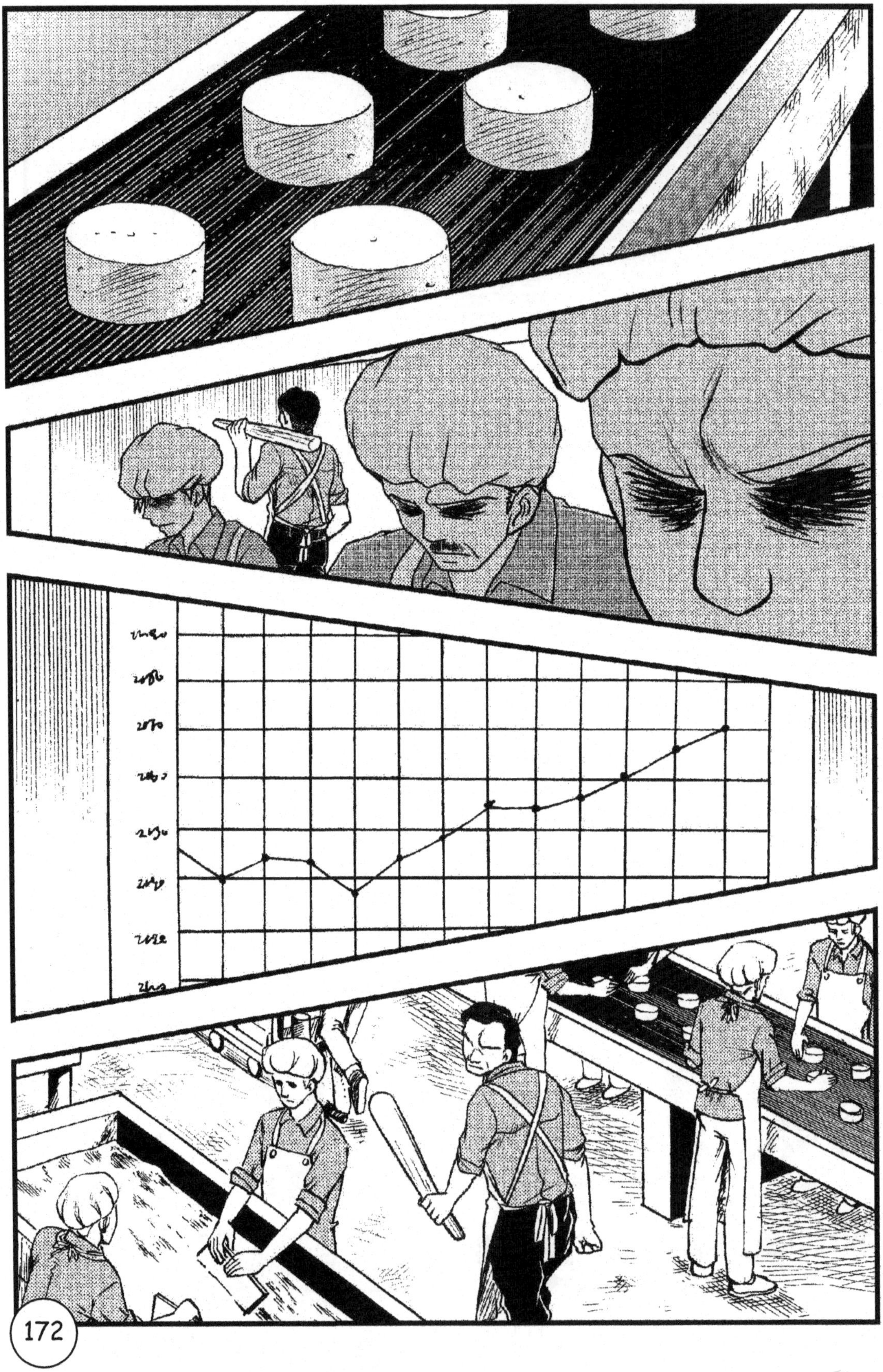

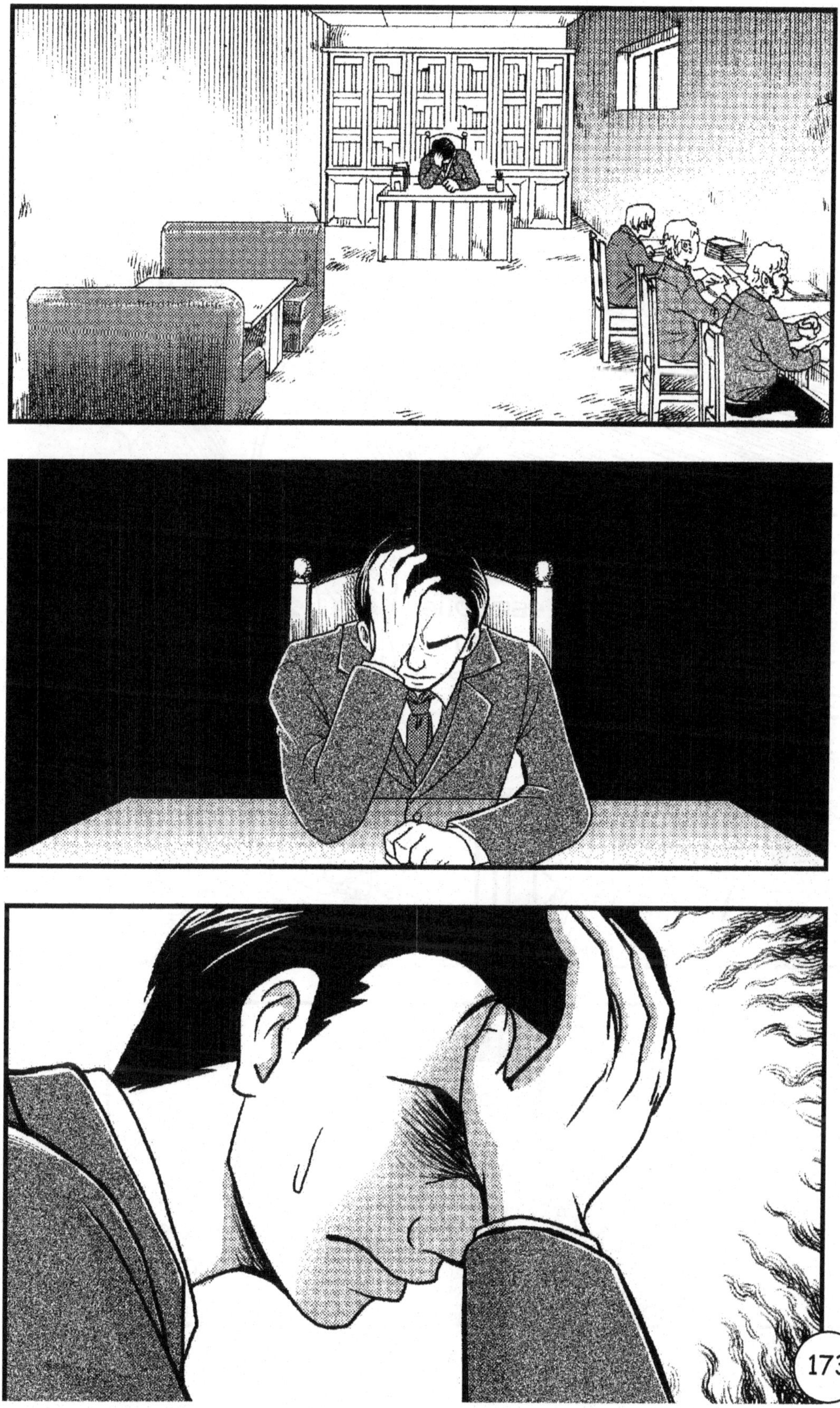

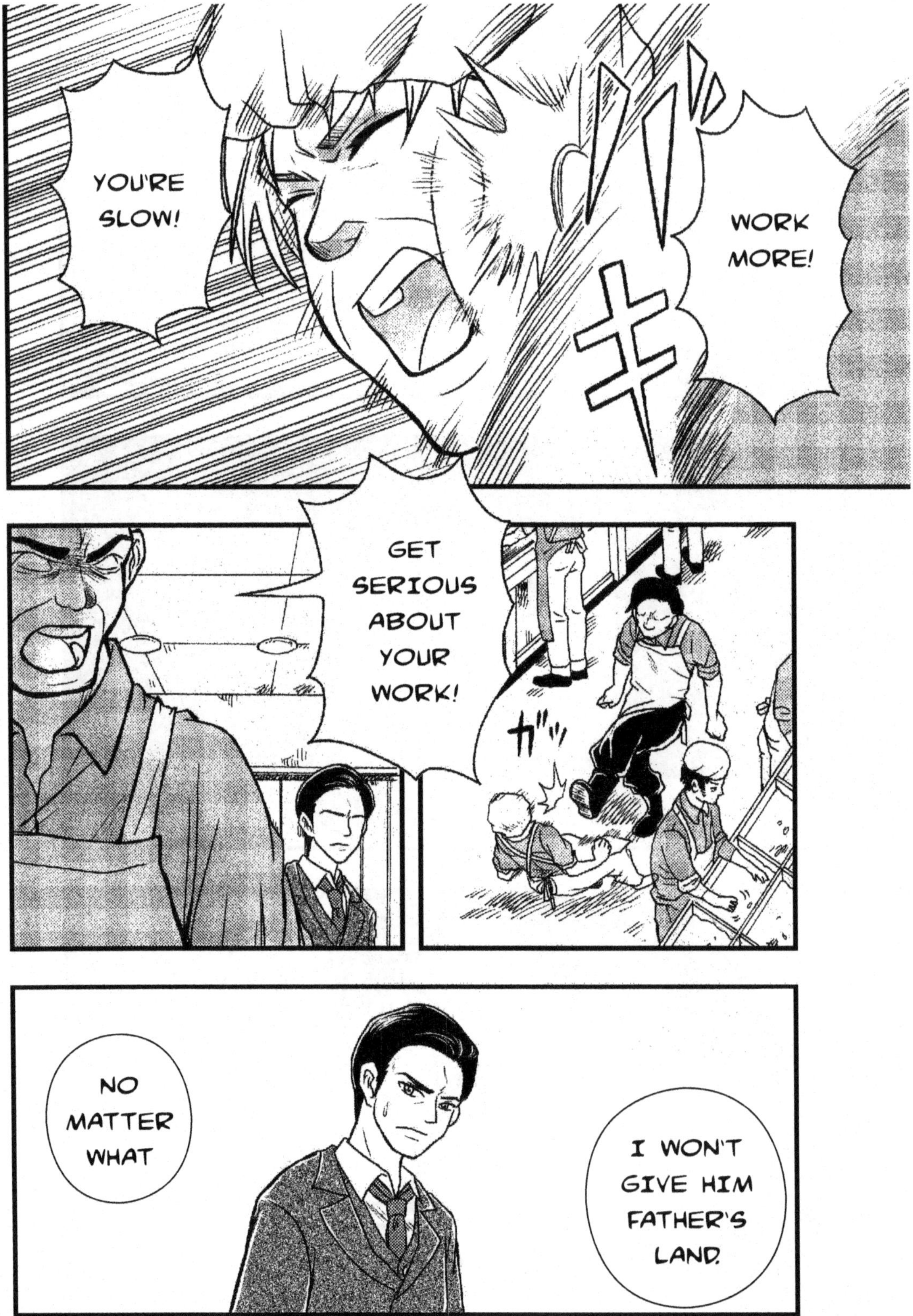
YOU'RE SLOW!
WORK MORE!
GET SERIOUS ABOUT YOUR WORK!
ガッ
NO MATTER WHAT
I WON'T GIVE HIM FATHER'S LAND.

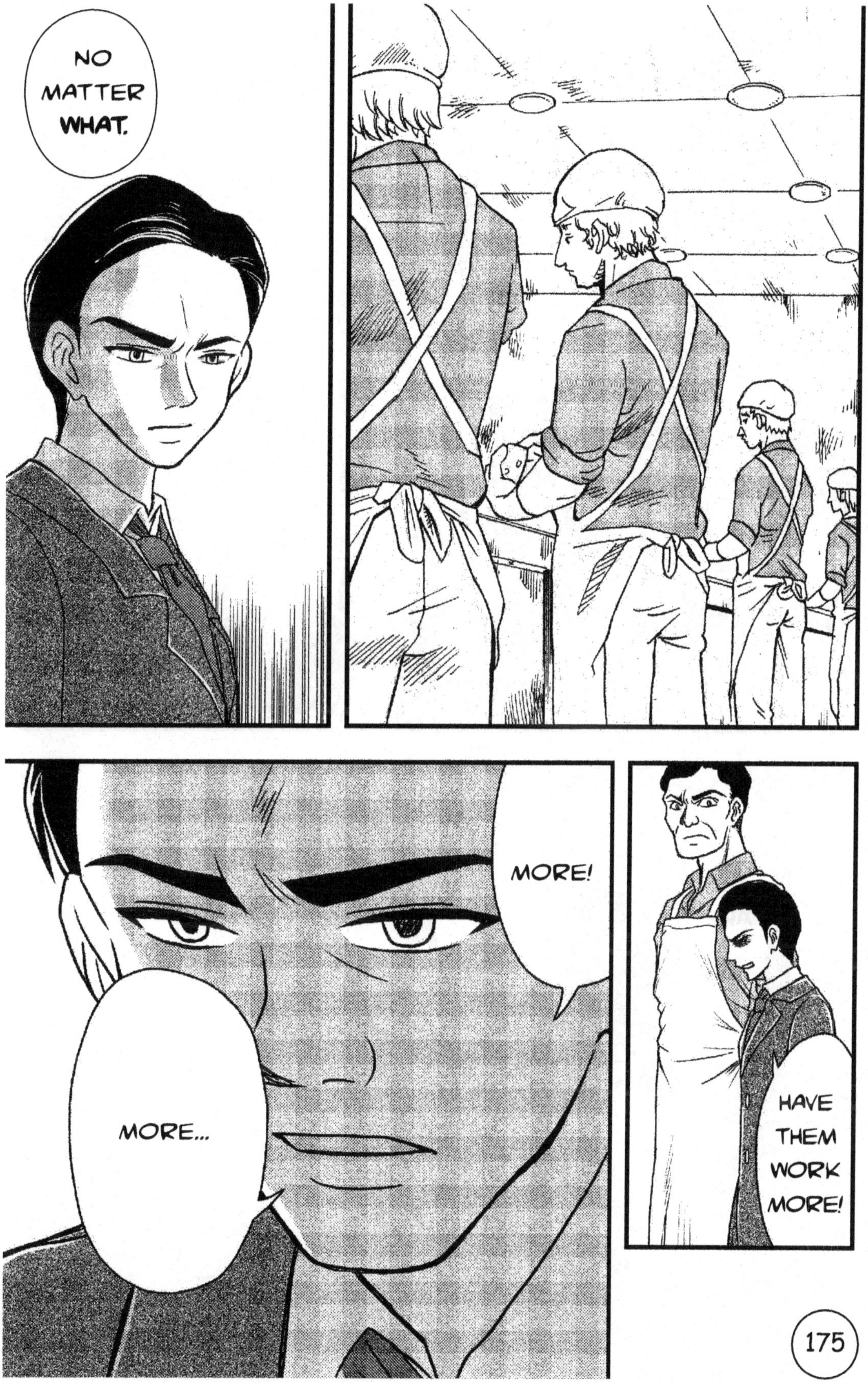
NO MATTER WHAT.
MORE!
MORE...
HAVE THEM WORK MORE!

WE ARE

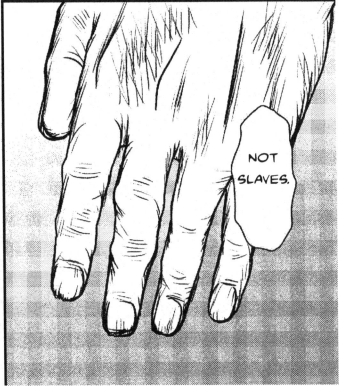

NOT SLAVES.

176

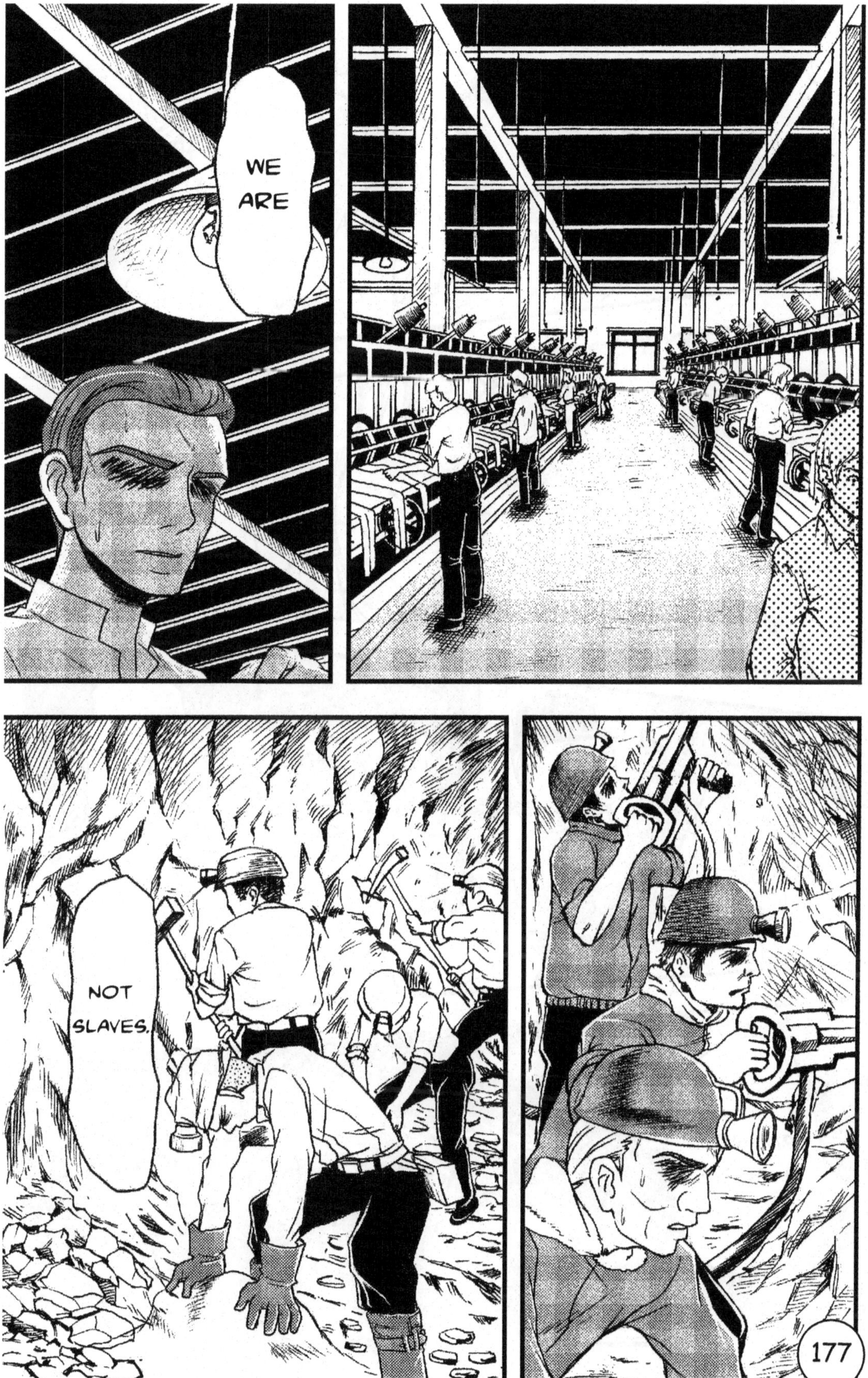
WE ARE
NOT SLAVES.

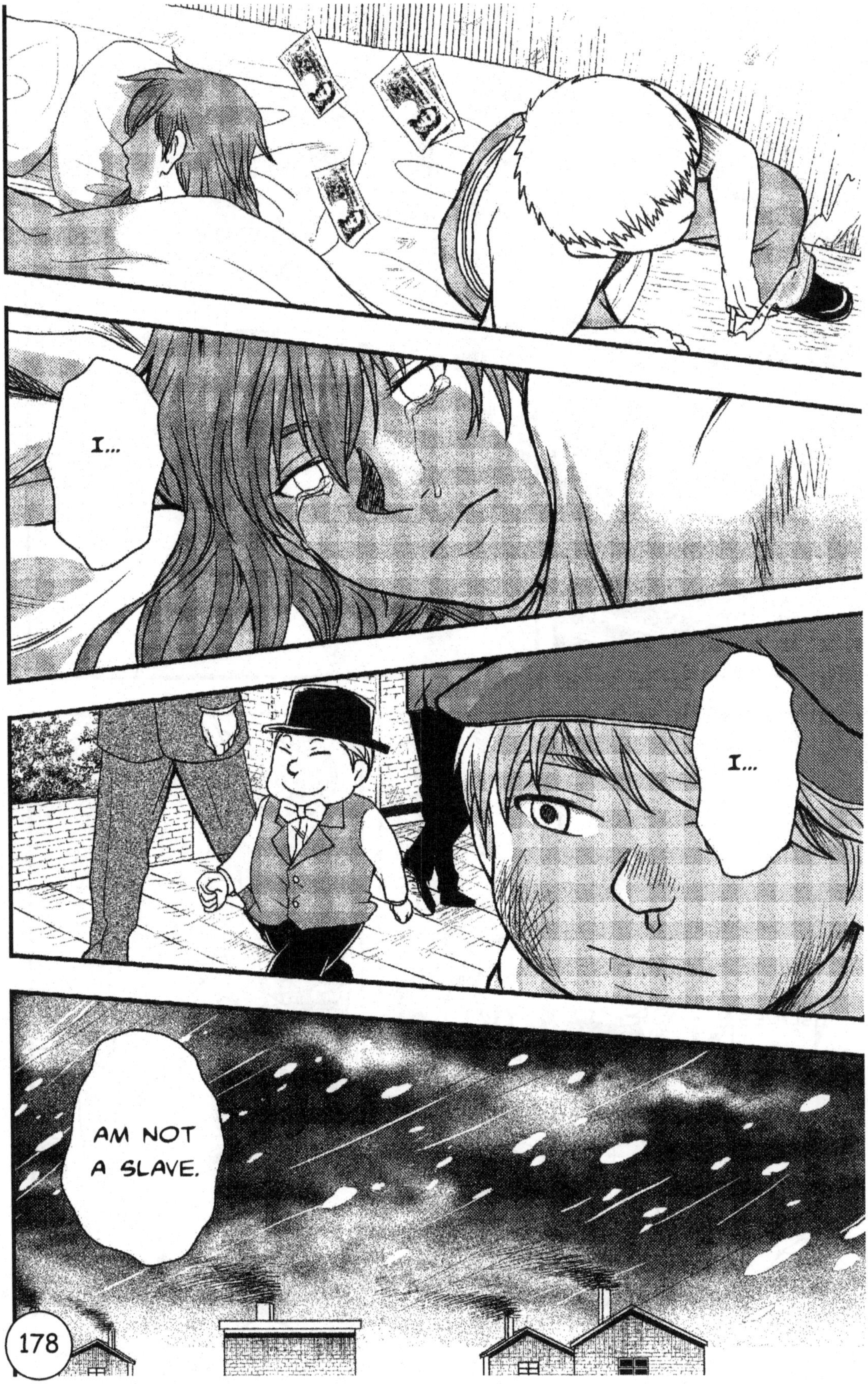
I...
I...
AM NOT A SLAVE.

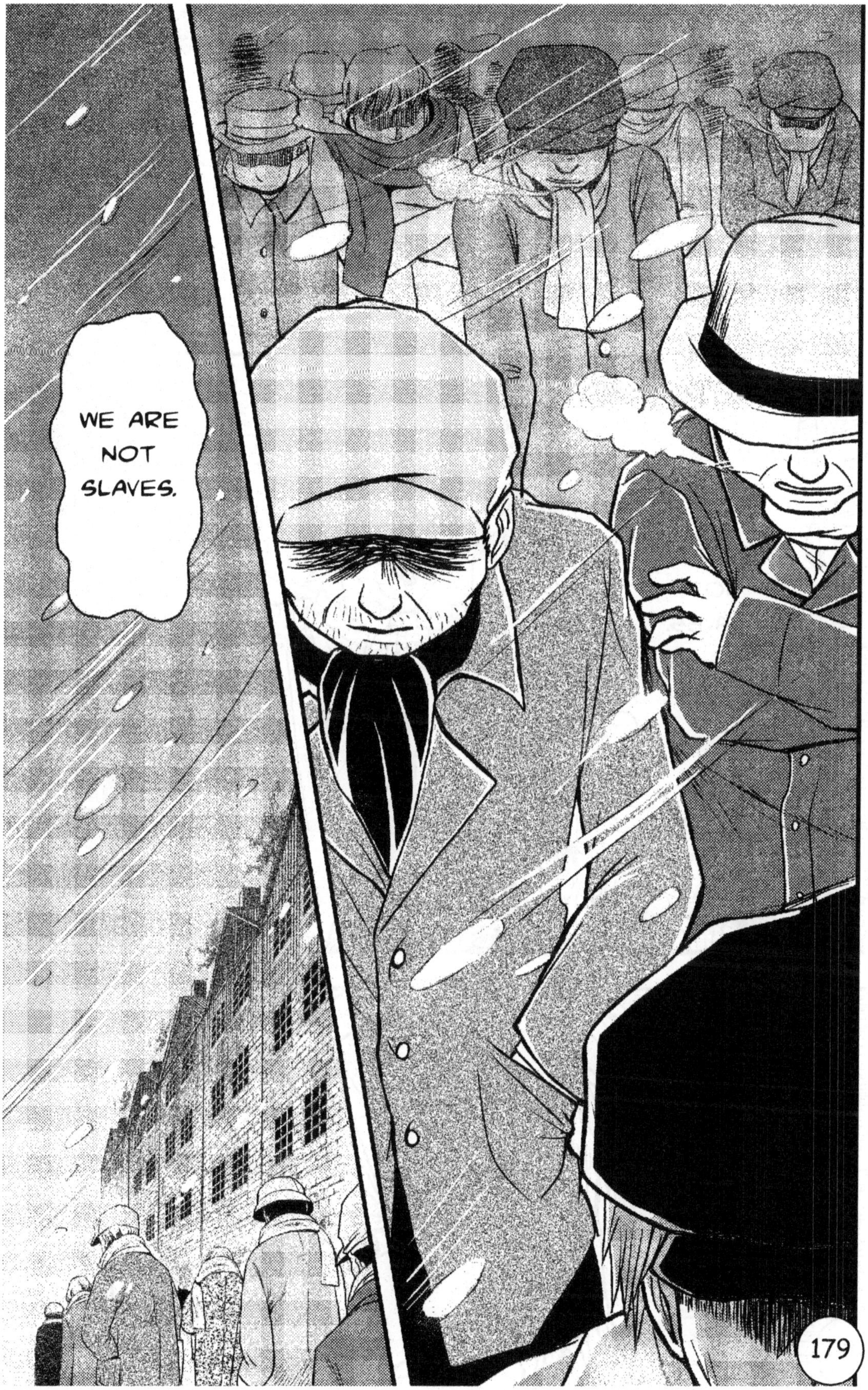
WE ARE NOT SLAVES.

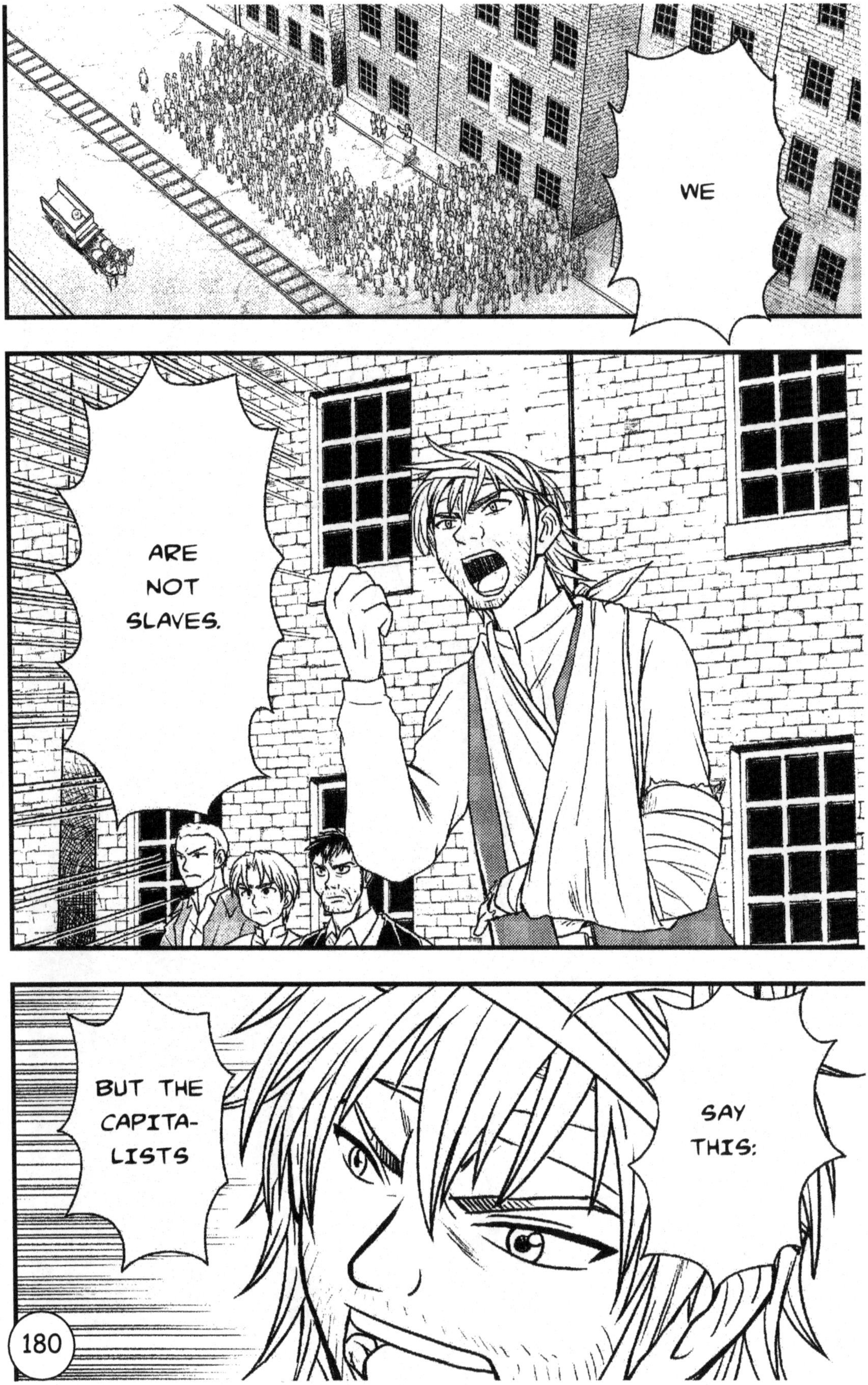
WE
ARE NOT SLAVES.
BUT THE CAPITA-LISTS
SAY THIS:

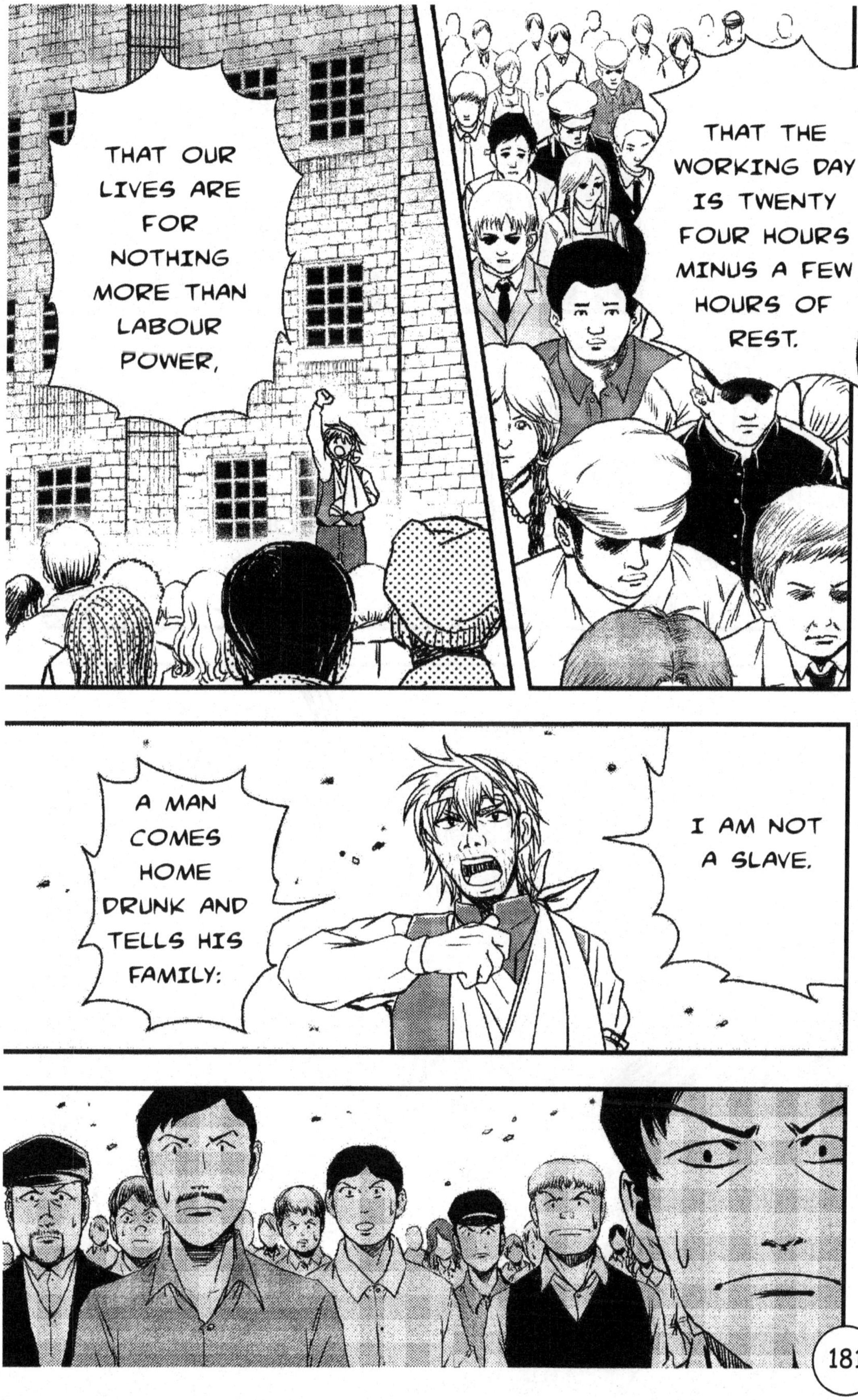
THAT OUR LIVES ARE FOR NOTHING MORE THAN LABOUR POWER,
THAT THE WORKING DAY IS TWENTY FOUR HOURS MINUS A FEW HOURS OF REST.
A MAN COMES HOME DRUNK AND TELLS HIS FAMILY:
I AM NOT A SLAVE.

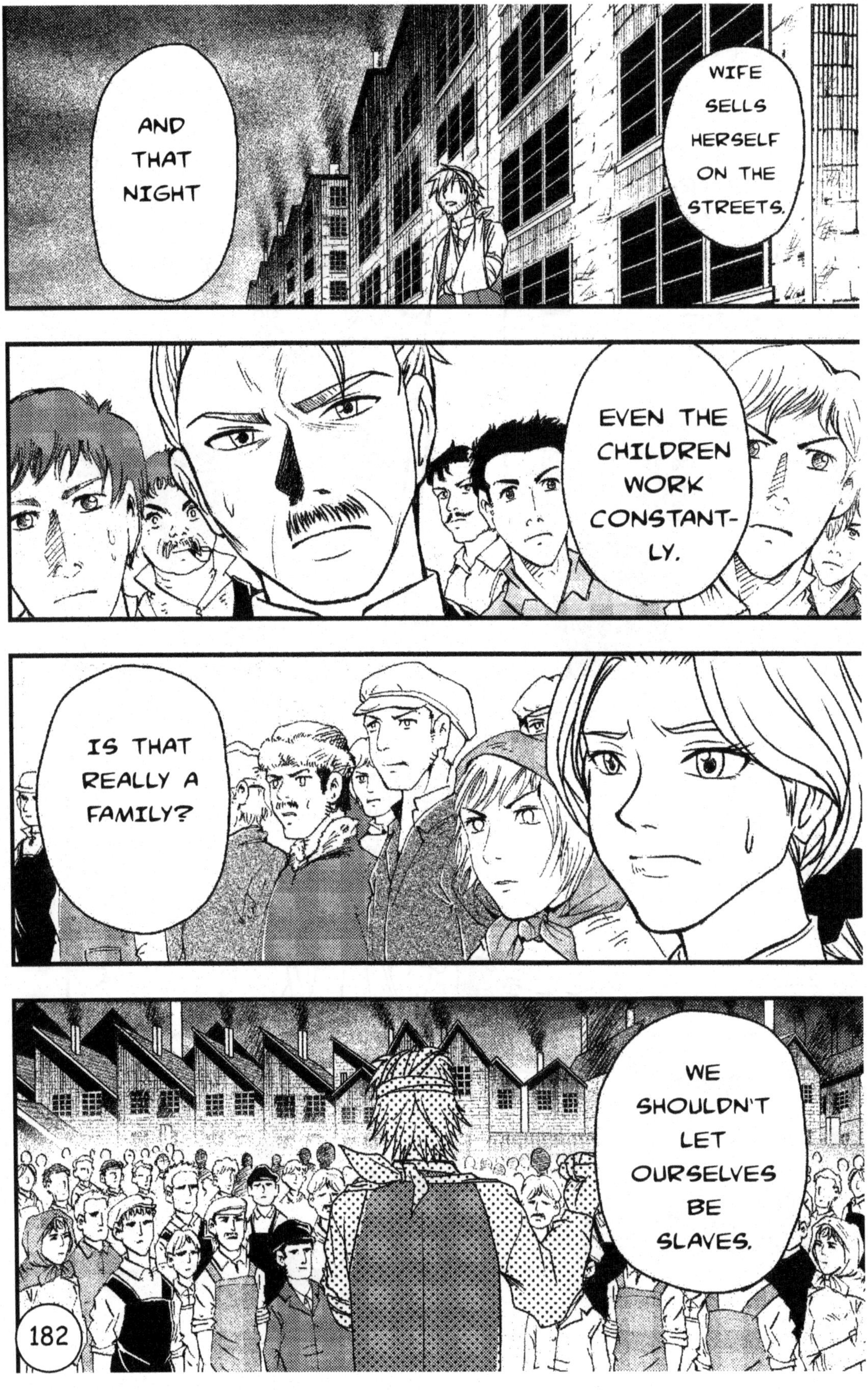
AND THAT NIGHT
WIFE SELLS HERSELF ON THE STREETS.
EVEN THE CHILDREN WORK CONSTANT-LY.
IS THAT REALLY A FAMILY?
WE SHOULDN'T LET OURSELVES BE SLAVES.
182

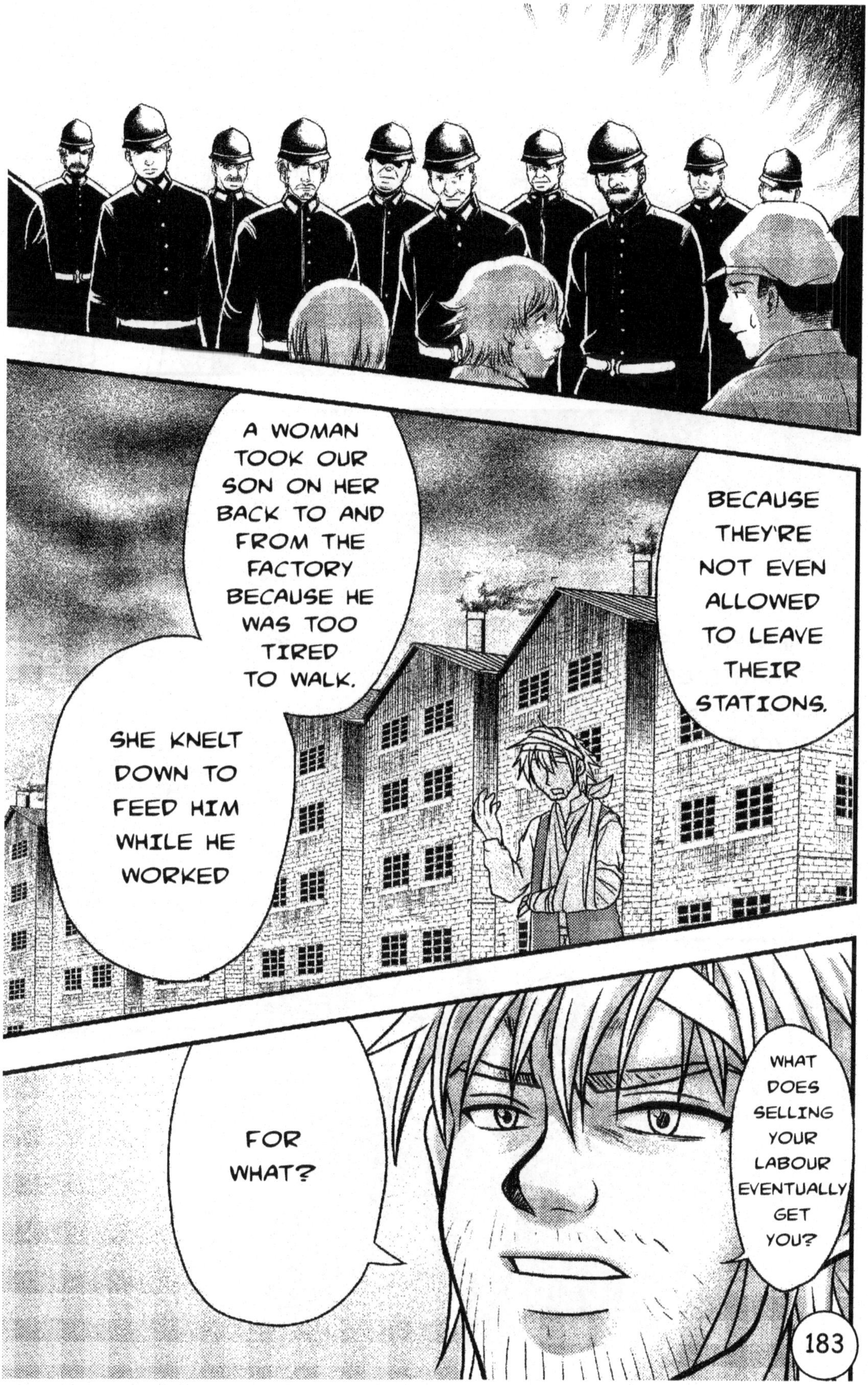
A WOMAN TOOK OUR SON ON HER BACK TO AND FROM THE FACTORY BECAUSE HE WAS TOO TIRED TO WALK.
SHE KNELT DOWN TO FEED HIM WHILE HE WORKED
BECAUSE THEY'RE NOT EVEN ALLOWED TO LEAVE THEIR STATIONS.
FOR WHAT?
WHAT DOES SELLING YOUR LABOUR EVENTUALLY GET YOU?

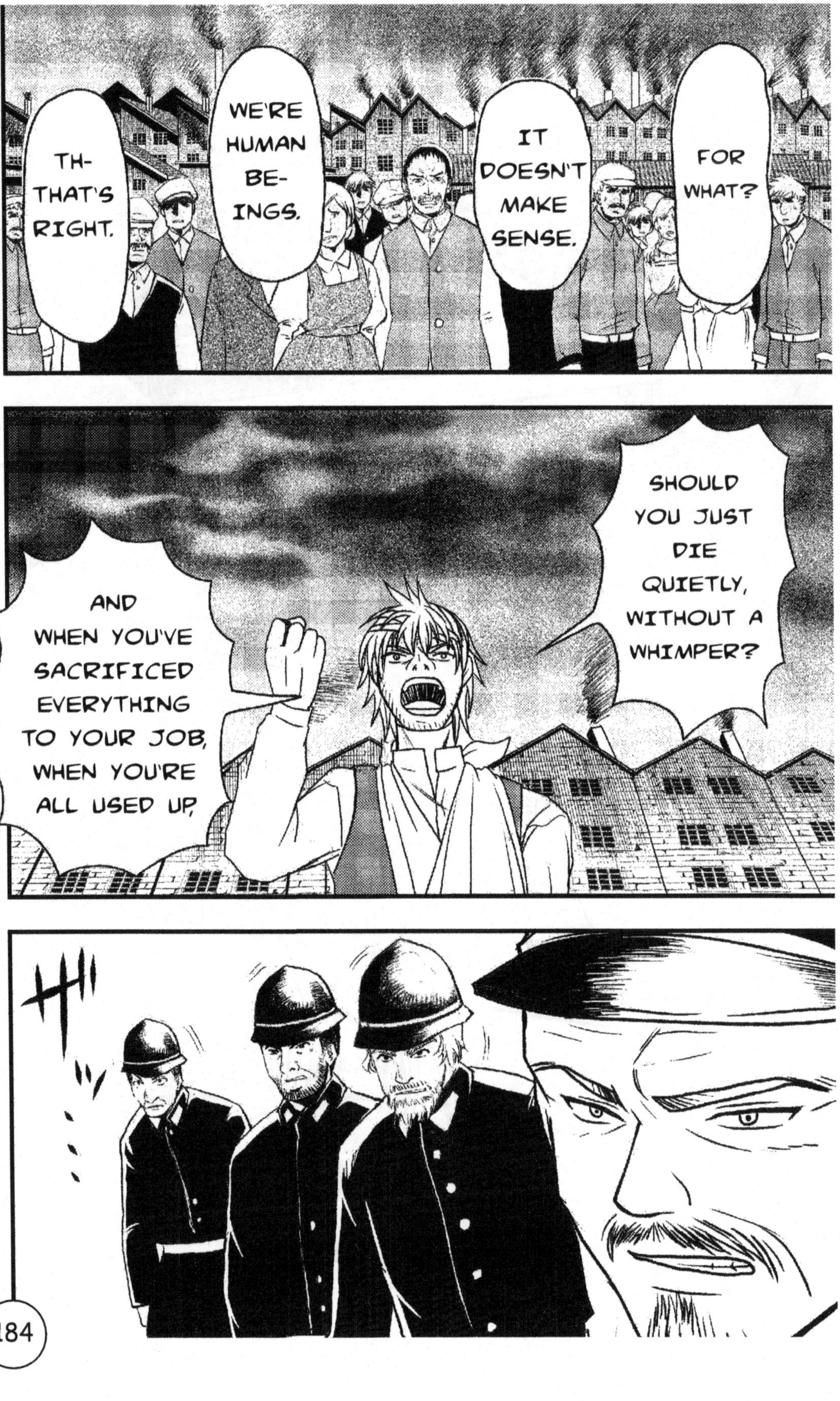
TH-THAT'S RIGHT.
WE'RE HUMAN BE-INGS.
IT DOESN'T MAKE SENSE.
FOR WHAT?
AND WHEN YOU'VE SACRIFICED EVERYTHING TO YOUR JOB, WHEN YOU'RE ALL USED UP,
SHOULD YOU JUST DIE QUIETLY, WITHOUT A WHIMPER?

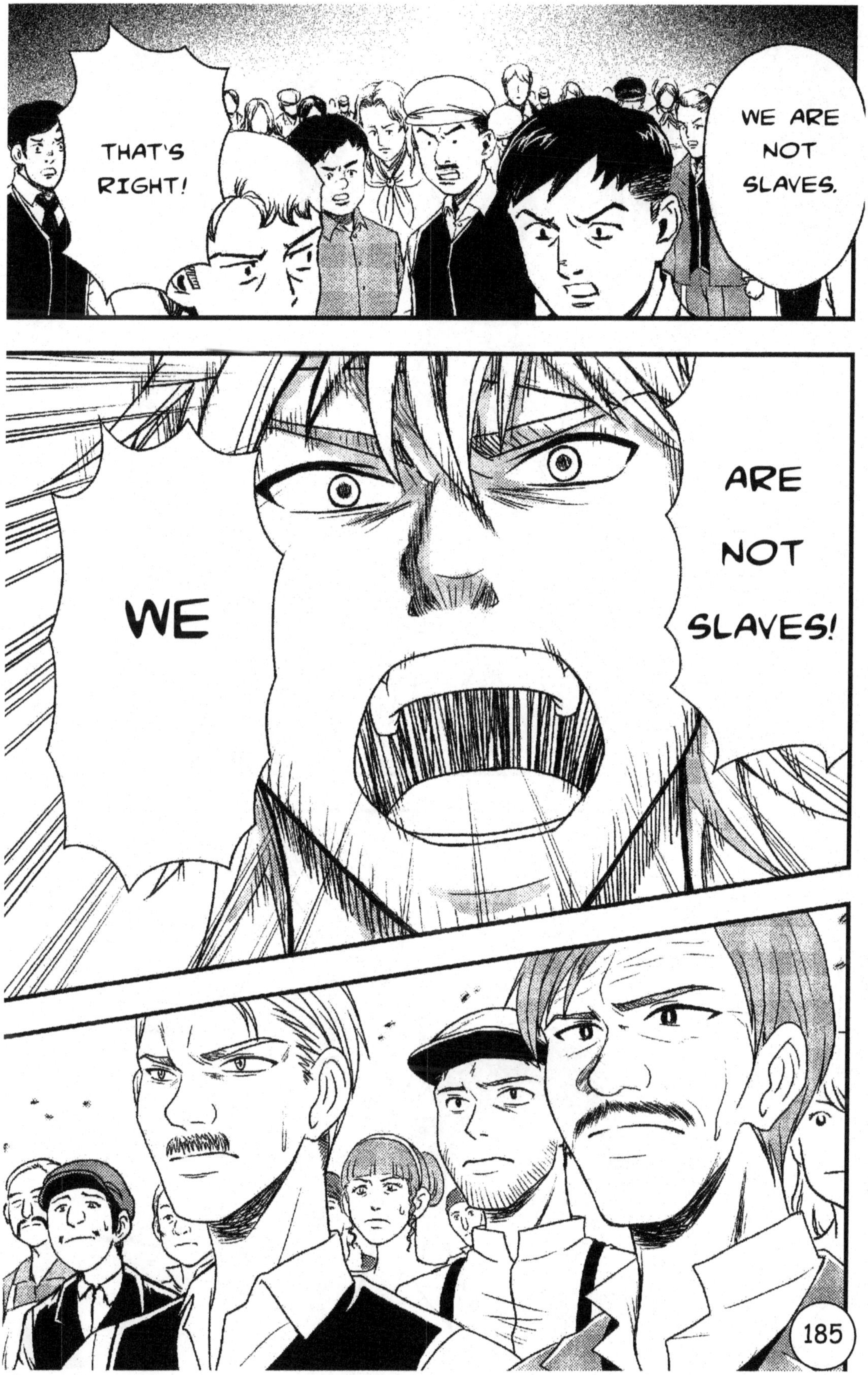
THAT'S RIGHT!
WE ARE NOT SLAVES.
WE
ARE NOT SLAVES!

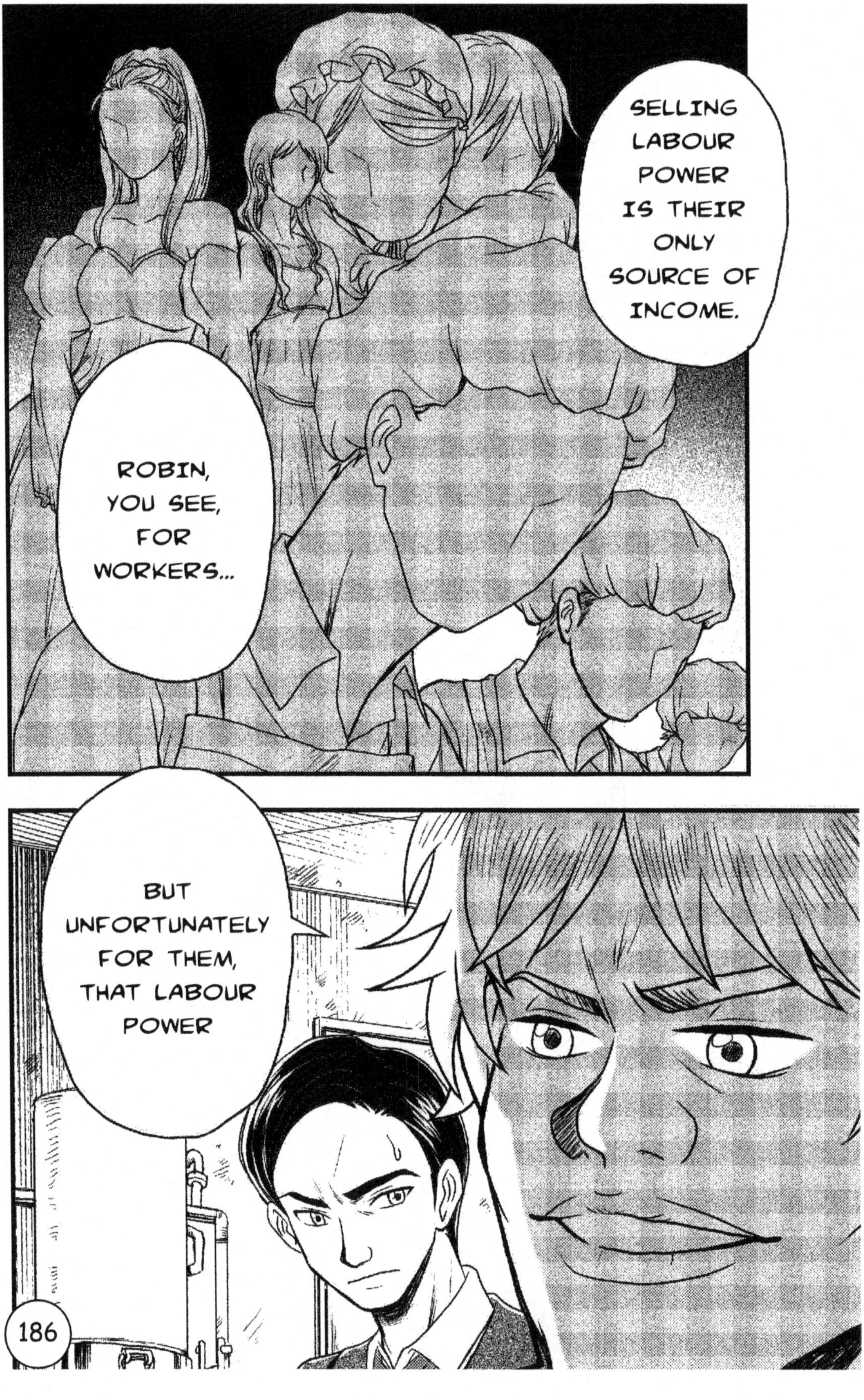
ROBIN, YOU SEE, FOR WORKERS...
SELLING LABOUR POWER IS THEIR ONLY SOURCE OF INCOME.
BUT UNFORTUNATELY FOR THEM, THAT LABOUR POWER

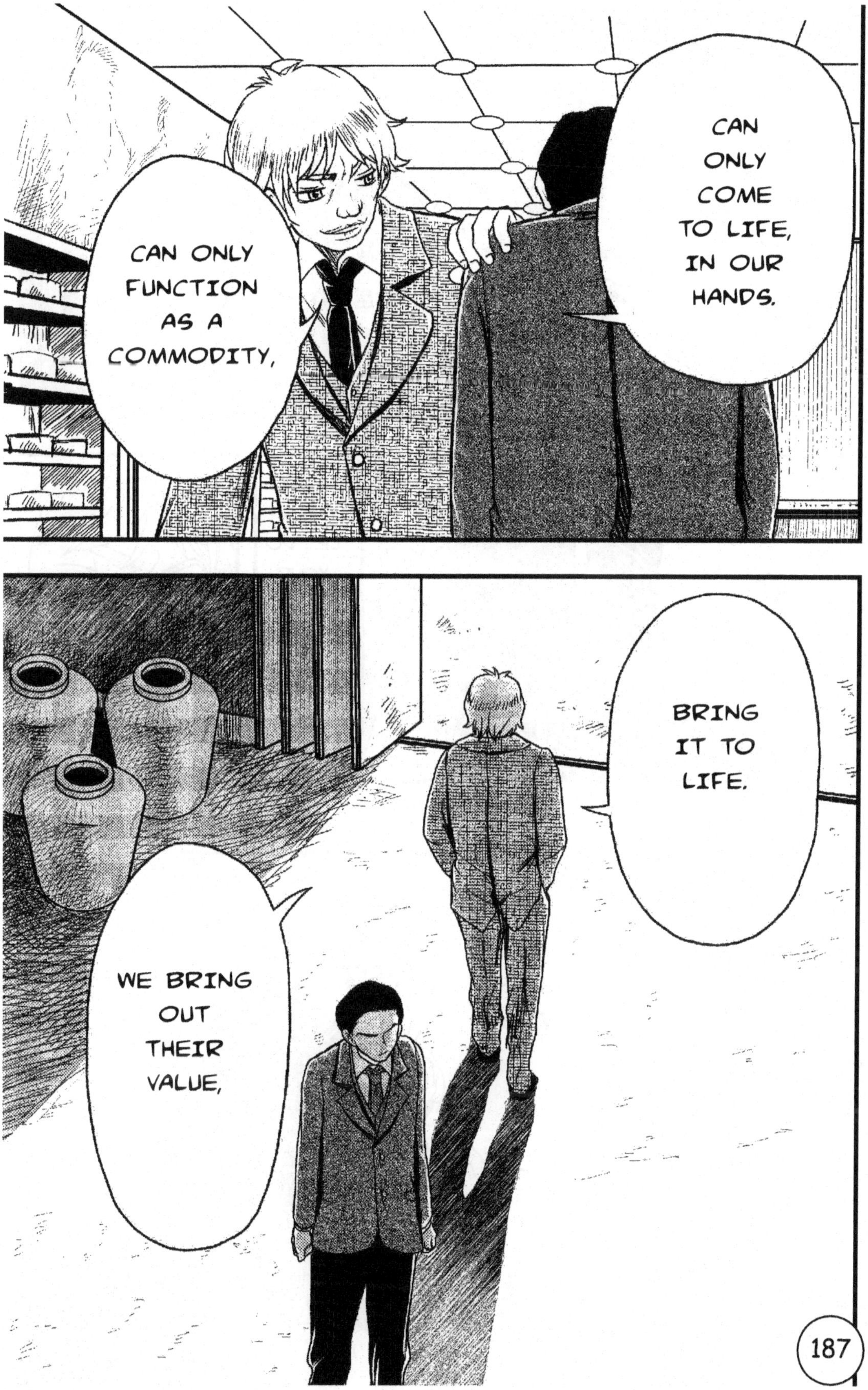
CAN ONLY FUNCTION AS A COMMODITY,
CAN ONLY COME TO LIFE, IN OUR HANDS.
WE BRING OUT THEIR VALUE,
BRING IT TO LIFE.

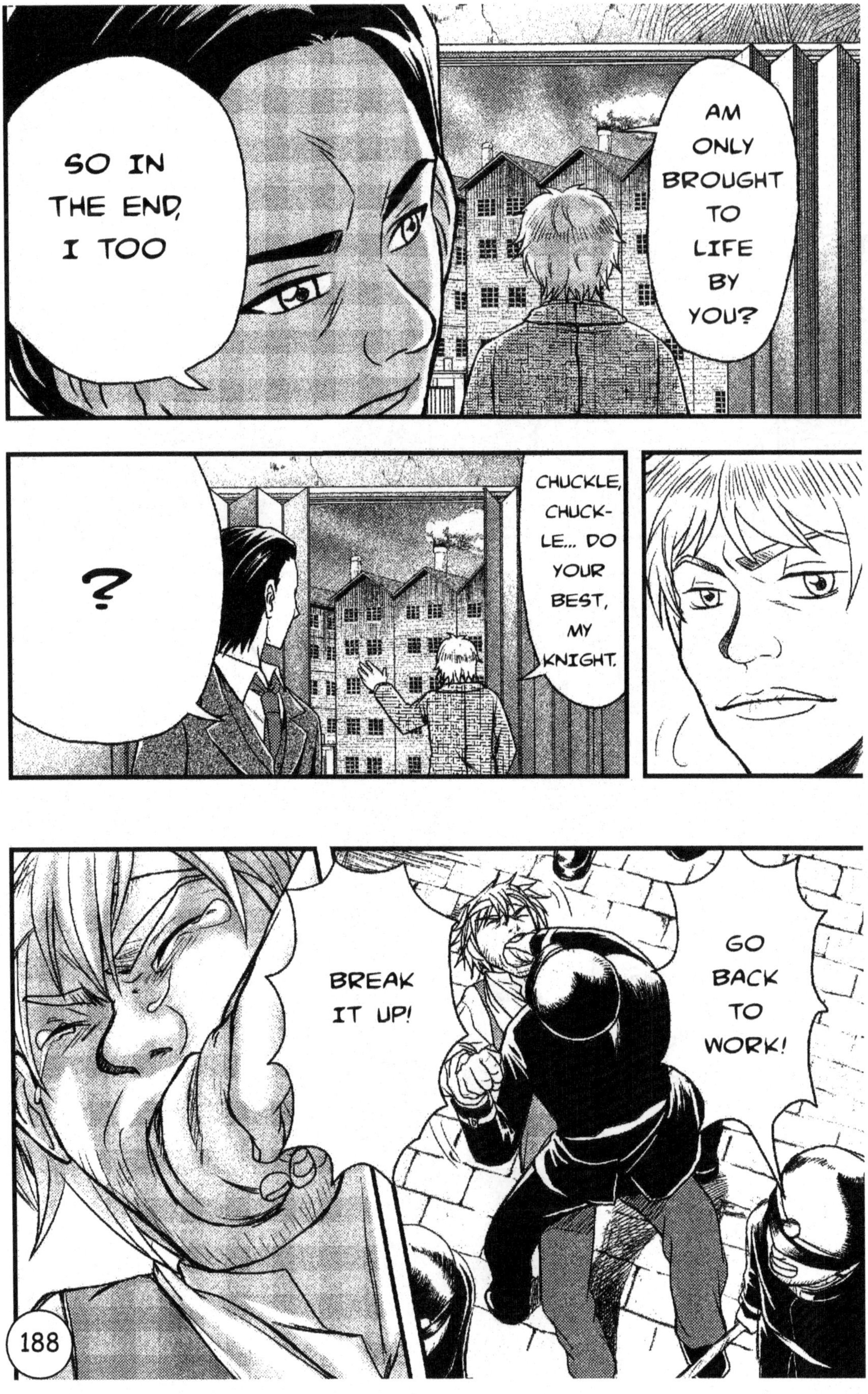
SO IN THE END, I TOO
AM ONLY BROUGHT TO LIFE BY YOU?
?
CHUCKLE, CHUCKLE... DO YOUR BEST, MY KNIGHT.
BREAK IT UP!
GO BACK TO WORK!

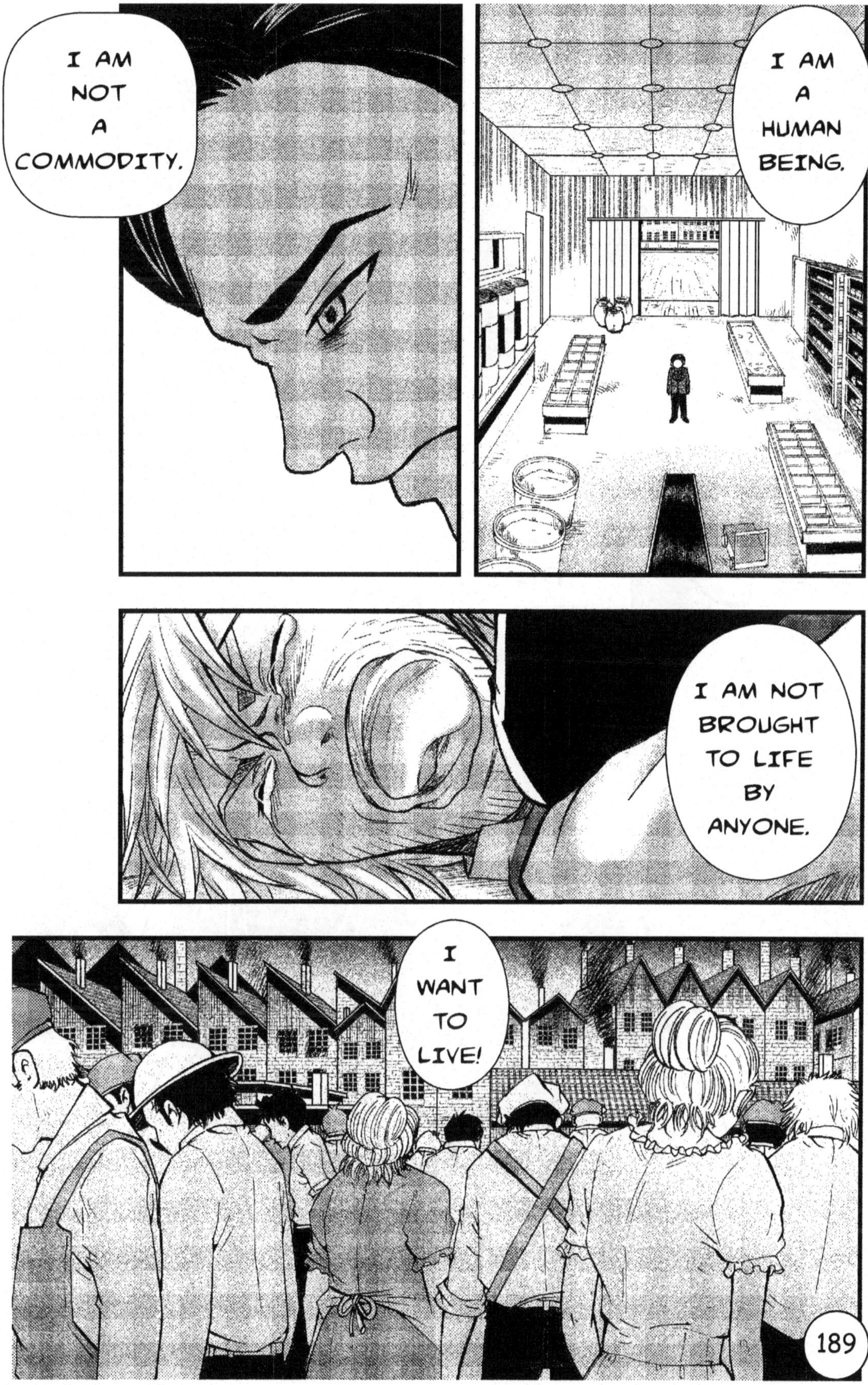
I AM NOT A COMMODITY.
I AM A HUMAN BEING.
I AM NOT BROUGHT TO LIFE BY ANYONE.
I WANT TO LIVE!

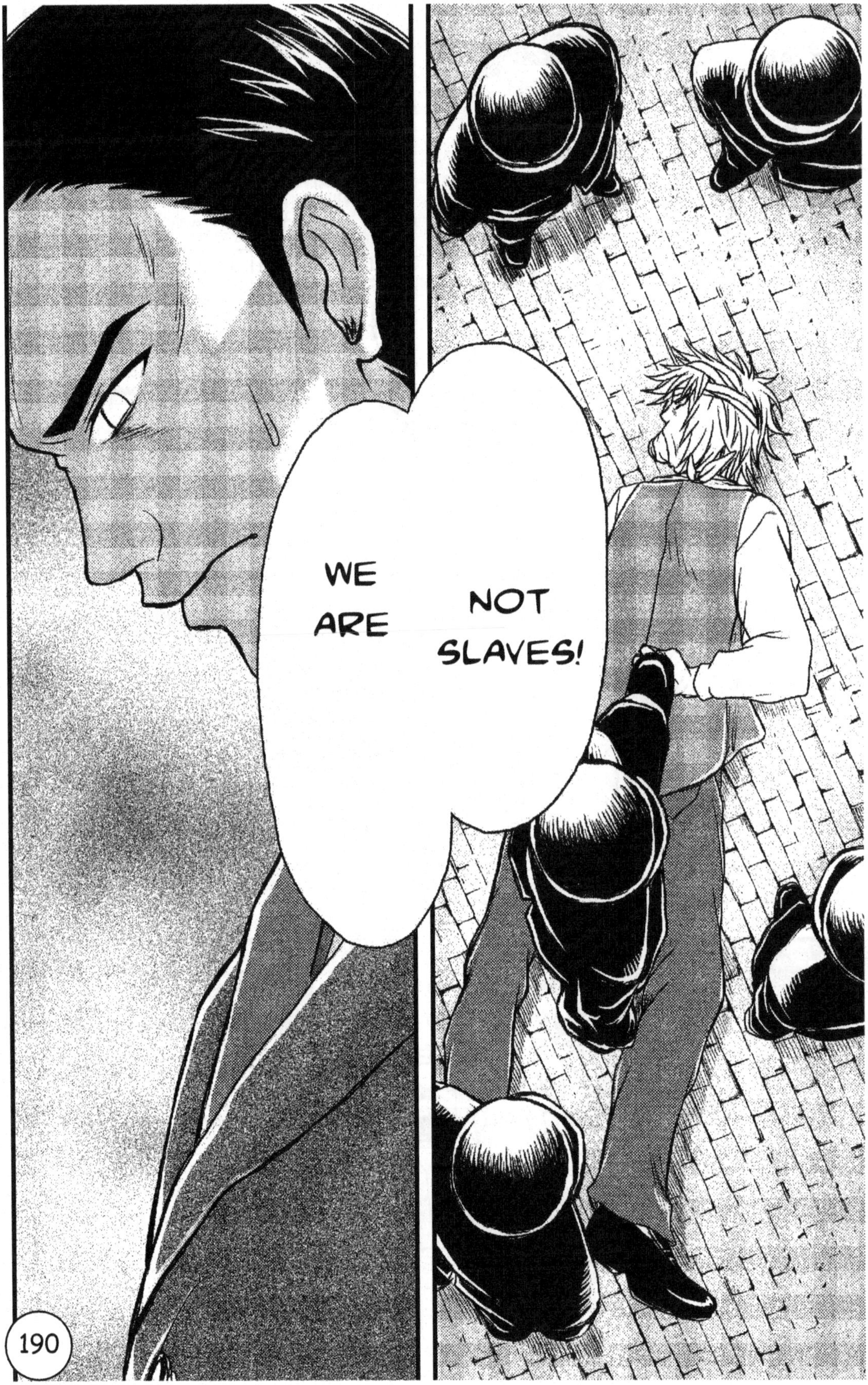
WE ARE NOT SLAVES!

THE END

Lightning Source UK Ltd.
Milton Keynes UK
UKOW04f1452280217

295528UK00002B/41/P

9 781926 958194